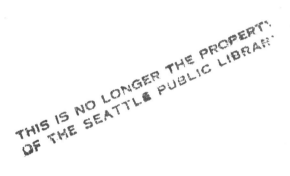

We Believe
the Children

We Believe
the Children

A Moral Panic in the 1980s

RICHARD BECK

PUBLICAFFAIRS

New York

Published in the United States by PublicAffairs™, a Member of the
Perseus Books Group

PublicAffairs books are available at special discounts for bulk
purchases in the U.S. by corporations, institutions, and other
organizations. For more information, please contact the Special
Markets Department at the Perseus Books Group, 2300 Chestnut
Street, Suite 200, Philadelphia, PA 19103, call (800) 810-4145,
ext. 5000, or e-mail special.markets@perseusbooks.com.

Book Design by Pauline Brown

Library of Congress Cataloging-in-Publication Data
Beck, Richard, 1986–
   We believe the children : a moral panic in the 1980s / Richard
Beck. — First edition.
      pages cm
   ISBN 978-1-61039-287-7 (hardback) — ISBN 978-1-61039-288-4
(e-book) 1. Child sexual abuse—United States—History—20th
century. 2. Ritual abuse—United States—History—20th century.
3. Child care workers—United States—History—20th century.
4. False arrest—United States—History—20th century. 5. Moral
panics—United States—History—20th century. I. Title.
   HV6570.2.B43 2015
   362.760973'09048—dc23

                              2015011572

First Edition

10 9 8 7 6 5 4 3 2 1

For n+1
and
for Garry Lee Snodgrass

CONTENTS

AUTHOR'S NOTE

In order to protect the privacy of children discussed in this book, pseu-donyms have been used in place of given names. These pseudonyms match those used in two other books on this subject: *Satan's Silence: Ritual Abuse and the Making of a Modern American Witch Hunt,* by Debbie Nathan and Michael Snedeker; and *The Witch-Hunt Narrative: Politics, Psychology, and the Sexual Abuse of Children,* by Ross E. Cheit. Where I mention children not previously discussed in either of these two books, I have assigned new pseudonyms. Furthermore, if a child is referred to by a pseudonym, his or her parents are as well.

I have made two kinds of exceptions to this practice. In cases where a child has made his or her real name a matter of public record by speak-ing out as an adult, I use the real name. Similarly, given names are used for parents who became public figures in their own right—who spoke to reporters on behalf of an activist group, for example—over the course of the investigations and trials. In the endnotes, I indicate whether a real name or pseudonym is used.

Why are the accused witches' confessions under torture so like the communications made by my patients in psychic treatment?

—SIGMUND FREUD, 1897

The average American is just like the child in the family.

—RICHARD NIXON, 1972

INTRODUCTION

In the late summer of 1983, residents of a beachfront city in southwestern Los Angeles began to suspect that their children were in danger. In August, the mother of a child who had attended the McMartin Preschool in Manhattan Beach told the police that her two-year-old son had been molested by one of his teachers. In September, police arrested the accused teacher and charged him with three counts of child abuse. They also mailed a letter to some two hundred parents of current and former McMartin students, alerting them to the investigation and requesting their assistance. These parents, by and large, were affluent and successful professionals, often working in real estate or the aerospace industry. Many of them had put their children on a lengthy waiting list in the hopes of getting them into what was, at the time, the most respected preschool in the city. In October, the Los Angeles County district attorney's office asked social workers to interview children who had attended the school, and by November the evaluations were under way. The McMartin Preschool closed down for good, after twenty-eight years of operation, in January 1984.

It would be almost another month before any news organization published or broadcast a report. By that point social workers had interviewed dozens of current and former McMartin students, and the police investigation had grown considerably. "Authorities now believe that at least sixty children were victimized," a reporter with the local ABC affiliate said.[1] Each of those sixty children, he went on to say, "had been keeping a grotesque secret of being sexually abused and made to appear in pornographic films while in the preschool's care, and of being forced to witness the mutilation and killing of animals to scare the kids into being silent." Police and district attorney investigators searched homes, local businesses, and an Episcopal church, and they also called up a national park in South Dakota in search of evidence. Six other former McMartin employees, including the school's seventy-seven-year-old founder, were arrested. Speaking to a news reporter, the mother of one of the children who had attended McMartin said that there was no doubt in her mind "or in anybody else's mind" that her son had been abused. "You cannot—*he cannot*—have made any of this up. There is no way."[2]

Bizarre as these allegations may have been—one therapist hired by the prosecution used the word "unthinkable" to describe what took place at McMartin—they were not without precedent, at least not in California.[3] Some 125 miles up Interstate 5, which cuts away from the coast into California's more conservative and agricultural Central Valley Region, a similar investigation was unfolding. In 1982, Mary Ann Barbour, a woman living in Bakersfield, obtained custody of her stepgrandchildren. Barbour believed that her stepdaughter Debbie's two daughters were being molested by Debbie's stepfather and that their parents were not doing enough to protect them from further harm. Over the course of interviews conducted by Kern County officials, the sisters reportedly said that they had been abused by Debbie's stepfather *and* their father. As these interviews progressed, the children gradually revealed that they had been suspended from hooks in a ceiling, beaten with belts and other implements, made to perform in pornographic film shoots, and rented to strangers in motels around the area. They said many other children had also been abused. In 1984 the girls' parents, along with two other members of what prosecutors said was a clandestine sex ring operating throughout Kern County, were given a combined sentence of exactly one thousand years in prison. More than thirty people were convicted of participating in a network of sex rings.

The word "epidemic" became an important feature of the political and rhetorical landscape in the 1980s. Whether the epidemics themselves were real, as in the case of AIDS, or imagined, as in the case of "crack babies," the rhetoric that surrounded them portrayed American society as menaced on all sides by conspiracies and dire threats.[4] Child sexual abuse officially took its place among these other threats at a 1984 hearing of the Senate Committee on the Judiciary, where Senator Arlen Specter of Pennsylvania said, "the molestation of children has now reached epidemic proportions."[5] His warning was confirmed by stories in newspapers and on television stations around the country. In Jordan, a tiny town to the southwest of Minneapolis, police investigators and FBI agents prepared to search the banks of the Minnesota River for bodies allegedly deposited there by a small boy's abusers. Twenty-four people, including two police officers and residents of a trailer park on the far side of Route 169, were accused of abusing dozens of children. The chairman of the Jordan school board told a reporter that many Jordanites had become "embarrassed to tell people where we even live."[6] In Niles, Michigan, the son of one preschool owner was sentenced to fifty to seventy-five years in prison. Children at the school said the man had photographed their abuse, made them take drugs, unearthed corpses, and sacrificed—not killed, but sacrificed—animals. In Malden, Massachusetts, the owner of a day care center and her two adult children were accused of abusing forty students in a place called the "magic room." In Chicago a janitor at a community child care facility was accused of boiling and eating a baby. Other staff members were charged with 246 counts of abuse and assault.

One witness at the Senate Judiciary Committee hearing testified to the difficulty of prosecuting cases that rested largely on the testimony of young and frightened children. She said courtrooms needed to have towels on hand for when kids "go in the back room and throw up all over you, they are so terrified." She said that children were "the perfect victims of the perfect crime."[7] One case in Miami, however, suggested that this witness may have exaggerated the difficulty of obtaining a conviction. In 1985, a thirty-six-year-old man on trial for the abuse of fifteen children at a home-based babysitting service asked that he be permitted to sit in the courtroom while his wife, who was also accused of participating in the abuse, offered testimony. "She cannot lie in front of me," Frank Fuster told the judge. "I need her to be here in person so she can see what's going on. When we see each other in person, have eye contact, my wife will not be able to lie."[8] Judge Newman granted the request, and so Fuster would eventually watch in person as Ileana told the jury that her husband had worn a white sheet and a strange mask, that he had sexually assaulted her with a crucifix, and that he had forced her to abuse the children along with him. "And he was naked," Ileana said, referring to one of the children, "and Frank was—was kissing the body. . . ." At this point Frank leapt from his chair and shouted, "You are a liar! God is gonna punish you for this!"[9] Ileana screamed, slumped down behind the wall of the witness box, and covered her face with trembling hands. Frank was found guilty. He received a sentence of six consecutive life terms, with additional time added for parole violation. In exchange for her testimony, Ileana received ten years. At her sentencing hearing she was seated next to Dade County state attorney Janet Reno, for whom the verdict represented a significant victory.

The dangers of babysitting services and day care centers became a national news media fixation. Plummeting enrollment numbers and surging insurance premiums forced many centers to close down, and newspapers reported that some day care directors were advising their employees to avoid physical contact with children if at all possible, advice intended not to protect children from molestation but rather to protect employees from accusations of sexual assault. Popular and academic presses published sociological studies on abuse, journalists' accounts of some of the early trials, and memoirs by parents of abused children. Their titles effectively suggest the tone of their contents: *Unspeakable Acts, Nursery Crimes, Not My Child.* All the while, allegations of sexual torture and child pornography production continued to emerge in El Paso and in suburban New Jersey. At the day care center run by the US Military Academy at West Point, rumors swirled about satanic ritual abuse and a possible connection to another army base in San Francisco. In 1984 and 1985, the television newsmagazine *20/20* aired "The Best Kept Secret" and "Why the Silence?," two lengthy examinations of the McMartin Preschool case, which still had not gone to trial. "Choose a nursery school very carefully," reporter Tom Jarriel warned.[10] "Almost every month has brought new stories from all parts of the country indicating that sexual abuse may be more common than any of us had imagined." Jarriel talked to "one of the army's leading authorities on brainwashing," who explained how the McMartin teachers were able to maintain their victims' silence for so many years.[11] At the end of one of these segments, Jarriel emphasized that "the defendants in this case are innocent until proven guilty." But rather than take up this line of thinking even for a moment, anchor Hugh Downs immediately pivoted back to the assumption that lay at the foundation of the whole broadcast. "How deeply marked are these children, Tom?" he asked. "Will they ever recover from it?"

"Psychologically, perhaps never," Jarriel replied. "One little boy, for example, asked his mother, 'Mommy, when I die, will the bad memories go away?'"

There was a brief pause. "My God," Downs said. "Thank you, Tom."[12] Legislatures took action to fend off the new threats facing the country's children. Multiple states passed laws that created new hearsay exceptions for trials involving abused children, meaning that parents, social workers, and police officers could take the stand and speak for the child victims they represented. The 1984 Child Protection Act removed all First Amendment protections from media defined as child pornography, which had been completely legal until 1977, and it also legislated millions of new children into being by raising the age of minority from sixteen to eighteen. Although the Reagan administration spent much of its time in power easing the federal government's financial commitment to social welfare programs, funds poured into new organizations and institutes looking to protect the country's most vulnerable class of citizens. These laws transformed the state's relationship to children, and they were aggressively pursued by law enforcement agencies and prosecutors' offices, often at the urging of activist groups organized and run by parents of children involved in the day care cases. Some states passed bills that allowed children to testify from outside the courtroom via closed-circuit television so that they would not have to undergo the further trauma of seeing their abusers in person. Many parents involved with the ritual abuse cases would have been otherwise unwilling to allow their children to testify in court, and without the child witnesses, prosecutors believed their cases were doomed.

Eyewitness testimony is a crucial component of many criminal proceedings, but prosecutors and parents working on the day care cases had good reason for special concern. As the defendants and their lawyers had been noting from the outset, police investigators were almost never able to find any physical evidence to corroborate the grotesque charges. Although this is true of most child sex abuse investigations, the majority of which involve fondling and other forms of contact that do not cause medically detectable injury or produce forensically detectable evidence, the day care ritual abuse trials were not anything like most child sex abuse investigations. In North Carolina, children said that their teachers had thrown them out of a boat into a school of sharks.[13] In Los Angeles, children said that one of their teachers had forced them to watch as he hacked a horse to pieces with a machete.[14] In New Jersey, children said their teacher had raped them with knives, forks, and wooden spoons, and a child in Miami told investigators about homemade pills their caretakers had forced them to eat. The pills, the child said, looked like candy corn, and they made all of the children sleepy.[15] Children in various cases said they had been taken to graveyards, sometimes to kill baby tigers and sometimes to dig up bodies, which were removed from their coffins and stabbed. In addition, the sex rings said to be operating in cities like Jordan, Minnesota, and Bakersfield, California, supposedly involved regular meetings, wild parties, elaborate religious ceremonies, and the production of child pornography, all witnessed by many people. (These wilder stories often took time to develop out of the more mundane allegations in which cases originated, but once they did develop they came to monopolize the attention of investigators and journalists.) Despite the numbers of people said to be involved, despite all of the different implements the defendants were said to have used, and despite the brutality of the violence they were believed to have inflicted on the children they cared for, prosecutors asked their child witnesses to do nearly all of the heavy lifting in court. No pornography, no blood, no semen, no weapons, no mutilated corpses, no sharks, and no satanic altars or robes were ever found.

Prosecutors, parents, and therapists dealt with this problem by repeating what became a common refrain. Set aside the lack of corroborating evidence, they said, and consider this basic fact: children all over the country were fighting through fear and shame to come forward and say they had been abused—how could a decent society ignore these stories? Therapists pointed to their own profession's long and inglorious history of ignoring children who tried speak out about abuse, and they said this was a mistake the country could not afford to repeat. "All children who are sexually abused anywhere," one abuse expert said at the National Symposium on Child Molestation in 1984, "need to have their credibility recognized and to have advocates working for them. Among the things that is most damaging is the sense of being alone and having no one to talk to."[16]

The social stigma associated with child abuse has a long, well-documented history, and today it remains a painful experience for many people who try to seek help or go public with accounts of victimization. As defense attorneys, journalists, and research psychologists associated with the day care trials eventually pointed out, however, this social stigma was not actually relevant to these cases because the allegations hadn't come from the children to begin with.

In New Jersey, an investigator with the Department of Youth and Family Services named Lou Fonolleras interviewed children who attended the Wee Care Day Nursery. One Friday in June 1985, Fonolleras asked a child about his experiences there:

Q: Did she make you do anything to her boobies?
A: No.
Q: What did she make you do to her vagina?
A: Nothing.
Q: Nothing. Okay. I'm going to ask you a couple more questions. So, you know Kelly's in jail, right? How do you feel that Kelly's in jail? . . . Are you happy or not?
A: No.
Q: No.
A: I don't like when Kelly's in there.[17]

As the interview continued in this vein, Fonolleras assured the child that "all the other friends" he had talked to told him about Kelly's abuse. "And now it's your turn to tell me. You don't want to be left out, do you?"

Q: Do you think that Kelly was—was not good when she was hurting you all?
A: [inaudible] wasn't hurt, wasn't hurting me. I like her.[18]

When the boy said, "No," in response to a question about whether Kelly had made people take their clothes off, Fonolleras said, "Yes." When Fonolleras asked the boy whether Kelly had ever kissed his penis, the boy replied, "No. Did Kelly kiss *your* pee-pee?" Fonolleras said that she hadn't, "because I never met her yet."[19]

By the time children involved in day care investigations spoke to an interviewer or therapist, many of them had already been questioned repeatedly by their parents, who described themselves to journalists and in books as being made physically ill by anxiety, anger, and fear. These undocumented conversations could, however, be dramatized, as in a 1989 made-for-TV movie in which a mother interrogates her son Teddy six times before he finally opens up. "They said you'd die if I ever told," Teddy says.[20] Professional interviewers often used these earlier conversations as the foundation for their own questioning, and in some interviews children referred back to their parents as a means of explaining, both to their interviewers and to themselves, the strange situation they now faced. In Miami a therapist named Laurie Braga asked a little girl how she felt about Frank Fuster being put in jail.

A: I'm glad.
Q: You're glad. How come?
A: Because [inaudible] now I found out that he was bad. . . .
Q: No. What is it that makes you think that he is bad?
A: My mom told me.
Q: Did she tell you what he did that was bad? [pause] Don't you wonder? No?
A: Do you know what he did?[21]

Interviews could last for hours, and the children being questioned were often five, four, or even three years old. When children failed to provide answers that corroborated allegations of abuse, interviewers repeated the questions. In Los Angeles one five-year-old boy who had attended the McMartin Preschool became frustrated with his interviewer, a woman named Kee MacFarlane:

Q: Where did Beth get touched?
A: She didn't get touched.
Q: You can help tell her yucky secrets and she won't have to tell. Wouldn't that be nice?
A: She didn't get touched.
Q: She never did? How about on the other side. Maybe she did.
A: She never even got touched.[22]

As these interviews pressed on, children who did not provide affirmative answers to questions about abuse found themselves being asked the same questions all over again. So the children began to provide different kinds of answers. Later in the same interview, Kee MacFarlane returned to the topic of the boy's classmate.

Q: Here's Beth.
A: She got touched nowhere.
Q: Oh, I don't know if that's the truth. We have to tell the [video recorder] the truth. Maybe she got touched in the back, too, like Otis.

A: Huh-uh [negative].

Q: Maybe she got touched in the mouth.

A: Huh-uh [negative].

Q: How about in the mouth?

A: Mouth?

Q: Yeah. Yes? In the mouth?

A: [No audible response.]

Q: I thought so.[23]

As the decade wore on, defense attorneys began to present expert researchers and therapists willing to explain what this kind of interviewing meant for the reliability of the accusations that eventually emerged. But expert knowledge doesn't seem to be required to see what was happening in many of these cases. Around the country, therapists, social workers, and police officers unintentionally forced children to fabricate tales of brutal abuse. The children were then asked to repeat and reinforce these stories, both in courtrooms and in the years of therapy sessions that often followed. Children as young as three and almost never older than nine or ten, children who previously understood their time in day care as essentially normal, whether happy or not, had their lives reorganized around the idea that they were deeply and irrevocably traumatized. No amount of benevolence and well-intentioned concern on the therapists' part can cover up the clearly coercive manner in which children were made to believe these things. "Are you goin' to be stupid, or are you goin' to be smart and help us here?" one interviewer asked a child who was failing to provide information.[24]

The coercive interviewing, the complete lack of physical evidence, and the incomprehensible strangeness of the allegations themselves began to make prosecutors' jobs difficult, and as the decade entered its second half, a number of cases fell apart. In Minnesota, when the state abruptly dropped charges against twenty-one people after a jury acquitted the first two to have been tried, the prosecutor issued a statement claiming the charges were dismissed to prevent the release of documents pertaining to a related but secret investigation involving as many as six child homicides.[25] In Miami members of the jury that acquitted a sixteen-year-old boy of ritual abuse in 1989 wrote a letter to Janet Reno in which they asked why her office had failed so spectacularly to present a convincing case. They did this in spite of what they described as their firm belief that "something did happen to the two children in question."[26] And in Los Angeles, where the McMartin trial would eventually drag on for seven years, becoming the longest criminal trial in American history, proceedings took on an atmosphere of surreal, geographically specific, black comedy. In 1985 a ten-year-old boy testified that a Los Angeles city attorney had slaughtered hundreds of animals alongside Ray Buckey, that he had been abused by priests and elderly nuns at a dozen separate satanic rituals, that he had been subjected to brutal beatings with a bull-whip, and that after all this the McMartin teachers had capped off their orgy of abuse by forcing the children to eat "peppers and other stuff that was raw" at a health food store.[27]

People who think they are being wrongly persecuted by the legal system will often compare themselves to the Puritans who were accused of witchcraft in Salem, Massachusetts. Those accused in the day care cases were no exception. In Manhattan Beach the defendants' supporters ran newspaper ads reading, simply, "SALEM MASSACHUSETTS, 1692. MANHATTAN BEACH CALIFORNIA, 1985."[28] These ads were rhetorically powerful but also accurate in more ways than the defendants may have realized. The Salem witch trials were the first legal proceedings in American history to involve the testimony of child witnesses, and in both the seventeenth-century witch hunts and the day care investigations, the question of a child's ability to distinguish fact from fiction was central.[29] In each episode, children were thought to have been abused by a secretive group of conspirators, and each time it was the adults who first began to suspect that a conspiracy was at work. Initially the girls in Salem did not even report that anyone was harming them. Some scholars have hypothesized that their outlandish episodes and fits were primarily expressions of ecstatic religious fervor. Descriptions of the girls' nonsensical outbursts strongly resemble modern accounts of speaking in tongues, and the girls described visions of angels, celestial light, and God's glory just as frequently as they talked of terror and witchcraft.[30] But the adult villagers ignored these expressions of religious ecstasy and joy, just as 1980s social workers would ignore those children who described benign experiences at day care. Again and again they asked their children, "Who is it that afflicts you?"[31]

Salem and the day care cases were also investigated and tried in many of the same ways. In the 1980s, doctors examined the genitals of the alleged victims and often diagnosed abuse on the basis of nearly micro-scopic variations in skin folds and hymen measurements, variations that are now understood to be completely normal. In Salem, physicians and midwives also conducted painstaking examinations of the accused, on the lookout for something called a "witch's tit."[32] This tit, which could be any odd protuberance or irregularity in a person's flesh, was frequently "dis-covered" within close proximity to the genitals, and it was thought that succubi came to the tit at night to feed. Also attributed to the accused in Salem were terrible psychological and spiritual powers, such that victims risked further trauma if required to occupy the same room as their abus-ers. As one of the accused witches was led into a courtroom, her victims cried out in what one observer called "extreme agony," and when she bit her lips, the girls said they could feel her teeth on their own skin.[33] Similar concerns were used in the 1980s to justify laws that allowed children to testify via closed-circuit television.

After the panic died down in Salem, however, there were apologies and reparations. In 1697 Samuel Sewall, who had presided over the trials, asked that a formal apology be read before the congregation in Boston's South Church, so that he could "take the Blame & Shame."[34] Twelve of the trial jurors asked for forgiveness, and although it was to take another fourteen years, the governor of Massachusetts authorized monetary com-pensation to twenty-two of the accused. No such apologies followed the day care ritual abuse trials, and there hasn't been much in the way of rep-arations either. Of the many hundreds of people who were investigated in connection with day care and ritual abuse cases around the country, some 190 were formally charged with crimes, leading to at least 83 convictions. Undoing these convictions proved to be a slow, halting, and very painful process. In Massachusetts it took eight years for the state to overturn Vio-let Amirault and Cheryl Amirault LeFave's convictions, and it would take nine more to release Gerald Amirault, Cheryl's brother and Violet's son, from prison. Kelly Michaels spent five years in prison after her 1988 con-viction in a New Jersey courtroom. In El Paso, Gayle Dove was released from prison only to be tried and convicted again, and it would be another two years before she was freed for good. Fran and Dan Keller of Austin, Texas, were released in 2013, the same year in which a San Antonio prison freed Anna Vasquez, Elizabeth Ramirez, Kristie Mayhugh, and Cassandra Rivera. This is to say nothing of the challenges people convicted in these trials face after their term of incarceration. Jesse Friedman of Great Neck, New York, remains a registered "Level 3" sex offender despite his 2001 release and despite the mountain of evidence testifying to his innocence.

Even as convictions were overturned in some parts of the country during the 1990s, new investigations and trials occasionally popped up elsewhere. Some of these became famous miscarriages of justice. Three Arkansas teenagers who were falsely convicted of murdering young boys in the woods, in part because of their interest in heavy metal, became the subjects of a sympathetic HBO documentary that included a soundtrack by Metallica. The "West Memphis Three" were released in 2011 after eighteen years in prison. Other episodes, however, remain almost entirely forgotten, including the sex ring investigation in Wenatchee, Washington, in which forty-three adults were arrested on more than twenty-nine *thousand* charges of sex abuse involving sixty children. Eighteen of the defendants, nearly all of whom were poor and on welfare and some of whom were illiterate or mentally handicapped, were convicted in the mid-1990s. The last of them would not be released until 2000. The panic has also turned out, like much else in American popular culture, to have a powerful international appeal. Cases similar to those that characterized the American ritual abuse panic appeared in Norway, the Netherlands, and much of the Anglophone world, including the United Kingdom, New Zealand, and Canada. As recently as 2010, a mentally handicapped man in Jerusalem was arrested on allegations of child sexual abuse. By 2011 many people in the tight-knit neighborhood of Nahalot were convinced that a sophisticated pedophile ring, governed by an elaborate secret hierarchy, had been operating in their midst for years, possibly generations. Children alleged ritual abuse at the hands of undercover Christians, and they described witches and magic doors.[35]

In order to cope with the implausibility of their allegations and the lack of physical evidence, supporters of the day care and ritual abuse prosecutions turned again and again to the importance of belief. In private homes, in court, and in the media, one's belief in the children and the adults who spoke for them became the central issue around which the whole issue of child sexual abuse (and, to a certain extent, sexual violence in general) revolved. To an extent this development followed naturally from the long history of society's inadequate response to abuse. Teenage girls alleging abuse at the hands of a relative or teacher were often dismissed as manipulative Lolitas, and adult women who went to the police with allegations of rape frequently watched as their credibility, rather than that of those they accused, became the crux of judicial proceedings. In the late 1960s, writers and activists began to point out that addressing the problem of sexual abuse in a just and constructive way would have to entail a new social willingness to take victims seriously when they spoke up. In the 1980s, however, the widespread emphasis on belief did not lead to children being taken more seriously. People associated with the day care and ritual abuse cases only believed children when they told stories that conformed to their adult advocates' conspiracy theories and lurid fantasies.

These fantasies of imaginary abuse also influenced how society started to think about the abuse that really does happen every day. The hysteria cemented the child molester as society's most feared and loathed criminal figure. When someone is convicted of a serious sex crime against a child, he—and in at least 95 percent of cases it is a "he"[36]—becomes the ward of a prison system in which pedophiles constitute a particularly reviled group and in which he will be vulnerable to sexual and physical assault himself. This vulnerability to beatings and rapes, which many people believe incarcerated pedophiles completely deserve, is the premise of many jokes about child abusers. When a sex offender finishes his sentence, laws in at least twenty states and hundreds of additional municipalities prevent him from living within a certain distance of places where children "congregate," meaning not only schools and playgrounds but also parks, bus stops, and even homeless shelters. (In Miami these restrictions were so onerous that a group of offenders in Dade County briefly formed a tent city under a highway bridge, there being nowhere else to legally reside.)[37] Politicians and their constituents enthusiastically support these laws in spite of a large body of research showing that child abusers almost never first encounter their victims in a "place where children congregate"; usually they encounter their victims, to whom they are often related, in private homes.[38] These laws, in turn, both respond to and reinforce a set of widely shared beliefs about the psychology of the sex offender who victimizes children, who is understood to have an illness, to have no self-control whatsoever, to be utterly helpless in the face of his desires. Again, studies showing that child molesters actually have a rather low recidivism rate relative to those convicted of other violent crimes have done little to modify the public perception of the pedophile as a uniquely monstrous figure.[39] This psychological caricature has shaped nearly three decades of thinking and policy about child sex abuse with destructive effects. Resources that might have been directed toward addressing the real causes of child abuse—simply put, these are poverty, the relative powerlessness of women and children within nuclear families, and the patriarchal organization of many workplaces, schools, and other social institutions—were instead used to fend off bogeymen. This misrecognition of the problem of child abuse and the misallocation of money and energy that resulted were, in a sense, part of the point. As disruptive and painful as the day care sex abuse cases were to those involved, addressing the real causes of child abuse would have been a much more difficult and disruptive task. Proponents of the day care panic sensed this and looked for ways to avoid the issue head-on.

A simpler way of putting all this may just be to say that the witch hunt worked. The climate of fear that surrounded these cases influenced a whole series of arguments about women, children, and sex that had been intensifying in American politics and culture for some twenty years. In the 1960s and 1970s the sexual revolution and then, especially, the second wave of the feminist movement upended the long-standing assumption that the nuclear family, organized around the lifelong, monogamous marriage of a breadwinning husband to a wife who oversaw things at home, was the indispensible foundation of American society. Women demanded equal access to employment and pay, divorce lost its social stigma, and the cult of motherhood and domestic bliss began to lose its sheen. By the 1980s, however, with Ronald Reagan in office and evangelical Christianity at the height of its political influence, conservatives were mounting efforts to roll back these changes and shore up the old domestic order. These efforts gained so much momentum that even some feminists joined in, arguing that the liberalization of sex had gone too far and produced not freedom but anarchy, danger, pornography, victimization, and psychological trauma. Some cases also drew on long-standing anxieties about homosexuals' supposed predisposition to pedophilia: four lesbian women in San Antonio and a gay nineteen-year-old teacher's aide in Massachusetts were among those convicted. The day care trials were a powerful instrument of the decade's resurgent sexual conservatism, serving as a warning to mothers who thought they could keep their very young children safe while simultaneously pursuing a life outside the home. As some of the country's most basic social arrangements began to shift, the trials dramatized the consequences of that shift in the manner of a gothic play.

This book is primarily a work of history, not of investigative journalism. The panic received enormous amounts of coverage as it took place. Some of this coverage was fearless and intelligent, and some of it was clumsy and stupid. In any case, the events recounted here are not breaking news, and my work is not a substitute for these earlier journalistic efforts. My goal is to understand why, after this initial tide of media coverage receded, so many of these cases fell so quickly into almost total obscurity. McMartin retains some wider function as a metonym for the panic as a whole, but Country Walk, Kern County and Bakersfield, the Bronx Five, Little Rascals, and Scott County, Minnesota, (to offer only the beginning of a much longer list) are unlikely to signify anything at all to people other than those who were directly involved. This is a large gap in recent historical memory, and it is not incidental to the panic's meaning; it is a central part of it. These cases were forgotten because the issues that brought them into being—especially conflicts surrounding the transformation of family life—remain very much unresolved. This book is an attempt to understand how hysteria both responded to and shaped these new social arrangements. It is also an attempt to make a lasting, stable place for these investigations and trials in the country's cultural and social history.

Chapter 1

The Discovery
of Child Abuse

In the years following the end of World War II, American doctors, psychiatrists, and social workers discovered that young children were sometimes beaten by the people who cared for them. For decades the question of what to do about child abuse—or whether to do anything at all—had been answered almost exclusively in private homes, with each family addressing the issue on its own in the manner it thought best. Now abuse became a public concern, a social problem. People began to look for a solution. How could child abuse be stopped?

The discovery that children were regularly subjected to acts that are now universally recognized as "abusive" might actually be called a rediscovery. The Victorian era had also been preoccupied with the things certain groups of parents did to their children at home. In 1874 concerned neighbors of an eight-year-old living on West 41st Street in New York City raised the alarm about the girl's maltreatment at the hands of her foster parents. As the neighbors reported to local officials in an unsuccessful attempt to goad the police into action, Mary Ellen Wilson's guardians starved the girl, beat her with leather straps, and sent her out into cold weather wearing little more than rags. It wasn't until a Methodist missionary contacted Harry Bergh, the founder of the American Society for the Prevention of Cruelty to Animals, that Mary Ellen was removed from the home. Bergh and the missionary, a woman named Etta Angell Wheeler, took the foster parents to court, and the sensational trial that followed was a staple of newspaper coverage for weeks. The trial ended with a one-year sentence for the foster mother, but more lasting was a decision made by Mary Ellen's lawyer, Elbridge T. Gerry, to found the New York Society for the Prevention of Cruelty to Children. Gerry's idea caught on across the United States, and by the turn of the century poor neighborhoods in many cities were filled with "anti-cruelists," crusading reformers who scoured immigrant communities for signs of abuse. By 1910 more than 250 separate organizations devoted to child protection, primarily comprising members of the philanthropic upper classes, operated in the country's urban areas.[1]

The anti-cruelists derived part of the moral impetus for their work from the Victorian elevation of childhood as a sacred and precious time of life, but as would also be the case in the 1980s, this earlier explosion of interest in combating child abuse provided cover for a completely different set of political concerns. American cities took in some 20 million immigrants during the second half of the nineteenth century, and many people regarded these immigrants with tremendous suspicion and resentment, with special attention paid to their lack of education and training. Viewed in light of the high birth rates that prevailed among the newly arrived immigrant populations, this lack of education potentially threatened social stability itself.[2] The anti-cruelists accordingly paid more attention to immigrants, whom they referred to as "the brutal poor," than to any other group of potential child abusers.[3] In 1924, however, quotas imposed by the National Origins Act set off a rapid decline in immigration rates, and so public concern about the brutal poor and their child-rearing habits went into a decline as well.[4] The first wave of enthusiasm for child protection remained a feature of American life for half a century and then disappeared just as quickly as it had emerged.

Child abuse completely disappeared from the public agenda for nearly forty years, but in 1946 a pediatric radiologist named John Caffey encountered something unexpected in the course of his work. On six separate occasions, Caffey made X-rays of infants admitted to the hospital for treatment of chronic subdural hematomas (swelling or bleeding immediately underneath the skull) and found recent fractures of the long bones in the children's arms and legs.[5] Caffey also observed scattered thickenings in children's bones, evidence of past healing from previous traumas. Caffey was a radiologist, so he didn't have contact with the children whose X-rays he examined, nor did he speak to the children's parents; he was left more or less to his own devices in trying to understand the cause of their injuries. "In not a single case was there a history of injury to which the skeletal lesions could reasonably be attributed," he wrote. In a different article published that same year, Caffey discounted scurvy, rickets, syphilis, and "neoplastic disease" as plausible causes. He also considered but then discounted violence inflicted on the children by someone else.[6] Caffey wondered whether the fractures and hematomas might be associated symptoms of some new children's disease.[7] Whatever their cause, Caffey wrote, the injuries clearly deserved further attention and study.

Evidence continued to accumulate in the late 1940s and early 1950s, as other radiologists began to report similar infant injuries. In 1953 a physician named F. N. Silverman rather tactfully identified parental carelessness as a potential source of injury. He suggested that physicians obtain detailed patient histories for injured infants, but he also wrote that doctors should not ask too many questions or seem overly suspicious.[8] It was hoped that these patient histories could be obtained without alarming (or angering) the parents. In 1955, however, two other American physicians observed that many infants admitted to medical facilities with very serious injuries were "unaccompanied by readily volunteered and adequate account of injury," and after looking into the infants' family backgrounds, the doctors determined that they "came invariably from unstable households with a high incidence of neurotic or frankly psychotic behavior on the part of at least one adult."[9] Finally, in 1957, more than ten years after his initial discovery, John Caffey reevaluated his original data set and concluded the children had probably been injured by their parents, not by some new disease.[10] One might wonder at the medical profession's decade-long reluctance to question or challenge any aspect of parents' conduct toward their children. How powerful the sense of embarrassment must have been in order for these doctors to avoid the most obvious conclusion for so long. It speaks volumes about the nuclear family's status in postwar society: the prestige, the respect, and especially the extraordinary degree of privacy that families regarded as their natural right.

The turning point came in 1962, when a Denver physician named C. Henry Kempe published "The Battered-Child Syndrome" in the *Journal of the American Medical Association* (*JAMA*). Kempe had reviewed injury reports from seventy-one hospitals around the United States and identified 302 cases in which injuries appeared to have been intentionally inflicted by the child's parents. He argued that although the condition "may occur at any age," affected children are generally "younger than 3 years," and he further noted that one hospital in Colorado had provided treatment to four children "suffering from the parent-inflicted battered-child syndrome" in just a single day. He wrote that symptoms varied widely, manifesting as everything from "very minor skin changes" to "life-threatening damage to vital organs," and that although child-beaters could often be diagnosed as "psychopathic or sociopathic characters," it was often the case that "the guilty parent is the one who gives the impression of being the more normal."[11]

"The Battered-Child Syndrome" was the most direct acknowledgment to date that physical violence against children was a common practice of American family life, and yet it is easy to see that the authors were uncomfortable with their findings. They arrive at their conclusions slowly, even reluctantly, and they also acknowledge, in an editorial that accompanied the article, that many physicians would have difficulty following the clear trail of medical evidence to its logical conclusion. "The implication that parents were instrumental in causing injury to their child is often difficult for the physician to accept," they wrote. "But, regardless of how distasteful it may be, the history should be reviewed for possible assault and the necessary laboratory studies performed in order to confirm or reject the suspicion."[12] Once the diagnosis of parental assault had been made, they went on to write, physicians had a moral obligation to act on that diagnosis: "The consequences of improper disposition are often so tragic that the physician must, in good conscience, call on social agencies and legal authorities to make certain that proper protection is given the child."

A certain queasiness surrounding the issue is further suggested by the fact that child abuse was first identified as a *medical* problem rather than a social one. Murder, robbery, assault—these are crimes, problems society usually asks cops, lawyers, and juries, rather than doctors, to solve. When the medical profession does get involved, as in the case of an insanity plea, the purpose is to remove some degree of moral or personal responsibility from the defendant. Kempe's decision to describe child abuse as a "syndrome" served the same purpose. The year before his article was published in *JAMA*, Kempe organized a panel discussion at the annual meeting of the American Pediatric Association. Although Kempe had originally planned to choose a title for the panel that accurately reflected the subject of his research—that is, the physical abuse of children—colleagues warned him that such a title might scare people off. They suggested that Kempe choose a less threatening title, and after a bit of trial and error, the

Battered-Child Syndrome was born.[13] By medicalizing and psychologizing the issue, Kempe successfully fended off a different interpretation of child abuse, one that, in identifying abuse as a social and criminal problem, could have more forcefully assigned moral and social responsibility. But this other interpretation would not make its way into the public discourse for almost another decade.

With its careful documentation and obvious concern for the special intricacies and difficulties of pediatrics, Kempe's article is a model of professionalism. But it was a press release that made Kempe's work a sensation. In the wake of his paper's publication, Kempe convinced the American Medical Association to send a release out over the Associated Press wire, and within weeks dozens of articles had picked up the news reported in "Parental Abuse Looms in Childhood Deaths."[14] In her study of the emergence of child abuse as a political issue, Barbara J. Nelson writes that professional research journals published just 9 articles on child abuse in the decade preceding the publication of "The Battered-Child Syndrome." In the decade following Kempe's article that number rose to 260, and that number, in turn, was dwarfed by the number of newspaper and general interest magazine pieces that repeated and amplified the contents of the AMA's press release.[15] In the *New York Times* a report on Kempe and his work didn't actually discuss any of that work until after the author had run through a disturbing list of sensational child abuse cases from around the country: in Cincinnati doctors had treated a "baby girl suffering from 20 cigarette burns"; in Boston a mother had beaten two teenage girls with a frying pan; a woman in Washington, DC, had taken out "her anger on her six-week-old baby by throwing him across the room."[16]

The *Saturday Evening Post*, with its readership of millions, took a similarly lurid approach:

[Children] are strangled, thrown, dropped, shot, stabbed, shaken, drowned, suffocated, sexually violated, held under running water, tied upright for long periods of time, stepped on, bitten, given electric shocks, forced to swallow pepper or buried alive. The reports of the injuries read like a case book of a concentration-camp doctor: bruises, contusions, welts, skull fractures, broken bones, brain injuries, burns, concussions, cuts, gashes, gunshot and knife wounds, ruptured vital organs, bites, dislocated necks, asphyxiations, eyes gouged out.[17]

In *Time, Life, Newsweek,* and elsewhere journalists focused at length and in detail on the variety and brutality of abuse, but they consistently did so within the medical framework set out by Kempe and his colleagues. The *Saturday Evening Post* headline said it best: "A Tragic Increase in Cases of Child Abuse Is Prompting a Hunt for Ways to Select Sick Adults Who Commit Such Crimes."

Medical professionals and state legislatures began to feel that some kind of a response was needed, and they tailored that response to fit the spirit of the times. By the middle of the 1960s, President Lyndon Johnson's Great Society programs were well under way. The Economic Opportunity Act of 1964 established an office aimed at addressing the roots of poverty as well as a Job Corps designed to provide vocational training. The federal government also established programs and passed legislation to fund public schools, protect large tracts of wilderness from industrial development, build low-income housing, establish suffrage for nonwhites, provide basic health care to the poor, and raise safety standards for consumer products. The country was experiencing a surge of optimism about the federal government's ability to solve social problems with legislation, and the doctors who rediscovered child abuse at the beginning of the decade felt that they should not be left behind. In 1963, California became the first state to pass a law mandating that physicians report any suspected instances of child abuse to the authorities. Just four years later, Hawaii became the fiftieth state, along with the District of Columbia and the Virgin Islands, to pass such a law.[18] Even in the midst of the period's intoxicating political optimism, the reporting laws were adopted with astonishing speed. In most cases those who reported their suspicions received immunity from civil or criminal lawsuits, and although the specific list of responsible professionals varied from state to state—some also included dentists, social workers, or pharmacists—the laws all agreed on a basic principle: for the first time, some people had a professional obligation to look for and speak up about child abuse.

The historian Judith Sealander has described Florida's initial experience with reporting laws as typical. The state's department of protective services only reported 16 cases of abuse across the state in 1965. Over the next eight years, however, Florida publicized a toll-free hotline number that citizens could call to report abuse and also ran television and radio ads describing the provisions of the reporting law. By 1971 protective services had recorded 250 cases of child abuse, and by 1974 the number would explode to more than 28,000.[19] It was at this point, as states scrambled to adequately staff their new reporting agencies, that the rhetoric surrounding child abuse began to change. Child abuse had initially been publicized as a syndrome, a collection of associated symptoms inflicted on children by adults who often displayed symptoms of mental illness as well. In the early 1970s, however, a different medical term began to appear in newspaper headlines and at professional conferences. Now the country was facing an "epidemic."

The first people to attempt a political analysis of child abuse—what caused it, what its consequences were, and what it said about the country's social arrangements—were members of the women's liberation movement. On April 17, 1971, a psychiatric social worker named Florence Rush made a presentation at Washington Irving High School in New York City. She was delivering her talk at a conference and speak-out on rape that had been organized by a group called New York Radical Feminists. At fifty-three, Rush was a few decades older than most of the young activists and thinkers who provided radical feminism with its initial surge of energy, and despite her years of organizing experience, she was more or less unknown to the younger feminist generation.

Her presentation, "The Sexual Abuse of Children: A Feminist Point of View," stunned the audience.[20] Rush historicized child sex abuse, explaining that the sexual culture of the Victorian era had given rise to both the idea of the innocent child as well as that innocent child's illicit erotic appeal. Departing from the popular view of child sex abuse as the product of psychological deviance—this remains the popular view of child sex abuse today—Rush analyzed abuse in terms of the power structures that made it possible, writing that psychiatrists had ignored "a social milieu where male sexual power over women and children is institutionally integrated."[21] Her talk attacked conservatives who believed the family was a benign institution based on love and affection, but she also criticized leftists who argued that the sexual revolution would eventually cause the taboo of pedophilia to fall harmlessly away. Both of her critiques were founded on the argument that the causes *and* the consequences of child abuse stemmed from inequalities that were built into the basic structure of the nuclear family. Rush's insistence on thinking through a problem that was often described as "unthinkable" made her talk a sensation, and she received the conference's lone standing ovation. Following Rush's lead, many radical feminists would come to believe that in order to eradicate child abuse, the family itself would have to change.

Although more moderate progressive groups were not interested in mounting such a direct attack on the country's most sacred institution, they did try to link violent child abuse to other aspects of child welfare, including poverty, education, and the problems working women faced in trying to keep jobs while caring for children. They believed it would be impossible to understand or prevent abuse unless the problem could be situated within a more general picture of children's lives. In 1971 the National Organization for Women (NOW), which was then the largest and most powerful feminist group in the country, spent enormous amounts of energy and money supporting a bill called the Comprehensive Child Development Act. A textbook example of Great Society optimism and ambition, the bill would have funded the single-greatest expansion of federal children's services in the country's history. Conservatives wanted nothing to do with it. A particular flashpoint was a set of provisions that would have provided federal day care services to parents across the country, with a set of sliding fees in place to accommodate a range of incomes. NOW and other feminist organizations had fought hard to encourage women to leave the domestic sphere and enter the workforce, and now that women actually *were* beginning to make their way into white-collar workplaces, feminists hoped that the federal government would provide them with much-needed support.

The bill, which one observer described as "one of the most heavily lobbied human services bills" the country had ever seen, passed through both houses of Congress, but in December of 1971 President Richard Nixon vetoed the Act.[22] The veto's language was direct: "For the Federal Government to plunge headlong financially into supporting child development would commit the vast moral authority of the National Government to the side of communal approaches to child rearing over [and] against the family-centered approach."[23] This was a major defeat for NOW and also for Minnesota senator Walter Mondale, who had introduced and sponsored the Comprehensive Child Development Act. The significance of Nixon's use of the word "communal" was easy to understand in Cold War America, and he went on to say that the bill had "family-weakening implications."

When Mondale then made a second attempt at passing major child-welfare legislation, he made sure not to repeat his earlier political mistake. On March 13, 1973, just a few years before he would join Jimmy Carter's ticket as a candidate for vice president, Mondale introduced a piece of legislation called the Child Abuse Prevention and Treatment Act. The act created a National Center on Child Abuse and Neglect to supervise and track research, instituted a program of grants to fund abuse prevention initiatives, and established a commission of nongovernmental observers to study the effectiveness of reporting and other prevention laws. "Development," with all its connotations of social engineering and government-run child rearing, was out.

A Senate Subcommittee on Children and Youth held hearings on the bill over the course of four days in the spring of 1973. Senator Mondale chaired the subcommittee, and he kept a tight grip on proceedings as several dozen witnesses testified. Two witnesses in particular caught the attention of Mondale, the other members of the subcommittee, and the national press. The first was David Gil, a professor of social policy at Brandeis University. In the late 1960s, Gil worked with the US Children's Bureau to publish the findings of the most comprehensive series of child abuse studies that had been conducted to date. He was one of the country's preeminent experts on the social and economic contexts of child abuse.[24] When he appeared to testify before the subcommittee, however, Mondale did everything he could to make sure that Gil was ignored. It was in the interest of appeasing more conservative members of the subcommittee that Mondale had used the Child Abuse Prevention and Treatment Act to sever physical and sexual abuse from other social problems in the first place—the bill was specifically designed to keep economic and racial inequality out of the conversation. So when Gil began to raise exactly those issues in his testimony, Mondale rushed to defuse the situation before things got out of hand. Although "physical abuse of children is known to occur in all strata of our society," Gil said, "the incidence rate seems significantly higher among deprived and discriminated-against segments of the population." Mondale immediately asked Gil whether he would yield for a question:

Mondale: Would you not say that the incidence of child abuse is found as well in the families of middle-class parents?

Gil: Definitely so.

Mondale: And upper income parents?

Gil: Yes.

Mondale: While the incidence may strike the poor, as you later argue,
more heavily than the rest, yet this is a national phenomenon that is
not limited to the very poor.

Gil: Definitely.

Mondale: You may go into some of the finest communities from an economic standpoint and find child abuse as you would in the ghettos of
this country.[25]

Gil, an extremely courteous witness throughout his testimony, agreed
again, but he tried once more to make the point that Mondale hoped to
avoid. He acknowledged that "the factors that lead to abuse among the
well-to-do are the same that also lead to abuse among the poor," but Gil
also tried to point out that "the poor have in addition many more factors."

"I know you are going to get to that," Mondale replied. "But this is not
a poverty problem; it is a national problem."[26]

A subsequent witness did a better job of describing this national problem in terms that pleased the Senate subcommittee. Mondale and his colleagues heard from a woman who lived in Southern California's Redondo
Beach. She testified under the pseudonym Jolly K. In 1967, as Jolly K told
the Senate subcommittee, she had been seeing a psychiatric social worker
named Leonard Lieber. She wanted to figure out why she had abused her
child and how she could keep herself from doing it again. Jolly K had
abused her daughter on two occasions: once by strangling her for lying
and another time by throwing "a rather large kitchen knife" at her from
across the room.[27] One day Lieber suggested to his twenty-nine-year-old
patient that she speak to another patient of his who was working through
similar problems. The pair became a small group, and then the group
became a larger group, and eventually Lieber and Jolly K gave the group a
name: Parents Anonymous. In her testimony, which she delivered with
her psychiatrist seated nearby, Jolly K described how she had abused her
child—verbally, aside from the two incidents previously mentioned—and
provided a psychological explanation for her acts.

Jolly K: To simplify it, to me this child reflected my negative self, who I
viewed for years as a rather rotten, worthless person due to the fact
I was raised much similarly to the way she was raised in the first
6½ years.

Mondale: Is that what psychologists call where you hate something you
   sense in yourself?

Jolly K: Yes. It is kind of like who is the abuse for. You are using the body
   of the child but it is your identity. Is it homicide or is it extended
   suicide?[28]

Jolly K further reassured the subcommittee with her description of the
typical Parents Anonymous member. "The average parent in our group,"
she said, "is middle class, white, educated to anywhere from 10th grade on
up."[29] The average member was, in other words, not black, not poor—not
a member of the groups that most interested David Gil. The contrast between Jolly K and Professor Gil was so obvious that Mondale asked Jolly
K about it directly:

Mondale: You heard Dr. Gil before you. . . . Don't you think there is some
   value in identifying these extreme cases of the kind you personally
   experienced, that you try to deal with those the best we can while
   society is being perfected, but not wait for a perfect society?

Jolly K: We have to. It is ridiculous. It is way too idealistic to assume—
   well, let me go back to the national priorities. . . . I think we need to
   look at the more fundamental, more realistic things of working with
   the person where they are and giving them the inner resources to go
   on after some more realistic things on their own, such as the motivation to want to go back to adult schools.[30]

The focus on individual psychology, the dismissal of sociological
idealism, the appeal to the individual's "inner resources" as the key to
preventing further abuse—Jolly K's testimony accomplished everything
Mondale could have hoped for. When the Child Abuse Prevention and
Treatment Act became law in 1974, the medical and psychiatric conception of abuse that had begun to take shape in the 1950s finally became
not only a matter of media hype and professional opinion but of federal
policy. It remains the consensus view today.

When Jolly K told Walter Mondale that the child she abused had "reflected her negative self," when she suggested that her anger and violence were the products of her own childhood, when she wondered aloud whether her aim was "homicide" or "suicide," she was speaking a particular language. This language had been invented and refined in Europe during the late nineteenth and early twentieth centuries. It had made its formal American debut in 1909, and by the middle of the century it dominated the way Americans talked about and understood themselves and one another to an extent that can now be difficult to understand or believe. One did not have to receive any specialized training or certification to learn the language—it would be more accurate to say that it diffused throughout society through writers and editors in the mass media, advertising of all kinds, and the popularizing works of academics. The language of Sigmund Freud and psychoanalysis was simply a basic part of the mental atmosphere in which midcentury Americans lived and breathed, and it provided much of the rhetorical foundation for the panic that would eventually begin in the early 1980s.

Freudian thought played a central role in the history of American attitudes and beliefs about child abuse, because the Freudian account of human experience is, at its core, an account of the persistence of childhood throughout adult life. In Freudian psychology, childhood fantasies, traumas, and dreams determine the shape and character of adult desires. Should these desires cause sufficient mental distress to the adult who experiences them, they can be pushed into the realm of unconscious thought—but not forever. Freud also held that these uncomfortable desires make themselves known during sleep, presented by dreams in a kind of code that draws on fragments of childhood memory and the events of the previous day. Freud's most famous psychological concepts, including penis envy and the Oedipus complex, were all derived from childhood. (Many commentators have noted that Freud devoted many more pages of writing to the analysis and interpretation of childhood sexuality than he did to the sexual lives of adults.) In the middle of the twentieth century, Freudian thought provided Americans with a way of understanding the relationship between childhood and adult life. As the public began to re-acknowledge the existence of child abuse in the sixties and early seventies, it instinctively drew on a vocabulary with which it was already intimately familiar and that seemed perfectly suited to explaining the subject at hand.

The sixties and seventies, however, were also a period during which everyday Freudian orthodoxy came under attack. The first group to challenge Freud's theories and their persistence in American culture was the women's liberation movement. This effort began in 1963, when a journalist and magazine writer named Betty Friedan published *The Feminine Mystique*. Opening with its rousing analysis of "the problem that has no name," Friedan's book identified the widespread boredom and despair of educated housewives as the product of systematic social oppression. "I seem to sleep so much," one Long Island woman told her. "I don't know why I should be so tired. . . . It's not the work. I just don't feel alive."[31] In addition to her discussions of the role played by media in encouraging women to find total fulfillment at home, the paralyzing psychological effects of trying to fill an entire day with housework, and the way university professors told women to give up their worldly ambitions just as the women gained the skills and knowledge to realize them, Friedan devoted an entire chapter to what she called "The Sexual Solipsism of Sigmund Freud." It was the opening salvo in a war that would last for more than twenty years.

"It would be half-wrong to say it started with Sigmund Freud," Friedan wrote. "It did not really start, in America, until the 1940s."[32] The "it" in those sentences did not refer to Freud's ideas themselves—"No one can question the basic genius of Freud's discoveries," Friedan wrote—but to the way psychiatry and news magazines had applied these ideas to the lives of postwar women.[33] Friedan believed that although Freud was an extraordinarily perceptive observer of human personality, his views on female sexuality had been irredeemably limited by the repressive culture in which he lived. Freud believed that women were docile and submissive by nature, that they were ill-suited to authority or public activity, and that when confronted with matters of sexuality, they tended to respond with hysterical outbursts.

Because Victorian culture really did punish people, especially women, who failed to repress their sexual desires, and because repression really did tend to produce hysterical neuroses, Freud's ideas had been fairly well suited to their environment, even if they were also symptomatic of it. But Friedan believed that psychology had made many important advances in the first half of the twentieth century, that the profession, along with society itself, had moved somewhat beyond the repressive atmosphere in which it had been formed. In addition, the general situation of women had drastically changed. Many midcentury women, for example, had significant experience working outside the home, whereas none of Freud's female upper-class Austrian patients led anything other than a completely domestic life. Friedan argued that her own era's rigid adherence to Freudian doctrine was simply a product of the fact that psychoanalytic thought had become "the ideological bulwark of the sexual counter-revolution in America. Without Freud's definition of the sexual nature of women to give the conventional image of femininity new authority, I do not think several generations of educated, spirited American women would have been so easily diverted from the dawning realization of who they were and what they could be."[34]

By the middle of the 1970s feminists were holding Freud responsible for many aspects of sexual inequality, such that anti-Freudianism became one of the defining features of women's liberation. Anne Koedt, in a classic work of early radical feminism, accused Freud of promoting the myth that women could only attain full sexual satisfaction through vaginal intercourse.[35] The Freudian idea that a clitoral orgasm was just a pale imitation of its more mature vaginal manifestation, Koedt wrote, was a lie designed to make women feel that a life without a male partner was not a life worth living. Two other radical feminist intellectuals, Kate Millett and Shulamith Firestone, carried out more general attacks, describing Freud, respectively, as the architect of a "domestic psychodrama more horrific than a soap opera" and "a petty tyrant of the old-school."[36] Anti-Freudianism became so commonplace among second-wave feminists that it sometimes became more of a shibboleth than an intellectual position. In her 1970 book *The Female Eunuch*, Germaine Greer didn't actually argue with psychoanalysis at all—she just cracked jokes. "Freud is the father of psychoanalysis," she wrote. "It had no mother."[37] She referred to all of psychiatry as "an extraordinary confidence trick."[38] In Boston one women's group kept a photograph of Freud on the wall so members would have a target for darts during their free time.[39] These writers didn't confine their criticisms to Freud's theories either. Some feminists also tried to undermine psychoanalysis by half-ironically subjecting Freud himself to the psychoanalytic technique. Freud's relationship with his mother—a "classic Jewish matriarch" with "a castrating and important personality"—came under suspicion, as did his rigidly monogamous marriage to Martha Bernays.[40] Even by Victorian standards, Friedan suggested in *The Feminine Mystique*, Freud may have been unusually repressed.

To these psychoanalytic attacks on the founder of psychoanalysis, feminists, along with a number of dissidents from inside psychoanalysis itself, added important re-appraisals of Freud's clinical practice. Florence Rush's 1971 presentation on child abuse had first put the issue on the feminist agenda, but it wasn't until 1977, when Rush published a lengthy essay in the journal *Chrysalis*, that feminism moved beyond scandalized "awareness" and began to form a plan of action. The essay was titled "The Freudian Coverup," and it focused on an important sequence of events from the earliest stage of Freud's career. Freud spent the middle years of the 1890s analyzing cases of hysteria with the physician Josef Breuer, and in 1896 Freud presented the startling results of this work at the Viennese Society for Psychiatry and Neurology.[41] In almost every case of adult hysterical neurosis, Freud said, analysis had eventually uncovered traumatic childhood sexual abuse—he called it "seduction"—as the primary cause. The argument became known as the Seduction Theory, and for a brief period of time it was the foundation of Freud's entire project. A year after his presentation at the Viennese Society, Freud wrote to a close friend, stating that he had adopted a new motto: "What has been done to you, poor child?"[42] In correspondence Freud was completely carried away with enthusiasm for his new theory, referring to it as "the great clinical secret," his first major discovery.[43] "Just think," he wrote in a jubilant letter from 1895, "among other things I am on the scent of the following strict precondition for hysteria, namely, that a primary sexual experience (before puberty), accompanied by revulsion and fright, must have taken place."[44]

Only two years after he presented "The Aetiology of Hysteria," however, Freud began to back away from the Seduction Theory and its implications. The problem had to do with fitting the Seduction Theory in with the more general theories of neurosis, hysteria, and mental illness to which Freud subscribed at the time. One of these theories said that on its own, sexual abuse was *not* sufficient to produce the kinds of hysterical symptoms that could be discovered and analyzed in therapy. After all, not every victim of sexual abuse went on to become hysterical. In order for hysteria to develop later in life, other events and factors, both mental and environmental, must come into play. For Freud, this meant that the instances of childhood sexual abuse revealed by hysterical neurosis constituted only a fraction of the abuse that actually took place. In order for the Seduction Theory to be correct, therefore, childhood sexual abuse would have to be nearly universal in Victorian society, occurring within almost every household, and Freud ultimately decided that "such widespread perversions against children are not very probable."[45]

Freud came to think that the stories of abuse he had encountered in therapy, in many instances—not all, but many—were not true memories but instead fantasies. Because he hadn't yet invented psychoanalysis, Freud couldn't say exactly where these fantasies had come from. He wondered whether his patients had made them up for some obscure reason; he hoped that *he* hadn't suggested the idea of abuse to his patients or unconsciously forced them to accept these memories as true. Whatever their source, Freud believed that although these fantasies of abuse might not have much to say about the truth of the outside world, they had the potential to reveal important truths about the workings of each individual's inner world. It was *this* belief, this turn from the outer environment to the depths of mental experience, that provided the foundation upon which the entire theory of Oedipal conflict—everything people came to understand as "Freudian"—was built.

Rush and other critics had a very different reading of Freud's intellectual development. They believed Freud had been right the first time—that with the Seduction Theory he had unveiled the secret festering at the heart of the most elaborately patriarchal society in Western history. They further believed that Freud had changed his theory not out of intellectual conviction but out of cowardice. Perhaps the most outspoken critic of Freud's abandonment of the Seduction Theory during this period was a young and charismatic Sanskritist-turned-psychoanalyst named Jeffrey Moussaieff Masson. Masson had conducted important original research at the Freud Archives in Munich, and in 1980 he began offering incendiary interpretations of Freud's decision to leave the Seduction Theory behind. Following the presentation of "The Aetiology of Hysteria," Masson argued, Freud had been ostracized by the very people he depended on for professional advancement. Freud had essentially accused everyone in his professional world of committing child abuse, and Masson believed that Freud "suffered emotional and intellectual isolation as long as he held to the reality of seduction."[46]

The critique advanced by Masson and many feminists was straightforward and damning: after making a truly important and disturbing discovery about the extent of childhood sexual abuse in Victorian society, Freud had been ostracized by his peers and forced to confront the shortcomings of those closest to him. Rather than make a hopeless intellectual stand, Freud adjusted his theory so as to cover up child sex abuse once more. Worst of all, by making an elaborate theoretical fiction out of the lie that children really had not been abused, Freud provided psychiatry and society at large with the only excuse they would ever need to keep ignoring child sex abuse for another seventy-five years. Speaking to the *New York Times*, Masson said his discoveries were sure to have dire consequences for psychoanalysis: "They would have to recall every patient since 1901. It would be like the Pinto."[47]

The crux of these arguments, the one issue around which everything else was organized, was belief. These dissident feminists and psychoanalysts argued that Freud's belief in the literal, historical truth of his patients' stories of abuse had led him directly to one of the era's most important psychological discoveries. "Freud was the first psychiatrist who believed his patients were telling the truth," Masson wrote.[48] When Freud abandoned that belief, then, he had betrayed not only his patients but also his own conscience and intellectual history. "Freud began a trend away from the real world," Masson wrote, "that, it seems to me, is at the root of the present-day sterility of psychoanalysis and psychiatry throughout the world."[49] Accordingly, if psychiatric therapy wanted to be able to say with a straight face that its aim, as a profession, was to help people, it would need to learn to hear and believe the stories that patients wanted so desperately to tell.

For some, this injunction took on the qualities of a dare. While Masson researched and wrote his book, therapists began to conduct analyses that might be described as experiments in radical belief. In 1973 the results of one of these experiments were published under the title *Sybil: The True and Extraordinary Story of a Woman Possessed by Sixteen Separate Personalities*. Written by a magazine journalist named Flora Rheta Schreiber, the book purported to tell the story of Sybil Dorsett, a shy and lonely woman who, in 1953, had "embarked on one of the most complex and most bizarre cases in the history of psychiatry."[50] The book reconstructed the therapeutic encounters between Sybil and her heroic, Upper East Side psychoanalyst, and it laid out the awful discoveries brought to light during Sybil's time on the couch.

"Sybil Dorsett's" real name was Shirley Mason, and her psychoanalyst was Cornelia Wilbur. The two first encountered one another in 1945, when

Mason, then a college student, went into psychotherapy with Dr. Wilbur. The two saw one another, with good results for Mason, for six months, and then doctor and patient went their separate ways. By 1953, however, Mason felt that her nerves were acting up again, and as it happened, both she and Dr. Wilbur had moved to New York City from the northern Midwest. Sybil thought that maybe a handful of sessions, a little psychiatric reunion, would help keep her steady. Dr. Wilbur agreed, and the pair resumed meeting.

Shirley Mason grew up in a Minnesota farm town where her Seventh-Day Adventist parents prohibited novel reading, story writing, and making drawings with weird colors in them—all activities that Shirley loved. Pretending was also expressly forbidden, but Shirley had imaginary friends named Vicky and Sam, though the rigid, self-lacerating piety of the church sometimes made their company difficult to enjoy. She had an intimate and confusing relationship with her mother, who sometimes alternated between bouts of nervous energy and long episodes of impenetrable depression. Shirley's adolescence was nervous and difficult: she missed school, frequently came down with colds and other minor illnesses, and worried her house would burn down or blow away while she was out for walks. She washed her hands furiously after reading—she thought the pages carried venereal disease or cancer.[51]

Although Mason's nervousness eventually developed into social anxiety and anorexia, she maintained a quietly tenacious scholarly ambition into adulthood, and it was this shared trait that drew Mason and Cornelia Wilbur to one another. The best evidence of Wilbur's ambition is the fact that in prewar America she went off to college with the intention of studying chemistry, a field that at the time held strong aversions to including women in any capacity. Wilbur's interests eventually landed on psychiatry, and she became fascinated by the diagnosis and treatment of hysteria. Wilbur's father had been a chemist and an inventor, and although she may have resented his efforts to keep her from attending medical school, she admired her father's achievements and sought to live up to them with achievements of her own. When Wilbur had early success in the treatment of hysterics, she believed she had found a line of work to which she was exceptionally—even uniquely—well suited. Years later she would describe her clinical abilities as those of a "genius" and "a magician." She also referred to herself as a maverick. In the years preceding her move into psychoanalytic practice, Wilbur consistently found herself working, sometimes recklessly, at the experimental frontiers of clinical psychiatry. She conducted a number of experiments with barbiturates, administering large doses of these powerful drugs to psychotic patients and noting the results. Wilbur was interested in shock therapy, and she also assisted on some of the first couple of hundred lobotomies performed in the United States. Debbie Nathan, in her history of the Shirley Mason case, described Dr. Wilbur as "a kind of Rosie the Riveter for mental illness."[52]

Mason's second round of therapy with Dr. Wilbur proceeded without incident until one day in late winter, when Mason sat down and began telling Wilbur about some odd situations she had gotten into. Mason said that on multiple occasions over the course of her life, she had suddenly found herself in antique shops with no memory of having gone to any antique shop. She would often be surrounded by broken merchandise she could not remember having touched. Or, she said, she would end up in some hotel or unfamiliar part of the city—again with no idea how she got there—and then would try to find her way home. Wilbur thought these stories were extremely interesting. She told Mason that she was experiencing fugue states, in which a person could behave like a completely different person for hours or even days at a time, and then sent her patient on her way. By this point Wilbur had also given Mason prescriptions for Demerol, Edrisal, Daprisal, and Seconal, the last of which is a highly addictive barbiturate. A week and a half later, Mason arrived at Wilbur's office for a weekday appointment, and there seemed to be something different about her. "I'm fine," Mason said, "but Shirley isn't. She was so sick she couldn't come. So I came instead."

"Tell me about yourself," Wilbur said, and Mason replied, "I'm Peggy!"[53] That Mason should have turned out to have Multiple Personality Disorder, of all things, was very exciting on its own—the condition was vanishingly rare in the 1950s. But within two sessions Mason had displayed four separate personalities. Wilbur had never heard of a documented case of four separate personalities. She decided to psychoanalyze all of them.

The book Flora Rheta Schreiber eventually wrote about Shirley Mason portrayed Wilbur's treatment as heroic and pioneering: "The analysis, Dr. Wilbur decided, would have to be an unorthodox one. She smiled as she thought; an unorthodox analysis by a maverick psychiatrist. She did consider herself a maverick and knew that it was this characteristic that would stand her in good stead in dealing with this extraordinary case."[54]

When it was finally published in 1973, *Sybil* included a list of the sixteen personalities that Wilbur eventually found inside Mason, complete with birth dates and personality characteristics. Victoria Antoinette Scharleau, born in 1926, was a "sophisticated, attractive blonde." Peggy Lou Baldwin, born the same year, was an "angry pixie with a pug nose." Mason had male personalities as well: Sid Dorsett was a carpenter and a handyman.[55] *Sybil* describes Wilbur teasing out these personalities, one by one, gaining their trust, playing them off one another in search of information. It is a long and arduous process. Some of Mason's personalities are so wary of Dr. Wilbur that she doesn't even learn of their existence for months. The personalities know all about one another, however, and unbeknownst to the host personality—that's Shirley—they argue and exchange information as part of a big, collaborative effort to help Mason survive the trauma that brought them into being in the first place. It takes nearly 150 pages, but eventually Mason's personalities decide the doctor is worth speaking to. "Then Marcia Lynn, Vanessa Gail, and Mary put into execution an internal grapevine through which the message ran loud and clear: *This Dr. Wilbur cares about us*," Schreiber wrote. "After that Marcia Lynn, Vanessa Gail, Mary, and everybody else held a conclave and decided that 'We'll go and see her.'"[56]

Toward the middle of the book, Mary, one of Mason's "alter" personalities, mentions a "pain" that all the personalities collectively feel. "What pain, Mary?" Wilbur asks. "You'll know in time," Mary replies.[57] As Mason's personalities presented themselves in therapy, *Sybil* suggests, they kept Mary's promise in spectacular fashion. One alter tells Wilbur about midnight walks Mason took with her mother, Hattie. Filled with resentment toward the wealthier members of their small hometown, Hattie regularly crept onto the lawns of elite neighbors, "pulled down her bloomers, squatted, and with ritualistic deliberateness and perverse pleasure defecated on the elected spot."[58] At home Mason's conservative, fundamentalist parents would bring their young daughter into the bedroom at night and force her to watch as they had sex.[59] In the woods Hattie would gather up neighborhood children and take them to a secluded place. "'Now lean over and run like a horse,' [Hattie said]. As the children squealed with delight at the prospect, Hattie would motion them to begin. Then, while the little girls, simulating the gait of horses, leaned over as they had been instructed, Hattie from her perch on the floor, revealed the real purpose of the 'game.' Into their vaginas went her fingers as she intoned, 'Giddyap, giddyap.'"[60]

In 1962 Cornelia Wilbur would serve as one of the editors of an influential study of homosexuality identifying the phenomenon as an "illness," one most frequently caused by improper mothering, and this belief is reflected in *Sybil*'s descriptions of Hattie's abuse.[61] Hattie orchestrated lesbian orgies in the forest. Hattie separated Mason's legs with a wooden spoon, suspended the small girl from the ceiling, upside down, and then administered enemas. "'I did it,' Hattie would scream triumphantly when her mission was accomplished. 'I did it.' The scream was followed by laughter, which went on and on."[62] *Sybil* described Hattie's motivation for these abuses as her pathological hatred of men. "'You might as well get used to it,' her mother, inserting one of these foreign bodies, explained to her daughter at six months or at six years. 'That's what men will do to you when you grow up. . . . They hurt you, and you can't stop them.'"[63]

Wilbur obtained these stories by slowly and methodically turning Shirley Mason, who never displayed her "alter" personalities to anyone other than her analyst and her roommate, into a drug addict. When Mason had a particularly bad day, Wilbur would regularly give her up to five times the prescribed dose of Daprisal, Amytal, Demerol, or any number of other medications, and as therapy progressed, Wilbur added a powerful antipsychotic called Thorazine. At the center of this pharmaceutical regimen was Sodium Pentothal, a barbiturate so renowned for its ability to lower patients' inhibitions that it was colloquially, though inaccurately, known as "truth serum." Wilbur administered Pentothal injections with such frequency and in such large doses that Mason would often come out of a therapy session unable to remember anything she had said. "Under Pentothal," she once confessed in a letter to Wilbur, "I am much more original."[64] As Mason's personalities multiplied, and as the stories those personalities provided became more horrifying and more lurid, Wilbur decided a book had to be written about the case. To ensure Mason's cooperation, Wilbur said she would cover Mason's living expenses in exchange for her full-time devotion to therapy. Mason agreed. She spent at least fifteen hours a week in Dr. Wilbur's office, and as a consequence of the drugs she consumed, she slept for roughly the same amount each night. As Nathan put it in *Sybil Exposed*, "she was a professional multiple personality patient."[65] Mason would stay on the job for more than a decade.

The prose in *Sybil* seems specifically designed to be put on a movie or television screen. "Forcing herself to keep moving," Schreiber wrote, dramatizing one of Sybil's post-fugue-state wanderings in Philadelphia, "she listened for sounds, for life. There was only the wind. Block after block along glassy streets failed to reveal a single street sign. The hope of a telephone became ever more vain."[66] *Sybil* the made-for-TV movie, starring Sally Field in the role that would launch her dramatic career, aired in 1976, but even the most optimistic network executive could not have reasonably dreamed that it would be watched by more than 40 million people, slightly less than one-fifth of the population of the United States. The book itself sold more than 7 million copies.

One explanation for *Sybil*'s runaway popularity is that it provided an elegant companion narrative to the growing consensus that child abusers committed their crimes not because of social conditions but because they were mentally ill. The tendency to see abusers as pathological aberrations from a healthy norm made them more interesting and less frightening: they could either be treated and then returned to nonabusive normalcy or, in cases that resisted treatment, they could be cordoned off from society for the rest of their lives without any misgivings. In any case, one would not have to get involved in a tricky conversation about what many people regarded as parents' right to subject their children to disciplinary violence if they wanted to. By giving the *victims* of abuse a mental illness of their own, *Sybil* accomplished much the same thing, pushing attention away from the circumstances that cause abuse to happen in the first place and toward the elaborate treatments that might be administered after the fact. Though Multiple Personality Disorder had not been subjected to anything like rigorous scientific scrutiny, the reasons for its emergence and the narrative of its treatment and healing made intuitive Freudian sense to many people who heard Shirley Mason's story: childhood trauma had produced mental illness in adulthood. Some of the readers who wrote to Schreiber took the book as a cautionary tale, and some understood Sybil's ordeal as a metaphor. "Am I a whole person?" one letter read. "I spend a long time thinking about things. . . . I am confused on who to be. How will people react if I act my true self?"[67] Another reader wrote asking for help—she loved her husband but couldn't bring herself to have sex with him. "Ever since my first boyfriend," she wrote, "I would turn [men's] love into a kind of parental love and found it impossible to have any kind of sex with them." Years of psychiatric treatment hadn't helped, and reading *Sybil* made her think she had been dealing with a different problem all along. "I realized it's the story of my life except for one thing," she wrote.

"I don't think I have 16 separate personalities although some would say I have at least 3."[68] Other readers didn't really know what they thought of the story other than that they found it absolutely captivating. "When I read that part," one eighth-grader wrote, referring to a scene of sexual torture, "I got deeply involved like I was there watching."[69]

Sybil also occasionally touched on a fear of occult religions and rituals that was percolating around the country in the 1970s, and this aspect of Schreiber's book became more important as the decade progressed. In 1966 a San Francisco musician and entertainment-world social butterfly named Anton LaVey founded a new religious sect based on pseudo-Nietzschean principles of individualism, hedonism, and epicureanism. He called it the Church of Satan. LaVey, who had been born with the name Howard Levey, had extraordinary showbiz instincts, and in Satanism's early years he used these to turn his church into a media phenomenon. He published *The Satanic Bible* in 1969, following it with a companion guide to religious practice (*The Satanic Rituals*) and a how-to seduction guide for women (*The Compleat Witch*). He used nude women as altars, and he televised both a satanic baptism and a satanic wedding.

LaVey's combination of media savvy and anti-Christian provocation was attractive to those who took him seriously and absolutely irresistible to those who did not. Hollywood took up Satanism in 1968 with *Rosemary's Baby* and then again with *The Exorcist* in 1973. Satanism also became a regular feature of evangelical cautionary tales about the dangers of a pleasure-seeking life. Mike Warnke, who became one of the country's most popular "Christian comedians" in the 1970s, got his start with *The Satan Seller*, a sensational memoir of the young Warnke's descent into Satanism, group sex, alcohol, and drugs.[70] As Satanism became a more prominent feature of the country's secular and religious entertainments, a number of Schreiber's prose decisions in *Sybil* took on increased significance. Mason's nighttime walk with her pooping mother "began as a casual stroll" but ended as "a demonic ritual." Hattie carried out her acts with "ritualistic deliberateness."[71] The abuse with enemas and the wooden spoon—that was another "favorite ritual."[72]

Schreiber's book never said these rituals were specifically satanic, but in the same year that *Sybil* was published, a psychiatrist working in British Columbia began seeing a new patient. Dr. Lawrence Pazder was in his early forties, a married Catholic with children, when he embarked on a course of intensive psychotherapy with a twenty-seven-year-old patient named Michelle Proby. He ran his psychiatric practice out of the Fort Royal Medical Centre in downtown Victoria, British Columbia, and he shared facilities with four other psychiatrists.[73] In 1980, having left their respective spouses and married each other after seven years of off-and-on treatment, Pazder and Proby, the latter using the pseudonym Michelle Smith, published their coauthored account of what they had discovered together. It was called *Michelle Remembers*.

The book is a tour-de-force of un-self-awareness. It is, on the one hand, an unwittingly faithful document of the sequence of therapeutic disasters whereby doctor and patient came to believe that Michelle had not only been abused as a child by her psychotic mother but also that she had been handed over to an organized and secretive satanic cult whose leader was named Malachi. On the other hand, the book also fails to avoid documenting the doctor-patient love affair that grew out of therapy and served as that therapy's true motivation and substance. Their descriptions of each other read like classroom love notes passed from one desk to another. Michelle, when she makes her first appearance in the book, is described as possessing "a heart-shaped face, a delicate mouth, and bountiful brown curls."[74] Pazder, when he makes his, is "warm, manly, soft-spoken—what people who live elsewhere consider the typical Westerner."[75] (He is also "tall, blue-eyed, and tanned even in February.")[76] When the two sit down for their first psychiatric consultation, the book records that Michelle "liked him immediately, partly because he looked nothing like her idea of a psychiatrist." "His style was slacks and a sweater," she writes (or he writes, or they write), "his manner open and friendly, in contrast to the pinstripes and wingtips and careful reserve that characterized many in his profession."[77]

The therapy Dr. Pazder conducted with Proby in many respects mirrored that conducted by Cornelia Wilbur with Shirley Mason. Both cases involved an initial therapeutic encounter that proceeded without incident and ended successfully. For four years Pazder and Proby diligently combed through Michelle's unhappy childhood and identified the symptoms expressed in Proby's adult life. Her father, after drinking, had sometimes beaten her mother, which terrified Michelle. And although Michelle's mother would usually show affection and tenderness in the wake of these rages, she was otherwise irritable and cold and had a quick temper. As an adult, Proby had also endured three miscarriages, which understandably produced their own collection of psychic difficulties. None of these events are in dispute, and the therapy that addressed them was conducted carefully and professionally. A short while after this analysis had reached its end, however, Proby returned to Dr. Pazder with a terrifying dream. "I dreamed that I had an itchy place on my hand," she told Pazder. "And when I scratched it, all these bugs came out of where I was scratching it! Little spiders, just pouring out of the skin on my hand. It was just—I can't even tell you how it was. It was so terrible."[78]

According to *Michelle Remembers*, Pazder immediately recognized this dream as "blatantly symbolic," as connecting "subconsciously to something very important." He asked that the two begin to see one another again, but within a few weeks Pazder, like Cornelia Wilbur before him, believed that an unorthodox approach was required: "all the normal ways they had worked together were of no value now."[79] Michelle began to lie on Pazder's couch, whereas she had previously sat upright in a chair. She lay motionless for twenty minutes at a time, unable to speak. She asked Dr. Pazder to sit closer. Then the pair decided it might be good for them to have some kind of physical contact during particularly difficult moments. And one Saturday, in the middle of a special weekend appointment they had arranged, Michelle, with Dr. Pazder's hand resting on her head, screamed in terror for twenty-five minutes. Then she began to speak: "It's . . . it's . . . it's all black. Black. It's black! It's all *black*. No! Oh, please help me. Help me! Oh, help me! *Help me!* [More screaming, which eventually dissolved into agonizing tears.] *Oh, God help me! Oh, God help!* I don't know what to do. I feel so sick. I feel like my heart's going to stop. . . . Oh, I hate this. I'm on this bed. . . . I'm in the air. I'm in the air, and I'm upside down. . . . There's this man and he's turning me around and around."[80]

Michelle told Dr. Pazder that the man's name was Malachi, and she told him not as an adult woman but in the frightened voice of a five-year-old girl. This little girl, Pazder came to believe, lived inside Michelle's unconscious and functioned as a kind of mental black box, storing up memories of trauma and keeping them away from the fragile woman Michelle had become. Pazder thought that if he could comfort that inner child—in part by snuggling with Michelle on the couch during therapy—if he could gain her trust, then he and Michelle, who had no recollection of Malachi until her episode on the couch, would be able to learn what had taken place years ago. In subsequent therapy sessions, Michelle's child personality revealed that Malachi and his cult members had forced Michelle to watch and participate in ritual sex. She said she had been placed in a car with a woman's corpse and that the car had been set on fire and then pushed down an embankment into a ravine, landing her in the hospital. She said the satanic cult maintained an operating room and that doctors had once surgically implanted horns and a tail into Michelle's tiny body. At home, Pazder took phone calls from Michelle and sat in comforting silence as she cried on the other end of the line. At the office both doctor and patient wound up crying together at the end of marathon sessions that lasted for as many as six hours. "In her depths, Michelle was like a child, and like a child she needed contact," Pazder recalled thinking. "Sometimes she would have her head on his shoulder. But he was careful about the way he touched her."[81] He also told his patient, "I'm always moved at how your innocence has been your only ally."[82] For both, the experience was clearly powerful and consuming.

Michelle's child alter saved the most awful revelation for last. For weeks Michelle was held captive by cult members in a round room with a dirt floor; the cult wanted to summon Satan himself, and Michelle was clearly to play some crucial role in the ritual. At certain points Satan's voice would become audible, reciting bad poetry: "I can do much to destroy and then / Replace with words of hate and despair / Words as stupid as love and care."[83] When Satan finally did emerge out of the fire at the center of the ritual, he grabbed Michelle around the waist by his tail and began dragging her away. It was only the intercession of a mystical figure Michelle called "Ma Mère"—clearly the Virgin Mary—that saved the little girl. With this spectacular climax, Michelle's memories came to an end. Proby converted to Catholicism, and she and Pazder began to bring their story to various Catholic authorities, who treated it with varying degrees of seriousness. They recorded one priest as citing Hannah Arendt's concept of the "banality of evil"—originally designed to explain the actions of prominent Nazi Adolf Eichmann during the Holocaust—as a means of explaining the satanic poems Michelle claimed to have heard. "It would be a great mistake to underrate these rhymes," the priest said. "The *very* mistake Satan wants you to make."[84]

Although the text of *Michelle Remembers* refutes itself, external evidence refutes it as well. No newspaper articles from anywhere in the Victoria area reported a car crash like the one Michelle claimed to have been involved in when she was five. A pediatrician did tell Dr. Pazder that he had a vague recollection of treating Michelle for some burn, at some point, in her childhood, but there are no records of any hospital visits by

Michelle. Proby also attended the first grade and was photographed for the school yearbook during a period when she should have been locked in the basement confronting the devil.[85] Finally, it turned out that although Proby had not mentioned them at all in the book, she had two sisters, Tertia and Charyl, and in interviews these sisters would eventually state that their middle sibling had never taken part in any satanic or abusive rituals. But this did nothing to stand in the way of the book's publication. Proby and Pazder received a $100,000 hardcover advance for *Michelle Remembers*, with an additional $242,000 to follow when the book went into a paperback edition. Proby made a formal conversion to Catholicism and went on a thirty-nine-day publicity tour to promote the book, which, helped along by full-page newspaper ads and reviews that ranged from bemused to horrified to bewildered, sold well. For his part, Dr. Pazder gave a presentation on the book at the 1980 meeting of the American Psychiatric Association in which he coined a term that would come into wide circulation over the next ten years: "ritual abuse."[86] In interviews Dr. Pazder insisted that Michelle's experiences had taken place, that her memories were too consistent and too detailed to be written off to some internal fantasy or therapeutic error. "In the beginning I wondered if she had made things up," he told a reporter. "But if this is a hoax, it would be the most incredible hoax ever."[87] The meaning of Pazder's appeal to the consistency and precision of Michelle's memories was clear: she had to be believed.

Even in these earliest documents of recovered memory and ritual abuse, however, the therapist's belief seems to depend on the patient providing a particular kind of story. Nearly four years after she had begun to see Cornelia Wilbur in her Manhattan office, Shirley Mason decided to write her therapist a letter. During the previous year, Dr. Wilbur, realizing that Mason had become addicted to Pentothal, refused to continue providing the drug. Then she rather optimistically declared Mason cured, or "integrated," and then she watched as Mason sprouted a host of completely new personalities. By the time Shirley wrote the letter, she had no life outside of therapy, her friendship with Dr. Wilbur, meandering walks through New York, and a lesbian roommate who sometimes tried to get into bed with her. The letter was written as a four-page entry in a therapy diary that Mason maintained and allowed Dr. Wilbur to read. It began with a kind of forensic analysis of the doctor-patient relationship in which Mason found herself:

At various times over the years you have told me you thought I was more than average in intelligence, or that I was clever, or that I was sensitive, imaginative, creative, original, etc. Well, I am. And, you see, I am also egotistical. . . . But I have played on it long enough now. It isn't getting me anywhere, so this time I will be honest. . . . I have tried to tell you this before, but I couldn't hold out very long when you showed doubts. . . . A person likes to be admired, and so I let it slide rather than to disappoint you or risk your anger if you should become convinced. I felt I couldn't lose you again.

After three paragraphs building up in this way, Mason came out with it, writing, "I do not have any multiple personalities. I don't even have a 'double' to help me out. I am all of them. I have been essentially lying in my pretense of them, I know. I had not meant to lie in the beginning. I sort of fell into a pattern, found it worked, and continued to build on it." While Mason thought it possible that there were real cases of Multiple Personality out there, she suspected that others diagnosed with the disorder could be cases "just like mine, hysterics with nothing better to do than 'act a part' and put off onto 'another personality' the things they cannot quite dare to pretend themselves, and then act as if they had forgotten in order to avoid punishment or feeling some sort of guilt or shame for the lie."

She also told her therapist that she was "only distraught and desperate the day I acted 'like Peggy,'" that she was "trying to show you I felt I needed help." What makes the letter so sad is Mason's detailed and sophisticated sense of self-awareness. She knew much more about what was wrong with her than she had let on. She explained, in detail, that she didn't know how to handle success, whether in "art or teaching or music or whatever." After a momentary rush of happiness, she would be overwhelmed by the "urge to do some fool thing." She specified that the fool thing, for a while, had been "to disappear and make people think I had no knowledge of what I had done or where I had been. Quite thrilling. Got me a lot of attention." As for the elaborate stories of abuse, Mason couldn't say exactly where they had come from. They "just sort of rolled out from somewhere, and once I had started and found you were interested, I continued." She said she made up all the stories about fugue states and Philadelphia, and she asked that Dr. Wilbur stop demonizing her mother, Hattie. She may have been anxious and controlling, but she hadn't been a sadist, and she hadn't raped Shirley with a flashlight.[88]

Though the letter had obviously been difficult for Shirley to write—she had no idea what Dr. Wilbur would make of it—the result was clear-headed and comprehensive. Mason seems to have been surprised to find herself in a state of mind where such honesty was possible, and she didn't want to waste the opportunity—usually she was either high or sleeping. Dr. Wilbur's response to this letter, which she regarded as "a major defensive maneuver," was to tell Mason that her confession was a sign of "resistance." It showed that Mason was frightened of the memories she had yet to uncover, that her mother really *had* tortured her, and that she needed to prepare for the important work that remained. The implication was that Mason could either agree to have Multiple Personality Disorder or she could stop seeing Dr. Wilbur. Mason went home and composed a second letter. Some irresponsible alter had written the first one, she said. She started seeing Dr. Wilbur five times a week.

Two decades later, in 1981, Lawrence Pazder was asked about the police. In his book and in many interviews, Pazder claimed that a murderous satanic cult was really out there, that it had kidnapped and tortured a five-year-old girl for more than a year, that it had orchestrated a fiery car crash as well as the cover-up. So, given the sophistication of the cult's organization and the brutality of its actions, was he planning to speak with law enforcement? Pazder said that although some efforts had been made to learn the details of the crash, the records had been destroyed, and in any case, "it is not our desire to go and cause a witch hunt."[89]

Chapter 2

McMartin—Allegations

Virginia McMartin opened her preschool in southwest Los Angeles County in September 1966. Her daughter, Peggy, worked as the school's administrator, and Peggy's husband, Charles Buckey, built playground equipment for the yard. Peggy and Charles also had two children, Peggy Ann and Raymond, and eventually they began to teach and help out at the school as well. By 1980 a child's admission to the McMartin Preschool was a coveted social prize for the aerospace and real estate professionals who had moved out to Manhattan Beach during the previous decade. Two videos made by investigators shortly after Ray Buckey was first accused of abusing children at McMartin make it easy to see why.

In the first video a cameraman, trailing a long power cord behind him, tours the McMartin Preschool. The classrooms are painted in different shades of lime green, and they are filled with Charles Buckey's ingenious handmade furniture. Colorful wooden panels on the wall display the alphabet and single-digit integers. The closet doors make a clown face, and there is a fake wooden refrigerator in which the children keep fake plastic food. Little coats hang on a wooden giraffe. There are chairs, unfinished art projects, little chalkboards. There is clutter and activity everywhere. There are children too, watching the cameraman pass through, and every once in a while he speaks up in a loud voice and asks a child to show him something or open a cabinet. The cameraman looks into each bathroom— they are all tiny—and flips the lights on and off. Out in the playground children are running and shrieking as cars race by along Manhattan Beach Boulevard, but the camera ignores the children, the cars, and the octopus seesaw, and it zooms in on a little boy. He stands quietly to the side and leans against a pole.

The second video replicates the tour, but this time there is a guide. The video is dated January 12, 1984, and the guide is Peggy McMartin Buckey, the school's administrator. She wears a dark dress with polka dots. She is a big person and moves quickly, with her shoulders thrown back. "This is the stove," she tells the camera, standing in the kitchen. She looks uneasy, or maybe annoyed. "These are the cupboards where we keep all of the supplies. This is the refrigerator where we keep the juice that we make. And this is where the parents sit when they come in to talk. And this is the other cupboard where we keep other crackers. And this is where we keep our juice and the other things." In between sentences she looks up at the camera and then looks back down. "This is a drawer where we keep spoons and forks and everything that we need to use."

As she walks from room to room the camera occasionally catches her face from a sufficiently close distance to reveal that her colorful and extravagant clothes and makeup resemble the interior of the preschool. She wears outlandish costume jewelry, jangly medallions, lots of rings, long nails. She has big gray hair and big, spectacular glasses and red lipstick. "This is our happy face closet," she says. "This is where I keep my supplies. And this is the bulletin board. Each month we do a different thing. There's some more toys down here." She gestures toward big yellow buckets. If the date in the corner of the screen is correct, this is the last day Peggy will ever spend at work. The school closed on January 13, never to reopen. As the camera follows Peggy out into the yard, it sees that she has a red flower in her hair too, and then she goes through a door that says "Charlie Room" on the front. She says, "This is where Ray Buckey sat right here."[1]

In March of the previous year a woman named Judy Johnson had called the McMartin Preschool to ask about enrolling her two-and-a-half year-old son. She was told the school could not accept any new children for the time being, but Johnson was determined and a little desperate. She had recently separated from her tax auditor husband, leaving her to look after the boy full-time. On March 15 she put a note in her son's lunch bag explaining who he was, dropped him off at McMartin, and drove away. Peggy McMartin hadn't previously known Judy Johnson or her son, but she decided the woman must have been under enormous stress to do something so rash. She let the boy stay.

Peggy McMartin Buckey's mother, Virginia McMartin, was seventy-six years old, and by 1983 she had spent more time in Manhattan Beach than almost anybody else in the city—her residency dated back to the Great Depression. Then, as in the 1980s, Manhattan Beach was a long, narrow municipality running along the coast, with bungalows, houses, and little businesses crowding down toward the surf. "We moved from Inglewood because I loved to swim in the ocean," Virginia told an interviewer.[2] She worked as a riveter during World War II, which she thought was "fun," and then one day in the early 1950s one of the teachers at a church nursery school where Virginia volunteered told her that she was very good with children. After a few years of night classes she got certified as a teacher. Then Virginia paid $10,000 for "Miss Dawn's" preschool and replaced the sign with one bearing her own name. In 1966 she moved into a new building on one of Manhattan Beach's busiest streets, and that is where she stayed until the early 1980s. She was an acerbic and imposing presence even later in life, when she was confined to a wheelchair. A parent of a child who had attended McMartin once brought her dogs along to pick up her children. One of them urinated on bushes in the yard in view of Virginia, and the parent felt that Virginia was chilly toward her from that point on.[3] But it is a fact that the preschool Virginia ran was universally beloved in Manhattan Beach, no matter what parents would eventually say to reporters and to one another about hints they should have picked up on, ominous signs to which they should have paid closer attention. Over the course of twenty-eight years, 5,330 children attended Virginia's school. "Every morning, year-round, I swam from 16th Street to the pier and back," she said. "But not in the heart of the winter. I taught my children to swim in the ocean by holding them up by their suits."[4]

Things briefly calmed down for Judy Johnson. She and her husband made their separation permanent, and she also found a job in retail. In the summer of 1983, however, Johnson became concerned about the condition of her son's anus. One day in July she took Matthew to the emergency room and told the doctor that her son's anus was itchy. The doctor wasn't terribly concerned. Judy and Matthew went home.[5] A month passed. On August 12 Johnson called the Manhattan Beach police. Her concerns were the same as in July, except that now she suspected criminal rather than strictly medical causes. She told police detective Jane Hoag that when she had sent Matthew to school the previous morning his anus had been normal, but when she had brought him home at the end of the day it had been red. There was only one male teacher, Ray Buckey, working at McMartin.

Johnson said that Matthew had recently begun to play doctor, running around pretending to give people shots or check them for fever, which Johnson found very alarming. Repeated questioning finally induced Matthew to reveal that he had learned this behavior from Ray Buckey. Johnson believed the "thermometer" had been Ray's penis. Detective Hoag advised Johnson to take her son to the hospital, and at 8:30 that evening, after examining Matthew at the Kaiser Hospital in Harbor City, a doctor filed a suspected child abuse report. Over the weekend Johnson further questioned her son about what had happened at school, and then on Tuesday she called the police to provide Detective Hoag with two names; Johnson said Matthew had identified these other children as victims of Ray Buckey. On Wednesday Matthew was examined again, this time by two pediatricians at the Marion Davies Children's Clinic at UCLA. His examining physicians filed a second suspected child abuse report. A week later, no warrant having been issued for his arrest, Ray Buckey boarded a flight for South Dakota. He was going to visit his sister, Peggy Ann, who was spending the summer at Wind Caves National Park.

Around this time, Judy Johnson began to reach out to other parents whose children attended McMartin. She called the parents of one of the children Matthew had named to inform them of her suspicions. The parents talked to their son and then called Judy back: the boy didn't like Ray, but he denied having been molested at preschool. Johnson persisted. Detective Hoag, by this point, was making inquiries of her own. In the space of two days she called the parents of five other McMartin children, all of whom reported back that nothing had happened to their children. None of this eased Judy's mind. She was disturbed by an incident in which Matthew had wandered into her room while Johnson was partially undressed. The boy looked at his mother and said, "Matthew wear bra." Johnson told the police that Matthew had eventually revealed that Ray made him wear women's underwear at McMartin.[6]

Ray Buckey played a lot of volleyball on Manhattan Beach, and among the surfers and other young men who spent their days on the Pacific, prevailing fashions dictated big, baggy shorts or swim trunks with no underwear beneath. When Manhattan Beach police arrested Ray on September 7, they made special note of the fact that Ray "was not wearing any underwear beneath his shorts."[7] The Buckeys sought help from an attorney,

Don Kelly, who had previously assisted Ray with a drunk driving incident. Earlier that week police had searched the McMartin-Buckeys' homes for pornography and other evidence of molestation, but they failed to turn up anything up. Without any evidence to corroborate Johnson's allegations and the doctor's suspected child abuse reports, they briefly held Ray and then released him on $15,000 bail. The day after Ray's arrest, the police decided it was time to expand the scope of their investigation.

The police department worked up a list of some two hundred children who were attending or had previously attended McMartin and then mailed a letter to their parents. The letter read as follows:

September 8, 1983

Dear Parent:

This Department is conducting a criminal investigation involving child molestation (288 P.C.). Ray Buckey, an employee of Virginia McMartin's Pre-School, was arrested September 7, 1983 by this department.

The following procedure is obviously an unpleasant one, but to protect the rights of your children as well as the rights of the accused, this inquiry is necessary for a complete investigation.

Records indicate that your child has been or is currently a student at the pre-school. We are asking your assistance in this continuing investigation. Please question your child to see if he or she has been a witness to any crime or if he or she has been a victim. Our investigation indicates that possible criminal acts include: oral sex, fondling of genitals, buttock or chest area, and sodomy, possibly committed under the pretense of "taking the child's temperature." Also photos may have been taken of children without their clothing. Any information from your child regarding having ever observed Ray Buckey to leave a classroom alone with a child during any nap period, or if they have ever observed Ray Buckey tie up a child, is important.

Please complete the enclosed information form and return it to this Department in the enclosed stamped return envelope as soon as possible. We will contact you if circumstances dictate same.

We ask you to please keep this investigation strictly confidential because of the nature of the charges and the highly emotional effect it could have on our community. Please do not discuss this investigation with anyone outside your immediate family. Do not contact or discuss the investigation with Raymond Buckey, any member of the accused defendant's family, or employees connected with the McMartin Preschool.

THERE IS NO EVIDENCE TO INDICATE THAT THE MANAGEMENT OF VIRGINIA MCMARTIN'S PRESCHOOL HAD ANY KNOWLEDGE OF THIS SITUATION AND NO DETRIMENTAL INFORMATION CONCERNING THE OPERATION OF THE SCHOOL HAS BEEN DISCOVERED DURING THIS INVESTIGATION. ALSO, NO OTHER EMPLOYEE IN THE SCHOOL IS UNDER INVESTIGATION FOR ANY CRIMINAL ACT.

Your prompt attention to this matter and reply no later than September 16, 1983 will be appreciated.

HARRY L. KUHLMEYER, JR.
Chief of Police

JOHN WEHNER, Captain[8]

The letter threw Manhattan Beach into an uproar. As Kuhlmeyer should have known they would, parents of McMartin children ignored his request that they not discuss the investigation outside their immediate families, and before long they were calling one another on the phone to trade rumors, exchange information, and seek corroboration for their own children's stories. One parent who received the letter, Ruth Owen, immediately called another, Donna Mergili, who hadn't, to let her know about the investigation. Ruth cried as she delivered the news, and then the two women hung up and spent the weekend asking their children what had happened to them. Ruth asked her daughter, Nina, whether kids at McMartin were ever made to take their clothes off, and although Nina said no, Ruth would later report to the police that she did not feel her daughter had been telling the truth.[9] For her part, Donna Mergili immediately learned from her daughter, Tanya, that the children often played games with Ray at McMartin. Donna told the police and other parents that these games had likely served as a pretense or cover for sexual abuse. Tanya named two, in particular, that would become focal points for the long investigation that was to follow: the "horsey" game and "naked movie star," the latter a fragment of a children's rhyme that was popular in the early 1980s: "What you see is what you are / You're a naked movie star." The following Monday, Ruth took her daughter to the police for more questioning.

The city's anxiety intensified through the end of September, with parents constantly stopping one another in church or on Manhattan Beach's long, beautiful ocean promenade to learn the latest. One child told his parents that Ray Buckey took photographs, though he would not say of what or how often. Another parent went to the police to repeat her daughter's revelation that she had "seen 'Mr. Ray's' penis and had touched it," information which, according to the parent, the girl had been "very reluctant" to give.[10] Other parents came to the police with more frightening information, saying their children had reported being sodomized by Ray or that Ray had forced the kids to perform oral sex on him. Around Manhattan Beach, it became common for parents to look back on little incidents from the last few years and to drastically reevaluate their significance. One parent who had been told by a doctor that her child's vaginal infection was caused by poor hygiene began to suspect a different explanation.[11] Another wondered about an episode where her daughter, in the bathtub with her young brother, had suddenly tried to grab at her sibling's penis. Another was disturbed by her child's curiosity about breastfeeding. All told, the police received what they recorded in phone logs as eight "positive" responses from parents in the wake of their mass mailing.[12]

Even at this early stage, however, the investigation had problems. For one thing, some of the McMartin children's stories had rapidly expanded beyond the accounts of fondling and nonpenetrative molestation that constitute the vast majority of child sex abuse, to the point that police seemed to be dealing with a set of crimes that could not possibly have gone unnoticed by the other teachers at McMartin. Parents were calling police detectives with stories of children tied up, anal penetration, photographs of the abuse, and yet none of the children had suffered injuries, no photographs or photographic equipment could be found, and none of the other McMartin teachers said they had witnessed any wrongdoing by Ray Buckey. One child told investigators that she had alerted Babette Spitler, another teacher at McMartin, to Ray's abuse, and that Spitler had immediately called the police. But Spitler denied being told anything of the kind, and the police had no record of any call.[13] And although many parents became convinced that Ray had abused their children, other parents were not convinced at all, and they soon began to resent what they saw as police detectives' weird insistence that their children must have been victimized. One parent remembered ten phone calls from the police over the course of the fall, each of them informing her that her daughter's name was repeatedly coming up in other children's stories. At the detectives' request, she questioned her daughter many times about McMartin, but every time her daughter said Ray hadn't done anything wrong, and her mother believed her.[14] For an investigative team that was trying to put together an internally consistent story about what had gone on at McMartin, all of this should have thrown up rather large red flags.

Although a number of McMartin parents supported the school's staff in their claims of innocence, their support was not particularly active or vocal, and on October 6 the Buckey family's attorney, Don Kelly, released a statement announcing that the school's enrollment had dropped from forty-five students to just fifteen. Less than a week later, the Buckey family filed a $4.5 million lawsuit against the police department and the city of Manhattan Beach. The suit claimed that the family's reputation and business had been ruined.[15] Meanwhile the investigation continued to expand, this time beyond Manhattan Beach's city limits into the political institutions of greater Los Angeles.

The city's district attorney at that time, Robert Philibosian, was a little-known gubernatorial appointee, and his prospects in the upcoming election were not good. Opposing him for the office was a city attorney and career politician named Ira Reiner, a man with such widespread name recognition that a significant number of Californians thought he was already the state's governor. As Philibosian and his staff cast around for a campaign issue to call their own, they came across a surprising public opinion poll. The poll asked Angelenos to identify the crime issues that most concerned them, and there at the top, right along with drugs, was child abuse.[16] Philibosian decided that the Los Angeles district attorney's office would open its own investigation of the McMartin Preschool, separate from the one being carried out by the police in Manhattan Beach, and he assigned Jean Matusinka, head of the DA's sexual abuse prosecution unit, to take the lead. One of Matusinka's first decisions—certainly her most important one—was to contact a local organization named Children's Institute International and ask for Kee MacFarlane.

Kee MacFarlane first encountered the problem of child abuse in 1970 when she began working at a center for neglected children in Tucson,

Arizona. She was twenty-three years old and just out of college with a degree in fine arts. Her time at the Arizona Children's Home completely changed her life.[17] Moved by her work with the children she met in the southwest, MacFarlane eventually enrolled at the University of Maryland for a degree in social work, and among other activities in the early 1970s she worked to establish new branches of Parents Anonymous in Baltimore and New Jersey.[18] In 1976 she joined the National Center for Child Abuse and Neglect (NCCAN), which had recently been opened as a result of Walter Mondale's child abuse legislation, as a sex abuse specialist. Excited by her work and well funded by the federal government, MacFarlane distributed grant money, built up contacts with specialists from around the country, and absorbed the psychotherapeutic approach to child abuse treatment around which NCCAN was organized. This work continued until 1982, when, as a result of the Reagan administration's budget cuts, MacFarlane was laid off. She packed her bags that January and moved across the country to Los Angeles. She wanted to write a book.

In Washington, NCCAN had been an important and innovative participant in what was then still a rather new and underdeveloped field, but its ambitions had been restrained somewhat by the government supervision that came along with the government funding. California was different. The state had served as a kind of incubator for new institutional responses to child abuse, especially child sex abuse, since the early 1970s. Parents Anonymous, for example, the group whose founder, Jolly K, had pleased congressional Republicans with her testimony in 1973, was based in California, as was Parents United, a self-help group for incestuous families that was founded in Silicon Valley. In the southern half of the state, other professionals pioneered models of incest treatment and response that would soon take hold around the country. These models were usually organized around therapeutic programs designed to keep families together in the wake of incestuous abuse. The idea was to avoid an over-reliance on law enforcement, which tended to break families apart.

Michael Durfee, a doctor and the director of the Los Angeles County Health Department's child abuse program, played a number of important roles in the evolution of child abuse detection and treatment. He reviewed infant death records, looking for cases in which probable homicides had been misclassified as death by accidental or natural causes. He developed an interest in traumatic dissociation and Multiple Personality Disorder in the wake of the publication of *Michelle Remembers*, and he began working with a woman who claimed to have recovered memories of childhood abuse at the hands of a violent satanic cult. He helped her report the ritual murders, for which no evidence was ever found, to the FBI. Most important, however, were his efforts to have preschoolers regarded as a group particularly threatened by sexual abuse. In the early 1980s he organized dozens of area abuse specialists into something he called the Preschool-Age Molested Children's Professional Group. The group met six times per year, looking for ways to make the region's courts, hospitals, and legislatures more responsive to these vulnerable children. Kee Mac-Farlane began to participate in these meetings soon after her arrival in Los Angeles.[19]

Some of the group's ideas were rather sensible. Its members noticed, for example, that suspected child abuse victims were often repeatedly interviewed over the course of an investigation and that the frequency and intensity of these interviews could be traumatic.[20] First, a child might be interviewed by someone at Child Protective Services. Then a doctor might conduct another interview to obtain a medical history before conducting an exam. Then police detectives might visit a child, maybe more than once, and then the child might be asked to tell his or her story again, either before a grand jury or in open court. MacFarlane and a few other members of Dr. Durfee's group hit upon the idea of videotaping the child's first interview. If conducted in a sufficiently thorough and competent manner, a recording of this interview could then theoretically satisfy the needs of investigators working in many different departments and prevent the child from having to confront yet another strange adult in some fluorescent-lit government building.

MacFarlane and her colleagues also embraced some riskier ideas that were being developed around this time. Although the idea was completely unfamiliar to law enforcement, psychotherapists had long used different forms of play as a means of connecting with child patients and encouraging them to open up. A casual drawing or coloring session might precede more serious therapeutic conversation. Toys would be made available to the child for use during breaks. The use of hand puppets was common. MacFarlane believed these techniques could also be helpful in *forensic* interviews with suspected child abuse victims, interviews in which the main priority, by definition, had to be the accurate recall of events rather than the emotional well-being of the child.[21] And because she had started work at a nonprofit called Children's Institute International shortly after she had joined Dr. Durfee's professional group, she soon had a chance to put her theories into practice.

In Manhattan Beach a number of McMartin parents complained about the police department's investigation, saying that Detective Hoag was too aggressive in her interviewing. Assistant District Attorney Matusinka requested that children be interviewed at CII, partially in the hope that children could be interviewed "in a non-traumatic therapeutic setting." This was a seemingly benign thing to hope for, but it went on to cause problems for the interviewers at CII, and it became the subject of major debate at the trial that was eventually to come. Trial transcripts suggest that Matusinka, MacFarlane, and the others at CII were not entirely on the same page about the purpose of the interviews that were about to take place.[22] In a purely therapeutic setting the doctor or social worker can sometimes make the decision to prioritize a patient's psychological or emotional truth over the truth that is actually out there in the world. However, a forensic interview needs to elicit statements that can hold up before a judge and a jury in criminal court. And although MacFarlane and CII had evaluated child abuse victims for the DA's office before—one assistant district attorney described their work on those cases as excellent—they had not previously taken on anything like a case of this size.[23] MacFarlane's untested efforts "to try to combine" these two types of interviews—the therapeutic and the forensic—were therefore brought to bear on a type of case with which CII was totally unfamiliar.[24]

Once Matusinka's request came in, however, MacFarlane prepared to begin very quickly. Her interview room was filled with children's toys and tiny furniture, and the walls were coated in bright paint. MacFarlane brought in assistants to work the video equipment and conduct interviews of their own, and she dressed them and herself in colorful, goofy clothes. They decided to encourage their interview subjects to speak through puppets—a Pac-Man doll, an alligator, a dog named "Detective Dog"—when they wanted to communicate some "yucky secret" they were too frightened to share on their own. Finally, MacFarlane planned to use anatomically correct dolls, which came in both child and adult versions and included penises, vaginas, breasts, and pubic hair. Kids would be encouraged to use the dolls to demonstrate how their abuse had taken place. (This eventually gave rise to the cliché, "Show me on the doll where the bad man touched you.") Two weeks after Matusinka's letter MacFarlane was ready to start.

For detectives in Manhattan Beach, the interviews could not have started soon enough. Throughout October Judy Johnson had deluged Detective Hoag with elaborate and surreal allegations. On September 30, according to a police report, Johnson reported "that in further discussion had with Matthew he related having been sodomized by Ray while his head was put in the toilet. Matthew also mentioned something about Ray wearing a mask to his mother."[25] Johnson also told Detective Hoag that Matthew had been acting out, including a number of incidents in which her son attempted to tie her up. On October 17 Johnson called the station again:

> Judy Johnson provided [reporting officer] with additional information obtained from Matthew: Matthew related that a song "Peter, Peter, Pumpkin Eater" was sung after which Raymond Buckey sucked said victim's penis; Matthew related having been masturbated by Ray; Matthew said he had been put in a closet by Ray and in a high place; Matthew hurt by Ray following a Hide N Seek game. . . . Ray apparently took Matthew's blood pressure and sometimes the blood pressure cuff had Ray's penis in same; Matthew was given a shot by Ray. . . .[26]

On October 19, Judy called Detective Hoag again: "Matthew related to his mother that he had seen Ray wear some kind of a cape. Matthew also related having sat on Ray's lap and that it hurt. The victim has described Ray as having inserted some kind of an air tube in his rectum." The next day Judy called to say that Ray once dressed up like a minister while abusing her son.[27] The detectives investigating the McMartin Preschool were not much given to expressing doubts, but one might notice a bit of uncertainty in Hoag's use of "apparently" in her October 17 report. Somebody needed to sort and verify these allegations before they made the case totally impossible.

Kee MacFarlane conducted her first interview with a McMartin student on November 1, 1983. The subject was a four-year-old girl named Ella Baldwin, and MacFarlane took her time to build up a rapport. The pair chatted about pets. Ella said her family kept a snake and that although they had also kept a dog, the dog had died. "Aww," MacFarlane said. "Was he just old?" Ella nodded her head, and MacFarlane said, "Old dogs die," and then Ella heard about MacFarlane's cat.[28] This went on for a while: coloring, comments about the toys in the room, ordinary questions about

Ella's classmates at McMartin. It isn't until the thirty-third page of the interview transcript that MacFarlane alluded to the subject of the police investigation at all, and even then the allusion was oblique:

Q: Was it, your teacher was a boy?
A: Yeah.
Q: Oh, what was his name?
A: His name was Ray.
Q: Ray. . . . I see. Did you like him? Was he a good teacher?
A: No.
Q: No?
A: He was bad.
Q: Oh he was bad. What did he do? Why was he bad?
A: Because, sometime he, my ma, my mom said sometimes he tied up kids.[29]

Here, already, the complications involved with investigating a case like McMartin were clear. No sooner had MacFarlane obtained her first statements about Ray's criminal acts than the child attributed those statements not to her own experience but rather to something her mother told her. With Ella, as with a number of other children interviewed in November, MacFarlane proceeded carefully, at least at first. Four times she asked Ella whether she had personally seen Ray tie up kids, and all of Ella's responses were negative. MacFarlane let the subject drop and soon brought out a set of anatomically correct dolls. Together, MacFarlane and Ella undressed the dolls to get a look at their special features. "She has her hole under her," MacFarlane said, spreading a female doll's legs. "See her little hole? Just like you, right?"[30] They reviewed a boy doll as well, and then, with Ella still absorbed with poring over the boy doll, MacFarlane asked, "Did you ever see any of the kids in your old school take their clothes off?" Ella said, "Nope," and again MacFarlane didn't press her point. More games follow. Holding an adult male doll, Ella assumes a dad's voice and tells the other dolls to have dinner and take a bath. "Anybody ever take a bath in school?" MacFarlane asked. Again, "Nope." Ella then ignored a few more questions about Ray.

For a brief moment, the child seemed to allude to something that might have interested MacFarlane, identifying Ray as the teacher who told her "not to talk about it."[31] But the "it" to which Ella was referring—whether

Ray ever took her clothes off—was something she had already said, earlier in the interview, didn't happen. When MacFarlane asked her to pretend the dolls were other children from her class at McMartin, Ella mentioned five names, none of which matched the names of any of her classmates. Then Ella told MacFarlane, "No one gets tied up," and when MacFarlane kept to the subject anyway, Ella said that she did get tied up but that it happened outside, on the playground, which was right beside one of Manhattan Beach's busiest streets.[32] She also said that Ray did nothing while she was tied up and that her clothes were on. The variety and inconsistency of Ella's statements suggest that she was not speaking from memory but simply playing, which is essentially what MacFarlane had asked her to do in the toy-filled room. After MacFarlane asked again whether clothes ever came off, Ella says that Ray undressed two girls who, again, were not in her class.[33] Then Ella made the Ray doll fondle one of the tied-up children. MacFarlane seemed to be getting somewhere, but then this exchange occurred:

> A: A big, a big mommy came around.
> Q: A big mommy came into the room?
> A: Yep. And she, she camed up. . . . She tied up him.
> Q: Is that the truth?
> A: No, it's just a story.
> Q: Oh, that's just a story. What about the part with Julia, was that the truth?
> A: It's all a story.[34]

MacFarlane spent the rest of the interview circling back to the question of whether Ray had put his finger in or on Ella's vagina, and although Ella eventually agreed this had occurred, she also said that she hadn't personally seen it happen. "My mom must have looked," Ella explained. "Cause she told me who was doing it."[35] Ella did not go on to become a formal complainant in the district attorney's case.

MacFarlane interviewed fourteen more children in the month of November, refining her interviewing technique as she went along. She began to refer to the microphone, which had piqued the curiosity of a number of children, as the "secret machine." She told kids that if they were holding onto "yucky secrets" from their time at McMartin, revealing those secrets to the machine would make them go away. "We have to tell the secret machine the truth," she told one boy.[36] Her tone steadily changed as well. Whereas her questions for Ella Baldwin, though frequently repeated, were asked in a neutral and usually open-ended manner, interviews from later in the month featured a different approach. When some children said they hadn't played a certain sexual game or that they hadn't seen Ray remove anybody's clothes, MacFarlane replied that a sibling or a friend from McMartin "told already."[37] When one five-year-old boy maintained that nobody had scared him into not talking about naked games being played at McMartin, even after Mac-Farlane tried this new approach, MacFarlane became very direct:

Q: Anybody ever tell you something bad would happen to you?
A: No.
Q: Anything bad happened to your mom and dad?
A: No.
Q: No?
A: No.
Q: Why don't you want to tell me what happened at school?
A: Well somebody was going to hit me and I said don't hit me. They sat on
   the bench. They said who cares I'm going to hit you.

(The boy appears to be talking about a playground confrontation with another *child*, who then got in trouble and was made to sit on a bench as a form of "time out.")

Q: I think you're scared to tell me about Mr. Ray.
A: I'm not scared.
Q: Why won't you tell me?
A: I could go and tell my mom.
Q: Tell it in here. . . . Tell what happened to the other kids.
A: I don't know.
Q: Did they get touched?
A: No.
Q: How about when you played the naked games, is that a secret?
A: No.
Q: That's not a secret?
A: No, that's a bad secret and we have to throw it away.
Q: Now we got rid of the bad secret.
A: Did all the secrets go away?

This last remark—*did all the secrets go away?*—is ambiguous. One possible interpretation is that the boy really was scared, despite his protestations, and that he was looking to MacFarlane for validation as he hesitantly unburdened himself. Another interpretation, though, is that he was asking MacFarlane, who was so insistent about the necessity of throwing away bad secrets, whether she was satisfied, whether the interview would now be allowed to end.

Q: Mr. Ray ever do anything bad?

A: I don't know. How would I know?

Q: Did you know he ever did anything bad?

A: No.

Q: Ever see him do anything to the other kids?

A: I never saw it.

Q: Ever see his pee pee?

A: No. Who's [*sic*] pee pee?

Q: Mr. Ray. . . . I wonder when you used to play the naked games with Mr. Ray and the other kids if anything else happened that might be bad. Other kids remember things and they told me you were there. So don't you remember seeing some of that?

A: [Shakes head no.]

Q: You're just afraid.

A: No I'm not.

Q: You're just a scaredy cat. How come you won't tell me?[38]

MacFarlane genuinely believed that someone had terrified the children into silence, but her approach in this interview borders on bullying, and it suggests a mounting frustration with her lack of success to that point. Only three of the children interviewed in November made sufficiently incriminating statements to eventually wind up on the official list of trial complainants. MacFarlane was convinced, however, that nearly all of the children interviewed that month had been abused. In her view and in the view of the police, the scope of the case was growing.

On the afternoon of November 30, Judy Johnson called Detective Hoag again. She said Matthew had revealed more details of his abuse and that McMartin teachers other than Ray had been involved. Babette Spitler, Johnson said, made Matthew vomit by stepping on his stomach, and there was a stranger, an old woman, who came to the school and held Matthew's feet down while he was sodomized. Matthew had also been forced to perform oral sex on Peggy McMartin Buckey, the school's administrator. According to Detective Hoag's report on the call, Matthew also told his mother about "being taken to some type of a ranch far away where there were horses and he rode naked." Ray took pills. Ray gave himself a shot. Ray killed a dog and put a cat "in hot water."[39]

The December interviews did not go any better for MacFarlane or her CII colleagues. Of the eighteen children interviewed during that month, only two would end up on the criminal complaint filed by the district attorney in May of 1984, and neither of those children would appear at the eventual trial. This was not for lack of trying on MacFarlane's part. She seemed to be less tolerant of the children's unwillingness to provide details of abuse, and she abandoned many of her more open-ended lines of questioning, bringing up the "tie-up game" and the "naked movie star game" whether children mentioned it or not. She called a second child a "scaredy cat," and when the girl still refused to say that she had been abused, MacFarlane brought in the girl's mother to ask questions of her own.[40] MacFarlane also appears to have stopped attending to the implications of the playful dynamic that she had encouraged in the first place, taking statements clearly made in the context of some imaginative game as straightforward accusations of abuse. On December 9 her persistent efforts to elicit abuse stories from a boy named Jeremy Morse produced a semicomic sequence in which the two seemed to be playing three or four games at once, with no way to separate the boy's flights of fancy from his memories. MacFarlane spent much of the interview asking who had photographed the children—CII workers had begun to suspect that child pornography had been produced at McMartin. The way she and Jeremy talk across one another in the transcript is like something out of Abbott and Costello:

> Q: Here's the camera. Now, who takes the pictures?
> A: Him [indicating the plastic Ken doll].
> Q: Who's Him?
> A: Who is he?
> Q: I don't know. Who used to take the pictures?
> A: Miss Peggy.
> Q: Miss Peggy took the pictures? . . .
> A: He's going to take the pictures.

Q: Mr. Snake? But who in your class took the pictures when you used
   to play?
A: Snake.[41]

The interview devolved into snake play for a time, as Jeremy fed the
snake a length of string and then a pair of doll pants. The boy turned on a
toy police car with a loud siren, and when MacFarlane tried to direct his
attention back to the interview by asking whether he wanted to tell some
secrets to the secret machine, Jeremy said, "I want to listen to that car."[42]
The boy eventually seemed to claim that Ray had touched his penis, but
then he offered a clarification: the "Jeremy" doll was actually Jeremy's
friend, Benjamin, and the Ray doll was Jeremy.[43] Technically, Jeremy's
claim was that *he* had once touched *Benjamin's* penis, but MacFarlane
pressed on. Toward the end of the interview Jeremy used a toy syringe to
strike the "Ray" doll's penis. MacFarlane said, "That pee-pee touched a lot
of people, didn't it?"[44] By the end of the month more than 30 children had
been interviewed at CII. MacFarlane and her colleagues would eventually
talk to some 375 more.

Despite the fact that the December interviewees said little that their
November predecessors hadn't already said, and despite the fact that so
few of them became formally involved in the criminal complaint and trial,
they were important to the development of the case as a whole. Criminal
complaint or no, MacFarlane was absolutely convinced that nearly all of
the children she saw over the first two months had been abused, that Ray's
"pee-pee" had "touched a lot of people." But during December she also
came to believe, as Judy Johnson believed, that teachers other than Ray
were involved and that the crimes they had committed went well beyond
what investigators normally saw in sex abuse cases. As MacFarlane sat on
the floor in the middle of the room and interviewed each child, the person
operating the video camera kept a written log of what was said. (These logs
were made so that particular exchanges could be tracked down after the
fact, without having to go through an entire transcript.) These logs document CII's growing conviction that the teachers at McMartin had not only
been abusive but, bizarrely, elaborately so: Peggy had watched Ray molest
a student; Betty Raidor had taken photographs during the naked movie
star game, removed her own clothes in class, and driven a tied-up child
to an unidentified home in the area where she had taken more pictures;
and Babette Spitler had not only organized but played the naked movie

star game. In some instances CII therapists entered these claims in logs summarizing interviews in which children had not actually made those claims.[45] With twelve months of additional interviews to come, CII made up its mind about what had happened at McMartin.

In the thirty years since these interviews were conducted, a number of commentators have tried to excuse MacFarlane's mistakes on the grounds that social workers and therapists working with suspected sex abuse victims in the 1980s simply could not have known any better. As a discipline, the forensic interview was in its infancy, and the body of psychiatric research on the dynamics of conducting forensic interviews with children was tiny. In his recent book *The Witch-Hunt Narrative*, Ross E. Cheit acknowledged that some of the techniques used at CII "are now recognized as inappropriate," but the "now" in that phrase does more to exonerate MacFarlane than to criticize her, as though she were simply the unfortunate product of scientifically unenlightened times.[46] Incomplete scientific knowledge, however, does not seem to account for MacFarlane's approach to her interview subjects, nor does it account for the video operators' mistaking the interviewer's questions for the children's answers in compiling the logs.

When children said "no" in response to MacFarlane's questions, she tended to believe that they would have said "yes" except for their teachers' intimidation. She acquired this belief, at least in part, from a local psychiatrist named Roland Summit. Working out of the Harbor UCLA Medical Center in nearby Torrance, Summit was officially a "community psychiatrist." In the 1970s he helped Jolly K organize Parents Anonymous's first board of directors, and he encountered both victims and abusers in the course of advising police departments and other organizations. He wrote papers based on his clinical work in which he tried to taxonomize child sex abuse, describing incest as a kind of familial love run amok. "Snuggling with children under the covers on a cold Sunday morning," he wrote in a 1978 paper, "can be one of the great joys of family living. A woman may remember fondly the warmth and strength of her father's body against her."[47] Problems arose, he wrote, when this affection overstepped the bounds family roles assigned to it: "A child is regarded at times as something other than a child, or as a surrogate of someone else."[48] This "someone else" was almost always the mother, who was "no longer invested either in endorsing her husband's ego needs or in trying to wring pleasure from a tired relationship." Burying herself in "a job, church, or social commitments," the mother can "count on her daughter to take her place." The victim of incest, meanwhile, is almost always a girl on the cusp of adolescence, a developmental stage at which she is "learning to transmit the magical vibrations our society requires of the emergent woman."[49] (Summit's words often took on this slightly honeyed quality, which, given the subject matter, was unfortunate. In one newspaper interview he ventriloquized the incestuous father's point of view by describing children as "delicious little creatures.")[50]

Although Summit was an early adherent to the feminist idea that incest was a woefully underacknowledged social problem, his theories about incest's causes were more deeply rooted in prefeminist, midcentury psychiatric doctrine, with its transference, its Oedipal fantasies, and its menagerie of unwittingly seductive children and frigid wives and mothers. He also shared with midcentury psychiatric orthodoxy the idea that family preservation took priority over most other considerations. Some of Summit's work involved reintegrating incestuous fathers into the families that had been torn apart by their actions. He believed that healthy family life was organized around limits and that "incestuous activity begins when the father needs to bend those limits and the mother chooses to ignore them."[51] He began regularly working with Kee MacFarlane shortly after her move to Los Angeles.

Summit saw no children as patients, nor had he conducted any peer-reviewed original research on child sex abuse, but by the late 1970s he was well established throughout Southern California as an expert on the subject. He made what is undoubtedly his most influential contribution to the field in 1979, when he began work on a paper that would eventually be published under the title "The Child Sexual Abuse Accommodation Syndrome" (CSAAS).[52] "Since the events depicted by the child are so often perceived as incredible," Summit wrote, "skeptical caretakers turn to experts for clarification. . . . Every clinician must be capable of understanding and articulating the position of the child in the prevailing adult imbalance of credibility." To facilitate this understanding, Summit proposed the CSAAS, which was in essence a narrative describing the process by which children did or did not disclose the abuse they had suffered. For many therapists, investigators, and prosecutors who would become involved with massive child sex abuse cases during the 1980s, this narrative would become a sort of hymn. An oddly self-regarding tone prevails throughout the paper, which describes psychiatric professionals as leaders in society's effort to bring the problem of child sex abuse out into the light.

The syndrome included five "categories":

1. Secrecy
2. Helplessness
3. Entrapment and accommodation
4. Delayed, conflicted, and unconvincing disclosure
5. Retraction

The first three concerned the child's experience of abuse as it happens. Of the first, Summit wrote that child abuse "happens only when the child is alone with the offending adult, and it must never be shared with anyone else." He provided a long list of examples, things a molesting adult might say to a child to underline the importance of keeping the secret: "Nobody will believe you"; "If you tell anyone (a) I won't love you anymore, (b) I'll spank you, (c) I'll kill your dog, or (d) I'll kill you." Basing his argument in large part on reports and anecdotes he received from other clinicians at professional conferences and symposia, Summit argued that "any attempts by the child to illuminate the secret will be countered by an adult conspiracy of silence." In the face of such a dynamic, a child victim might naturally move into the second stage of the CSAAS: helplessness. Summit discussed the power imbalance that characterizes all adult-child sexual encounters, an imbalance produced not only by the disparity in size and strength but also by the caretaking or authoritarian role played by the adult. "Small creatures simply do not call on force to deal with overwhelming threat," Summit wrote. "Children generally learn to cope silently with terrors in the night. Bed covers take on magical powers against monsters, but they are no match for human intruders."

Trapped in an abusive relationship with someone who wields such enormous power and authority, the child progresses into the third stage of Summit's syndrome, "entrapment and accommodation." Summit describes how the abused girl eventually learns to accept her situation—the paper only discusses girls as victims, citing the difficulty of obtaining reliable clinical data on the abuse of boys—not because she enjoys the abuse but because she must find a way to survive. This involves accommodating not only the abuse itself, which Summit says tends to escalate in severity as time passes, but also the child's growing awareness that what is happening is wrong, that it is a betrayal, and that her father has abandoned his proper role in pursuit of his own desires. This abandonment, Summit writes, is an extremely violent and disfiguring psychological experience for the child, one that resonates throughout the rest of a person's life. Summit writes that entrapment and accommodation lie at the root of "much of what is eventually labeled as adolescent or adult psychopathology."

To this point in the paper, the psychological dynamics Summit describes, although outlined in a melodramatic way, are more or less in line with clinical observations subsequently made by thousands of counselors, therapists, and social workers. Toward the end of the third section, however, Summit introduces a more radical idea. Describing the effects of accommodation, Summit says on multiple occasions that the process breaks the child's psyche apart. He approvingly cites another researcher who wrote, "This is a mind splitting or a mind fragmenting operation," Self-hate produces "a vertical split" in the child's sense of reality, and a few paragraphs on, Summit describes the "inevitable splitting" of moral values that attends the experience of abuse. Writing in the wake of *Sybil* but before the publication of *Michelle Remembers*, Summit became one of the first physicians to write that victims of child sexual abuse "may develop multiple personalities"—one to handle the feelings of rage, another to suffer in silence, and so on—or that victims frequently "dissociate" from their own bodies during abuse so as to avoid experiencing its full horror.

The fourth aspect of the CSAAS is "delayed, conflicted, and unconvincing disclosure." It refers to victims' common reluctance to tell others about the abuse, adult family members' desire to seek other explanations for what is going on, and a wider social failure to credit those rare allegations that actually do make it into the criminal justice system. (Then, as now, child abuse remains an underreported crime.) This, again, outlines a psychological dynamic that is widely recognized among child protection and mental health professionals. Summit went a step further, however, in describing what he saw as the therapist's appropriate role in the drama of disclosure. "The psychiatrist or other counseling specialist has a crucial role in early detection, treatment intervention, and expert courtroom advocacy," he wrote. Faced, first, with children reluctant to disclose, and second, with parents and judges who hesitated to believe those disclosures that did manage to come out, the task of exposing and insisting on the truth fell squarely on the psychiatrist's shoulders. Summit had essentially asked a group of healers to start working as investigators and prosecutors as well. Like much of Summit's writing from this period, "The Child Sexual Abuse Accommodation Syndrome" has a bit of a messianic gleam in its eye.

In the paper's final pages Summit wrote, "It has become a maxim among child sexual abuse intervention counselors and investigators that children never fabricate the kinds of explicit sexual manipulations they divulge in complaints or interrogations." Though presented as therapeutic common sense, this was actually Summit's most radical claim. He wrote that no more than two or three children per thousand invented or exaggerated abuse claims and that among those children who misrepresented reality at all, the prevailing tendency was to *minimize* what had taken place. Summit's argument was essentially that if children say they are abused, then they are always telling the truth. No less radical was Summit's description of the final stage of the CSAAS, "retraction." "*Whatever a child says about sexual abuse,*" Summit wrote, adding the italics himself, "*she is likely to reverse it.*" Summit argued that in the wake of disclosing abuse, the child is likely to face intense emotional pressure from those around her. Her father will accuse her of tearing the family apart. Her mother will ask how she could say such things about the man who has provided and cared for her. As a result, Summit wrote, a child following "the 'normal' course" of things will eventually admit that her story was made up. The quotation marks that Summit put around the word "admits" suggest that only in this one instance, in the case of retraction, is suspicion of the child's truth-telling capabilities appropriate.

In later years Roland Summit would write articles and give presentations bemoaning the unscientific way in which some therapists, prosecutors, and police detectives had used his CSAAS, but here he has only himself to blame. CSAAS was easy to use in an irresponsible way because it is an irresponsible paper. Summit made the therapist out as a kind of hero detective, someone uniquely well suited to persuade children to reveal their darkest secrets. Once those secrets did come out into the open, the paper implied, the investigator's work was essentially done—if children were psychologically incapable of lying about sexual abuse, then corroborating evidence was just a superfluous adjunct to a truth the therapist already knew. And if a child should eventually retract her allegations for any reason—including accusations of overzealous or coercive interviewing—the therapist should not trouble himself too much. Given that Summit described it as a completely normal part of the disclosure process, a therapist might even be justified in seeing retraction as *supporting* the veracity of the child's initial claims.

MacFarlane and her colleagues at CII put Roland Summit's theories into practice. In the interviews conducted during the first month of 1984, MacFarlane's suspicion that the children's denials were masking secret pain hardened into a conviction. A January 24 interview with a boy named Keith Doherty is very easy to interpret: the child repeatedly said that nothing bad happened at McMartin and that he did not play naked games or go into a bathroom with Ray. Again and again, MacFarlane encouraged him to come up with different answers. MacFarlane conducted much of the interview via puppets used by her and by Keith, a tactic thought to help children maintain some measure of psychological distance from the events they were about to recount. Early in the interview, as MacFarlane introduced these puppets, she explained their purpose to Keith:

> We and the puppets are trying to figure out secrets. That's what we do in here. And this microphone is called our secret machine. And the way it works is that we tell it secrets, and they go down in that wire, and they go into the box, and they go into the TV, and then they're gone. And that's how it works. . . . We found out that there's some secrets going around from your old school. And the puppets have been trying their best to figure it out. And all the kids from your old school have come to tell—help the puppets tell.[53]

The first puppet Keith picked to use was a Looney Tunes rooster named Foghorn Leghorn, and as he tried it on, MacFarlane introduced a distinction that would become one of the interview's themes. "Do you know anything?" she asked Foghorn. "Are you smart, or are you dumb?"[54] Keith assured MacFarlane that he was smart. Keith was somewhat older than many of the other children interviewed at CII, and MacFarlane told him that these younger children were "too little to tell us, because they're babies." "What we're trying to do is talk to the older kids," she said, mentioning his name along with the names of a few peers, "because they're the smartest kids in the whole school and they can help the little kids." MacFarlane said, "We can figure out the games. That would be simple if you're smart."

"Yeah, I'm smart," Keith said.[55] MacFarlane also told the child that she had talked to his parents and that while they hoped he would be able to tell some secrets, they didn't know if their son had "a good enough memory."

Keith replied, "Well, I have a good enough memory."[56]

But when MacFarlane started to ask Keith about specific games and abuses, he refused to play along. He said Ray did not ride children around like a horsey, and he said the horsey game was not played naked. At this point MacFarlane asked Keith to use a new puppet, an alligator, who maybe could be more helpful. "All right Mr. Alligator," she said through her own bird puppet, "are you going to be stupid, or are you going to be smart and help us here?"

"Well, I'll be smart," Keith said.

Now MacFarlane asked the Alligator to talk about the naked movie star game. "Do you remember that game, Mr. Alligator," she said, "or is your memory too bad?"[57] Keith said he did not remember a naked movie star *game*. All he remembered was "a little song," someone in his class singing, "naked movie star, naked movie star" as a joke. MacFarlane told the alligator puppet that he "better not play dumb." When Keith again denied that he had ever seen anyone playing a game called "naked movie star," MacFarlane said, "Well, what good are you? You must be dumb."[58]

At the end of the interview, after he had given in and agreed with MacFarlane that Ray had touched kids, he even tried to clarify that the allegations weren't being made because of anything he had experienced. Speaking to each other through puppets, MacFarlane thanked Keith for being such a help. "Well, Keith told me," said Keith, through the puppet, and then he added, "Well, his mommy and daddy told him, then he told me." Finally, as the interview was winding down, Keith appeared to become anxious about what he had just said. "Some of the stuff I sort of forget," he told MacFarlane, "and like then I remember, and I'm not really sure."[59] MacFarlane cut him off, but he tried to bring it up one more time:

A: If I forget something like—or maybe I accidentally said the wrong thing.

Q: What would make you think that you could have said the wrong thing?

A: Some—

Q: You told the truth, didn't you?

A: Well, some of the things—I wasn't sure.[60]

Four months into the investigation there was also evidence that the churches, grocery stores, and private homes of Manhattan Beach were fertile grounds for rumor and speculation. From almost the very beginning children interviewed at CII had occasionally mentioned learning about Ray's crimes from their parents. Now, at the beginning of the new year, the stories children provided to Kee MacFarlane became more surreal. One boy said that Peggy Buckey was the teacher behind the naked horsey game, that she would mount her students and ride them around in the nude.[61] He denied that Ray was involved in the abuse, but he said that Virginia McMartin had killed animals at the school. Because police detectives do not hire stenographers to monitor every potential witness and suspect at home, it is impossible to know exactly who spread which rumor, who heard a story and added a detail of their own before passing it along, who misheard something over the telephone. But the way the stories told at CII intensified over time suggests that the extreme length of the investigation was crucial in shaping the case. By the end of the process, children coming in to talk to MacFarlane had spent nearly a year living among neighbors, friends, and parents convinced that Manhattan Beach harbored a secret evil. In January the boy who accused Virginia of killing classroom pets also told MacFarlane that teachers had taken the children off school grounds for abuse in various locations. He said he had been put in a car and gone to a hotel, a car wash, and a church. When the district attorney filed a criminal complaint three months later, that boy's name was included.

Sixty-three children spoke with Kee MacFarlane or her assistants during the first three months of interviews at CII. When an investigative journalist with the local ABC affiliate finally broke the story on February 2, he reported that "at least" sixty children had been identified as victims.

Wayne Satz learned about McMartin early on from a KABC colleague whose children had been involved with the investigation. He spent months gathering information—almost half a year after Judy Johnson's first call to the police, not a single news report on the case had been published or aired. Satz took special care during the fall and winter to cultivate Kee MacFarlane, who became his most important source and eventually his girlfriend. He had a long nose and brown hair, and he spoke with a soft and slightly thin voice. He wore tan jackets on camera, and he worked at the tail end of the period when men could wear facial hair—in his case a full beard—on television. "Scores of children from the McMartin school," he said in his first report, "boys and girls, have now reportedly told [Kee MacFarlane] that they had been taken to locations away from the school and been filmed, presumably for sale as kiddy porn, and had been sexually abused, repeatedly, and in every imaginable way."[62] He was always careful to say the word "alleged" before he said "crimes," "victims," or "abuse," and yet his stories left no doubt—the only question was how many victims the police would eventually turn up and how many adults would eventually be charged. "I don't think the depth of terror that can be put into a child should be underestimated," MacFarlane told Satz. "In my thirteen years of working in this field, I've never seen a situation that compares with this one."

Satz broke the McMartin story before District Attorney Philibosian took the case to a grand jury, before the grand jury returned an indictment, and even before Philibosian announced its existence. With six weeks to go before the grand jury began to consider the case, other journalists scrambled, unsuccessfully, to catch up to KABC. Satz had his sources—and the story—all to himself.

In his initial report Satz said that in addition to the testimonial evidence being gathered at CII, a Ventura doctor had found medical evidence of abuse. "Dr. Bruce Woodling is a specialist in finding the sometimes subtle signs that a child has been molested," Satz said. "And he is said to have made positive findings after examining these preschool children."[63] If true, this would have been a major coup for the district attorney. Law enforcement had long struggled with the fact that although rape and other violent forms of sexual assault produced physical evidence, chronic forms of nonviolent abuse did not; a parent could fondle a child repeatedly without leaving any marks.

Bruce Woodling had spent the better part of his career trying to help prosecutors find a way around this problem. He graduated from the medical school at the University of Southern California in 1972, and it was shortly after he settled at the county hospital in Ventura that he received a call from the Los Angeles district attorney's office. The DA asked whether he would be interested in doing on-call work examining rape victims. Woodling took to the job, which paid very little, with enthusiasm and a sense of purpose, and before long he was known around Southern California as a sex crimes expert. By the middle of the decade he was looking for ways to find medical evidence of chronic abuse in children.

His eventual findings had two parts, both variations on the idea that physicians needed to examine suspected abuse victims more closely than had been previously done. First, as Debbie Nathan and Michael Snedeker have explained in their book on the child care sex abuse panic, Woodling revived a set of Victorian theories about the physical consequences of gay sex and adapted them to children. Nineteenth-century physicians had looked hard for ways to identify homosexuals in court, and one popular belief had it that if a physician began to perform a rectal examination on a patient who regularly engaged in sodomy, the anus would spontaneously open up, whereas normal anuses would tighten. Although this theory had been discredited by the time Bruce Woodling entered medical school, many physicians continued to believe in it, and Woodling saw no reason why it shouldn't hold true for children as well. During exams he began using a swab to touch a spot near the young patient's anus. If it opened, he concluded that the child had been sodomized.[64] The wider the opening, the more regular the abuse had been. Woodling called this the "wink response" test.

Woodling's second innovation in child sex abuse forensics was technological. Around the time that Woodling published his wink response findings, an article in the *American Journal of Forensic Medicine and Pathology* began to publicize a new examination instrument called the colposcope. This was essentially a magnifying device that could be hooked up to a film or video camera, and it had recently been introduced to forensic exams in Brazil as a means of conducting virginity checks (legally a woman could only be raped in Brazil if she had never previously had sex).[65] Woodling acquired a colposcope and began using it to examine children, and he soon developed a vocabulary to describe the things the instrument allowed him to see. Blood vessels, miniscule abrasions, and tiny variations in the size and shape of a girl's hymen were suddenly visible, and Woodling's reports quickly filled with words like "microtrauma," meaning a wound that only the colposcope could see, and "synechiae," meaning scar tissue. Woodling also adopted the now-discredited idea that any hymenal opening greater than four millimeters is a marker of sexual trauma. The adoption of this last notion more or less completed the theory of sexual abuse forensics that would come to dominate the McMartin investigation.

At Children's Institute International, forensic interviews with McMartin students were usually followed by medical exams. Although Woodling did not personally conduct the majority of CII's medical exams, he trained Astrid Heger, who did.

Astrid Heger joined CII in 1983. She had nearly a decade's worth of experience in pediatrics but little experience examining victims of sexual assault, so she called Woodling, whose work she had followed for a number of years, and asked him to give her a course in forensic examination. She absorbed Woodling's theories about microtraumas and the four-millimeter hymen, and she acquired a colposcope. When she first began examining McMartin children at CII, she had conducted fewer than a dozen examinations of repeatedly abused children, most of which had been conducted with the supervision of a more experienced colleague.[66] The results of her McMartin exams validated the conclusions drawn from Kee MacFarlane's interviews: Heger concluded that 80 percent of the 150 children she saw had been abused.[67] Many of these diagnoses were based on Woodling's microscopic abrasions and hymenal variations, but Heger also diagnosed sexual abuse where she herself had found no positive evidence of it. This was based on the conviction—one she shared with Roland Summit—that medical professionals had a special social role to play in bringing the problem of child abuse out of the shadows.

Instead of clarifying or challenging the claims elicited in Kee Mac-Farlane's interviews, her reports validated them. Even perfectly normal physical findings were sometimes described as "consistent with history of sexual abuse."[68] Because abuse often fails to scar or mark the victim in any medically detectable way, this is technically true. But another feature of this language would certainly seem to be its helpfulness to prosecutors. Shortly after the McMartin examinations, Heger appeared in an instructional, "how-to" video on conducting forensic abuse exams. In the video, Heger talked about the importance of keeping the courtroom in mind while performing an exam: "[the medical record] should be prepared with the thought that it may become part of the legal proceeding," she said.[69] She also said that "the recognition of sexual molestation in a child is entirely dependent on the individual's inherent willingness to entertain the possibility that the condition may exist." At CII Heger seems to have taken this idea to its logical extreme and concluded that the social recognition of child abuse was also dependent on the individual's refusal to entertain the possibility that abuse had not occurred. Neither Heger nor her mentor, Bruce Woodling, whose "wink response" paper was coauthored with an employee of the district attorney's office, appears to have worried too much about the effects such a close alliance with prosecutors might have had on their work. Heger simultaneously acted as a pediatrician and as a police detective with a white lab coat.

CII billed the state of California $455 for each interview and medical examination, and these continued into the spring of 1984.[70] Like Mac-Farlane, Astrid Heger sometimes refused to take no for an answer from patients who would not provide a medical history that included sexual abuse. "I don't want to hear any more 'no's,'" Heger told one girl who had refused to disclose. "Every little boy and girl in the whole school got touched like that."[71] By this point investigators believed that almost every teacher in the school had been involved as well. Judy Johnson was still making regular calls to the Manhattan Beach police, reporting what she claimed were allegations made by her son, Matthew, who was now three years old. The police reports that document these calls, however, suggest either that Judy was dutifully and neutrally reporting her son's increasingly surreal allegations, or that her mental health was deteriorating:

> Matthew feels that he left L.A. International in an airplane and flew to Palm Springs. . . . Matthew went to the armory. . . . The goatman was there . . . it was a ritual type atmosphere. . . . At the church, Peggy drilled a child under the arms, armpits. Atmosphere was that of magic arts. Ray flew in the air. . . . Peggy, Babs and Betty were all dressed up as witches. The person who buried Matthew is Miss Betty. There were no holes in the coffin. Babs went with him on a train with an older girl where he was hurt by men in suits. Ray waved goodbye. . . . Peggy gave Matthew an enema. . . . Staples were put in Matthew's ears, his nipples, and his tongue. Babs put scissors in his eyes. . . . She chopped up animals. . . . Matthew was hurt by a lion. An elephant played . . . a goat climbed up higher and higher and higher, then a bad man threw it down the stairs. . . . Lots of candles were there, they were all black. . . . Ray pricked his right pointer finger . . . put it in the goat's anus. . . . Old grandma played the piano . . . head was chopped off and the brains were burned. . . . Peggy had a scissors in the church and she cut Matthew's hair. Matthew had to drink the baby's blood. Ray wanted Matthew's spit.[72]

The Manhattan Beach police do not seem to have dismissed these claims entirely. They may not have gone looking specifically for goat men or decapitated infants, but by March detectives believed that the case involved not only teachers at McMartin but other adults in the area as well, and they executed search warrants on eleven residences across the South Bay. The month saw a frenzy of activity. CII held regular meetings with the McMartin children's parents to bring them up to date on new developments. Over the course of two weeks, a Los Angeles grand jury—the one whose existence had been revealed by Wayne Satz at KABC—heard testimony from eighteen children who had been interviewed at CII. After hearing this testimony, the grand jury filed a 105-count indictment against five McMartin teachers: Ray Buckey, Peggy McMartin Buckey, Peggy Ann Buckey, Betty Raidor, and Babette Spitler. In a phone interview broadcast on KABC, Virginia McMartin angrily cut off an interviewer who asked whether she thought her grandson had ever had any sexual contact with children. "I certainly do not think that my grandson has one thing wrong with him," she said. "He is a very fine young man with a natural understanding of children."

"So you think you're just being framed, huh?" the reporter said.

"You're darn tootin' I think we're being framed," Virginia replied. "I don't think it, I know it!"[73] Virginia would soon be jailed herself. So would Mary Ann Jackson, who taught at the preschool.

Around this time, Ray hired a lawyer named Danny Davis as his new defense attorney. Davis first met the McMartin-Buckeys in the offices of Don Kelly, who had taken a small retainer before deciding he wanted nothing to do with the rapidly and ominously expanding case. When Davis received Kelly's phone call, he was in his backyard in west Los Angeles planning a vacation with his girlfriend. Davis had spent much of the previous five years defending young, wealthy Americans with "boutique" drug operations, and his most recent defense, of a pilot caught with six hundred kilos of cocaine, had gone very well. "It was a big success," Davis said. "Everybody was very happy with what happened." Davis had never handled any kind of molestation case before, but he had heard a little bit about the McMartin investigation, and the kinds of drug cases he liked best were becoming rare; larger, organized cartels were pushing smaller operations out of business. He drove over to Kelly's office "with 'yes' already on [his] lips," and then he saw the McMartin-Buckeys and decided that what he saw lined up with what he had heard on the news. "They had those hard-boned, chiseled, criminal-looking features," he said. "Not knowing whether or not they did it, I acted on my experience and presumed they did." Unlike prosecutors, who theoretically do not expect to bring charges against any defendant who is innocent, criminal defense attorneys are very open about the fact that many of the people they represent really have committed crimes. "My line is, there's never been a long line of innocent people waiting outside my office," Davis said.[74] As Davis began to plan a defense with his new client, the other six McMartin defendants sought out lawyers of their own.

One night in early April, someone jumped the fence surrounding the McMartin Preschool and lit the building on fire. The blaze caused around $10,000 worth of damage, and as the arsonist left the grounds, he or she spray-painted a message on one of the school's stucco walls: "ONLY THE BEGINNING." The story made local papers like the *Easy Reader* and *Daily Breeze* and also the *Los Angeles Times*. With the grand jury's indictment formally released, with a prosecutor named Lael Rubin assigned to head the state's case, and with the district attorney himself, Robert Philibosian, making a highly unusual appearance in court seated at the end of the prosecutors' table, McMartin was now front-page news all over the city.

In addition to the horrible news coming out of Manhattan Beach, these reports described a city with growing doubts about the safety of day care in general. "A child abuser," one *Times* article said, "intimidates the child to keep it a secret."[75] Efforts to crack down on unlicensed preschools and child care centers had been under way since the beginning of the decade, but even a license, another article said, was "no safety guarantee," and social services representatives claimed that abusers were often smart enough to evade detection for long periods of time. "You are not going to find out about abuse by visiting," one director of community care licensing told the *Times*. "Most have enough sense to stop beating or molesting children when we arrive."[76] McMartin was held up as a perfect example of social services' helplessness in the face of such a threat. "They're administering day care centers as if they were Burger Kings," one McMartin parent said of the state's licensing agencies. "They're measuring square footage and doorway widths, counting teachers and checking the sliding boards for splinters while our children are being molested."[77]

Turning to law enforcement, it seemed, was the best hope for protecting the city's children. All around Los Angeles, parents began to call the cops. In May the Peninsula Montessori School, less than ten miles down Pacific Highway 1 from Manhattan Beach, was closed as a result of child molestation allegations. In late July police executed a search warrant for the Manhattan Ranch Preschool in Manhattan Beach. The Children's Path Preschool in Hermosa Beach closed in October, and the Learning Game Preschool followed in December. By that point Michael Ruby, a seventeen-year-old who had previously worked at Manhattan Ranch, was on trial. The preschool run out of St. Cross Episcopal Church shut down the following spring. Teachers who worked at preschools that did manage to stay open noticed that parents were reluctant to leave their children at a day care that employed men. "McMartin's was *the* place—it was the cliquey little place," said a dental assistant who had given lectures on hygiene at McMartin. She hadn't noticed anything suspicious. "How could we have been so blind?" she said.[78]

Chapter 3

Prosecutors

McMartin was part of a national phenomenon from the beginning. Two other cases involving alleged conspiracies to sexually abuse dozens of very young children—one in central California, the other just outside of Minneapolis—had got under way well before McMartin became a major news story. One of these cases even predated McMartin by more than a year. As the Los Angeles district attorney's office worked to finalize charges against the McMartin teachers in the spring of 1984, a jury some 125 miles to the north, in the working-class oil and farm town of Bakersfield, delivered a verdict. Alvin and Debbie McCuan and Scott and Brenda Kniffen were all convicted of selling their children for sex in area motels and abusing them while the children hung from hooks in the ceiling. Their combined prison sentences totaled exactly one thousand years.

Around the same time, in a tiny Minnesota town called Jordan, a judge set trial dates for two other married couples who had been arrested and charged with abusing children between the ages of two and eleven during the previous summer. That brought to twenty-two the total number of people who had been arrested for similar crimes in Scott County over the previous few months.[1] Detectives believed that two or maybe three organized child sex rings had been operating in secret for at least the previous year, throwing private parties during which games of hide-and-seek devolved into indiscriminate abuse. Jordan was a conservative, Christian community of about twenty-seven hundred people, a place reflexively described by both visiting national news reporters and its own inhabitants as "typically small-town U.S.A."[2] As the investigation widened, distressed residents wrote letters to Jordan's local newspaper, the *Independent*. "The

65

saddest part of all of this," one wrote, "is the large amount of children that were abused while no one seemed to be aware of it! Are we all too busy with ourselves that we don't have time to care?"[3]

In Bakersfield the district attorney who tried the case against the Mc-Cuans and the Kniffens owed both his career and the power of the office he occupied to his work on crimes against children. Ed Jagels was a combative but little-known Kern County prosecutor when police found fourteen-year-old Dana Butler's body on a highway shoulder in April 1979. The girl had been stabbed forty times. An investigation quickly identified a man named Glenn Fitts as the obvious primary suspect—eyewitness testimony, blood samples recovered from Fitts's carpet, and pubic hair recovered from Butler's corpse all suggested as much. That Glenn Fitts regularly invited teenagers to his home and provided them with drugs and alcohol was also a fairly open secret in Bakersfield, at least among the teenagers. The problem was that Glenn Fitts was the former training coordinator of the Kern County Police Academy. For weeks the police officers who had trained at that academy failed to make an arrest, and in the wake of the scandal that followed, Kern County's district attorney decided he would not seek reelection.[4] Ed Jagels made corruption, which had nearly allowed Glenn Fitts to go free, and children, whom Kern County had failed to protect, the centerpieces of his campaign. He promised that under his supervision those who broke the law would be punished—every time. Speaking to a television news reporter, he said, "We've simply got to jail a lot more criminals for a lot longer."[5]

Some eighteen hundred miles away, in Minnesota, Scott County had a passionate and charismatic prosecutor of its own. Kathleen Morris had taken a circuitous route to the law. She spent much of her time at Southern Illinois University playing pinochle in the student union, and then she moved to Champaign-Urbana to teach high school. She joined the Yippie Party and lived in a commune, where she didn't mind the fact that she was the only employed person. "Everybody said you had to do your part to contribute," she said, "and mine was to bring in money."[6] Then she left teaching, the commune, and the Yippies for Hamline University. As a law student, she appealed a misdemeanor case to the Minnesota Supreme Court, and by 1978 she was an assistant county attorney, prosecuting drug cases against high school students. In 1981 she attracted statewide attention for her work prosecuting six members of the Cermak family—two brothers, their elderly parents, and their wives—for sexually abusing a number of children, mostly their own. The brothers each received forty-year sentences, and Morris said the long prison terms handed down to the Cermaks created the false impression that her primary prosecutorial aim was revenge; her real focus was on obtaining psychological treatment for both the abusers and their child victims. Whether such treatment could be sufficient to protect children from those Morris prosecuted, however, was a different question. "I would like to just put a sign on their houses that says: 'Pervert Lives Here,'" she said.[7] By the time the Cermaks were sent to prison, Morris was thought to be one of the most promising political figures in the state. Journalists and attorneys thought she would eventually run for attorney general.

As Kern County district attorney, Ed Jagels demonstrated none of Morris's interest in therapeutic rehabilitation for those who committed sex crimes against children. But like Morris, Jagels recognized and turned to his political advantage a growing perception among middle-class people that children were in desperate need of protection, that what most threatened children were sex crimes, and that the legal system, especially judges, made it harder for ordinary people to keep their children safe. This perception yoked together both the massive increase in attention paid to child abuse that had begun in the 1970s and a more general fear of crime that emerged in response to the protests and social disorder of the 1960s. Throughout his campaign Jagels received unwavering support from a group of parent-activists called the Mothers of Bakersfield. The group's leader, Jill Haddad, had previously testified before Congress on the dangers of child pornography. One of the first prosecutors in the country to form an alliance with the crime-victims movement, Jagels attacked judges who granted early parole to violent offenders, chased an overly inquisitive news photographer up a courthouse staircase, and promised to put more power in the hands of the one legal figure who could truly be said to have an uncomplicated interest in protecting the public from criminals: the prosecutor.

Jagels kept his promises. He brought in staffers whose zeal for radical change matched his own, and his office's aggressiveness, both in investigating cases and trying cases, earned Jagels frequent reprimands from judges. "The instances of misconduct are legion," one panel of a state appeals court wrote of Jagels's conduct during the prosecution of an armed robbery case.[8] The appeals court only declined to throw out the conviction Jagels had obtained because there was so much evidence against the defendant, including clear testimony from two eyewitnesses. In other words, the defendant would have been convicted even without what the court described as Jagels's "rantings, ravings, constant apologies, characterizations of defense counsel and defense counsel's objections, personal attacks, allegations of impropriety, attacks on defense witnesses, improper questions, defiance of rulings, and the need for the court to continually admonish counsel."[9] Jagels had a boyish face, a very small mouth, and the kind of hair that politicians want to have. He seemed to enjoy confrontations with the media just as much as he had enjoyed confrontations with judges in his courtroom days. He was an extraordinarily effective reformer. Within a few years of his election, Kern County was imprisoning more people per capita than any other county in California, a state that already imprisoned more people per capita than any other state in the United States, a country with the largest prison system in the world.

That prosecutors could be reformers at all—much less prominent or effective ones—was, in the early 1980s, a relatively new feature of American politics. Beginning with the Omnibus Crime Control and Safe Streets Act of 1968 and continuing through the 1970s, state legislatures and the US Congress passed hundreds of laws designed to shift legal power away from those accused of committing crimes and toward those who wanted the accused in prison: police officers, prosecutors, and victims. Through the middle of the twentieth century, the judge had been the representative figure of the American legal system and also, to a certain extent, of American government as a whole. By virtue of the political neutrality of their offices, judges commanded deference inside the courtroom and public esteem outside of it. The Supreme Court's series of landmark civil rights decisions in the 1950s and 1960s also suggested that the judiciary answered a high moral calling, that it was through judges that the country might manage to realize the promise of its Constitution.[10]

Beginning in the 1970s, however, the series of policy reforms comprising what is known today as the War on Crime permanently altered judges' position within the legal system. Where the public had previously tended to see judges as impartial arbiters of the law, many—especially conservatives—now saw a group of unelected, unaccountable officials who frequently used their powers of discretion to let dangerous criminals off the hook. And if those powers of discretion were now a problem, the solution was to take them away from judges and hand them over to prosecutors. In the 1970s, for example, judges were the only officials with the power to determine whether a juvenile defendant would be tried as an adult. Today, in almost every state, that decision belongs to the prosecutor.[11] The introduction of mandatory minimum sentences for those convicted in court further eroded the judiciary's discretionary powers, making the prosecutor's decision to bring charges—rather than the judge's assessment of the circumstances surrounding the case—the key factor in determining the length of a convict's prison term. These incremental shifts were soon reflected both in the country's incarceration rates, which increased dramatically during the eighties, and more generally in the campaign promises and stump speeches of office seekers around the country. When mayoral, congressional, or presidential candidates describe themselves as "tough on crime," they are trying to sound like prosecutors.

Ed Jagels became an early master of this kind of political rhetoric during his race for Kern County district attorney. His favorite campaign themes were the irresponsibility of the county's judges and the threat they posed to public safety. At one debate, Jagels arranged for Jill Haddad to speak from the audience and accuse Jagels's opponent, a Superior Court judge named Marvin Ferguson, of sending a four-year-old girl back to her abusive parents, who eventually killed her. Journalists later discovered that Ferguson was forced to send the girl home only because of the then–district attorney's failure to actually send a prosecutor to the hearing, but this news came too late to be of any help to the judge.[12] There was also the press conference at which Jagels, incensed over a California Supreme Court decision to strike down a law that would have allowed illegally obtained evidence to be presented in court, said, "If a couple of victims of these homicides wore appellate black robes instead of being gas station attendants and ranchers and jewelry store clerks, we'd start getting a little bit different decisions," he said. "I guarantee that."[13]

Jagels was still a few years away from the district attorney's office in 1977 when a woman named Mary Ann Barbour began to worry about the safety of her step-grandchildren. Mary Ann's life before her marriage to Gene Barbour had been eventful and fairly unhappy. Her father died in a road accident, and she had also once accidentally fallen out of a moving car, sustaining injuries that left a metal plate in her head. Her mother remarried twice after her father's death, and she left home for good at the age of fourteen (the specific reasons for her departure are unclear). By the time she met Gene she had three children and two marriages behind her. Gene had two daughters of his own from a previous marriage. One of them was named Debbie, and when Debbie was twelve she left her mother's home and said she wanted to live with her father. She said her stepfather, a man named Rod Phelps, had tried to molest her. Debbie got married to Alvin McCuan a few years later.

Debbie and Alvin had two daughters named Bobbie and Darla. Mary Ann was delighted with the girls, but between 1977 and 1980 she became increasingly convinced that Phelps was abusing Bobbie and Darla. She frequently examined the girls' genitals, which she found to be red and swollen, and she insisted that Debbie stop leaving the children with Phelps. In January 1980, Mary Ann called a pediatrician to report that Bobbie had told another young relative about being molested by Phelps. The pediatrician examined Bobbie and came to the opinion that she had been sexually penetrated. A few days later, Gene Barbour told his wife about the allegations Debbie McCuan had made against Phelps when she was a teenager. Although Debbie eventually retracted those allegations, there is evidence that she too was worried for her daughter. In 1979 she asked a pediatrician to have a look at Bobbie's "pubic area," which was bruised. She told the doctor that Bobbie had fallen on a wire fence, but the doctor said this could not possibly explain the bruising.[14] This revelation so upset Mary Ann that she left home for a few days before returning on January 14 at four in the morning. Gene called the sheriff's department and said he was worried about Mary Ann—she hadn't been sleeping, and she was also making threats. When the police arrived at the Barbour home that same day, Gene was restraining Mary Ann, there was a knife on the counter, and Gene said Mary Ann had threatened to kill him. According to the police officer who then spoke to Mary Ann, she appeared to be extremely paranoid—among other things, she said the Welfare Department was out to get her. Mary Ann was briefly hospitalized and given antipsychotics.[15] A social worker named Velda Murillo was called in to interview Bobbie and her parents, and eventually Bobbie said that on one occasion Phelps had put his hand down her underwear and his finger in her vagina. Police tracked down Phelps for questioning. Alvin and Debbie, for their part, promised to keep Phelps away from their home and offered to put their daughters into therapy.

Soon after her hospital release, Barbour asked an acquaintance at the Welfare Department for help with getting Debbie McCuan's day care license revoked, but a surprise inspection failed to uncover any problems. Barbour then made contact with Jill Haddad, who would be so instrumental to Ed Jagels's political career. As the leader of an area chapter of the victims' rights organization Stronger Legislation Against Molesters (SLAM), Haddad received copies of every sex-crime arrest report produced by the Kern County police, and she also drove the creation of a "sex abuse coordinator" position within the district attorney's office. She gave Mary Ann both a friendly hearing and a means of accessing Kern County's rapidly developing child sex abuse investigation machinery. In October 1981 Mary Ann told a probation officer that despite their earlier promises, Alvin and Debbie McCuan had allowed Rod Phelps to see their two daughters and that the abuse had started up again. After interviewing Bobbie and Darla again, Velda Murillo reported the girls had accused both Phelps *and* their father, Alvin McCuan, of molesting them. Alvin was arrested. At his preliminary hearing, the girls described being abused by their mother as well, so Debbie was arrested too. After a juvenile court proceeding, custody of the girls was handed over to Gene and Mary Ann Barbour in February 1982.[16]

To this point, Kern County police were dealing with a relatively ordinary investigation of intrafamilial abuse. That changed a few months after Mary Ann Barbour obtained custody of Bobbie and Darla. On April 2, Mary Ann met with Velda Murillo to report a number of shocking allegations the girls had allegedly furnished her with during the previous night. She said there were orgies, that the girls were having nightmares and were afraid of fire, that they had been made to watch snuff films and had seen another little girl killed right in front of them. She also said that Scott Kniffen and his wife, Brenda, had participated in the orgies. The Kniffens were family friends of the McCuans, getting together several times a year to catch up and play cards. In preparation for his trial, Alvin had asked Scott to testify on his behalf as a character witness. Scott later remembered that when police officers arrived to arrest him at work, he thought it was a prank, "like a singing telegram."[17] Scott and Brenda's two sons were immediately placed in a juvenile home.

Child interviews were conducted in a special room, furnished with a box of toys and bowls of candy, in the Kern County district attorney's office. The Kniffen boys eventually corroborated Mary Ann's allegations of motel orgies and wads of cash, but they failed to corroborate the part of the story where the cash was actually used to pay for things. Instead, one of the children elaborated the story to the point of implausibility, describing a scene in which six naked adults ran out into the parking lot, all of them

clutching money in their fists—money that should have been handed over
to Scott and Brenda Kniffen, according to the detectives' working theory
of the case. There is no evidence, however, that Kern County investigators
were skeptical of any of these stories. The McCuans had suddenly gone
from domestic sexual abusers to members of a county-wide network of
sex rings.

In court, the prosecution presented testimony from Bruce Woodling,
who would eventually do so much to shape Kee MacFarlane and Astrid
Heger's understanding of medical evidence and child abuse in Los Angeles. Woodling described his "wink response" test and testified that his
examinations of the Kniffen boys had revealed proof of their abuse. The
jury also heard from the Kniffens' two sons, who, after eighteen months
in foster care, said that their parents had handed them over to strangers
in motels and that they had referred to those strangers as "customers." In
the spring of 1984, each of the four defendants received a prison sentence
of at least 240 years.

Alvin McCuan, the first of the group to be accused, received 268 years
on 75 convictions. "You know," he later said, "it sure does change your
way of looking at the system."[18] The verdict form was 550 pages long, and
the court clerk needed two and a half hours to read out its 345 separate
decisions, which the jury had reached after less than two days of delib-
eration.[19] A letter published in the Bakersfield Californian a month after
the trial's conclusion pointed out that, "assuming [the jurors] ate, slept
and took potty breaks, that calculates out to approximately two minutes
per verdict," with each guilty verdict carrying an eight-year sentence.[20]
District Attorney Jagels, having obtained some of the longest prison sentences in California history, described the McCuan-Kniffen convictions
as one of Bakersfield's finest moments. Brenda Kniffen was sent to a unit
that had been constructed to house the women accomplices of Charles
Manson, and Scott Kniffen occasionally played chess with Sirhan Sirhan,
who had shot and killed Robert Kennedy.[21] With the hearing that sent the
Kniffens and McCuans to prison, the initial stage of the Kern County sex
ring investigation came to an end.

———

In Minnesota, Kathleen Morris never matched Ed Jagels's single-minded
passion for conviction and incarceration. To Jagels, criminal defendants

represented a kind of crucial anti-constituency, a group deserving of nearly unlimited punishment and scorn. In order to make the punishment of criminals politically useful, however, the War on Crime–era prosecutor also needed to identify and mobilize victims, people whose lives dramatized the dangers of American society and the need for politically empowered prosecuting attorneys. Because she was the first female county attorney in Minnesota history, Morris attracted attention from the moment she took office, but it was as a fierce advocate for crime victims that Morris got herself onto insiders' lists of potential candidates for statewide political office. Today many female political candidates know that in order to project toughness without alienating or threatening voters, it can be useful to talk and act like a mother determined to protect her children. This is exactly how Morris presented herself as her sex ring investigation swept through Jordan in 1983 and 1984, including in her choice of office décor. As her office interviewed dozens of children who police believed had been abused at wild parties, Morris began making photocopies of their little hands, palms down on the Xerox scanner. She arrayed these photocopies on the wall behind her desk, posing in front of the display when newspaper journalists came for interviews.[22] The intent may not have matched the images' effect, however, which is of many children reaching up to press against shut windows.

As in Bakersfield, the Scott County sex ring case began with relatively ordinary allegations. In September 1983 a twenty-five-year-old woman named Christine Brown called Jordan police and told them her children had been abused by a neighbor named James Rud. Police made an arrest, opened an investigation, and soon discovered that Rud already had two prior convictions for child sex abuse—one in Virginia, where he had been stationed during a brief period in the army, and one in Apple Valley, Minnesota, where he had moved following his "other than honorable" discharge.[23] In Jordan, Rud lived in the Valley Green Trailer Court and worked as a trash collector.

Jordan was an old farming town that had also supported two breweries for many years. It sat on the south bank of the Minnesota River, and it was filled with stands of old, beautiful elm trees.[24] Much of the town's social life was organized around church. St. John's Catholic Church and Wisconsin Synod, a Lutheran congregation where services had been held in German until World War II, were two of the community's focal points.[25] In the years leading up to Rud's arrest, however, new residents began to arrive from nearby Minneapolis in intermittent waves, and some of the town's inhabitants resented the idea that Jordan had been reduced to a big-city suburb. "Twenty years ago you'd know 95 percent of the people you saw on the street," one local doctor told a reporter. "And you'd know them well. Now it might be 10 or 15 percent."[26] Nothing embodied these changes more clearly than the Valley Green trailer park, whose residents were transient and frequently poor or working class. The trailers were separated from downtown Jordan by State Highway 169, a road that split the town in half and had also been partially responsible for the recent influx of so many unfamiliar faces. For longtime Jordanites—or "Hubmen," as they sometimes called themselves, after the local high school football team—Rud's arrest confirmed suspicions they had been nursing for years. An older resident told a writer that the trailer park was built on ground that had previously been spread with "sludge"—human waste from the septic system. He said the ground was ideal for raising corn and that it should have stayed that way. "Valley Green is located on a pile of shit," he said. "It's just shit on shit."[27]

Kathleen Morris took on the case in November 1983, by which point police investigators had more than they needed to win a conviction against Rud. For months Rud had taken advantage of his friendly rapport with local children and persuaded their parents to hire him as a babysitter. Children occasionally spent nights at Rud's home, and police interviews, which were initially conducted with caution and skill, soon uncovered what had transpired in Rud's trailer:

Q: OK, now do you know why you are down here?

A: Yes.

Q: OK, can you tell me about that incident, when this took place?

A: No.

Q: You can't? Let me rephrase the question. I'll ask you in a different way. Did a man touch you?

A: Yes.

Q: Did he touch you in personal areas of your body?

A: Yes.

Q: OK, when did this happen?

A: When I was staying with him.[28]

The child went on to provide Rud's name and address, the date of her stay at Rud's home, and a perfectly clear account of how she spent the afternoon, evening, and following morning in his company. Other children's stories about meeting Rud in the game room of a local bowling alley, where he would supply them with quarters, were corroborated by Rud himself.[29] More disturbingly, it seemed that in at least one case a child's mother had known about Rud's pedophilia, had even been in a home with Rud as he took her daughter off to a separate room, but had failed to stop or report any abuse—she and another parent were also arrested.[30]

Police continued to interview children, and before long they were using many of the same tactics that Kee MacFarlane would come to depend on in Los Angeles. "I don't know," one child said in response to an interviewer's question about sexual games played at Rud's house. "Did he take your underpants off?" the interviewer asked. "Can you say yes? Say yes."[31] Another boy claimed that when he once cut across Rud's yard with some friends, Rud came outside, hit the boy on "the wiener," said, "You're gay," and then walked back into his house and sat down in front of the television. Later, the boy said, Rud tore pages out of a stack of *Playboy* magazines, used scissors to remove the breasts and genitals from the pages, then jumped all over them. "He just went crazy," the boy said. "He had a real funny laugh and he was going 'Haaaaa haaaaa' and stabbing these girls in the face and everything."[32] Five more people were arrested by the end of November, including two residents of the Valley Green trailer park, one of them the woman who had made the very first allegations against Rud. "We believe from the statements we've taken from all of the children so far involved," said Police Chief Alvin Erickson, "that this thing goes back possibly two years." A newspaper article claimed it was the biggest sex ring investigation in state history. The article also noted that all of the women involved were either divorced or separated from their husbands.[33]

"How did this happen?" Morris asked. "It happened because children who didn't know better were told that they had wonderful, special and beautiful bodies, how sexy they were. And they kept quiet out of fear and threats."[34] Police now believed that Rud and his accomplices had abused at least thirty children, and as investigators conducted interviews in nearby towns in search of additional victims, Jordan residents tried to patch up their deeply wounded feelings of small-town pride. Margaret Duke, a woman affectionately referred to as the "grandmother of the trailer court," recalled friendly hordes of children banging on her door during previous Halloweens. This year's crowd, however, was noticeably thin. "You'd expect something like this to happen in Minneapolis," one woman said, "but not in a small little community like this."[35]

Many residents worried that Jordan had some special flaw that had made Rud's crimes possible, and in order to demonstrate to itself and to the world that this was not the case, Jordan committed every resource at its disposal to the fight against child abuse, including the town's only computer. In December the *Independent* reported that "the Scott County computer has been reprogrammed to keep track of costs, victims, and defendants in the expanding investigation of the countywide sex abuse ring." The county controller said the reprogramming had not been expensive—a pair of programmers took care of it over a weekend.[36] This allocation of resources helped to reassure Jordanites, with the mayor even suggesting that it was really the town's unique commitment to stopping child abuse (rather than the child abuse itself) that had caught the media's eye. "A main reason that we have received so much public attention," she wrote, "is that our law enforcement officials have been unusually diligent in their investigations and in seeing that those responsible are brought to trial and convicted."[37]

Jordan also did its best to understand why the world had suddenly become such a dangerous place for children. "I see the real problem as the deterioration of families," one woman wrote to the *Independent*. "The nation, right down to this small community, is sacrificing family life to better living standards."[38] Although most child abuse actually occurs *within* the private domain of family life, whether at the hands of immediate relatives or close family friends, many Americans believed then and believe today that child abusers are usually strangers, middle-aged men in old clothes hanging around bus stops and playgrounds. (A similar misconception sustains the popular image of the rapist as a stranger who drags women into alleyways. In reality the vast majority of rapists know their victims.) It was this belief, in part, that helped the Scott County sex ring case to grow to such enormous proportions. In November, as Jordan police arrested their eighth suspect and promised that more arrests would follow, Kathleen Morris explained that the Rud investigation had a much wider scope than her prosecution of the Cermaks. "The Cermaks abused children primarily in their own families," the *Independent* reported. "In this case the abuse was primarily outside the family."[39] Rud menaced not just individual children but also an entire way of life. "Until we turn our priorities around and work on better and stronger family standards," one resident wrote, "sexual abusers [and] pornography producers . . . will eat their way right through our communities."[40]

In January 1984 police began to make arrests outside the Valley Green trailer park. Husband and wife Robert and Lois Bentz were arrested and charged with child sexual abuse, and then so were Greg Myers, a Jordan police officer, and his wife, Jane. Their son was eleven at the time, and he was immediately removed from his home, as were his two siblings. "They insisted that I was abused," he later remembered. "They questioned me for, like, two hours that night."[41] The interrogations continued on an almost daily basis for three months, with therapy and foster care all seamlessly integrated into the process of criminal investigation. "We were asked to report any information to Kathleen Morris's office," said Susan Phipps-Yonas, a therapist who interviewed many of the children involved with the investigation.

Phipps-Yonas said that today psychiatrists understand that therapy and detective work have different goals and that it is important to clearly separate the two. "Those boundaries were just a mess back then," she said. "We were being forensic interviewers, we were being expert witnesses. It was nuts."[42] As a result of these messy boundaries, Greg and Jane Myers's son would not be allowed to see or communicate with his parents for a year and a half, and he said this is why he eventually began to fabricate stories of abuse. "I was just sick of being badgered," he said. "I didn't think, I mean, I was even going home. . . . I figured if this is going to be the way life is, I might as well make it a little more tolerable for myself."[43] He said his parents held orgies in the woods. By this point one local paper was reporting that the county was suffering from "a severe shortage of foster parents."[44] Arrests continued into the summer.

In Bakersfield, things were getting out of hand. In the wake of the McCuan and Kniffen convictions, new allegations of mass molestation exploded across Kern County. In Oildale, a suburban town just west of the Kern River Oil Field, a woman locked in an awful custody dispute became convinced that her stepchildren had been molested by their biological mother and stepfather. When the children said no such thing had happened, she beat them and denied them meals until they changed their stories, and then she called the police.[45] Another man, John Stoll, was called back to court every few days for weeks and told at each hearing about a new child who had accused him of abuse. "Now it was a whole big passel," he said. "Now there's this whole giant molestery."[46]

There were also more traditional pedophilia investigations, starting out with a single defendant and a small number of accusers, that grew to encompass entire neighborhoods. By 1985 police believed they had uncovered *eight* distinct molestation rings, and the county's rate of arrest for sex crimes against children was twice the state average.[47] SLAM and the Mothers of Bakersfield were joined by another parents' group called Kids Are People Too, whose members protested outside the courthouse during Stoll's trial. News footage shows a little boy, not more than four or five, who had been outfitted with a sign reading, "Help Me! Stop Child Molesters!" "The town was convinced," John Stoll said, "that this herd of child molesters had just fallen out of the trees all at once."[48]

Donny Youngblood, the county sheriff's detective commander, later said that police did not go looking for these cases, that "they were thrust upon us."[49] But as the state attorney general's office would eventually document, Youngblood's remark, if sincerely meant, was very naïve. The following is an exchange that took place between a Kern County social worker and a suspect:

Q: You know when children, when children tell law enforcement or Child Protective services—

A: Uh huh.

Q: —about somebody, we believe children, okay.

A: Uh huh.

Q: Especially little, ah, would involve children but these are just, you know, four-, four-, five- and six-year-olds.

A: Uh huh.

Q: Okay, and they don't have, they shouldn't have knowledge of this stuff, they have a lot of knowledge, a lot of explicit details, knowledge, they say cream was being used . . . lotion.

A: Have you seen, you know, TV nowadays though, the parents let their kids watch?

Q: Okay, people often do accuse TV, but still children don't fantasize about sexual abuse and they don't implicate their own father.

A: Uh huh.

Q: Okay?

A: Uh huh. . . .

Q: Let alone themselves, especially when they're, when they are feeling so badly about and they know it's wrong.

A: Uh huh.

Q: Okay, it's just they, some you know, if they aren't gonna, if they're mad at their dad and that's when they may say *physical* abuse.

A: Uh huh.

Q: But, ah, they're not gonna say sexual.

A: Uh huh.

Q: It just doesn't happen.

A: Uh huh.

Q: So we, we do believe the children.

A: Uh huh.

Q: Okay, that you are involved.

A: Then no matter what I, what I say doesn't even matter then?

Q: Well, yeah of course it matters, but, but our stand is that we believe the children.

A: Uh huh.

Q: At all cost, cause that's our job and that's, that's what our belief is.[50]

As in Los Angeles, this belief was contingent on the child's willingness to say that he or she had been abused. "I remember telling them no for about four hours," one woman said, "and I was just tired. I wanted to go home, so I said what they wanted me to say."[51] Brian Kniffen remembered Andrew Gindes, the prosecutor who tried his parents' case in court, bullying him into providing false testimony. "He would slam books down," he said, "yell when we wouldn't cooperate."[52] And a number of people retain vivid memories of one deputy sheriff in particular. According to Michael Snedeker, an attorney who represented a number of defendants in the Kern County sex ring cases, this deputy began whispering "hypnotic, graphic repetitions of sex acts" during one interview with a boy who could not recall being molested. A different mother called Jagels's office to complain that the officer had slapped her daughter in the mouth when the girl refused to disclose abuse. That girl's sister was subject to similar coercion. When she told the officer that her earlier allegations had been made up, he twisted the girl's arm, told her, "You're lying!" and then described "very detailed, filthy" sex acts. He didn't let go of her arm until the girl retracted her retraction.[53]

In the 1970s feminist activists and writers had criticized the vulgar, pseudo-Freudian idea that children who accused adults of sexual abuse were only fantasizing. It was a valid criticism then and it remains so today that "deep down, she actually wanted it" is a direct descendent of "she's just fantasizing." But in the early 1980s the relationship between sex abuse allegations and fantasy underwent a strange inversion. Although a very small number of children seemed to relish the opportunity to tell awful, scary stories about people they knew, the *adult* accusers were the ones who fantasized Kern County's sex rings into being. By the summer of 1984 the "Pitts" ring investigation, which began with a single disgruntled stepparent and a custody battle, had grown to include seven defendants, all accused of staging and filming weekly orgies with as many as thirteen children in a single ten-by-twelve-foot room. After a trial, during which prosecutor Andrew Gindes made repeated references to the Bible and told the jurors that Jesus Christ would believe the children's allegations, all seven defendants were handed a combined prison sentence of more than twenty-five hundred years. When asked about these remarkably long prison terms, Judge Gary Friedman said the sentences fit the crimes. He said that he had personally seen photographs of the abuse—"every perversion imaginable."[54] But the photographs to which he referred were never produced. One assumes that if this definitive proof of the crimes actually existed, the prosecution would have made use of it at trial.

Social hysteria is born of an unmanageable surplus of anxiety and fear, and as a result panics themselves behave in excessive ways, improvising a series of crises and fabrications that build until the whole process breaks down under the weight of its own internal contradictions. But Ed Jagels was a talented politician and manager, and the investigative apparatus he built to pursue sex offenders could bear a lot of weight. Soon after the Pitts ring convictions, things escalated dramatically.

Brad Darling was a Kern County police lieutenant. He worked extensively on the ring cases, and in addition to believing all of the children's allegations, he believed much worse. In a multi-issue *Bakersfield Californian* series on the sex rings, Darling claimed the defendants were exporting the child pornography they made to Europe.[55] His wife, Carol Darling, was a social worker and sexual abuse coordinator for the district attorney's office, and she interviewed many of the alleged victims involved with the ring cases. As a California Justice Department investigation would later document, Brad Darling came to believe that Satanism played a role in the abuse taking place in Kern County and that people working within Child Protective Services, the sheriff's office, and other official agencies were involved in the satanic conspiracy.[56] In the spring of 1985, with interviews still occurring on a regular basis, a number of social workers attended a training seminar at which copies of *Michelle Remembers* were made available to supplement a discussion of the role devil worship played in child molestation.[57] One of these social workers was employed at Shalimar, a residence for suspected victims of abuse that had become home to many of the children Kern County police had removed from their homes. Soon after the social worker's return from the training seminar, Darling received a call from Shalimar reporting that multiple children had been made to worship the devil. Darling drew up reports and asked the district attorney to bring charges against eleven people.[58]

The first child to make allegations of satanic abuse originally came to the attention of police during the investigation of a sex ring supposedly centering around the Nokes family. The girl said that while being molested she had been made to drink the blood of sacrificed animals in a "bad" church.[59] Other children claimed their abusers wore black robes and brandished inverted crosses, that they had been forced to stab "little bears, little wolves, and little birds."[60] On their own these claims were not unprecedented—detectives had previously heard of abusers harming animals in order to frighten their victims into silence. But the satanic stories also introduced allegations of homicide, and these were new. Therapists reported accounts of women giving birth on dark altars so that their newborn infants could be eviscerated and thrown into pits. Sixteen babies had been murdered and eaten in a single night, according to one child, and police eventually calculated that they needed to find dozens of small corpses in and around Kern County. The search began with the formation of an official Ritual Abuse Task Force led by Brad Darling.

"You've got to realize how crazy this thing got," John Stoll said. "Here they are digging up this land, with a backhoe, doing infrared, looking for bodies."[61] Darling's task force took their investigation all over Kern County, and they felt the urgency of their task very keenly. Three times police sent men with construction equipment to excavate grounds where Satanists were believed to have disposed of their sacrifices, and each time they found nothing. They also sent divers into two lakes, with similar results.[62] Even worse, from the investigation's point of view, were the discoveries that, first, none of the alleged sacrifices' names matched any missing persons reports and that, second, a number of the supposed victims were found to be perfectly alive. These disappointments only reinforced the task force's belief in the magnitude of the threat Kern County now faced. Having dismissed defense accusations of child "brainwashing" by social workers and therapists for months, police now advanced brainwashing theories of their own, with one officer speculating that cult members had either "set up and programmed" the children to provide implausible stories or else tricked them with fake, staged murders.[63]

Programming may have also explained why some of the children began to accuse even members of the Ritual Abuse Task Force of participating in the satanic cult, although there was some internal disagreement on the subject. Brad Darling thought it plausible that cult members might have infiltrated Kern County law enforcement. When he traveled to Los Angeles to meet with investigators working on the McMartin case, he said that police suspected doctors, deputy sheriffs, a mortuary owner, and two ministers of cult involvement. He thought an enormous cover-up was under way.[64]

Ed Jagels was furious with the paranoid theories being advanced by members of the task force. A number of ring cases were coming to trial in the next few months, and Jagels believed that tales of mass baby slaughter without any dead babies to back them up would turn both the local media and the public against his office's efforts. Since March the task force had managed to avoid attracting any media attention while carrying out its investigation, and according to a prosecutor who worked on the sex ring cases, Jagels worried that if the satanic allegations became public it would do significant damage to his political reputation around the state. To work around this problem and keep satanic abuse out of the newspapers, the district attorney's office devised a neat trick. Prosecutors created an imaginary suspect, made up a file folder for him, and then put all documents pertaining to satanic activity in that folder. Because this imaginary person was completely unknown to anybody outside the prosecutor's office, defense attorneys filing discovery requests on behalf of actual suspects never knew to file the one request that would have produced documents pertaining to Satanism.[65] This prevented defendants, their lawyers, and— perhaps most importantly—juries from understanding the full extent of Kern County law enforcement's overreach and suspension of disbelief.

Much of this eventually came undone. The media learned about and began to report on the Ritual Abuse Task Force in the summer of 1985.

The Kern County grand jury, which coordinated oversight of local government, initiated its own investigation of prosecutorial misconduct in connection with the ring cases. John Van de Kamp, attorney general for the state of California, produced a report on the child abuse investigations that, despite its pointed criticisms of the task force's conduct, made only tepid recommendations for improvement and reform, including increased supervision and training. Jagels dismissed charges against a small number of people following the report's publication. Despite these setbacks, it is hard to view the early stages of Jagels's twenty-seven-year tenure as district attorney as anything other than a massive prosecutorial success. More than fifty people were charged as ring participants or satanic ritual abusers, and twelve others who avoided prosecution were still determined to be sufficiently suspicious for their children to be taken away. At least twenty-eight people were sent to prison, and despite public doubts about many of their convictions, most of them remained there for many years.

As Kathleen Morris prepared to take her cases to trial in a Scott County courthouse, her investigators continued to struggle to find physical evidence to corroborate their child victims' stories. This was a problem also faced by prosecutors working on the other two earliest major day care and sex ring abuse cases in Bakersfield and Manhattan Beach. But then, in 1984, an adult witness came forward in Jordan, Minnesota, and said he was prepared to make a full confession.

The witness, James Rud, was also the case's central defendant. Over the course of four days, he provided a lengthy statement to three investigating officers describing the sex parties he had attended over the previous two years, identifying the adult participants and the children they brought with them and explaining the "rules" by which various sexual games were governed. In exchange for this statement and an agreement to testify against other defendants, Morris dismissed 98 of the 108 charges pending against Rud, who pled guilty to the remaining 10. "This is the best thing that could happen to children," Morris said. "I think so many would like to believe children would lie, and now we have an adult saying they didn't lie at all."[66]

Rud's interviewers began by asking about the crimes he had committed before coming to Scott County, and his answers to these questions were short, simple, direct, and also characterized by the little uncertainties and memory gaps that would be expected of any account of events that had transpired years in the past. When the conversation turned to his more recent involvement in Jordan's sex rings, however, Rud's speaking style underwent a dramatic change. He described his sexual encounters with children as well as those he had witnessed in florid, extremely specific detail, and he seemed to adopt what he saw as a law-enforcement register and vocabulary. Describing an episode in which he had taken Marlene Germundson and her children to his parents' home, he said, "During this time I assumed that Marlene met my mom and she was already in the house and they were having a conversation. I don't know what it was about." Describing a sexual encounter he subsequently had with Marlene's daughter inside the house, he said, "Ten minutes or so into the game or so I had unbuttoned VK's pants. During this time I started fondling her inside her clothes on the outside of her vaginal area. . . . My feelings toward that was I was turned on by it."[67] Then he described coming out of the bedroom to find that his parents had also, without any prior planning or discussion, embarked on an encounter of their own with Marlene and her other children:

> When I got toward the kitchen area, I saw that my parents were sitting on the couch and Marlene was on the floor. The way it looked to me was that dad was coming on real heavy with my mom and if I recall, the twins were sitting with Marlene on the floor, both of them. I couldn't exactly see what Marlene was up to at this point. She was in sort of a blind spot for me. I went a little further in and I noticed Marlene had the twins on the floor. The twins had their pants down. I want to correct myself. When I came out of the bedroom, my dad was on the couch with Marlene and my mother was on the floor with the twin girls. What I saw when I come out of there was Marlene had her panties on and her bra and my mom, all I saw was her back but to what I saw she was still dressed. I couldn't see her front at this time.

How did Rud react to this spontaneous bout of group sex between his parents and Marlene, who had met just fifteen minutes before, and the two girls? "I sort of acted a little bewildered but not too surprised," Rud said. "I didn't think my mom and dad and Marlene would get along this well."[68] Rud wanted to be as helpful as he possibly could. When asked to define a "blowjob," Rud said, "It's when another person either of the same sex or opposite sex puts their mouth around my penis and sort of masturbates with his or her mouth."[69] His constant hedges and qualifications—"about this time," "sort of a blind spot," "maybe five minutes, maybe a little longer"—seem designed to guard against any inconsistencies that might emerge as a result of too-direct speaking over the course of four days of mostly fabricated testimony. When Rud did make mistakes, however, he was happy to fix them as quickly as possible. Toward the end of the first day Rud was asked whether he had seen his father "involved in any of the sexual contact" with any of the children he had been discussing; Rud said that he hadn't. The interviewer asked Rud whether he was sure, and Rud said that he was. Then the following exchange took place:

> Q: Jim, I'd like to refresh your memory just a little bit. . . . In this incident
> as you described to them earlier, I believe you make some mention of
> one of the children, I believe one of the girls, being
> involved with your father just prior to you folks leaving the trailer
> that day. Do you recall that incident?
> A: Yes, I do now.[70]

The next day, Rud began to describe the sex parties. He said he had attended three large gatherings at which nearly all of Kathleen Morris's suspects were present. He said these parties began "a little after six—sixish" and that he could remember seeing eleven children there. At a certain point—Rud didn't remember exactly when—word started going around—Rud didn't remember exactly how—that it was time for the game to start:

> Okay, the rules of the game or at least the way we played it was that
> the kids were to stay within a boundary around the house, either in-
> side or within this boundary on the outside. They were to hide but
> not real discreetly, you know, somewhere you know it would be pretty
> much easy to see them or at least pick them out of someplace. . . .
> From there the adults go seek whoever, seek in this general area. And
> whoever they found, male or female—it doesn't make any difference
> who the kid was, if it was a relation or not—they had a choice of either
> taking that person to wherever they felt like. If in a bedroom, bath-
> room, wherever they could be with another person, another couple in
> the same room or privately, and between them sexual acts would go
> on. After the sexual acts it doesn't make any difference how long, we
> usually limit it to around between five and ten minutes.[71]

Rud's confession takes on a kind of awful, hypnotic quality when read in its entirety. But individually very few of his statements make very much sense. Consider Rud's description of how the children were supposed to hide, and then imagine a group of adults trying to say the following to a group of very young children: "We need each of you to go outside—or stay inside, it doesn't matter—and pick a hiding place, but not a hiding place that falls outside this imaginary boundary, if you go outside, and also please be sure not to hide too discreetly. Just pick someplace where we can either already see you or pick you out without too much trouble. Now, get to it."

According to Rud, the game continued, with children hiding and adults finding them again, until "around the latest eight-thirty, or in that area." Rud said that although adults could play the game in the nude, most of the adults who played outside kept their clothes on, which explained why nobody had noticed a crowd of naked people chasing kids around in the yard. Rud said that once the game wound down, everybody got dressed. Then one of the adults lit the barbecue. Rud's interviewer wanted to know who provided the food. "Did you each have to bring something?"[72]

The scenes Rud described over the next two days read like unsettling dream sequences. Rud almost never remembered anybody saying anything; in his telling, orgies were organized and disbanded spontaneously, by silent general agreement, and children—who were also more or less silent participants—were handed off from one adult to another without so much as a single instance of hesitation, conflict, or logistical wrangling. A number of Rud's narrative tics also became more apparent as his days with the detectives wore on. When describing someone in a state of undress, he almost always specified that his or her pants were pulled halfway down, just below the knees. The general picture that emerges from Rud's confession is of a complicated sexual frenzy that proceeds in an oddly methodical and orderly fashion, one stage leading seamlessly to the next until everyone becomes hungry for dinner at exactly the same time. What makes the dreamlike qualities of Rud's account disturbing is the realization that his interviewers essentially encouraged a convicted child abuser to fantasize into a microphone for nearly a week, used those fantasies as the foundation of their prosecutorial efforts, and then handed Rud a reduced sentence in exchange for his services.

The trial of Robert and Lois Bentz began less than two weeks after Rud made his statement. This was the first of the Scott County sex ring cases to be presented to a jury, and it attracted so much publicity that a judge ordered that proceedings be moved to nearby Carver County. Morris called Rud to the stand on a Monday and asked him to begin by identifying the defendants. Rud identified Lois Bentz. He could not identify Robert. On cross-examination the Bentzes' defense attorney, a man with the wonderful name Earl Gray, pointed to another attorney and asked Rud, "Is this Bob Bentz?" Rud said it was not. Then Gray asked, "Who is Bob Bentz?" Rud did not know. When Morris, on redirect, asked Rud to describe Robert Bentz's appearance in September 1983, the period during which many of the alleged crimes took place, Rud said, "I can't right now." Speaking to reporters later that day, Morris said that Rud's inability to identify the defendant had not surprised her at all. "You think I don't know my own case?" she said.[73]

Many things contributed to the Bentzes' eventual acquittal, but first among them was the simple fact that Kathleen Morris performed very poorly in court. Soon after the prosecution's unfortunate debut, the trial judge ruled that all of Rud's testimony would be thrown out entirely. Morris told reporters that the decision did not weaken her case, that in fact she looked forward to convicting the Bentzes solely on the basis of her child witnesses. "What I've been saying all along [is that] it's time we listen to kids," she said. "You either believe them or you don't believe them."[74]

In addition, Morris's aggressiveness in the media and inside her own office—an aggressiveness so pronounced that a state commission would eventually find that Morris had physically and verbally abused a number of her employees[75]—seemed to disappear inside the courtroom. She declined to cross-examine Ralph Underwager, a psychologist and Lutheran minister whose expert testimony was crucial in undermining the jury's confidence in the children's testimony, and then she also declined to cross-examine Robert and Lois Bentz. "This isn't *Perry Mason*," she told reporters after failing to pose a single question to the defendants. "I'm not going to stand up and say something brilliant and get them to break down."[76] The Bentzes' defense attorneys made some puzzling and morally questionable tactical choices as well. Barry Voss told jurors that as it is in a scorpion's nature to sting, so it was in one child witness's nature to lie.[77] In another instance, Earl Gray drove a girl to tears on the witness stand when he suggested that she was nervous about having her lies tape-recorded. "You're just helping Bob and Lois get out of this stuff, this child-abusing stuff," she replied. "I'm not lying; you guys are. It's the truth. They hurt us."[78] This outburst did not persuade the jurors, who set the Bentzes free after three days of deliberations.

Morris told reporters that she had no idea why the jury had returned a "not guilty" verdict. "We still believe the kids," she said. "I have to go tell the kids why adults don't believe them. . . . [I'm] always surprised when people don't believe children. . . . It's about time people started to believe children."[79] She vowed to fight the Bentzes' efforts to have their three children returned from foster care.

Morris still had an additional twenty-one defendants awaiting trial. Donald and Cindy Buchan were scheduled to hear opening arguments in less than a month. When prosecutor Gehl Tucker actually rose to deliver her argument, however, she did not discuss the Buchans' alleged crimes; instead, she announced that all charges against the married couple would be dropped. Later that day Morris's office announced that all charges against *all* of the remaining sex ring defendants would be dropped as well. In place of criminal prosecution, she would use the family court system to try to keep the children away from their parents, all of whom Morris said she still believed were guilty.

In a statement Morris explained this stunning development by claiming that the sex ring cases had been dropped for the greater investigative good. "The state had been ordered to release sensitive documents which relate to another ongoing criminal investigation," she wrote—"an active criminal investigation of great magnitude." Complying with these discovery motions, she wrote, "would have subjected the child witnesses to additional stress and trauma." The best path forward, then, was to "[protect] the children from further involvement in criminal proceedings."[80]

As journalists soon revealed, these discovery motions had their roots in an exchange that had taken place between Earl Gray and a child witness during the Bentz trial. On the eighth day of the trial, a child recounting his sessions with the police mentioned that the detective asking questions had made handwritten notes throughout the interview. Despite having previously submitted requests for "any and all materials or information within the prosecutor's possession . . . which is favorable to the defense," the Bentzes' attorneys had only received typed reports—never handwritten notes.[81] Morris, a state commission would eventually find, still had these documents in her possession and had intentionally concealed them from defense attorneys. Like the contents of the fictitious John Doe file created by the Ritual Abuse Task Force out in Kern County, these handwritten notes made it clear that the investigation had lost touch with reality.

In late 1983, nearly a year before the Bentz case went to trial, a ten-year-old boy told an investigator about a party at which children were whipped by women wearing "real dark mascara" and "see-through clothes." "They just called everybody 'honey child,'" the boy said of the adults in attendance. "They just were crazy." He also described being pulled into a black limousine by James Rud and a man who "had millions of cameras."[82] A girl said she knew the pornographic films in which she had appeared were sold because "that's where I got all my spending money." She also said one defendant forced her to eat the intestines of a squirrel, a fox, and her pet gerbil along with a cat that was eaten "fur and all." Other children said they had seen murders, the bodies wrapped in canvas, thrown into trucks, and driven away.[83] Despite knowing perfectly well that such allegations, if made public, would be damaging to the prosecution's case, a number of detectives and therapists were absolutely convinced the children were telling the truth. "I personally believe that this kid actually saw someone die," one interviewer said, citing the level of detail in a child's description of murder.

Therapist Susan Phipps-Yonas, for her part, said that she did not credit the hypothesis being floated by some that the defendants may have only *pretended* to kill people as a means of frightening children into silence. Staging the corpse disposals in a convincing way, she said, would have been complicated.[84] The terror they exhibited, she said, as well as the specificity of the dollar amounts being exchanged ("sometimes $1,000 or more") indicated that kids had been scared by the real thing. She said that many therapists could not begin to understand the sheriff's office's reluctance to begin the search for bodies in and around Scott County. "The therapists involved have basically been raving, 'Why not?'" she said. "We questioned very openly and directly why hasn't there been the kind of search that would aid in locating bodies or in getting some kind of concrete evidence, given the fact that we have these accounts from several different children."[85] Phipps-Yonas eventually got her wish when Scott County deputies, disguised as fishermen, combed the banks of the Minnesota River in search of a gravesite. "We're looking for dead bodies of kids," one anonymous source said. "We may have gotten into this too deep."[86]

Soon after these allegations became public, Kathleen Morris handed control of the investigation over to Minnesota Attorney General Hubert Humphrey III, who released a report the following February announcing that a joint investigation conducted by the Bureau of Criminal Apprehension and the FBI had uncovered no evidence of homicides or of a Scott County–based child porn industry. No additional criminal charges would be filed. James Rud told the Minneapolis TV station WTCN that he had lied in implicating others in his crime, and a month later the two boys who had provided detectives with most of the tales of murder and bizarre group encounters in the woods also admitted their stories were false. Rud was sentenced to forty years in prison in January 1985.

The *Jordan Independent* reported that despite some data entry irregularities, the county computer's estimate of the total cost of the sex ring investigations had come to $251,266.87.[87] And although the prospect of criminal prosecution was now gone for good, the havoc that Scott County had brought upon itself lingered in many ways. Civil suits filed against the county by a group of defendants worked their fruitless way through the court system for months, and family courts were similarly slow in returning the children to their homes. Shortly after recanting his allegations, an eleven-year-old boy who had spent eighteen months in foster care and been interviewed on at least seventy-four separate occasions, suffered a psychological collapse. He was hospitalized for six weeks. And although Roland Summit was correct in later noting that the boy said he was "desperately afraid of any contact with his parents," it wasn't because he feared abuse. "I didn't want to go home then because, I mean, of all the stuff that was coming out of my mouth," he said. "I figured I'd never be able to go home now. I mean I just called my parents everything from sexual abusers to murderers. I mean, it wasn't real. It was like being in a movie, it wasn't real. It wasn't real at all."[88]

Other children found the investigation had upended their homes for good. Robert and Lois Bentz were divorced shortly after their acquittal. "We spent our 15th anniversary in court," Lois said. "You can't take it out on the judicial system, so you take it out on each other."[89]

"Sources have said that Morris acted as an investigator as well as county attorney," the *Star and Tribune* reported as the investigation wound down, "that therapists acted like cops and cops acted like therapists, that social workers went along on a search warrant party."[90] In many communities prosecutors can exert a more direct and tangible influence on the textures and rhythms of people's daily lives than any other government official. By expanding her office's reach and blurring the lines that separated prosecution, law enforcement, and mental health services, Morris changed how Jordan's residents thought about their community, their neighbors, and their children. Her office turned the helping professions into instruments of criminal investigation, and it also taught children and adults to scrutinize everyday interactions for subtle signs of trouble. At the height of the investigation, schools began to put on a new kind of presentation that tried to explain the difference between good (appropriate) and bad (abusive) kinds of touch. The *Star and Tribune* sent reporters to a nursery school to gauge the kids' reactions:

> For example, [teacher Kathie Voss] says, "Sometimes moms have to clean us up when we get dirty." She pulls out a drawing of a child being bathed. "What's this?"
>
> "Bubbles!"
>
> "What's happening to this person here?"
>
> "Drowning!"
>
> "No. This is a bathtub. Do moms and dads have a right to help us take a bath?" There are some yeses—and some no's.
>
> "Of *course* they do. Do you like to take a bubble bath?"
>
> "Yes!"
>
> "You like to have mom help you?"
>
> "No!"
>
> "Oh, come on!"[91]

The presentation was titled "Touch," and it told children that it was usually okay to be tackled while playing football—so long as you were a boy—and usually not okay to be hugged by an adult who wasn't also a relative. Although the students had trouble parsing some of the surprisingly fine distinctions separating good touches from bad ones, one may assume that parents, the presentation's true intended audience, got the message just fine.

Chapter 4

McMartin—The Preliminary Hearing

More than four hundred children had been interviewed at Children's Institute International by the end of 1984. Only forty-one would be named as complainants on the district attorney's charging documents, and only thirteen would testify at the preliminary hearing. Most people involved with the prosecution's side of the case, however, clearly believed that hundreds of children had been abused at McMartin, no matter what it said on the charging documents. Those hundreds of children had parents, and in the spring of 1984 many of them began to organize.

Nearly a year after Judy Johnson first called the police, the investigation was moving along at a slow pace, and parents looking to work off anger and nervous energy wanted to know how they could pitch in. The district attorney's office furnished them with a list of forty locations to which children said they had been taken. "We're out here playing Dick Tracy," one father told the *Los Angeles Times*. Parents met up to form search parties, piling into cars with kids in the back and driving around town, hoping some storefront or bungalow would ring a bell. They wondered why no suspects beyond the original seven had yet been arrested. They shared information among themselves and with detectives. They took down suspicious license plate numbers outside restaurants and went through people's garbage.[1]

One of the parents was a real estate broker named Bob Currie. His children attended McMartin between 1972 and 1981, and when the abuse allegations first surfaced, Currie and his wife sent these children to Kee

MacFarlane. The two sons apparently did not make allegations that were sufficiently credible for the DA to list them as complainants, but then *none* of the parents most actively involved in independently investigating McMartin, with the exception of Judy Johnson, were ever formally involved with the case. Whether Currie's exclusion from the legal proceedings caused him to look for alternative means of involvement is unclear, but a legal proceeding is only one part of what happens to a community during a criminal investigation. McMartin gave Currie a reason to change his whole life.

Currie provided photographs of buildings, suspects, and license plates to the FBI. He coordinated drive-arounds and other little reconnaissance missions. By late 1984 he was contacting the police with regular updates on his progress. He said children had been taken to a street called Sorrel Lane in Palos Verdes. He couldn't be sure of the exact address at which abuses had occurred on that street, but it was either 7, 9, 18, or 20. He said his son had been taken to a farm in a "very clean restored Ford Mustang convertible." He believed that Ray coordinated some of his activities from out of state, so he called the park rangers at Mount Rushmore to determine whether the Buckeys had any kind of ranch or compound nearby. When children described being flown out of Los Angeles in a six-passenger airplane, Currie conducted a stakeout at Hawthorne Airport and took down airplane registration numbers. Ten miles to the south, at Torrance Airport, Currie observed the comings and goings of pilots. He noted one in particular: "a female pilot who may be a lesbian."[2]

Not all parents associated with the McMartin case subscribed to these conspiracy theories, nor did all of them even believe that any molestation had occurred at the preschool. Some people sent their children to Children's Institute International, listened as Kee MacFarlane described the secrets she had uncovered, decided that what MacFarlane described made no sense, and stopped returning investigators' phone calls. These parents largely kept their heads down during the investigation's early stages. Their silence would go totally unnoticed in noisy Manhattan Beach, especially given the amount of attention drawn by Bob Currie. In March 1985 he led a group of parents to the McMartin Preschool grounds. For months stories had circulated about teachers slaughtering classroom pets—rabbits, birds, cats—as a means of frightening the children into silence. Hoping to corroborate these stories with physical evidence, Currie brought in a backhoe to excavate a vacant lot next to the school. When the backhoe didn't find anything, parents used shovels. By Saturday afternoon some fifty parents (with twenty children in tow) were pitching in, milling around, catching up. Then somebody found a turtle shell in the ground. "We didn't touch anything," Currie's wife said to a journalist who arrived to report on the dig.[3] Investigators then took a more professional look at the lot. Their team of expert surveyors was unable to locate any "trapdoors, tunnels, subterranean rooms, or hidden doors."[4]

A career in local real estate does not usually provide many opportunities for camera time, but Currie discovered and then tapped into an immense talent for media provocation. When asked what he thought of people who refused to believe that child molestation could be so widespread and violent, Currie said, "The soldiers who went to Auschwitz didn't expect to find six million dead, either."[5] In 1985 Currie was arrested for illegal possession of a loaded weapon in a public place. He had followed one of his leads to Pico Rivera in East Los Angeles, and of the gun, which he had borrowed from another activist parent named Jackie McGauley, he said, "It's better to have [a weapon] with you than not to have it with you sometimes."[6] Currie paid his $1,000 bail and went home. Some people were put off by these press conferences and other performances. One columnist was at pains to point out that Currie's group had "been dismissed as cranks and fanatics by police officials and most of the media."[7] But calling someone a crank is not the same as not paying attention to him. Journalists could dismiss Currie even when they shared his belief that mass-molestation had been concealed for years at McMartin, as though a small subset of mediagenic extremists was needed to reassure those in the panicked mainstream of their moderate, rational thoughtfulness.

One possible motivation for these bursts of activity was the parents' desire to atone for what they now saw as previous failures to protect their children. Parents in Manhattan Beach had to deal with the normal feelings of concern and grief that would obviously accompany the news that a crime had been committed against one's child, but these feelings were compounded by the fact that the abuse was said to have taken place for such a long period of time. "The last thing in the world I would have ever dreamed of is child abuse," said John Cioffi, a McMartin parent who was also a member of the Hermosa Beach City Council.[8] He and many other parents wondered how they could have failed to see what was going on, and some people felt that if the crimes really were as elaborate as the DA said, parental negligence was the only plausible explanation. "To me the parents aren't listening," said one school director, and another preschool owner agreed that neglect was "the only way that I could see it could have happened."[9] But it wasn't only feelings of guilt that had Bob Currie reporting potential lesbians at airports. The investigation energized him and many others whose children had attended McMartin. The case offered mothers who spent their days socializing and tending to their homes an opportunity for personal and political transformation, a chance to become fiery activists. Of Cioffi, who was already engaged in a political career as city councilman, the case demanded swift, decisive action in a time of crisis.

More generally, McMartin lent a sort of heroic glow to the very idea of parenting. Worries about the anomie and selfishness of upper-middle-class Americans were a staple of Sunday newspaper editorials during the early eighties, and Manhattan Beach was an affluent place with its share of boredom and restlessness. McMartin reimagined life there as a battle to preserve that peaceful, comfortable way of life. The local chapter of Society's League Against Molestation mobilized its flood of new members to put on abuse prevention workshops around the area. A mother launched a campaign that included support for mandatory sentencing minimums, public awareness campaigns, and a victims assistance telephone hotline run out of her home. A *Los Angeles Times* article that described the campaign mentioned three different kinds of abusers: the McMartin teachers, a sexual psychopath who had been sent to death row in San Quentin, and "male babysitters," who were to be avoided in favor of their female counterparts if at all possible. The article did not mention family members—statistically the most frequent perpetrators of child abuse—except to laud parents' efforts to bring abuse to an end. In Los Angeles parents saw themselves as the only thing standing between their children and sexual peril. "We have learned that there is no such thing as too much parental love and reassurance," the mother said, "to a child who has been molested."[10]

Though not everyone agreed with Bob Currie's ideas about the complexity and reach of the McMartin conspiracy, parents were soon entertaining some pretty unlikely scenarios. Therapists at CII elicited stories involving strangers and camera equipment out of the children they interviewed, so in November 1984 parents and their allies formed a group called Parents Against Child Abuse (PACA), and at its first press conference the group announced a $10,000 reward for "any verifiable piece of child pornography involving any child who attended the McMartin Preschool that will lead to the conviction of the seven defendants presently charged in this case."[11] The wave of nursery school and day care closings that swept over the area in 1984 also bolstered the idea that McMartin was not some isolated aberration. PACA members told reporters they believed that as many as two hundred other adult abusers remained to be discovered.

These claims only differed in degree—not in kind—from those made by official investigators. One judge made a blunder during an early hearing and publicly announced that police detectives had a list of thirty uncharged suspects in the case. Thirty isn't three hundred, of course, but both numbers suggest a fairly elaborate plot.[12] PACA's child pornography reward also seems less quixotic in light of the fact that investigators had already raided a local photography shop in search of incriminating evidence and flown to a national park in South Dakota that employed Peggy Ann Buckey during the summer of 1983. They thought Ray might have hidden child porn somewhere in the park when he flew out to visit his sister.

In 1984 a number of parents filed civil lawsuits against the police for their alleged mismanagement of the case. They wanted to do something that would finally goad the MBPD into accelerating the investigation or bringing in some extra help. They succeeded. Police contacted the FBI's Los Angeles office, and for a few weeks federal investigators went door-to-door, interviewing people involved with the case. Police were confident that the kinds of hard physical evidence they so badly needed would soon surface. FBI agents spoke to a former teaching assistant at McMartin who remembered finding it odd that Ray never talked about dating any women. She said that she had been to Ray's house and that Ray had a weird "pyramid structure" hanging over his bed.[13] They talked to parents who remembered that Ray had been arrested for drunk driving several years ago and that soon afterward his mother had made him get some kind of counseling from a local pastor (Peggy McMartin Buckey was raised as a devout Christian Scientist and remained religious as an adult).[14] Maybe that counseling was for something more disturbing than a few nights of heavy drinking.[15]

When Judy Johnson spoke to the FBI, she made it clear just how concerted an effort parents were making to expand the parameters of the case. "She is in contact with various parents," the FBI investigator noted in his report, "and those parents have very specific information concerning elaborate photographic equipment used to photograph their children." Johnson told her interviewers she had strong evidence that children had been taken "out of state into the Las Vegas, Nevada area and/or the Palm Springs area."[16] (Probably without knowing it, Johnson joined a long tradition of conspiracy theorizing here by only alluding to this evidence rather than producing it.) Reading Johnson's FBI statements, it is apparent that the investigation was taking a toll on her mental health. She said her other child had also been molested, years earlier, at a different preschool.

In Los Angeles the parents worked to influence the course of the McMartin case in particular, but in Sacramento they began to push for legislation that could influence cases throughout the state. They knew that their children would soon be called to testify against their former teachers in court, and they believed this experience would retraumatize kids who were already dealing with severe psychological damage. Standing between the parents and a solution to this problem was the confrontation clause of the Sixth Amendment, which stipulates that criminal defendants have the right to hear testimony against them in person, face-to-face. Parents hoped to carve out an exception that would allow children under the age of fourteen to testify from outside the courtroom via closed-circuit television. They worked with a state senator named Art Torres to craft SB46 and shepherd it through the legislature. The bill, Torres said, would not trample on the Constitution; all he wanted was to equip the legal system with "contemporary" tools. The Founding Fathers, after all, could never have "envisioned child molestation as epidemic as it is today."[17]

The Senate passed the bill by a 28–8 vote in February 1985, and when the gavel came down on the final vote, parents who made the trip up from Los Angeles hugged and cheered in the back of the chamber. Other bills were passed by the end of the summer, all of them transferring power from defense attorneys to prosecutors in the name of protecting traumatized children. Child abusers who killed their victims became eligible for the death penalty. In cases where a child was under the age of eight, hearsay evidence could be admitted in court, allowing parents to tell juries what their children had told them about what the abusers allegedly did. For children under the age of sixteen, pretrial testimony could be videotaped and shown in court so that the actual child did not have to make an appearance. These last three measures were all part of a single bill that sailed through the State Senate without debate and with unanimous approval.[18]

That taking the stand was traumatic to children was more an article of faith than a documented fact among therapists and parents. For journalists who actually covered the McMartin preliminary hearing and other day care sex abuse trials in the Los Angeles area, the experiences of child witnesses did not seem to be so one-dimensional. A girl who cried when asked to describe her "private parts" might take a long break, return, and then smilingly claim that her day care teacher had been standing "on his head, probably" when he subjected her to oral sex.[19] Another might provide vivid testimony and then immediately admit on cross-examination that nothing had happened at all. Another might seem to be not so much terrified as bored.[20]

But when Lael Rubin, the prosecutor who would soon be trying the McMartin case, flew to Washington and testified before a US Senate subcommittee, she said that "the Sixth Amendment right does not grant constitutional status to the defendant being able to intimidate any witness by his physical presence."[21] If children failed to seem traumatized on the stand, it was then only a matter of waiting for the inevitable psychological consequences to make themselves known. "It's not clear why these kids are not exhibiting symptoms," Roland Summit said of a few children who testified without apparent difficulty at the McMartin preliminary hearing, "[but] going to court to testify in a child molestation case is a no-win situation. You're exposed, you're denuded by it."[22]

A preliminary hearing is conducted before a judge, and it is not designed to determine actual innocence or guilt. The prosecution's goal is simply to prove that its charges carry sufficient weight to merit the consideration of a full trial. In many criminal cases the preliminary hearing is little more than a judicial formality. The McMartin prelim began on August 7, 1984, and everyone expected it to be brief. Few people in California had ever heard of one running longer than a couple of months.

Like the investigation that preceded it, however, the McMartin preliminary hearing often barely seemed to be moving forward at all. Part of this was due to SB46, which introduced a number of complications and delays, but most of it was by design. The McMartin prelim moved slowly because that's how Ray Buckey's lawyer wanted it.

Danny Davis had a home-brewed theory of social panic on which he based many of his decisions about strategy. The theory divided a panic into different stages. The first stage, "social event," referred to the set of conditions or circumstances that made the panic possible. Davis believed

that McMartin had been precipitated by affluent baby-boomers' feelings
of guilt about their soft lifestyles and lazy parenting habits. In the second
stage, "scapegoating," society looked to shift blame away from those who
really deserved it. Ray Buckey was the scapegoat. Finally, Davis said, after
lots of destructive energy had been expended trying to punish the scapegoat, you reached a phase called "shameful retrospect," in which people
realized their mistake and then wished they had not acted so recklessly.[23]
Davis wanted to give southwestern Los Angeles time to make it to "shameful retrospect" before a jury was asked to deliver a verdict, and to that
end he announced that he would present what is called an affirmative defense at the preliminary hearing. Rather than sitting to the side while the
prosecution glossed its case against the McMartin teachers, Davis cross-
examined witnesses and filed subpoenas for prosecution documents before a jury was even selected. He hoped a lengthy preliminary hearing
would give the panicked atmosphere in Manhattan Beach time to subside,
and he also thought it would give him the opportunity to conduct an
ad hoc form of discovery, with courtroom cross-examinations standing
in for the pretrial depositions that are usually only allowed in civil, not
criminal, cases.

Stretching out the hearing in this manner would also give Davis
time to map out exactly when each of the child complainants had attended McMartin, which revealed that some of the children had never
actually been under Ray Buckey's supervision at the preschool. The preliminary hearing became a "protracted, serial, comprehensive pre-trial
deposition."[24] Then Davis convinced the six lawyers defending the other
McMartin teachers that they should join his affirmative defense, and then
he convinced Aviva Bobb, the relatively inexperienced judge assigned to
preside over the hearing, that the seven defendants should all be treated
as part of a single, massive case. That decision gave each of the seven
attorneys the right to individually cross-examine any witness called in
connection with any defendant.

When they weren't in court or poring over the MBPD's investigation
reports, these seven attorneys tried to look out for their clients in different ways. Forrest Latiner, a long-time attorney with the public defender's
office, represented Ray Buckey's sister, Peggy Ann. He was very good at
using his enormous mustache to convey moral outrage in interviews with
the press. Dean Gits had a quieter personality, and he represented Ray's
mother, Peggy McMartin Buckey. Both lawyers feared for their clients'

safety in jail—inmates once tried to light Peggy Ann's hair on fire, and Peggy McMartin Buckey sustained minor injuries when she "tripped on a cord"—and so they initially spent much of their time trying to get them out. In June 1984 a judge finally set Peggy Ann's bail at $250,000 and her mother's at $1 million, but Ray was denied bail entirely.

Davis kept his client occupied by meeting with him almost every night to watch and transcribe CII interviews, but he also wanted to make sure jail didn't wear Ray down physically. Ray was in perfect health, and he needed to stay that way. "He was, I think, substantially vegan or vegetarian," Davis said of Ray, "and he had theories about fruit and vegetable juices and why it's better to keep the fiber in it, and everything had a detail." Davis believed that in long and difficult court cases there is very little a defendant can do to meaningfully contribute to his or her own defense, except for one thing, which is to "be in the best shape of your life. . . . Sleep comes with it. Rest comes with it. Handling stress comes with it, and you can control it." Davis bought two treadmills and donated them to the Manhattan Beach Police Department. One was for the police and one was for Ray.[25]

In court Davis's tactics reflected the larger strategy. *Easy Reader* columnist John A. Jackson described his demeanor:

> The attorney's style is distinctive and maddening. Enduring [Danny Davis's] cross-examination is like invading Russia without a map. One can expect to be lost most of the time—and to find oneself at last neck-deep in snow.
>
> In a representative 30-minute period last week, Davis asked questions on 19 different topics, moving as though at random from one to another and back again.
>
> From time to time, even one of his fellow defense attorneys will object to a Davis question as vague, irrelevant or without foundation. His slow, soft voice creates a miasma, a thick mental fog; he seems as full of torpor as a basking rattle-snake—and then he strikes.
>
> Davis must be endured to be believed.[26]

Jackson was one of a small group of journalists who became part of the courtroom scenery. In order to avoid the publicity and snarled traffic associated with the 1984 Summer Olympics, the preliminary hearing was temporarily moved to the northwestern neighborhood of Van Nuys, but by late August it had returned to the downtown Los Angeles Superior Courthouse. These venue changes did not deter the reporters who had spent almost a year waiting for an actual courtroom exchange to transcribe and who now filed detailed pieces on a daily basis. The *Los Angeles Times* sent Lois Timnick, who had covered crime and psychology for years—the effects of incarceration on the mentally ill, a piece on child suicides, a psychological profile of the Hillside Strangler—before taking up McMartin full-time. The Torrance-based *Daily Breeze* was the first paper to publish sustained criticism of the prosecution, so angering McMartin parents that a group of them drove out to Torrance to stage a protest. The trial also attracted people from the profession's margins, such as Paul and Shirley Eberle, a married couple who sat through day after day of courtroom proceedings and eventually wrote a four-hundred-page book about the experience.[27] Their previous publishing ventures included the pornographic magazine *Finger* and a children's book called *The Adventures of Mrs. Pussycat.*

John Jackson's column had the largest initial impact. "McMartin Watch" quickly became essential reading for parents associated with the case. "The first truth that must be faced," Jackson wrote in the fall of 1984, "is that, *beyond any reasonable doubt,* the molestations did occur."[28] Although Jackson believed the McMartin teachers were guilty, he took no prosecutorial glee in the prospect of sending Virginia and her family to prison. On the contrary, the idea pained him, as did all the unhappy consequences of what had transpired inside the preschool, and he wrote in strings of anguished, hammy metaphors that allowed readers to refract his pain through their own. The preliminary hearing's slow pace, the way it seemed to stall completely for days and then weeks at a time, made Jackson especially crazy:

The hearing, before municipal judge Aviva Bobb, ends its seventh week today. So far, only two witnesses have completed their testimony against the seven present defendants, and one of the two testified in secret. Another 98 witnesses, more or less, are due to be called. . . .

Sitting in the courtroom, one feels trapped in a timeless, shapeless space, nibbled at by hordes of ravenous minutiae, droned upon by toneless voices speaking legal jibberish. One feels one is reporting ancient history—or smoke.

The appearances are deceiving. In front of you in the courtroom, Virginia McMartin, the school's 77-year-old founder, works listlessly on her daily crossword. But behind the surface, often just behind it, an immense human agony is trying to pour itself into the tiny, fragile, misshapen vessels of the law.[29]

Within weeks of its debut, "McMartin Watch" was one of the *Easy Reader*'s most successful features. John Jackson fan mail filled up space on the letters page.[30]

These local reports continued to spool out facts that had received national attention from a very early stage. But during late 1984 and early 1985, what might be called the atmosphere of McMartin—the suspicion, the pervasive sense of threat, the feeling that the pursuit of justice demanded the suspension of disbelief—went national as well. It began when Kee MacFarlane traveled to Washington, DC, to testify again before Congress. Speaking to Democrat Charles Rangel and other members of the Committee on Children, Youth, and Families, MacFarlane said she had spent her "whole 5½ years while I was in Washington screaming about this issue and trying to get Congress and the administration to listen."[31] She noted the irony of the federal government only developing an interest in stopping child abuse after she had finally abandoned the capital for a new life, three thousand miles away. Although she had never heard very much about the sexual abuse of preschoolers during her time in Washington—her focus had been on older children and adolescents, the most frequent victims of abuse—her work at CII had put her in "the eye of that storm."[32] Preschool-aged children were "perfect victims," she said, because "they are trusting, naïve about sex, compliant to the authority of adults, and they come at a developmentally perfect time of magical thinking, when you can convince them of almost anything."[33] She said that substantiated reports of child abuse had been doubling every year since 1976, that the crime knew "no racial, economic, or geographic boundaries," and that boys were just as vulnerable as girls, if not more so.

That was her preamble. What she said next appeared in the *New York Times* and other major newspapers the following day:[34]

What we are dealing with, and I have no idea how widespread it is, I have no idea how much Federal attention it merits, but I think you need to know that I believe we are dealing with no less than conspiracies in these cases, organized operations of child predators, whose operation is designed to prevent detection, and is well insulated against legal intervention.

Preschools in this country in some instances I think we must realize have become a ruse for larger unthinkable networks of crimes against children.

If pornography and prostitution are involved, which is sometimes the case, those networks may have greater financial, legal, and community resources than any of the agencies trying to uncover them.[35]

MacFarlane knew that her theory might strain credulity, so she came with reassurances. "If these things seem unimaginable to you," she said, "you are not alone. They have been unimaginable to us as well."[36] After all, she said, McMartin had begun as a routine case—just five interviews with five children—and within three months CII had what she described as "a waiting list of 300 hysterical families."[37]

National news outlets also broadcast paranoid reports on McMartin. In January 1985 the TV newsmagazine *20/20* aired a bizarre and lengthy report on the case called "Why the Silence?" The program addressed what had long been an annoying stumbling block for McMartin believers: if the abuses were really that bad, how had the teachers managed to keep so many children quiet for so long? Reporter Tom Jarriel explained that the teachers must have used mind-control. "If the seven teachers are indeed guilty of the child abuse charges," Jarriel said, adding the qualifier necessary to shield the network from libel suits, "it appears they may have also practiced a sophisticated form of behavioral modification. . . . The children's allegations fall into a pattern that is curiously paralleled to the classic brainwashing techniques used on prisoners of war."

To bolster this claim, Jarriel interviewed Colonel James Roll, "one of the Army's leading authorities on brainwashing." The specter of mind-control had occasionally popped up in different areas of American life ever since the Korean War, when people had sought explanations for a handful of humiliating defections by US soldiers. Roll explained that brainwashing involved a "conditioning process" that targeted several of the victims' key beliefs and sources of faith. During the broadcast, Jarriel also referred to a graphic depicting what experts had identified as "eight categories of behavioral modification." The graphic, in the manner of a phrenological diagram from the nineteenth century, depicted the head of a frightened child seen in profile, his brain divided into eight regions: "family," "isolation," "drugs," "torture," "religion & patriotism," and others. Jarriel illustrated each of these regions with a snippet from interviews he had conducted with three McMartin children, so that after mentioning "religion and patriotism," for example, the scene would cut to a child, his face obscured and his voice altered to an eerie croak, explaining how teachers forced children to bury communion wafers in dirt, while another said that children were raped with a flagpole with an American flag attached.

Teachers told the children that the Easter Bunny wouldn't love them anymore. Teachers locked a child in a refrigerator. Teachers made children "devour" things that had "come from their private parts." *20/20*'s litany of horrors and abuses is so extravagant and imaginative that even the show's anchors seem to have had trouble accepting what they heard. This is perhaps one of hysteria's underappreciated traits: it feels hysterical not only after the fact, in Danny Davis's "shameful retrospect" stage, but at the time, even to people who believe in it. And so at the end of the report, back in the studio, Barbara Walters asked Jarriel about the children's unexpectedly sophisticated vocabularies. "What about the language these children use," she asked, "like, 'oral sex,' uh . . . 'they *devoured* us.' This is not the language of little kids." The children's stories sounded off or somehow inauthentic, and Walters could tell. And it being another of hysteria's traits that a social panic will sometimes attempt to confess itself in veiled ways, as though to relieve internal pressure, Jarriel replied, "No, understand, these children have been through therapy, they have been thoroughly rehearsed. They know the story over and over because the doctors who have been working with them want to explain in words they can understand what has happened to them."[38]

Nobody in Los Angeles saw the *20/20* report. Fearing that the segment could "popularize exploitation of child witnesses," parents persuaded the local KABC affiliate, despite objections from the parent network, to preempt the segment.[39] Proceedings in and around the preliminary hearing, however, took on a surreal tone as the case moved into 1985. To begin with, Lawrence Pazder and Michelle Smith (Michelle Proby's pseudonym), coauthors of *Michelle Remembers* and now a married couple, traveled to Manhattan Beach to visit with the McMartin parents and trade stories about their experiences. Rumors and local TV news reports about weird, potentially satanic rituals performed at St. Cross Episcopal Church had been circulating for months, but after talking to the parents, Pazder concluded that the McMartin case was probably not related to "orthodox Satanism."[40]

Inside the courtroom, after months of testimony from parents, children finally began to take the stand, and this provoked a new surge in the media's interest in the case, among other complications. In Sacramento, final passage of the Senate bill that would allow children to testify via closed-circuit television was still months away, but prosecutors wanted to find some means of easing their witnesses' minds. They decided to invite comforting adults to join the children in the courtroom as "support persons," and the first person to accept their invitation was Laurence Tureaud, whose stage name, on television and in the wrestling ring, was Mr. T. It was only a series of successful defense objections that ultimately prevented Tureaud from appearing in court to encourage the testifying children.[41]

In the spring of 1985, however, it was prosecutors who were objecting to Danny Davis's attempt to have a television celebrity admitted to the courtroom. The reason had to do with a ten-year-old boy who took the stand in April. Although it is true that a majority of the children who testified only began to reluctantly fabricate their stories under intense pressure from therapists and parents, a few children took to making things up pretty easily. This ten-year-old was one of those few. During several disastrous days of cross-examination, the boy made one incredible claim after another, telling Danny Davis and other defense attorneys that he and other children had been forced to dig up graves on field trips to cemeteries, that teachers had killed classroom pets with knives and hypodermic needles "almost every day,"[42] and that on multiple occasions he had been beaten until he was bruised, bloodied, and barely able to stand. In a break from his usual outraged manner with the press, Forrest Latiner greeted reporters with loud laughter during a recess. "Picture seven little dwarfs with pickaxes marching to a grave in broad daylight," he said. "It's totally unbelievable." Prosecutor Glenn Stevens could only helplessly support the boy. "He was terrorized and taken to a cemetery," Stevens said, "and awful things happened."[43]

Stevens didn't say anything at all to reporters after the boy's second day on the stand; instead, he "literally sprinted" down the hall toward his office and then shut the door. Earlier that day, Danny Davis had told the boy he wanted to ask a few questions about the strangers the boy kept mentioning as being present at the Episcopal church, the cemetery, and elsewhere. Davis held up a piece of poster board with a bunch of photographs attached, and he asked the child whether he recognized any of the people on the board from his time at the church and the cemetery. Yes, said the boy, he did, and then he pointed to two photos. One was a portrait of James Kenneth Hahn, who was then city attorney–elect for Los Angeles and who would become the city's mayor in 2001. The other was a picture of the action star Chuck Norris.[44] Davis vowed to subpoena Hahn and Norris for testimony unless the district attorney dropped all charges associated with the ten-year-old witness. With lawyers, judges, and reporters alike all estimating that an actual trial was still probably at least a year away, Davis and the other McMartin attorneys had not just raised doubts, however small, about the prosecution's case—they had made parts of it look silly. Davis's strategy was working.

The lengthy preliminary hearing subjected the prosecution, its supporters, and Manhattan Beach as a whole to an awful kind of endurance test. The strictly adversarial nature of a criminal trial means that even those attorneys engaged in a noble effort to defend innocent people are also engaged in a less noble effort to make their opponents sorry they ever brought the case before a judge in the first place. Nobody felt this as keenly or with such exquisite sensitivity as John Jackson. Over the course of 1985 his *Easy Reader* column documented the process by which Jackson, without ever wavering in his belief that dozens, if not hundreds, if not one thousand children had been the victims of a conspiracy, came to doubt that justice in the South Bay was worth the cost. "The McMartin case's hallmark," he wrote in the spring, "seems to be its thunderous, soul-destroying inevitability. Every party to it seems like a boulder rolling downhill toward some greater ruin."[45] Like many people associated in peripheral ways with the prosecution, Jackson believed that the case was going to fail in some crucial way not because of human error or any flaw in the evidence but because the judicial system itself was inherently unequipped to address such a horror. "Beneath the steady courtroom drone of the McMartin preliminary hearing," he wrote, "one can often hear another sound, a sound repeated, deep and insistent, like a bass accompaniment: the crash of collapsing institutions."[46] The implications of this idea filled him with dread.

"I found myself trying to assess dispassionately the exact degree of terror felt by a crying child whom I could not reassure or even see," Jackson wrote, "while other adults, who were not frightened, squabbled all around me like beasts over her bones." Jackson wrote this in the middle of 1985, by which point his dread had turned into despair. Not only had his community failed to protect its children from abuse, but it had then compounded the error by leaving kids at the mercy of a heartless judicial machine. Here he was unwittingly half-correct. The children who endured hours of therapeutic interviews, parental questioning, and police visits only to wind up believing they had been raped by Satanists were certainly victims of *something*, as were the children who knew nothing had happened but said it had anyway. It is also true that the judicial system performed poorly in many respects. By September Jackson was reporting that in a single morning Judge Bobb threw out 81 of Danny Davis's 114 questions as "irrelevant, vague, already answered, or improper."[47] It is an obnoxious attorney who only asks 33 appropriate questions over the course of an entire morning, but it is also a completely overmatched judge, a judge with very little control over her courtroom, who can't get an attorney to cut it out with the inappropriate questions.

Jackson didn't know whether he could continue writing about the case:

> It seems to me that without a strong sense of community responsibility, one is certain to become a voyeur or a panderer, recounting these horrors for the thrills they may give and, therefore, becoming complicitous with them. . . . For me, distrust and frustration have become endemic. I no longer trust, for example, the prosecution's competence or its intellectual honesty. I no longer really expect justice to be done or my community or its molested children to be healed, even as I become ever more fully aware of how essential those results truly are.
>
> In the name of humanity, I am coming to hate and fear the touch of humankind.[48]

By November, Jackson was exhausted, and the *Easy Reader*'s editors needed someone whose coverage could provide a more skeptical view. "The hearing is not a terminal destination," Jackson wrote in his final column, "but a sort of funnel or refinery. Information goes in one end, and, to complete the metaphor, a type of poison comes out the other."[49]

The preliminary hearing ended on January 9, 1986, seventeen months after it had begun. Judge Bobb ruled that all seven defendants would stand trial on 135 counts. Eight days later, however, District Attorney Ira Reiner announced that only Ray and his mother, Peggy, would be prosecuted. His office dropped all charges against Virginia McMartin, Peggy Ann Buckey, Mary Ann Jackson, Betty Raidor, and Babette Spitler. Peggy McMartin Buckey made bail and went home after two years and one day in jail.

The poison to which John A. Jackson referred had obvious effects on the defendants, their families, those whose businesses suffered after a police search, and the pastor and congregation at St. Cross Episcopal Church. But those effects may have been most pronounced in the case of Judy Johnson, who ultimately found the investigation too much to bear. As her mind deteriorated over the course of 1985, so did her drinking increase. She once threatened a relative on her doorstep with a shotgun, after which she was hospitalized for a voluntary psychiatric evaluation. She was diagnosed with acute paranoid schizophrenia. Custody of Johnson's two children was handed over to her father, who lived in Washington State.[50]

Deputy District Attorney Glenn Stevens, who, along with Lael Rubin and Christine Johnson, was one of three prosecutors to work on McMartin, either left or was removed from the case shortly after the end of the preliminary hearing. His departure was precipitated by an article published in the *Daily Breeze* that described doubts Stevens had raised inside the DA's office about the validity of the McMartin students' accusations. Stevens was young and affable, very good with the media, and he could often be found surrounded by reporters after the day's courtroom business had come to an end. But the prosecution needed to project unwavering confidence in their case, so Stevens was out. He resigned from the district attorney's office and took a job with a group of criminal defense lawyers. Then, though the story would not become public until the end of 1986, he spent many evenings during the spring and summer at the home of a prominent Hollywood screenwriter, talking for more than thirty hours about what he and his former colleagues actually thought about their case. The screenwriter and his wife made tapes of everything Glenn Stevens said.

Abby Mann won an Academy Award for the screenplay to *Judgment at Nuremberg*, in which Spencer Tracy presides over the American military tribunals that followed the end of World War II, and he continued to mine trials for dramatic material for the rest of his career. He wrote a muckraking TV film about the Atlanta child murders of the late seventies and early eighties, and as cracks in the McMartin case began to appear, he saw another opportunity. He contacted many people associated with the case and asked them to talk, and Glenn Stevens returned the call and signed a contract. Talking over glasses of wine in the home Abby Mann shared with his wife, Myra, Stevens was both nervous and excited. "By the way, Myra, what do you do after all these tapes are transcribed?" he asked during one meeting. "Do you erase them clean?"

Myra answered, "Yeah, of course."[51]

Stevens must have known that the publication of what he was about to say would torpedo many of the professional relationships on which his career depended. But this anxiety had to be weighed against the prospect of being turned into the heroic, truth-telling protagonist of a film written by established Hollywood screenwriters. Abby and Myra Mann suggested that famous actors would be drawn to the part. "Like Abby says," Myra said during a meeting, "it's an incredible starring role for a male, you know, to be conflicted."[52]

Stevens said doubts about the case had gnawed at him for a long time. As the prosecutor assigned to organize and coordinate police searches of the McMartin teachers' homes and other areas, he was often the first member of the prosecution to examine the physical evidence firsthand. Again and again, nothing turned up where something was supposed to turn up. He watched all of the McMartin-Buckeys' home movies. "My god, did we end up with rolls and rolls," he said. "They were stupid movies about trips to Mexico, you know, 'us on the beach.'" Then he read through Virginia's diary and was disappointed to find another collection of "just regular stuff": "You know, 'Today Peggy called me from South Dakota,' and you know, mom stuff. Ah, 'Today UCLA played in the NCAA championship against Louisville and lost. Darn, I was so upset.' This is the kind of stuff she writes. She's a Lakers fan, I swear."[53]

According to Stevens's account, the early stages of the investigation revealed the McMartin-Buckeys to be exactly the kind of family their defense attorneys had always said they were: close-knit, devoted to life at the preschool, and led by a sports-obsessed matriarch who was once chastised by a judge for chatting with jurors about the previous day's Angels game. "It wasn't like going out and interviewing X number of witnesses in a murder case, and the leads all produce evidence," Stevens said. "Here, the leads all produced nothing. The leads turned to leads turned to leads turned to leads."[54]

Despite the lack of evidence, of course, the district attorney's office plowed ahead. Lael Rubin stood before a judge at one early hearing and said, "It's abundantly clear the horrors we have found at that nursery school have affected an entire generation of children." Stevens recalled this hearing at the Manns' and then said, "Keep in mind, none of that was proven."[55] He said the DA's office was sure that real evidence would turn up somewhere by the time the case made it through a grand jury to trial, and he said he and his colleagues had allowed themselves this over-confidence because they were ambitious. Philibosian, he said, "wanted to develop name identification." Lael Rubin, he said, "looked at McMartin as her own personal slingshot to get to starhood."[56] Rubin's ambitions were no secret around the DA's office, Stevens said—coworkers had even warned him against agreeing to work with her. But then Stevens had ambitions of his own: "I mean, I always knew what I wanted out of McMartin. You know, I wanted to be able to do hard work on getting convictions and then either, you know, get promoted into, to, ultimately the management in the district attorney's office or, or go along, you know, to a judgeship or whatever. And it was like that's just part of a career stepping-stone of mine."[57]

Stevens's self-regard seems to have made Abby and Myra Mann a little suspicious. Here was their leading man, the one member of the prosecution willing to speak up about what the Manns thought was an obvious miscarriage of justice. So then why, if Stevens really thought the case was a product of "hysteria," had he kept quiet for so long? Why hadn't he raised any of his doubts in public? Had he been gullible, or cynical, or what? Stevens needed to say that he had been neither, and so he found himself in the position of having to argue that in a certain light, from a certain angle, at a particular time, things had not looked that crazy at all. "We searched just about the entire city of Manhattan Beach and Hermosa Beach, and we came up empty," Stevens said. But there was another side to the story: "And the other side is the investigation was so botched from the beginning that [the defendants] had ample opportunity to destroy or get rid of every bit of evidence." There were also the children to consider. Stevens just didn't believe CII could have "brainwashed" that many of them. The only option was to "keep on plugging with testimony and keep plugging [with the] investigation and, uh, see what comes up."[58]

Parents—especially Judy Johnson—came up repeatedly. In his con-versations with the Manns, Stevens provided a detailed look at what those working for the prosecution thought of the McMartin parents as wit-nesses, as constituents whose favor and approval had to be courted, and, when prosecutors failed to secure that approval, as political and media adversaries. Stevens started work on McMartin in April 1984, and one of his first tasks was to look over leads phoned in by parents and decide which ones merited a search warrant. These leads were a mess: "'I heard from Mrs. Smith who heard from Mrs. McDonald that her daughter was at the McMartin school.'" Or, "'I remember my kid came home and said that, that Peggy took a carload of kids over to Mrs. Gooch's market.'"[59]

It was during this effort to sort out the chaotic tangle of suspicion and innuendo that coalesced around McMartin that Stevens met Judy Johnson for the first time. "She's really weird," Stevens remembered Lael Rubin telling him of "Judy J" in the spring of 1984. When he asked what exactly she meant by weird, Rubin said, "Well, you'll find out when you get to meet her." The district attorney's office quickly flagged Johnson as a problematic source, and Stevens drove to her home in an apprehensive mood. "Should Judy testify?" he remembered wondering. "I mean, is Judy nuts, as we all seem to think?" Meeting Judy briefly eased his fears—"She gives direct answers," he said. "She's not going off the deep end." But the interview with Judy's son was less reassuring: "Well, I sit down and I say, 'Hi, Matthew.' He'd look up and just smile. 'My name's Glenn. I'm your lawyer. I'm going to court with your mommy and I'm here to talk to her about the stuff that happened to you.' He never said anything."[60]

With Matthew apparently unable to communicate any of the substance of his allegations to Stevens, even the notion that Matthew had made allegations in the first place was little more than hearsay. Stevens had to trust that Judy was accurately reporting her son's accounts of preschool, and as word of her increasingly strange phone calls to the police began to circulate, this became difficult for Stevens to do. "I was always worried," he said, "that she would not be really sane when she came into court and that some of this bizarre stuff would start to come out on the witness stand."

As the investigation moved toward the preliminary hearing, Stevens made periodic visits to Judy, who would eventually testify. "Keeping track of her wasn't the hard part," he told the Manns, "but keeping track of her mind at the same time was tough . . . cause sometimes they'd be in two different places." Although the testimony she delivered in Judge Bobb's courtroom went relatively well, Stevens became concerned about Judy during the months that followed. Two weeks after she testified, Judy called to report that her home had been burglarized. "Nothing was taken,"

Stevens remembered her saying. "However, Matthew was sodomized."[61] Judy said the perpetrator was an AWOL Marine who had removed a window screen from outside and then entered the house. Judy didn't see the man commit the act, but Matthew's butt was red—the police needed to come immediately.

"It slipped through everybody's analytical process," Stevens said, "to sit down and wonder exactly what kind of woman this is and what is going on here."[62] The Manns asked Stevens whether he and Lael Rubin ever discussed Judy Johnson's mental health. "Sure, we got a good laugh about Judy," Stevens said, but he claimed they never discussed any of what Judy's mental decline meant for the case, the McMartin children, or the defendants. Stevens did not explain how he and Rubin managed to avoid having this conversation, but the instrumental logic of criminal prosecution may have helped. If Judy continued to make her court dates, her difficulties were not actually a problem for the prosecution, and even in the Manns' living room Stevens seems to have believed that what he knew did not need to affect the trial's outcome. Throughout the taped conversations Stevens insisted that nothing he said be made public until after the jury delivered a verdict. One could understand a prosecutor whose doubts about a case become so troubling that he feels he must speak out, but Stevens was pointedly not speaking out, even months after severing his professional ties to the case's outcome. One night Stevens made his case for keeping the Manns' film and his involvement under wraps until the trial's end:

Stevens: Abby, let me tell you something. You can't honestly believe that there is a chance in the world these people will be convicted, do you?

Myra Mann: They will not be convicted.

Stevens: There's no way . . .

Myra: That's why, that's why all these cowards . . .

Stevens: That's why this . . .

Abby Mann: Well, for our project . . .

Stevens: That's why this has got to wait.

Abby: For our project, they better not be.

Stevens: Yes, to our project. We drink to an acquittal.[63]

So long as Stevens's conversations with the Manns remained private, and so long as the Manns had to wait for the trial's conclusion to move forward with their film, the only immediate beneficiary of Glenn Stevens's crisis of conscience was Glenn Stevens. In addition to the money that came his way as a paid consultant to the Manns, Stevens was able to talk through his role in a case that obviously did weigh on him, at least sometimes.

He recounted one episode with Judy Johnson in especially vivid detail. At some point in the second half of 1984, Stevens said, Judy Johnson called from Seattle. She was in the hospital, and she didn't know why. "All she knows," Stevens said, "is that she was in her Volkswagen bus, and she was with the kids, and, ah, she was driving up to Seattle, and, ah, that they were being followed by a car with the Marine in it." Then Stevens didn't hear from her for a few days, and then she called to say that actually she had not been at the hospital—she had been staying with friends the whole time. On the way back to Los Angeles she called Stevens again from somewhere in Northern California and said the Marine was following her. Would Stevens please send an investigator to help? "Judy, you know, why don't you just get back to Los Angeles," Stevens told her, and she did. Then she called again to report that her son had been molested by Roberta Weintraub, a member of the Los Angeles County school board. "Matthew saw her on TV," Stevens remembered Johnson saying, "and said, 'Mom, she molested me.'" Stevens didn't explain exactly what it was that set this particular phone call apart from all the others, but it made Johnson's mental condition real to him for the first time. "All of a sudden," he told the Manns, "I just wanted to stuff a sock in her mouth."[64]

The conversations between Glenn Stevens and Abby and Myra Mann wrapped up by midsummer. Half a year later, on the same day a judge denied another of Ray Buckey's bail requests, police entered Judy Johnson's home and found her body in the bedroom upstairs. She died of internal hemorrhaging—friends said she had suffered from ulcers for years, and these may have been exacerbated by her alcoholism, which, in the last months of her life, became severe. "She made the McMartin case," said Bob Currie, one of Johnson's close friends.[65] When they found her there was food in the cupboard, an empty bottle of rum in the trash, and a subpoena from Danny Davis stuck in the mail slot.

Chapter 5

FBI, DSM, XXX

The panic swept across the country in the middle of the 1980s. In addition to the original trio of cases—McMartin, Kern County, and Jordan—allegations of bizarre or ritualistic abuse triggered investigations in dozens of communities. In El Paso, Texas, Michelle Noble and Gayle Dove, two women working part-time at the East Valley YMCA, were accused of taking many of the children they watched to Noble's home and abusing them. A number of men were also thought to have been involved in the abuse, a prosecutor said, but because the children had only seen them dressed as monsters and werewolves, these men had been difficult to identify.[1] In the Bronx five men were convicted of abusing children at day care centers throughout the borough, one of them almost entirely on the basis of testimony provided by a three-year-old who endured hours of police interviews. The investigation eventually expanded to include fourteen city facilities. A few hours to the north, in Pittsfield, Massachusetts, a nineteen-year-old teacher's aide named Bernard Baran was convicted of abusing five children and then sentenced to several consecutive life terms in prison. Baran was openly gay, and during his trial the prosecutor told the jury that hiring a gay man to work in a day care was like putting "a chocoholic in a candy store."[2] The day care cases lent new energy to the old homophobic idea that gay men were naturally predisposed to become child abusers.

Bizarre abuse involving rituals and defecation as well as the production of child pornography were alleged in two other Massachusetts cases, one of them in Malden and the other in New Braintree. Children in Maplewood, New Jersey, testified that a woman named Kelly Michaels had abused them during naptime, licking peanut butter off their genitals and also raping them with kitchen utensils. In Miami, District Attorney Janet Reno (eventually to become President Clinton's attorney general) led the successful prosecution of Frank Fuster, a Cuban immigrant, and his seventeen-year-old wife, Ileana, who ran a babysitting service out of their home in Country Walk, a small suburb. Both were accused of abusing the children in sadistic rituals and feeding them unspecified mind-altering drugs. Ileana was deported to her native Honduras after serving three and a half years of a ten-year sentence, and Frank continues to serve a sentence of six consecutive life terms. Other cases appeared in Memphis, Tennessee; Niles, Michigan; Spencer Township, Ohio; Chicago, Illinois; Clarkesville, Maryland; and at the military academy's day care center in West Point, New York.

For all that these cases had in common, there were also many differences among them, innumerable distinctions and details, both small and large. Some resulted in convictions, some in acquittals, and sometimes prosecutors dropped charges before they made it to a courtroom. Nearly half the accused were women. Some were in their sixties and seventies, and a few others were in their teens. Defendants came from the working class, the inner city, and affluent suburbs. And although many prosecutors' targets would eventually turn out to be completely innocent of the charges filed against them, there were also cases in which the tales of ritualistic, theatrical abuse obscured and buried abuse that seems to have actually occurred, abuse for which there is sadly no better word than "normal." In Pittsfield a four-year-old boy really did contract venereal disease, after which the boy's mother called the police to identify Bernard Baran as the likely culprit. When social services interviewed the boy, however, he unambiguously claimed to have been abused by his mother's boyfriend, who was never charged with a crime.

But although these details and the various social and legal situations that produced them had drastic consequences on an individual, case-by-case basis, they were not part of how the imagined child care sex abuse crisis described itself as it took the national stage. Local news was both useful and awful in all of the usual ways. Sometimes important facts would slip out in the midst of endless expressions of concern and anxiety, and sometimes they wouldn't. It was the national news reports, however, that helped people to understand ritual abuse as a larger phenomenon, a disturbing trend. Many of these reports used the word "increasingly." An article in *People* magazine on the Jordan sex rings, a report in the *New York Times* on Kee MacFarlane's Senate testimony, a cover story in *Time* magazine on a "wrenching" question, "Who's minding the kids?"—whatever their differences, all of these pieces of writing told the same simple story.[3] They were supplemented by the *20/20* McMartin reports and made-for-TV trauma narratives like *Something About Amelia*, which starred Ted Danson and Glenn Close and became one of the highest-rated programs in the medium's history.

The news media always makes for a convenient scapegoat when something goes wrong on a large scale, but a basic chronological problem suggests that it shouldn't receive too much of the blame for the panic's spread. For the most part the actual investigations and trials came *before* the national news reports about the investigations and trials. In many cases, by the time any national broadcast or print journalists made it to a town where ritual abuse was thought to have taken place, some, most, or all of the following would have already occurred. Police, having been presented with allegations of abuse and having found them credible, would have opened an investigation that targeted anything from a single individual to dozens of people. Therapists or detectives, having been asked to interview abuse victims, would have uncovered crimes on a scale neither the police nor the children's parents could have imagined. Parents would have organized search parties, founded political organizations, set up community meetings, and lobbied for new legislation, while grand juries would have delivered piles of charging documents to the city or county prosecutor. Professional organizations, legal and judicial institutions, friends, neighbors, and civic groups, all working together, got their respective local panics up and running well in advance of any sustained media attention. The media transmits and amplifies hysteria; it refines the stories told by paranoid fringe groups looking to frighten themselves. But hysteria doesn't take root in society until it can work its way into a community's most important institutions: the government, the justice system, the schools, medicine. In this respect it behaves just like any other issue around which people mobilize and around which social change takes place.

———

As police departments around the country began to take ritual abuse more seriously in the mid-1980s, one figure who popped up again and again in conference reports and law enforcement publications was the FBI's Kenneth Lanning. After years of work as a field agent, Lanning joined the Bureau's Behavioral Science Unit (BSU) in 1981. The BSU was established at the FBI Academy in Quantico, Virginia, in 1972, and the people who worked there trained aspiring agents in political science, sociology, criminology, and psychology. They did a lot of work on serial killers and child molesters, flying out to California to interview Charles Manson in prison and then working up "profiles" of different criminal types. Although the appearance of BSU agent Clarice Starling in the successful crime novel and subsequent film *The Silence of the Lambs* would lend the unit a measure of celebrity and glamour, Lanning's early work mostly revolved around teaching and research.[4]

Lanning also spent a lot of time teaching classes at the FBI's National Academy, where the students were not future employees of the federal government but local cops. The National Academy was founded in 1935, but an influx of government funding in the late sixties and early seventies drastically expanded its reach. Four times a year, police chiefs at local law enforcement agencies in all fifty states nominated officers they viewed as promising leadership material to attend a series of ten-week courses in Quantico. All of these courses were taught by people with graduate degrees—at least a master's—and their goal was both to specialize and professionalize the police, a group for whom, in much of the country, the only necessary qualification had traditionally been that your father was friends with the sitting sheriff. For accepted students the National Academy was an intense, sophisticated educational experience, following which they could return home with a new credential and all the prestige that went with it. For Lanning and his colleagues, people engaged primarily in academic research and the training of young and intimidated FBI recruits, the NA students provided a welcome influx of hands-on law enforcement experience, anecdotes, and case histories against which their theories could be tested or at least argued out.

Another happy by-product of the National Academy program became apparent by the early 1980s: student by student, class by class, the FBI had cultivated a lively network of law enforcement contacts from around the country. Former students would ask their old teachers to get on a plane and teach a class to other members of the local department, or they would phone to ask for some academic insight into a tricky case. Lanning remembers that by 1983 he was receiving more phone calls than he could keep up with, and that in addition to research and instruction, his job now included a substantial amount of consultation. The FBI's influence over the practice of American law enforcement had moved outside the classroom and into the field. One thing that Lanning found interesting was the fact that his colleagues in sociology and political science did not move into consulting. Local cops wanted to talk to the criminologists and the psychologists, and slowly, Lanning says, the line separating those two disciplines within the FBI began to disappear.

Lanning received his first phone call about ritual abuse in early 1983. A police officer had just interviewed a woman who described how she had been abused when she was a little girl by a group of people that included her parents. "It was a horrendous case," Lanning said, "involving killing people, mutilating bodies, drinking blood." The police officer wanted to know whether Lanning had ever encountered a similar set of crimes, and though he had worked on a variety of gruesome cases during his career, this seemed unusually extravagant. "I kind of never heard it all together in one case," Lanning said. A few weeks later he received a call from another law enforcement contact who wanted to talk about the strange abuses an adult woman claimed to have experienced as a child. "Jesus," Lanning thought, "I already heard about that case!"[5] But the two cases only sounded the same—the women involved were different people. A few weeks after that, Lanning received a call about similar allegations centered on a day care center, and within nine months the number of police departments soliciting his advice on ritual abuse investigations rose to twenty or thirty.

Lanning didn't know what to make of these phone calls. He said that from the beginning the idea that a group could torture and kill large numbers of people and then keep the secret for decades struck him as unlikely, at best. But it would be some time before he made any of these doubts public. Instead, he embraced the BSU's interdisciplinary approach and called the psychologists and other researchers he knew who worked on child sexual abuse. He knew Roland Summit. He talked to Jon Conte and Lucy Berliner, two academic social workers who had spent their careers on incest and other forms of abuse. He also talked to Ann Burgess, a feminist researcher who, in 1984, published an edited volume called *Child Pornography and Sex Rings*. These professionals, Lanning said, reinforced the idea that ritual abuse was a problem urgently in need of a solution. "I'm not saying every one of them used these words," Lanning said, "but the element is, 'We must believe the children.' That seemed to be a lot of what I was getting."[6] Meanwhile the consultation requests continued to pour in, and Lanning was told the BSU had a little extra money lying around. He decided to put on a conference of his own.

Lanning's Day Care Center and Satanic Cult Sexual Exploitation of Children seminar took place over four days in February 1985. The gathering assembled FBI agents and police officers along with a handful of attorneys, social workers, and academics from as far afield as the Bronx, Michigan, and California. Glenn Stevens was there, and so was Sandi Gallant, an intelligence officer with the San Francisco Police Department who for years had been warning of the dangers posed by cults.[7] The pamphlets and handouts distributed by the various attendees provide a fairly detailed picture of the proceedings. Years after the fact, Lanning said that he organized the seminar in the hopes of assuaging his doubts about the validity of ritual abuse allegations. His colleagues, however, with the possible exception of Glenn Stevens, did not share these doubts. They were eager to hear just how big the ritual abuse problem really was.

One packet provided a list of more than four hundred "occult organizations" around the country. California, with ninety-five such organizations, had the most, while Delaware, Hawaii, Montana, New Hampshire, Oklahoma, Utah, and Arkansas only managed one each. No information was included regarding the size, activities, or sophistication of any of these groups, nor was any effort made to distinguish between allegedly violent Satanists and the small countercultural spiritual organizations that have existed throughout the United States since at least the 1960s. (Womynscope, for example, a collective of feminist astrologers based in Minnesota, was on the list.) Another handout talked specifically about the importance of promptly obtaining search warrants in child sex abuse investigations, noting that pedophiles "collect sexually explicit materials consisting of photographs, magazines, motion pictures, video tapes, books, and slides which they use for their own sexual gratification" and that they "rarely destroy correspondence received from other pedophiles unless they are specifically requested to do so."[8]

The seminar's star pamphlet was Sandi Gallant's guide to investigating ritual abuse. A questionnaire promised to help police distinguish between brutal, grisly murders, which may only *seem* to resemble ritual abuse on the surface, and the real thing. "Were victims forced to devour mutilated parts?" Investigators could check "yes" or "no." The pamphlet also put ritual abuse into a kind of ersatz historical context, listing the dates of important occult festivals—"February 2nd, Candlemas or Ormelc"—and explaining that a circle is humanity's "oldest symbol." Most impressive, however, were the lists of "ritualistic indicators," which Gallant helpfully divided into subcategories:

A. RITUAL ITEMS/SIGNS

Cameras	Key of Solomon
Candles	Masks/Painted Faces
Cauldrons	Pentagram
Chalices	Robes
Circle of Power	Swastikas
Inverted Cross	Symbols
Jewelry	

B. RESTRAINTS/WEAPONS

Chains	Knives
Drugs	Ropes
Firearms	Swords

C. RITUALISTIC ACTIVITIES

Blood letting	Nudity
Chanting	Sacrifices
Crying	Screaming
Invoking Satan	Singing[9]

The handout provided no guidance as to the specific number of items, weapons, or activities that would actually suggest ritual abuse. In the classic paranoid style, these lists made the ordinary ("singing," "ropes," "jewelry") ominous through cataloguing and classification.

Perhaps more important than the pamphlet's contents, though, is the fact that it was distributed at the most prestigious law enforcement institute in the country. Many of the attendees had worked on ritual abuse cases in their various jurisdictions, and as they presented their findings to one another, this scattered collection of rumors took on an official, institutional reality that it never would have acquired without the FBI's help.

Some of these presentations were documented in notes made by Glenn Stevens for Lael Rubin and his other superiors back in the district attorney's office, and in addition to the usual litany of implausible allegations (taken largely at face value), these notes reveal the seminar's pronounced political conservatism. Although Sandi Gallant said that Satanists were frequently "normal, intelligent, working class men and women," she also blamed their attraction to Satanism on their inability to get ahead in life. "They will traditionally be underachievers," she said, people who, despite their "good backgrounds," will "settle into mediocre lifestyles."[10] She also gave voice to the widely held belief that Satanism was only the most extreme manifestation of a much wider social attack on conservative Christians. "Christians look for faith," she said. "They do not call out for the obtaining of power." Satanists, however, intentionally used perverted symbols of Christian worship (such as the inverted cross) in their own rituals "because they call upon powers which they need to obtain more and more in their lives." Everything Satanists do, she believed, "is done to defame the name of God and Christ."[11] As a law enforcement group whose primary goals are the conviction of criminals and the maintenance of order, the FBI has long been closely associated with political conservatism, and as the emergence of charismatic, law-and-order prosecutors like Ed Jagels illustrates, that association only grew stronger during the Reagan-era 1980s. Lanning's doubts about ritual abuse notwithstanding, the institution that employed him, the professional class to which he belonged, and the individuals he assembled in Quantico were all looking, first and foremost, to put criminals in prison.

In later years Lanning tried to reconcile his personal doubts and his professional actions by writing an article that blamed the trouble surrounding the idea of ritual abuse on a lack of professionalism. Those who believed wholeheartedly in ritual abuse, Lanning wrote, were members of a "witch hunt," whereas vocal skeptics comprised the "backlash." Lanning wrote that the two groups were as similar in their tactics as they were opposed in their respective outlooks. "Each side," he wrote, "tends to take an all-or-nothing approach to complex issues . . . relies heavily on raw emotion . . . [and] conveniently fails to define its terminology."[12] He accused both sides of deceiving themselves with "conspiracy theories," and by placing himself in the middle as an impartial, evidence-driven observer, he hoped to defuse the paranoid atmosphere in which he worked.

The solution he proposed was simple: "For child sexual abuse inter-veners concerned about the witch hunt or the backlash, the best approach is not to imitate their tactics but to respond with professionalism." According to Lanning, this meant evaluating information objectively, considering the middle ground, and critiquing oneself while guarding against the impulse to ascribe evil motives to one's opponents.

Lanning's principles may offer a nice guide for people involved in a formal debate, but collectively they present a strange and fatally incomplete definition of professionalism. Strange, because where is the middle ground supposed to be on the issue of organized conspiracies to commit satanic ritual abuse? That there are *some* national cult conspiracies, though not very many? And incomplete, because professionalism is also a process by which credentials, which signify competence and expertise, are handed out. It was precisely this aspect of the FBI's professionalism, the way it handed out credentials to police departments in the seventies and eighties, that turned it into an institution that validated local law enforcement's belief in ritual abuse. And it was precisely this aspect of the FBI's professionalism that Lanning was apparently unable to see.

The seminar featured a few presentations on topics other than the police investigations themselves. One attendee talked about how doctors obtained medical evidence from the child victims, describing the colposcope that Bruce Woodling and Astrid Heger had used to examine the McMartin children. The therapeutic interviews that produced many of the allegations in the first place received a little less attention. Two representatives of the Minnesota Bureau of Criminal Apprehension talked about how children in the Jordan case had been interviewed too many times.

No mention, however, was made of the therapeutic beliefs that determined how the Jordan interviews were conducted. These beliefs concerned the psychological experience of sexual trauma, the consequences of abuse for child victims, and the relationship between trauma and memory. They had their origins in the 1970s, when a group of dissident psychiatrists, social workers, and activists began to challenge the dominant, largely Freudian mode of American thinking about abuse. And as Lanning convened the Quantico seminar that made belief in ritual abuse professionally respectable in law enforcement, this new thinking about trauma and abuse was also finally making its way into the professional mainstream of American psychiatry.

Within ten years of the publication of C. Henry Kempe's paper on the Battered-Child Syndrome, a consensus had emerged that abuse represented a serious threat to the physical health of children. But the medical profession was much slower to adopt the idea that child abuse could also have serious psychological consequences. In 1975, two full years after Walter Mondale's famous hearings on the Child Abuse Prevention and Treatment Act, the nearly three-thousand-page-long *Comprehensive Textbook of Psychiatry* still contained no material on the mental health of abused children, nor did it mention any possibility that father-daughter incest could result in psychopathology.[13]

The connection between child abuse and mental illness would have to be forced on the profession from the outside, and as it happened, the psychological and psychiatric establishments were in the process of embracing large numbers of outsiders. In the 1970s psychoanalytic institutes began to train nonphysician therapists, or "lay" analysts, in an effort to breathe new air into a form of treatment that was seen by many as insular, obscure, and rarified. This opened the doors to those with no medical degree and no deep immersion in psychoanalytic texts.[14] Elsewhere in the profession, the invention of interpersonal therapy (IPT) dramatically increased the role of psychiatric nurses and social workers in day-to-day therapeutic practice. IPT was designed to provide short bursts of treatment—typically twelve to sixteen weeks—to people dealing with mild to moderate cases of depression and other common ailments, people who didn't need an intensive therapeutic intervention so much as sustained, empathetic attention and intelligent emotional advice. In other words, it called for therapists who could provide a slightly medicalized version of the services that social workers had always provided.

That people were seeking any kind of treatment at all for these kinds of everyday problems reflected psychiatry's growing role in American life. In earlier decades, most forms of treatment had been aimed at those with obvious and debilitating psychological illnesses, with psychoanalysis reserved for affluent and educated people in major urban centers. After the 1960s, however, psychiatry began to involve itself with a wider range of problems and experiences. Those whose marriages or jobs made them sad or anxious started to understand themselves as in need of medical assistance, and even those with no problems at all began to suspect that psychiatry or therapy could help them reach their full potential. Membership in the American Psychological Association grew by a factor of sixteen between the late 1950s and the late 1980s, and that figure does not account for the thousands of counselors, nurses, and social workers who went into practice over that same period. As it expanded, therapy deregulated itself: in most states no license was required to rent out an office and put the word "psychotherapist" on the door.[15]

Florence Rush was one of these social workers. Her 1971 presentation "The Sexual Abuse of Children: A Feminist Point of View," had been one of the first public expressions of the idea that Freud had discovered the true extent of childhood sexual abuse in society, been frightened by what he found, and then conspired to cover it up. Kee MacFarlane was another. She built her career entirely on the basis of her University of Maryland master's degree in social work. Along with their colleagues in rape crisis centers, shelters for abused women and children, and the women's movement, these people agitated at the margins of mainstream psychiatry for an increased focus on seeking a therapeutic solution to forgotten abuse. But it wasn't until the psychiatrist who rediscovered Multiple Personality Disorder got involved that they made any really significant progress.

Sybil made Cornelia Wilbur a famous doctor. Her discovery of a disorder as rare and as dramatically compelling as MPD in such an unassuming chemistry student, combined with her account of the sadistic abuse that had caused the condition to emerge, earned Wilbur invitations to many conferences and other professional meetings. There she told audiences that MPD was a fascinating and dynamic disorder, that treating it was an intellectual adventure. She described the process by which she had coaxed Shirley Mason's alter personalities into revealing themselves, exhibited the paintings "they" had made, and said the alters were talented artists and writers, meaning that Sybil made for interesting therapeutic company.[16] Alongside these tales of psychiatric discovery, Wilbur explained to audience after audience that childhood abuse, usually sexual, was the primary cause of MPD. She made this argument so frequently and so consistently that her colleagues started referring to it as the "post-Wilburian paradigm."[17] But Wilbur knew that it would not be enough to hear her name mentioned at conferences and symposia—she wanted to get MPD into psychiatry's handbook.

The first edition of the *Diagnostic and Statistical Manual of Mental Disorders* was published in 1952, and a revised second edition followed in 1968. Both volumes ran fewer than 140 pages, and they were written in a highly technical language aimed primarily, even exclusively at psychiatric

specialists. In 1974, however, the American Psychiatric Association decided that a third edition of the DSM was needed to address the rapidly
changing state of the profession—not only psychiatry's expansion into the
everyday lives of millions of people but also the emergence of pharmaceu-
ticals as a basic component of psychiatric treatment. An APA committee
spent six years preparing the DSM-III, which, when it was finally published in 1980, ran to 494 pages and included 265 diagnostic categories.
Written in everyday language designed to appeal to the social workers
and other nonphysician therapists who were filling up the field's professional ranks, the DSM-III employed a radically new diagnostic system
and immediately went into widespread use. It is considered a watershed
moment in the history of psychiatry, and "Multiple Personality" was diagnosis number 300.14.[18]

"The essential feature" of Multiple Personality, according to DSM-III,
"is the existence within the individual of two or more distinct personalities, each of which is dominant at a particular time. . . . Transition
from one personality to another is sudden and often associated with psy-
chosocial stress." The authors went on to explain that most patients were
unaware of the existence of their "subpersonalities," even though the subpersonalities usually knew about one another. Like Dr. Wilbur's "Sybil,"
the manual's archetypal Multiple Personality patient had "lost periods
of time," mysterious gaps after which the patient would find herself in
some strange part of town. "The individual personalities are nearly always
quite discrepant," the manual said, "and frequently seem to be opposites.
For example, a quiet, retiring spinster may alternate with a flamboyant,
promiscuous bar habitué on certain nights."[19] Though "the disorder is
apparently extremely rare," enough cases had been documented for the
manual to list "child abuse and other forms of severe emotional trauma in
childhood" as possible predisposing factors.[20] The number, 300.14, was for
the therapist to write down on forms when billing the insurance company.

Almost immediately after Multiple Personality made its debut in
DSM-III, therapists began to diagnose it with rapidly growing frequency.
Until 1970 fewer than two hundred people in the entire world had ever
been diagnosed with anything resembling MPD, but in 1980 a psychiatrist
who made extensive use of hypnosis in his therapy sessions published an
article describing fourteen cases that had recently come to light.[21] Dr. Wilbur, having successfully legitimized the diagnosis, now traveled from conference to conference in an effort to convince researchers and clinicians

to specialize in the disorder, and that effort was also successful. The International Society for the Study of Multiple Personality and Dissociation (ISSMP&D) was founded in 1984, and it quickly set out to lend a credentialed air, if not actual credentials, to its members. It founded a journal, *Dissociation*, and it sent certificates designed to look like medical school diplomas to those who became "Affiliates" of the Society. "Display your professionalism," an attached flyer read. "Be proud of your commitment to the field of multiple personality and dissociative disorders." A "handsome membership plaque" was also available for eighteen dollars.[22]

Dr. Bennett Braun, a founding member of the ISSMP&D, announced in 1984 that some one thousand cases had been identified, and in 1986 he established a unit specifically devoted to dissociative disorders at Chicago's Rush-Presbyterian St. Luke's Medical Center, a nationally respected hospital. The movement received an additional infusion of energy from the 1984 publication of *The Assault on Truth*, Jeffrey Masson's book-length polemic on Freud's cowardice in the face of child abuse.[23] Published by Farrar, Straus and Giroux, the book's prospects were damaged by a two-part magazine profile of Masson that came out around the same time (the profile's author, Janet Malcolm, portrayed Masson as a charismatic but intellectually shallow womanizer). Nevertheless, *The Assault on Truth* received a number of high-profile reviews, including an article titled "The 100-Year Cover Up" in the feminist monthly *Ms.* magazine.[24] Masson had given the MPD movement a history, which it needed in order to flourish. Amplifying a critique that had been circulating among many American feminists for more than a decade, Masson described Freud as the architect of a century-long campaign to ignore both the incidence of child abuse, especially sexual abuse, and its psychological effects. His story made the MPD movement, the social workers, the psychiatric nurses, and the therapists working at Children's Institute International into members of a revolutionary vanguard whose discoveries required not just intellectual daring but also political courage.

Yet Masson's argument in *The Assault on Truth* rests on a very shaky historical foundation. Freud's patients did not actually tell him that they had been sexually abused. His theory that hysteria was caused by repressed memories of childhood abuse was developed before any of his patients ever reported being victims of incest, and it was Freud who cobbled together the abuse narratives from stray memories and impressions elicited from patients under a mild form of hypnosis.[25] "Something has occurred to me now," one patient told him, "but you obviously put it into my head."[26] Freud admitted as much in his *Studies on Hysteria*, writing that in some cases of difficult therapeutic resistance he "laboriously forced some piece of knowledge on a patient."[27] Masson's account also gives the impression that many of the abusers identified by Freud's female patients were fathers, but this is inaccurate. Most were nursemaids, siblings, servants, and governesses. When patients identified male abusers, they tended to be men who were only slightly older than the patients themselves, such as brothers. Freud does not even mention fathers in "The Aetiology of Hysteria," the paper in which he publicly outlined his Seduction Theory for the first time.

Freud was open about his active role in producing his patients' stories. He made interpretive leaps that his patients would never have made on their own, writing that one patient's habit of kicking his legs about in bed before going to sleep meant he had previously tried to "kick away the person who was lying on him"—namely, an abusive servant girl.[28] Even when patients eventually agreed that abuse must have occurred in the way Freud suggested, they had "no feeling of remembering the scenes" and assured Freud "emphatically of their unbelief."[29] None of this dissuaded Masson and his supporters. Although MPD therapists didn't know it, one reason they liked the abuse narratives Freud initially claimed to have uncovered was because he uncovered those narratives using coercive therapeutic techniques very similar to their own. As the seduction theory revival gained momentum, the professionalization of the MPD field helped to make therapists' beliefs more durable. Peer-review made it possible for MPD advocates to put one another's findings inside a closed loop of citation and validation. In 1986 Cornelia Wilbur wrote an essay in which she cited Steven Marmer as arguing that childhood trauma was a crucial factor in the development of MPD. Marmer's essay, though, which had been written in 1980, actually did no such thing; instead, Marmer noted that some *earlier* reports on MPD had suggested a link between the disorder and childhood trauma. He also provided citations—to earlier cases that were first reported by Cornelia Wilbur.[30]

Therapists found MPD patients with dozens of alter personalities. Then they found MPD patients with hundreds of alter personalities. As the number of alters increased, so did the supposed violence and brutality of the abuse that had brought them into being. Cornelia Wilbur was one of the first really prominent advocates to talk publicly about the connection between multiplicity and something resembling ritual abuse. At the 1984 meeting of the ISSMP&D, while delivering a paper called "Multiple Personality Disorder and Child Abuse: An Etiologic Overview," Wilbur described a patient whose family had all been members of a murderous, racist cult: "How would you like to be exposed to multiple murders as an infant and a child, since your grandfather formed the first Klan and your father formed the second Klan and the family literally owned the town? I don't know how many murders this child saw . . . she tells me that a group of individuals in that part of the United States killed every single black person that came within their purview."[31] Wilbur said the patient had also watched her family kill "whites that were itinerant farm workers, including the children."

In 1986 the Washington Supreme Court heard *Tyson v. Tyson*, the first case based on an adult's repressed and then recovered memories of childhood sexual abuse at the hands of her father. Although the court ultimately decided to dismiss the case, a dissenting opinion laid out a line of reasoning that many courts would take up in the coming years. "Fundamental fairness," the dissenting judge wrote, "compels us to extend the discovery rule to adults who suffered sexual abuse as children and then repressed that abuse."[32] By 1987 the ISSMP&D's national meeting would feature eleven discussion papers on ritual abuse, and in that same year a revised edition of the DSM-III documented just how far MPD had come.[33] To begin with, changes in the volume's categorization system made MPD more prominent, as MPD became the first diagnosis listed under the heading "Dissociative Disorders (or, Hysterical Neuroses, Dissociative Type)." Those comparing the manual's description of the disorder to the early 1980 version also found that MPD itself had become more exciting. Whereas "classic cases" of MPD still featured "at least two fully developed personalities," the manual now noted that "in adults, the number of personalities or personality states in any one case varies from two to over one hundred, with occasional cases of extreme complexity."[34] The revised description also displayed increased certainty about MPD's cause and increased alarm about its prevalence. "Several studies," the authors wrote, "indicate that in nearly all cases, the disorder has been preceded by abuse (often sexual) or another form of severe emotional trauma in childhood." In addition, "recent reports suggest that this disorder is not nearly so rare as it has commonly been thought to be."[35]

One thing that didn't change was the idea that "a quiet, retiring spinster may alternate with a flamboyant, promiscuous bar habitué." Such an easy and unthinking embrace of the old, sexist Madonna-whore complex—itself an idea first proposed by Freud at his most sexist—might have seemed strange coming out of a professional group that owed so much to feminist thinking about abuse. Also strange, from this perspective, was the fact that women made up 90 percent of those diagnosed with MPD. In the 1960s and 1970s, feminists had complained loudly about psychiatry's habit of recasting the difficulties women faced in a sexist society as mental health problems for which each woman, individually, was to blame.[36] Yet here was another psychiatric disorder just for women, a malady for which the prescribed treatment was both debilitating and lengthy, often requiring months or even years of costly therapy and regular hospitalizations. Because boys make up some 40 percent of child sex abuse victims nationally, a small number of MPD researchers dutifully began looking for the "missing" male multiples, but they didn't look very hard. Cornelia Wilbur once proposed that you could find them in the prison system, as their childhood traumas would have eventually driven them all to crime.[37]

If some aspects of MPD made it a tricky or incongruous feminist project, they also made the diagnosis very appealing to conservatives. Evangelical Protestants made up a substantial and vocal wing of the MPD community, and in the mideighties this group enjoyed more political momentum and energy than at almost any other time in its history. Fifteen years of grassroots organizing had turned evangelical organizations like Focus on the Family and the Moral Majority into some of the most powerful political groups in the country and mobilized conservative Christians of many denominations around right-wing causes. The threat of satanic cults had been a consuming preoccupation among evangelicals since the early 1970s, with books like Mike Warnke's *The Satan Seller* describing a good Christian's fall into drug-fueled devil worship and subsequent redemption.[38] (A Christian magazine exhaustively discredited Warnke's claims in the early nineties.)[39] For some evangelical therapists the connection between MPD and abuse, especially satanic ritual abuse, was irresistible. In the patient's long road to "integration"—the reabsorption of all alter personalities by the primary personality—therapists saw an analogue to the evangelical's religious quest, which moved through sin and a difficult spiritual rebirth toward redemption and peace. The threat of ritual abuse also allowed evangelical therapists to view their own work in terms of religious war, with Satan as the enemy and recovered memory therapy as the weapon of choice.

MPD's evangelical therapists were mostly nonphysicians. Psychiatrists working on the disorder were more secular, and as a result they regarded the papers and presentations connecting MPD to ritual abuse with suspicion or overt hostility. Like Kenneth Lanning at the FBI, they must have known that by allowing these paranoid conspiracy theories to share conference programs with their own, comparatively pedestrian findings, they would only be inviting intensified scrutiny and skepticism later on. That the ritual abuse "true believers," as they were sometimes called, remained at the center of the MPD movement for so long makes little sense from an academic perspective; medicine is supposed to test new theories and dismiss the ones that don't manage a passing grade, and MPD could have been dismissed rather easily.

Medicine, however, is also a profession with political interests and considerations like any other, and the persistence of ritual abuse within the MPD world may best be understood as a doomed attempt to cope with a tough set of political pressures and changes. By the time Ronald Reagan won the presidency, these pressures were also changing how the feminists who had done much of the initial mobilizing against sex abuse talked about the issue. In the 1970s feminists had talked much more about rape than about child abuse. Rape, according to Susan Brownmiller and scores of other writers and activists, was a message from a patriarchal society to women. It told women they were a subordinate class, it reminded them that men understood access to women's bodies as a natural right, and it served as a punishment for women who stepped outside their prescribed social role. Conservatives objected to this description—they preferred to understand rape as a crime committed by mentally ill deviants—but when Susan Brownmiller published *Against Our Will* in 1975, all fifty states had laws on the books that said rape within a marriage was impossible, sex being just another of the housewife's lifelong obligations. After 1975 those laws began to change, and sexual harassment in the workplace became legally actionable as well. Feminists were able to say these things, in part, because of the extraordinary cultural and political momentum at their backs, a whole wave of liberation movements that had been upending the country's sexual and racial hierarchies since the 1960s.

The political situation looked very different in the mid-1980s. Conservative resistance to the women's movement was hitting its organizational stride. Focus on the Family and the Moral Majority were flourishing, and evangelical Christians, for whom social issues like homosexuality and the preservation of the nuclear family were crucial, imbued the antifeminist backlash with enormous energy. In Ronald Reagan these groups had a president whose administration was more open to evangelical influence than any other in the country's history. Legislators no longer wanted to hear, for example, about the role played by race and class in the incidence of sexual violence against adult women, nor did the culture want to hear about the way society's hierarchies tolerated or even condoned rape and other forms of abuse so long as it didn't happen to the wrong people or in the wrong place.

What legislators and pundits *were* still willing to hear, to the exclusion of almost everything else on the feminist agenda, was that the country's children were at risk. Over the course of the 1970s conservatives made the endangered child into a kind of political and rhetorical abstraction, a way of thinking about the country and its citizens that could help advance a wide range of policy initiatives. They opposed the counterculture on the grounds that rock and roll caused adolescents to lose respect for family life. They promoted the War on Drugs with racially tinged morality tales about addicted inner-city mothers and, crucially, the "superpreda-tor" "crack babies" to whom those mothers supposedly gave birth. (That particular epidemic was later shown to be a myth.)[40] And when Anita Bryant led a campaign to allow Dade County to discriminate against homosexuals in hiring teachers for public schools, she named the effort "Save Our Children." The fear that tied all of these campaigns together was of the ease with which children could be victimized or else corrupted and turned against the society that was supposed to nurture them. Even without its connection to ritual abuse, MPD would have been attractive to many conservative antifeminists: it was a diagnosis that ignored all the circumstances of a woman's adult life by claiming that what really mattered were the events of her childhood.

Slowly, some feminists hoping to stay politically relevant in the Reagan era adopted these conservative ways of speaking as their own. In the 1970s, feminist antipornography groups began to stage protests and publish articles denouncing the representation of women in sexually explicit media as well as the treatment of women who worked in the sex industry as performers. Women Against Pornography (WAP), founded in 1979 and based in New York City, became the most famous of these groups, thanks both to its roster of celebrity feminist supporters and its notorious guided tours of porn theaters and peep shows in Times Square. Despite WAP's public identification with radical feminist causes and beliefs, their office began to receive hundreds of letters from conservative Christian groups offering praise, soliciting advice on opposing pornography in other cities and towns, or looking to schedule a tour in New York. "Dear All You Wonderful People," Florence Rush wrote in reply to members of a South Carolina Methodist denomination that barred gays and lesbians, "Thank you so much for your interest and support. A letter like yours makes all our hard work worthwhile."[41] These overtures to the right wing alarmed some feminists inside the antipornography movement, and for feminists who thought targeting pornography was a mistake altogether, they validated many fears. But the Reagan administration, which had coasted into office on a wave of evangelical support, had stymied many of feminism's legislative efforts. WAP seemed to believe they needed all the friends they could get.

These uneasy alliances came into full view as antipornography groups around the country started trying to pass laws restricting explicit media. As Kathleen Morris's sex ring investigation was gearing up in late 1983, feminist lawyer Catharine MacKinnon, working out of the University of Minnesota along with the writer and activist Andrea Dworkin, drafted legislation allowing women to sue pornography's vendors and producers for civil rights violations. The Minneapolis Government Operations Committee held public hearings on the proposal over a few days in December. "We are proposing for your consideration," MacKinnon said in her opening remarks, "a statutory scheme that will situate pornography as a central practice in the inequality of the sexes, in specific, as a practice that is central to the subordination of women."[42]

Similar events followed in Indianapolis, in Massachusetts, and in Los Angeles, where the antipornography hearing was conducted just a few city blocks from the ongoing McMartin preliminary hearing. The antipornography movement was not directly involved with those investigating and prosecuting the sex ring and day care trials, but the two groups had many interests in common. In Minneapolis the Committee heard testimony from Sherry Arndt, a moderator and trainer with the Illusion Theater, which had put on plays about "good touch" and "bad touch" for the children of Jordan's elementary schools.[43] Jeffrey Masson appeared in Los Angeles to describe his work on Freud's seduction theory and to say "that pornography in my opinion is the expression of sexual abuse, no more a fantasy than sexual abuse is a fantasy. Thank you very much." He also modified the feminist slogan, "pornography is the theory, rape is the practice." According to Masson, "pornography is already the practice."[44]

The federal government took up the issue when the president appointed Attorney General Edwin Meese to study pornography and its effects on society. The Meese Commission, as it came to be known, was organized just fifteen years after the Johnson administration had conducted its own porn investigation. To the surprise of many, the original 1970 *Report of the Commission on Obscenity and Pornography* had found porn's corrosive social effects to be largely nonexistent. The commission found "no evidence to date that exposure to explicit sexual materials plays a significant role in the causation of delinquent or criminal behavior among youths or adults," nor could they find evidence that porn had any effect on citizens' "established attitudinal commitments regarding either sexuality or sexual morality."[45] The commission recommended that all laws restricting the sale of sexually explicit material to adults be repealed—a recommendation that was singled out as especially egregious when the Senate rejected the commission's findings by a 60–5 vote. The Reagan administration's opinion of the original commission's work was no kinder. Meese began work under the basic assumptions that porn was bad for people and that it needed to be more strictly controlled. His stated objectives were "to determine the nature, extent, and impact on society of pornography in the United States, and to make specific recommendations . . . concerning more effective ways in which the spread of pornography could be contained."[46]

The Meese Commission organized public hearings in various major cities during 1985 and early 1986, including Los Angeles, Miami, Houston, New York, and Washington, DC. Meese appointed three commissioners whose views on pornography and censorship could be described as liberal, but the commission's other nine members were largely conservative, including a prosecutor with a special focus on obscenity cases, a priest, and a former Nixon speechwriter who thought the commission should go after slasher films as well. These politics were reflected in the testimony presented at the commission's hearings.

WAP helped to organize a few dozen witnesses to testify about the harm they had suffered, including a cheerleader whose photographs had been published in *Playboy* without her permission and a woman who claimed that her husband's pornography consumption had caused him to turn violent. An overwhelming majority of the testimony presented was vehemently and emotionally critical of pornography's place in society, and although this could have been read as a signal that porn really did need to be subjected to tighter controls, a few commissioners pointed out that such simple conclusions made no sense in light of pornography's immense commercial success. "Such material is selling to millions of apparently satisfied customers," two commissioners wrote in a jointly signed statement. The problem was that none of those people were willing to talk about their satisfaction in front of a federal panel. "To find people willing to acknowledge their personal consumption of erotic and pornographic materials and comment favorably in public about their use has been nearly impossible. . . . It seems obvious that the data gathered is not well balanced."[47]

Some of the most powerful and widely publicized testimony came from Andrea Dworkin. She spoke at the commission's New York City hearing, and the transcript of her remarks does not do justice to her performance. She spoke in a deep voice with a rhythmic cadence, and her writing, which conveyed a similar sense of momentum and power, earned her a reputation as American feminism's Old Testament prophet. "I'm a citizen of the United States," she told the commission,

> And in this country where I live, every year millions and millions of pictures are made of women with our legs spread. We're called "beaver," we're called "pussy," our genitals are tied up. They're pasted, makeup is put on them to make them pop out of the page at a male viewer. Millions and millions of pictures are made of us in postures of submission and sexual access so that our vaginas are exposed for penetration, our anuses are exposed for penetration, our throats are used as if they're genitals for penetration. Uh, in this country where I live as a citizen, real rapes are on film and are being sold on the marketplace, and the major motif of pornography as a form of entertainment is that women are raped and violated and humiliated until we discover that we like it, and at that point we ask for more.[48]

She called pornography "a form of political persecution," she asked the government to enforce RICO statutes against studios and distributors, and she said that porn should be removed from federal prisons entirely: "It's like sending dynamite to terrorists."

When antipornography activists talked ominously about the porn industry's explosive growth, they weren't making it up. The number of published magazines had increased tremendously following the runaway success of the 1972 film *Deep Throat*. Although magazines featuring bondage and sexual violence remained on the margins of the pornographic mainstream (defined largely by *Playboy, Penthouse,* and *Hustler*), their numbers increased as well. The Meese Commission hearings, however, sometimes took on a paranoid tone that closely resembled that of the ritual abuse and multiple personality conferences that were taking place around the country at the same time. "We see the centrality of pornography in serial murders," Dworkin said during her testimony. "There *are* snuff films."[49] She was referring to an urban myth that held that in the darkest corners of the pornography world there existed a secret network of producers and directors who made sex films culminating in the actual, unsimulated murders of the women who performed in them. No evidence of such a commercial enterprise has ever been found, but Dworkin, MacKinnon, and others publicly referred to snuff films as the logical end point of pornography's misogynist hatred.[50] When police investigating day care and sex ring trials mentioned their belief that teachers and parents had produced and sold pornographic evidence of their crimes, it was this imaginary network of deviants that was thought to be taking care of distribution.

This was a bizarre and volatile political atmosphere. In the personal statement he composed for the commission's final report, Focus on the Family founder James Dobson wrote that he "passionately" supported the control of obscene materials, and then he specifically thanked Dworkin for her "moving testimony" and asked how anyone "could turn a deaf ear to her protest." He also repeated the slogan that had been invented by people who considered him a political opponent in every way, except for this one: "Pornography is the theory; rape is the practice."

It was in this environment that all the different professional threads of the child care sex abuse panic came together as well. Roland Summit testified in the Meese Commission's Miami hearing, and so did Kenneth Lanning, who appeared to discuss his behavioral profiles of pedophiles and child porn collectors.[51] The commission cited his work many times in the *Final Report*. Miami also heard from a woman who said pornography had been part of her three-year-old daughter's abuse at a preschool. Because the commission concealed her identity, there is no way to determine whether she was a McMartin parent, but her account matches the stories that came out of Manhattan Beach in every detail: "My daughter attended

[a] Pre-School in California. She was three years old when she began attending. During the six months she attended before the school closed, she was sexually molested on multiple occasions by teachers on the school grounds and was also taken off school property to unknown locations to be molested by persons unknown to me. Photographs were taken on many (if not all) of these occasions. She was threatened with physical violence with a knife and a gun and was forced to watch animals being killed."[52]

Finally, multiple personality made an appearance. The *Final Report* contained a section devoted specifically to "Amnesia and Denial and Repression of Abuse," and the commission heard from at least one woman who had been diagnosed with MPD.[53] "Like an internal sore," a witness at the Washington, DC, hearing said, "the repressed memories began erupting, baring all of my symptoms and anxiety."

> It has been extremely difficult for me to write my testimony. I am only now, because of the request that I testify today, beginning to remember the pornography to which I was subjected. The memories that I have relived completely have been of a physical nature, the extreme traumas which were responsible for my splitting. I feel that I have been so desensitized that the memories of having been shown pornographic pictures have seemed harmless and therefore, until now, there has been no need to remember them. . . . Each time I have reread what I have written I am so re-appalled, re-horrified, and re-traumatized myself that I decided it was more important to just tell you that I knew pornographic magazines played a large part in my stepfather's life.[54]

The commission was not thought to be a great success. Attorney General Meese made the mistake of announcing his findings while standing in front of a statue of Lady Justice, and many of the following morning's front pages featured a photograph of Meese denouncing sexual imagery while a marble pair of bare breasts loomed above him. The *Final Report* was also somewhat muddled by the liberal commissioners' refusal to sign on to some of the more ominous and unsubstantiated findings regarding the connection between pornography and violent sex crimes. Instead of one collaboratively written essay summarizing their shared conclusions, the commissioners wrote many individual pieces, each arguing with the others.

Still, the list of "Recommendations for the Justice System and Law Enforcement Agencies" that appeared at the beginning of the *Final Report* made it clear that Reagan had achieved at least some of his goals. Recommendation 11: "The Attorney General should direct the United States Attorneys to examine the obscenity problem in their respective districts, identify offenders, initiate investigations, and commence prosecution without further delay."[55] Recommendation 24, designed to give government officials an easy way of shutting down strip clubs: "State and Local prosecutors should enforce the alcoholic beverage control laws that prohibit obscenity on licensed premises." Recommendation 89, getting down into the fine details of adult entertainment: "Holes enabling inter-booth sexual contact between patrons should be prohibited at peep show booths." In the broadest sense, the commission recommended that the government shut down whichever parts of the adult industry it could.

The political alliances that made both the antipornography movement and the Meese Commission possible could not have come into being but for the shared belief that the country's children were in danger. Child protectionism has a long history in American politics, and Democrats and Republicans have each been eager to list the ways in which children would be harmed by their opponents' proposals and policies. In the decades following the 1960s and the sexual revolution, however, with the structure of America's social arrangements and sex roles in an unprecedented state of flux, conservatives came into full ownership of "family values." They described a country in which porn, gays, and women had run amok, and they argued that the confines of traditional family life, with its breadwinning husband and housewife mother, provided a shelter from social madness. So even as some of the country's most prominent feminist voices could be heard decrying porn and its effects on women and children alongside movement conservatives like James Dobson, the political benefits of their efforts were not so evenly divided.

This uneven distribution of political gains was part of what made antipornography so controversial within feminism itself. Although the media had always represented the women's movement as a unified campaign organized around a single set of goals, there were enormous disagreements between mainstream liberals like Gloria Steinem and feminism's more radical wing. As early as 1982, these disagreements over the role of sex and sexual expression in society had caused a feminist conference held at Barnard College to devolve into a series of angry denunciations. And if the antipornography position seemed to be consolidating its gains by the middle of the 1980s, that should not be taken as a sign that intrafeminist conflict over the issue had eased. As some of antipornography's harshest feminist critics pointed out, the 1980s were a decade during which the country experienced its most significant conservative retrenchment since World War II. When feminists contributed to the national mood of anxiety and fear about child endangerment, they were playing directly into their opponents' hands.

———————

The child care and sex ring trials were the purest expressions of these fears, but by the mid-1980s they were humming along with a quality that looked less like panic than efficient professionalism. One of the basic reasons the McMartin case took so long is that the people investigating and prosecuting it had to work out interviewing techniques and courtroom tactics all by themselves. Kee MacFarlane, Astrid Heger, Roland Summit, and Lael Rubin were pioneers, and like anybody breaking new ground in a new field, their work was plagued by its share of sloppy mistakes.

In Miami, however, State Attorney Janet Reno did not make the same errors as she organized the prosecution of Frank and Ileana Fuster, a married couple who lived in a suburban development called Country Walk. Frank was a thirty-five-year-old Cuban immigrant with a young son, Noel, from a prior marriage. Ileana was seventeen, an undocumented immigrant from Honduras, and she had been married to Frank for less than a year when the couple decided to run a neighborhood babysitting service out of their home. Frank handed out business cards: "Country Walk Babysitting Service—We don't say we're the best, but people do talk."

Children from around the neighborhood, most of them younger than six, spent time at the Fusters'. A little less than half a year in, one of these children was taken home at the end of the day and then asked his mother whether she would "kiss" his "body," meaning his penis. "Ileana kisses my body," he said. "Ileana kisses all the babies' bodies." Although the mother's alarm at these statements is understandable, it may well have been due to a simple cultural misunderstanding. Ileana had grown up in rural Honduras, a place where it is common for women to touch or kiss the genitals of young children to reassure them or to show casual, nonsexual affection.[56] A few months later a mother picking up her eighteen-month-old from his first day of out-of-home child care became convinced that her son had been drugged. The boy seemed tired, and at home he hit himself in the head with a block until she took it away. Word spread in the Country Walk development that something was not right with Ileana's babysitting, and a police detective was asked to interview five children. One of them had a speech impediment, and the others had very little to say.

There was one exception, a five-year-old boy who told the police investigator that Frank had taken photographs of naked children. He said the same thing over the following weeks to Joseph and Laurie Braga, a pair of child development specialists brought in by State Attorney Reno. The Bragas were significantly more responsible with their interviewing technique than the therapists at CII. They videotaped all of their interviews, they generally did not see individual children more than twice, and, with one glaring exception, they avoided the kind of openly confrontational tone that would cause the McMartin prosecution so much trouble at trial. Still, for each of the boy's incriminating statements—he said that Frank sodomized one of the children and also encouraged "caca" games, where kids were made to throw and smear feces around the house—the Bragas elicited a bizarre or implausible claim as well. The boy said a thirteen-year-old called "Ms. Booby" had stopped by one day and that he had been the only child who didn't laugh at her.[57] The boy said that the Fusters had drugged the children with homemade pills that looked like candy corn. He also vacillated nervously between describing himself as a participant in the games, as an observer, or as someone who had only heard things from other children:

> Q: You told me once, during one of our visits you told me that you saw Noel's daddy put his penis in his mouth.
> A: Right.
> Q: You did see that?
> A: Right.
> Q: So you just said that you never saw any of the games? Now what you're saying is different.
> A: I saw some games.
> Q: Oh, okay well can you—
> A: The games that they played with Noel. I saw.
> Q: Can you tell me what games with Noel that you did see? Can you tell me what they did? What you want to show me with the dolls what they did?

A: Hum . . . I just . . . I just . . . um . . . watched for a little while and
   then . . . hum . . . I had to leave then.

Q: So when you watch for a little while, can you tell me what you saw in
   that little while.

A: Um . . . they were uh . . . sticking, uh . . . penises in Noel's mouth.

Q: Who were?

A: Hum . . . Frank.

Q: Frank.

A: Yeah.

Q: And what was Ileana doing?

A: She was sending me home because my dad picks me up and she gets
   everything ready to leave.[58]

In a different interview he said the Fusters had played the sex game outside while he watched TV in the house. Other children who saw the Bragas failed to make any incriminating statements during their first interview, but then, weeks later, they would return for a second session, almost always at their parents' insistence. The neighborhood parents had been meeting every night to exchange information, and therapists aren't the only ones who can pressure children to disclose abuse. The Bragas ultimately conducted forty-six interviews with thirty-one children. For all their flaws, these interviews looked pretty good in comparison to Kee MacFarlane's more blatantly suggestive interrogations.

Frank's son, Noel, who was six years old when his father was arrested, also told the Bragas that nothing had happened to him, but then doctors took a sample from his throat and tested it for gonorrhea. It came back positive. With police unable to find any weapons, pornography, or feces smeared across the walls of the Fuster home, and with doctors unable to find any evidence of sexual trauma in their examinations of the children, Noel's positive gonorrhea test represented the first hard evidence of sexual abuse in the Country Walk case—or in any of the decade's child care and sex ring cases.

In later years this test would become the object of controversy among journalists and other observers. In 1988 researchers at the Centers for Disease Control reported that gonorrhea testing among low-prevalence populations like children produced a high rate of false-positive results—as much as one-third—and they specifically warned that the "RapID NH" test doctors had used on Noel might not be able to distinguish between

gonorrhea and other bacteria that naturally inhabit the respiratory system.[59] A later study confirmed the finding that the test was inaccurate
36 percent of the time.[60] In 1984, however, doctors were very happy with
their new test, which reduced the time needed to obtain results from two
days to just four hours. One study called it "accurate, reliable, and useful."[61] This may be why the Bragas decided to treat the boy very differently
from how they had treated any other child during their final interview
with him. They questioned Noel for seven hours: "Do you think it was
your father?" Joe asked, and Laurie followed up with, "Maybe it was your
dad?" All morning Noel insisted that he could remember nothing about
being abused, at one point driving Joe to say to him, "I know you are not
telling the truth because you said no one put their penis in your mouth."
They asked him to think it over after lunch, and when Noel returned he
admitted that Frank had abused him. Then he was allowed to leave the
interview room, and he reversed himself again.[62]

Frank and Ileana were arrested and jailed, and for months the pair
wrote love letters to each other every day. Frank was to be tried first,
and prosecutors used the Bragas' interview tapes to craft a lean and ingenious set of charges. Frank faced eight counts of sexual battery and
seven counts of lewd and lascivious assault against children, but prosecutors also included a final charge of aggravated assault. "On numerous
occasions," the document read, Frank had threatened the children, worn
frightening masks, locked kids in closets and given them drugs, danced
naked, fondled the children's genitals, and forced them to eat excrement.
The document connected each of these charges with an "and/or," making
the aggravated assault count a kind of clearinghouse for all of the children's stranger allegations. Under Florida criminal law, jurors only needed
to believe that one of these things had happened—it didn't at all matter
which—in order to return a guilty verdict.[63]

It did not help Frank Fuster that he was an awful defendant. Janet Reno's office discovered that Frank had two prior convictions on his criminal
record: one for first-degree manslaughter and the other, more ominously,
for lewd and lascivious assault on a minor. In 1982 Frank was convicted of
fondling a nine-year-old girl's chest and genitals through her clothes late
one night in a car after a party. Frank had always maintained his innocence, but that obviously looked very bad. His decision to marry a teenager
while in his thirties cannot have helped either. Frank also failed to make
a good impression in court. Against his attorney's advice, he repeatedly

held dramatic, rambling press conferences at which he would lash out at Reno, the district attorney's office, and the legal system in general. On the witness stand he went beyond denying that he had molested the children or danced with them in the nude, staking out some obscure technical grounds on which to claim that Ileana had not actually been running a babysitting service. He said he had never met many of the children he was accused of molesting, and when parents testified that they had often seen Frank in the house when they arrived to pick up or drop off their children, he called them liars. Once, he held a towel to his face, stopped answering questions, and seemed to go into a catatonic trance. His mother came over the railing, grabbed her son, and yelled in Spanish, "Be *strong*, Frank! Be *strong* like your mother! Be *strong* against the enemy."[64]

Ileana was a trickier case. Trying a strange, self-aggrandizing man with prior convictions for child abuse was one thing, but what to do with the shy, obviously naïve teenager? If the abuse had occurred in anything like the manner described by prosecutors, Ileana must have seen it, and according to the Bragas' interviews, she had also participated. Yet she sat in jail for months, alternating between long stays in solitary confinement and stints in the general population, maintaining her innocence all the while. She withstood fourteen sessions with a well-known Miami psychiatrist named Charles Mutter as well as pressure from her lawyer, Michael Von Zamft, who believed Frank was a pedophile and that Ileana should testify against him. She became so close with Shirley Blando, the jail's chaplain, that she began to call her "Mom Shirley," and in a later deposition Blando said Ileana frequently talked about a lack of trust in her attorney. "She was afraid of her lawyer," Blando said. "She would say, 'They want me to say something that is not true.'"[65] Ileana also allowed, in one of her conversations with Blando, that Frank had hit her once. Von Zamft hoped he could persuade Ileana to depict herself as another of Frank's victims.

Ileana was removed from the jail's general population and returned to isolation in the summer of 1985. Years later she claimed that she was periodically kept naked, cold, crying, and depressed in a cell numbered 3A1.[66] During her time in the cell she began to say that Frank had hit her not once but on multiple occasions, that he had pressured her into having sex with him soon after they met, and that he had also hit his son, Noel. This description of a relatively common form of spousal abuse was a start, but Ileana maintained through the end of July that she had never seen

Frank molest children, and a psychiatrist who examined her concluded that she "did not have any sort of amnesia or memory disturbance." So Von Zamft brought in another psychiatrist, Norman Reichenberg, to have a look at his client. He concluded that Ileana, in essence, was "an extremely needy child" who had fallen completely under the sway of her brutal and domineering husband. In a subsequent competency hearing, Von Zamft told a judge that Ileana's extreme psychological dependence upon Frank would make it impossible to defend herself while standing trial alongside him. "The only valid defense that counsel perceives in this case," Von Zamft said, "requires that this defendant be prepared to give testimony against the codefendant."[67]

Von Zamft had essentially promised Ileana's confession. Now Ileana needed to provide it. It was at this point that Country Walk's character changed, as for the first time, a ritual abuse investigation began to apply some of the techniques developed by multiple personality therapists to a defendant. Von Zamft contacted Michael Rappaport and Merry Sue Haber, two psychologists with a practice called Behavior Changers. The pair quickly developed an intense interest in Ileana. Later Michael told a journalist that he billed the state of Florida for between thirty-five and forty hours, and he told a judge that he spent more time with Ileana than he had with any other patient in his professional career.[68] He also told the judge that over the course of his sessions with Ileana he had come to understand, as nobody else did, the depths of Frank's evil as well as the effects it had on his wife. "If you were a prisoner of war or if you were forced to play the violin when the Nazis were killing the Jews in a concentration camp," Rappaport said, "you might understand that people can be forced to do things."[69]

Rappaport and Haber walked Ileana through "relaxation" and "visualization" exercises. They asked Ileana to close her eyes, and then they described allegations the children had made and asked her to confirm them. "They would tell me the name of the children," Ileana said. "I couldn't remember all of them, so they would correct me again. And we would do this over and over until I got the memory piece that supposedly was missing."[70] Although these exercises failed to produce anything Ileana could recognize as an actual memory, she began to have vivid nightmares about abuse at Country Walk. She told the psychologists about these nightmares, and they assured her that she was beginning to remember. These assurances were supplemented, according to Ileana, by several nighttime visits from Janet Reno, who reminded Ileana that her testimony against Frank was necessary to avoid a lengthy prison term.[71] "It's a lot like reverse brainwashing," Rappaport told a reporter. "We just spent hours and hours talking to her. . . . It's kind of a manipulation." They told her that confessing to the abuse and testifying against Frank was in her best interest. "It was very much like dealing with a child," Rappaport said. "You make them feel very happy, then segue into the hard things."[72]

Just a few weeks after her first meeting with Rappaport and Haber, Ileana said for the first time that she and Frank were guilty. Then she gave a series of depositions. She said Frank had repeatedly raped her, that he had forced her to have oral sex with the children, and that he had inserted an unloaded gun into her vagina and fired blanks. (Even without bullets, this last one would have caused extremely serious injuries.) She said Frank had hung her from the ceiling of their garage while children watched and that he had poured acid on her once while she was in the shower. She also said that Frank had brought a snake into the house, scared the children with it, and then put it inside and on her body before finally depositing it in a bucket on the porch. Rappaport sat through these depositions with Ileana, and when she had trouble recalling details or said she could not remember, the psychologist would request a break so that the two of them could speak privately in a separate room. When they returned, Ileana would have the required details ready. "What did he do to you that night?" Ileana was asked at one point. "I can't remember now," Ileana said.

"You can't remember," Rappaport interjected, "or you don't want to?"[73]

Ileana pled guilty. She testified against her husband in court, and then she was sentenced to 10 years in prison. At Frank's trial jurors viewed videotapes of the Bragas' child interviews, and then Roland Summit appeared to explain that, because of the Child Sexual Abuse Accommodation Syndrome, leading questions were sometimes needed to "push" children through the "window of disclosure." The jury deliberated for two days, and then it convicted Frank on all charges. He was sentenced to six consecutive life terms in prison plus 15 years for parole violation, with a minimum total sentence of 165 years. The speed and efficiency with which Janet Reno was able to obtain her convictions indicated just how much the legal, medical, and psychiatric professions had learned, how enthusiastically they incorporated what had recently been fringe ideas as part of standard procedure. All of this happened very quickly: when Fuster went to prison, the McMartin trial still had not yet begun.

Chapter 6

McMartin—The Trial

The private evening conversations at which McMartin prosecutor Glenn Stevens expressed his doubts about the case and about Judy Johnson's mental health to screenwriters Abby and Myra Mann were finally made public in November 1986, about half a year after they had taken place. The trial itself was still nowhere in sight—jury selection hadn't even begun. The case had been mired in motions and procedural hearings for nearly a year. Stevens's skepticism about the merits of the case, however, was extensively reported in the *Easy Reader*, the *Los Angeles Times*, the *Daily Breeze*, and other newspapers, and it sparked a brief media scrum that was reminiscent of McMartin's breathless early days. Myra and Abby were both summoned to testify about the Stevens tapes, and although Myra's testimony in particular was inconsistent and vague, the important facts were eventually established. The Manns had paid Stevens $1,000 for his time and had also promised him 5 percent of the profits from their future book and/or film. They were initially reluctant to give their tapes to the attorney general's office, Myra said, but their attorney had made it clear that not doing so left them vulnerable to obstruction of justice charges. At the end of her day on the stand, Myra apologized to reporters for her inconsistencies, explaining that she had been up late the night before, studying the tapes. "I was a banana head," she said.[1]

The tapes made problems for the prosecution that extended well beyond palace intrigue and workplace disagreements. Some of what Stevens said led to an investigation as to whether Lael Rubin had intentionally withheld information from Danny Davis and the other defense attorneys, including two documents that were obviously relevant to Judy Johnson's mental state in the initial stages of the investigation. One was a statement by Johnson in which she alleged that McMartin teachers had put staples in her son's ears and scissors in his eyes. The other was a letter Johnson wrote to an investigator claiming her son had been taken to Los Angeles International airport and then flown out of the city. The DA had originally received these statements during a time when the credibility of the children's allegations was very much up for debate, and Rubin was obligated by law to provide the McMartin-Buckeys' attorneys with any exculpatory evidence her office uncovered. Instead, Rubin filed the statements away, and the McMartin defense team went about its business completely unaware of Judy Johnson's mental health issues. "My negligence was responsible for it not being turned over," Rubin said on the witness stand. She said she had simply forgotten about the report "under the crush of work" and that there had been no malicious intent behind the lapse.[2] A judge believed Rubin and denied Danny Davis's motion to declare a mistrial. A few weeks later Glenn Stevens received partial immunity from criminal prosecution—he faced the possibility of being charged with obstruction of justice and unauthorized removal of a public record—in exchange for his testimony. He told Danny Davis about keeping Judy Johnson's strangest allegations secret, and then he said, "I no longer believe that [Ray Buckey] is legally guilty."[3]

Stevens's testimony capped a very bad couple of months for his former office. November had also seen the first nationally televised report expressing skepticism that the McMartin children had ever been abused. 60 Minutes was then the most prestigious news program in the country, and Mike Wallace's report provided both sympathetic portrayals of the defendants and straightforward critiques of the prosecutors and therapists. "The United States has the rottenest judicial system in the whole world," Virginia McMartin said. "Don't let anybody talk to me about Russia or South Africa or anything. We have it right here." Babette Spitler talked about having her own children taken away, and Peggy Ann said she wanted to get her teaching credentials back. The report gave District Attorney Ira Reiner some space in which to maneuver; he had replaced Robert Philibosian at the end of 1984, and he blamed his predecessor for filing charges against so many people without conducting a thorough investigation. "You're charging Philibosian with an unprofessional job," Wallace said in his interview with Reiner, who replied, "Well, that hardly begins to describe it."[4]

Lael Rubin appeared in the *60 Minutes* piece as well. The word for her affect is probably "embattled." "Very large numbers of children were molested at the school," Rubin said, refusing to address her case's diminished size following Reiner's decision to drop charges against five of the seven original defendants. "I don't see that at this point whether one says there were fifty, or one hundred, or two hundred, or three hundred—that is really beside the point at this point in time. . . . The issue is that children were molested at the school, whether there be two or whether there be a hundred!" Wallace responded by arguing that the difference between two molested children and one hundred molested children was actually very significant—two child victims and one adult defendant would never have received so much media attention. Then he asked Rubin about the allegations of Satanism that had floated around during the preliminary hearing, and Rubin would not disavow them entirely. "We did have testimony at the preliminary hearing," she said, "about some activities that I suppose one would refer to as Satanic."

The piece finally pivoted to Ray Buckey, speaking to a journalist for the first time since his arrest more than three years earlier. He was visibly angry. "You gotta have a scapegoat," he said, making use of the term at the heart of his lawyer's theory of social panic, when asked why Reiner had dismissed charges against all of the defendants except for him and his mother, Peggy. "You kept two people in jail for two years. You're gonna back off now and say, 'Sorry, they're innocent too'? It's an amazing fact that you can have the same evidence, with the same children testifying against all seven, but you can say there's weak evidence against five of them." Wallace asked Buckey what he planned to do if he eventually went free. "They've ruined my life," Buckey said. "I hadn't made up my mind of what I wanted to do in life. But they've put a scarlet letter on me that I can never get rid of. I don't know what kind of life I could have."[5]

The *60 Minutes* story, the dropped charges, and the Glenn Stevens debacle marked a qualitative change in how people talked and thought about McMartin, but the shift wasn't immediate. As attorneys prepared to work through what they expected to be a grueling jury selection process, a university professor surveyed Angelenos and found that 97.4 percent of those who knew about the case thought Ray Buckey was guilty (92 percent believed the same of Peggy McMartin Buckey). At the same time, the survey also found that 42.4 percent of respondents thought the therapists had planted ideas in the children's heads, with 22 percent believing that the

satanic allegations were absurd on their face.[6] Other developments around
the South Bay in early 1987 may have reinforced these beliefs. In Hermosa
Beach the Sheriff's Department told parents of some forty children who
had allegedly been molested at St. Cross Episcopal Church that the case
was being officially closed. This was the church to which some McMartin
parents believed their children had been taken in the middle of the night
for satanic rituals. The deputy district attorney in charge of the case said
her decision not to prosecute was based on the complete lack of physical
evidence and corroborative testimony. The St. Cross parents said they were
disappointed. "We can't go away because the pain won't go away," one said.
"Our children are still having nightmares from what happened to them."[7]

As therapists and police had formalized their techniques in the mid-
1980s, making them easier to disseminate to other parts of the country, so
now did skepticism of the child care and ritual abuse investigations take
on a methodical and systematic quality. Journalists began to work out how
these cases had come to trial in the first place, and by identifying the really
crucial institutions, legislative developments, and therapeutic and medical
practices, they began to make these bewildering trials intelligible to the
public. In March 1987, for example—jury selection in the McMartin trial
had *still* not begun—Kevin Cody wrote a cover story for the *Easy Reader*
called "A Rat in the Hall of Justice." Its subject was George Freeman, a
convicted felon who briefly shared a jail cell with Ray Buckey in 1984. He
testified at the preliminary hearing, and he also met with Wayne Satz at
KABC to submit to a polygraph examination. (American courts do not
admit the results of lie detector tests as evidence because of their inherent
unreliability.) He said Ray admitted to molesting children at McMartin,
even going into significant detail about the brand of lubricant he would
use. He also said Buckey confirmed the allegations about pornography
and interstate child prostitution. The whole McMartin family had been
shooting videos and dropping kids off around the country since Ray was
fourteen years old, according to Freeman. "*Eyewitness News* takes no
position whatsoever," Wayne Satz said on his evening broadcast, "as to
whether George Freeman should be believed or disbelieved."[8]

George Freeman probably didn't represent too much of a threat at
the upcoming trial. He had multiple convictions preceding his time in
jail with Ray Buckey as well as charges pending from arrests that took
place after the preliminary hearing. But Freeman was only one of *seven*
informants preparing to testify against Buckey—the *Easy Reader*'s story

was not about Freeman in particular but rather the DA's informant program as a whole. Cody identified a number of cases, mostly gang and
drug related, in which LA prosecutors won convictions solely on the
strength of informants' eyewitness testimony. Some of these informants,
he noted, had testified in as many as ten separate cases, making them
ostensible witnesses to a really extraordinary number of violent crimes.
In Ray Buckey's early days in jail, prisoners who worked as informants
were cycled through his cell in such quick succession that Danny Davis
asked him to carry a sign around the jail: "I do not talk or listen to other
inmates."[9] For the informants themselves, one public defender told Cody,
fabricating confessions had become something like a legal means of last
resort, the only way to make any kind of progress with their own charges.
"The name of the game in county jail is to be an informant," the attorney
said. "It seems if you want to get any type of action on your own case you
become an informant."[10] Another attorney said the problem became especially acute in cases that were already receiving lots of media attention.
"I don't think it's possible to have a client in county jail in a high publicity
case without having informants come forward," he said. "If you taped his
mouth shut you'd have informants saying he confessed in sign [language]
or in a note."[11]

Cody documented Lael Rubin's repeated use of jailhouse informants
in her work. In the last case she prosecuted before taking on McMartin
she asked a multiple child murderer named Manuel Cortez to testify at
the preliminary hearing of a man charged with the murder of a diplomat
at the Turkish consulate in Los Angeles. Cortez's testimony was the prosecution's only evidence that the murder had been politically motivated,
and when he suddenly vowed to rescind his statement if asked to testify
at trial, other informants were quickly rotated in to take his place. Some
attorneys wondered why, if the district attorney's office really believed these
defendants were so quick to talk about their crimes in jail, they bothered
trying to wrangle this endless procession of unreliable criminals. There
were other, perfectly legal ways of monitoring prisoners' conversations: "If
the DA wants to know what a defendant really said," Forrest Latiner, Peggy
Ann's attorney, asked, "why doesn't he get a court order to bug the cell?" In
fact, the DA *had* obtained a secret order to record conversations between
Ray and his mother as they were shuttled around in police cars to view the
CII tapes with their lawyers. Rubin told Cody that any evidence obtained
from those recordings would be presented at Ray's trial. None ever was.

One article of faith among those who supported the prosecution in child care abuse and sex ring investigations was that these cases had come out of nowhere. That such violence could be committed in such loving communities for so long seemed unreal and impossible. This partly explains why parents put so much emphasis on *belief* when they talked about the allegations. A certain blind faith was needed to bridge the gap that separated parents' memories and experiences of ordinary life from the horror stories that now occupied so much of their time. Without this faith, even those who thought all of the McMartin teachers were guilty had no way of understanding what had happened.

Cody's cover story, then, wasn't only important because of the light it threw on George Freeman's testimony; it also demystified McMartin by explaining how a small but very concrete element of the trial had come to be. It showed how a familiar institution—the same institution that handled robbery, drunk driving, and other common crimes—had contributed to a narrative that bordered on the supernatural. The informant program was such a well-established part of how criminal law worked in Los Angeles that workers in the DA's office informally referred to one county jail employee as the "snitch liaison," phoning him up when they needed someone to be housed next to an arriving inmate. The *Easy Reader* made McMartin seem less exceptional, more like other cases, more like other instances of prosecutorial overreach. This made McMartin easier to criticize in other ways too.

Parents responded to this growing skepticism quickly, though not always productively. In late spring two groups called Affirming Children's Truth (ACT) and We Believe the Children held a meeting to denounce society's denial of child sexual abuse. Some one hundred parents gathered at the Manhattan Beach Country Club and listened as Roland Summit argued that "it is hard to find parallels for our society's indifference to what happened to your children." Summit talked a little about Freud and the seduction theory, and then he gave what he thought was the appropriate analogy: "The parallel that comes to mind is Germany's treatment of its Jews during World War II." Another father mentioned war crimes. "Denial, cover-up, shifting of blame—the comparisons to My Lai are scary," he said. John Jackson, author of the defunct "McMartin Watch" column, was there, and so was Jan Hollingsworth, whose book *Unspeakable Acts* would serve for years as the definitive pro-prosecution account of the Country Walk case.[12] Jackson told the audience that skepticism had to be taken seriously and countered in public. "Public opinion, not the law, will be the deciding factor in the McMartin case," he said. "As custodians of your children's truth you must mobilize public opinion."[13]

Jury selection began in April 1987. Parents stood in the back of the courtroom with signs that read "I BELIEVE THE CHILDREN" as trial Judge William Pounders worked his way through a pool of five hundred potential jurors. Prosecutors and defense attorneys eventually agreed on seven men and five women. In the opening statement she delivered on July 13, Lael Rubin told those jurors to pay attention to the child witnesses. "You will need to listen to them," she said. "They have gone through a long and difficult process of disclosure, of retrieving, recognizing and re-calling events of the past."[14] In the opening statement he delivered the fol-lowing day, Dean Gits, Peggy McMartin Buckey's attorney, walked the jury through some of what had occurred during the previous three years. "There were 22 people employed on a full-time basis with the sheriff's task force in order to investigate other suspects connected with the McMartin Preschool," he said.[15] Gits added that he did not and probably never would know how many FBI agents had contributed to the investigation, "but we do know that as many as seven different FBI agents were working full-time on the case." What did all those people spend all that time doing?

> They searched 21 residences, seven businesses—when I say seven businesses, understand that that's seven. . . . They searched 37 cars and three motorcycles and one farm. And they searched for all these things here: child pornography, nude pictures of students, records, diaries, et cetera, evidence of mutilated or dead animals, bank ac-count records, evidence of scientific analysis and hidden wall and floor safes. Those were some of the things that they were investigat-ing. They also interviewed a lot of people. . . . At least 450 children were interviewed and probably a minimum of 150 adults.[16]

What else? "There were a total of 49 photo lineups that were shown," Gits said. "Presumably, unless the police department was making up suspects, somebody had pointed to each one of the persons in the 49 photo lineups." In addition, eighty-two separate locations, including four churches, "two food markets, two car washes, two airports, one photogra-phy studio, one exercise club, and one national park" had been searched. From the preschool police had seized twenty blankets, twelve items of children's clothing, nine rags, four towels, sheets, underpants, sponge mops, spiral notebooks, and soil samples.[17] They reviewed customs records, real estate filings, and utility records, and they sifted through thousands of pornographic images. This search, Gits said, had turned up no corroborative evidence whatsoever. "So we believe the money spent was well worth it," he said.[18]

Gits was able to make a few brief, sarcastic references to the satanic allegations because it is during the opening and closing statements that attorneys enjoy the most rhetorical freedom. The interactions between attorneys and witnesses that make up the majority of a criminal trial, however, are bound by a much narrower set of guidelines. In dropping charges against five of the seven McMartin defendants, Ira Reiner had also dropped the charges associated with those child witnesses whose testimony had provoked so much controversy during the preliminary hearing. Of the hundreds of children interviewed at CII, only thirteen were scheduled to testify at trial, and prosecutors intended to be much more careful about the kinds of testimony they solicited from these witnesses. It was important to avoid any more headlines about Chuck Norris's participation in satanic rites. As one report noted, a case that had originally made headlines as the "crime of the century" was now being presented as a "vanilla 288(a)," meaning, simply, "lewd and lascivious acts on a child under 14 years of age."[19]

Dropping these charges allowed prosecutors to avoid talking about some of the work they had been occupied with during the previous three years. With few exceptions, an attorney may only ask a witness about charges that directly pertain to that witness, meaning that much of the substance of the McMartin investigation would make no appearance at the trial. On the one hand, it is definitely better to be charged with molesting thirteen children than to be charged with molesting twenty or four hundred of them. On the other hand, the prosecution's lean new charging document meant the jury would not hear much of the information that made the McMartin investigation intelligible, that it would be insulated to the greatest possible extent from the skepticism that was beginning to circulate more freely in Los Angeles. A trial is a world of its own, and this is good and appropriate for the law but not so good for some other things.

The trial settled into a rhythm. One by one, each of the prosecution's complaining child witnesses testified, with parents appearing afterward to talk about nightmares and behavioral changes. One child told Rubin about being made to play naked movie star. "Did you hear anything that led you to believe that someone was taking pictures?" Rubin asked.

"Yes," the girl said. "Clicking." She and her classmates "assumed there were cameras," she said, and even though she never saw a person actually taking photographs during the naked game, she "could just see the lens sometimes."[20] The child said in a straightforward way that Ray had told her to remove her clothes, but much else in her testimony had a slight tinge of unreality, of being able to see the lens but not the person wielding it or of "assuming" there were cameras as opposed to seeing that there were cameras. Her description of Ray's threats had a similar dreamlike quality. After naked movie star, she said, Ray came into the classroom with a cat:

> Q: What, if anything, did Ray do with the cat when he came in the class-room with it?
> A: Well, he like brought it in and, like, on top of a paper bag, and he, umm, he just put it down on the table.
> Q: Did Ray say anything about the cat?
> A: No. But it was dead. And then he cut it in the side.[21]

The child also provided the standard recovered memory explanation for her initial denials. "It was, like, so far back in my mind," she said of the memories, "and it was starting to come forward, but I did not want it to." Rubin asked her why not. "Because it was, like, really scary and embarrassing."[22]

Many days were spent on the medical evidence. Astrid Heger and the other doctors who examined the children in 1983 and 1984 had used colposcopes to take photographs of the McMartin students' genitals and anuses, and now these slides were projected onto a screen in the courtroom. On direct examination expert witnesses for the prosecution said the giant, magnified anuses were "significantly deformed."[23] Then, on cross-examination, Danny Davis would show these witnesses slides they had not previously consulted and ask them to identify irregularities. The witnesses rarely picked out the same irregularities. These exchanges were very repetitive. Two journalists named Paul and Shirley Eberle attended almost every day of the trial, and the hours they spent staring at the col-poscopic slides seem to have marked them in ways that other aspects of the case did not. Listening to the lawyers discuss the hundreds of slides that were to be presented in the coming months, they recorded a lawyer sitting next to them as saying, "I wonder who are the real pornographers in this thing."[24] That is a bit of a cheap shot, but it is true that no other photographs of the McMartin children's genitals were ever found. Later, sitting quietly and staring yet again at a "blazing giant anus," a friend sat down next to them. "I see it's Anus Awareness Week again," she said.[25]

People can get used to almost any job, though. It wasn't more than a few months into the trial that Judge Pounders noticed that some of the jurors were not listening very diligently. He admonished one juror for his consistent late arrivals by accusing him of wasting taxpayer funds: "Just for the cost of this courtroom and the court staff—that doesn't have anything to do with the attorneys or their staffs—it costs us $7.70 a minute to keep this courtroom open."[26] Even when they did show up, it became difficult to keep some of the jurors awake. "I think we may have a problem with the jurors sleeping during the proceedings," Danny Davis told Judge Pounders one morning. "Enough people have brought this information to me that I felt it necessary to bring it to your attention."[27] Judge Pounders brought the jury into the courtroom and admonished them, as he would do many times in the future.

Outside the courtroom and outside Los Angeles, the struggle to mobilize public opinion intensified. Ellen Willis was a radical feminist writer and editor at the *Village Voice* in New York when she watched the *60 Minutes* report on McMartin. At the time, the *Voice* had national reach and regularly published investigative pieces on stories from around the country. Willis called Debbie Nathan, a journalist living in El Paso, Texas, and asked whether she would travel to Manhattan Beach and do some reporting. Nathan had a small child at the time and couldn't go, but as it happened, juries had recently convicted two former child care workers at El Paso's East Valley YMCA of abusing, raping, and photographing children. Gayle Stickler Dove, who was thirty-one years old when police arrested her at a Halloween party in 1985, received three life sentences plus 60 years. Michelle "Mickey" Noble turned herself in the day after Dove was arrested. She received a life sentence plus 311 years. Willis told Nathan she could look into that case instead.

These trials seemed to take on slightly more than their fair share of local color. If professional screenwriters could have a material influence on a day care trial that originated just twenty minutes south of Hollywood, then of course Michelle Noble in El Paso could have her trial overseen by a judge who referred to himself as a "cowboy" and also talked like one, saying once of the trial's enormous cost, "It ain't nothing new in the world. Justice runs high."[28] That said, there wasn't much that happened in El Paso that hadn't already happened in Bakersfield, Miami, or Jordan. A mother and father called the police after becoming convinced that somebody was molesting their son during his morning sessions at the YMCA. A detective and a social worker were called in to conduct interviews, which initially produced almost no useful testimony (the children were three and four years old). The social worker and the detective kept trying. Soon Noble and Dove were accused of driving the children to Noble's house, allowing them to be raped by unknown men, and forcing them to urinate and defecate while they made videos. Parents formed a support group called HELP, which stood for "Help Educate Little People," and they met every Wednesday to talk about new developments.[29] Dove and Noble were tried separately by Assistant District Attorney Debra Kanof, who called their alleged crimes "a murder of childhood, a murder of innocence."[30]

Kanof and her team benefited enormously from the investigations that preceded their own. The prosecutor said she knew El Paso had its own McMartin from the minute she saw the reports on the first boy to have alleged abuse. She kept in touch with Kee MacFarlane, whose work she admired. She responded to people who thought the child interviews were unreliable by talking about Freud betraying his "hysterics" in the nineteenth century.[31] When Marina Gallardo, the social worker, was confronted about her interviewing technique in court, she admitted that she had erred, describing a video of one of her own sessions as "one of the worst leading and suggestive interviews that I have ever witnessed."[32] She then fell back on an excuse previously used by Kee MacFarlane, saying, "I didn't care about the legal aspects of the case. I just wanted to get the truth out."[33] When asked about a child who recanted all of his allegations when interviewed in front of a video camera, she talked in the vocabulary of Summit's Child Sexual Abuse Accommodation Syndrome, claiming such reversals were common products of a child's desire to forget.[34]

They also benefited from legislation that others had pioneered. As Debbie Nathan finally reported in the *Voice* in the late summer of 1987, bills passed in 1983 made it possible for video of the child interviews in El Paso to be presented in court in lieu of the testifying children themselves.

This was a coup for the prosecutors. Parents are widely seen as the people best able to understand and interpret their children's needs and moods, and nobody expects them to videotape family conversations or adhere to a rigid set of interviewing protocols. Watching mothers and fathers take the witness stand, one after the other, and dissolve into anguished sobs just minutes into their testimony must also have been powerful. Nathan wrote that "because the parents were supposed to speak for their children, they tended to use baby talk, a style soon adopted by everyone from prosecuting attorneys to the press."[35] Lawyers had already made and distributed photographs of Michelle Noble's breasts to prove she had scars from a breast reduction surgery two years prior (despite claiming that they had been made to suck on Noble's breasts, none of the children mentioned the scars), and now Noble had to listen as parents and then prosecutors began to refer to her by the alliterative nickname her kids had used at the Y, "Miss Mickey."[36] One father, a retired police officer, imitated his child's inflection, tone, and vocabulary on the stand. Afterward he described his experience as cathartic. "I tried to be my son," he said. "I wanted to bring it out just like he told me. I wanted to feel like I felt when he was telling me."[37]

An important part of a trial attorney's job is to model, for the benefit of the jury, belief in either the defendant's innocence or guilt. Danny Davis occasionally joked around with Ray Buckey on the witness stand because of course you would only joke around with someone who *hadn't* sexually molested a bunch of children. By the same token, a prosecutor has to perform distaste for the defendant and demonstrate solidarity with the victims and their families. As Nathan documented at length, Debra Kanof put a lot of work into these performances. At one point during the trial the defense tried to address a child's claim that Michelle Noble had kept a decorated Christmas tree in her house when she brought children over for abuse. As the abuse was thought to have occurred during the summer, this was a strange allegation, but defense attorney Charlie Roberts then called one of Noble's former coworkers to the stand, and she explained that it was *her* house the children had seen, that she lived very close to the Y, and that they had come by one day in December and eaten cookies in front of her decorated tree. Kanof responded by speculating that Noble had deliberately set up a Christmas tree in her living room out of season so as to frustrate any future attempts by the children to describe their experiences.[38] Kanof also told reporters, on the basis of no evidence presented in any courtroom, that Noble had filmed the children in order to profit from her involvement in a "national porn ring out of Kansas."[39] She waited until Noble's husband, William, was seated in the witness box to inform him that, as he was now a suspect, he might want to retain legal counsel of his own. She saved her pet theories for moments that maximized their dramatic impact. In her closing arguments Kanof wondered aloud about the children's accounts of having plastic syringes inserted into their anuses. She pointed out that some children had also mentioned being made to defecate before a camera, and she said the syringes were likely the plastic tips of enemas. A reporter heard one parent sitting in the gallery exclaim, "Oh, God."[40]

Nathan's piece wasn't the only skeptical coverage Dove and Noble's trials received. Although the local news media had more than its fair share of lapses, it also noted Kanof's aggressiveness, the major implausibilities in the children's allegations, and Gallardo's leading interviewing techniques. But these reports didn't cover the material that Nathan explored in a second article she wrote that appeared in the same issue of the *Voice*. In "Sex, the Devil, and Daycare," Nathan called the day care sex abuse cases a panic and tried to explain why they were happening. She outlined a history of the country's waxing and waning interest in child abuse, tracing a line through the Victorians' sensational cases of violent battery, the Progressive era's fight against neglect, and physicians' attempts to detect traces of physical trauma in the 1960s. She pointed out the vanishing rarity of day care abuse as a proportion of child abuse as a whole, the vast majority of which is committed in private homes by relatives or close family friends. "A mere 1.7 percent of all reported child abuse—including beatings and neglect—is committed by teachers or other paid caretakers not related to the child," Nathan wrote. "And of that miniscule proportion, only one-tenth is thought to involve sexual abuse."[41] The implications of that last statistic are worth lingering over: for all the anxious news reports describing sexual abuse in day care as an "epidemic" in American life, it actually constituted less than two-tenths of 1 percent of the problem.

Nathan also tried to explain the origins of this strange obsession with abuse in day care. Her editor, Ellen Willis, had for years offered radical feminist critiques of antipornography feminists, arguing that activists like Catharine MacKinnon and Andrea Dworkin promoted narratives of helplessness and victimization that denied women's sexual curiosity and played into reactionary hands. Nathan's politics were similar—she believed the imaginary horrors of day care distracted people from the real issue:

> The people who have stared most unflinchingly at the glaring connection between sexual abuse and the patriarchal nuclear family have been feminists. They have examined power arrangements inside the family, then shown how child battering, wife battering, and incest are linked to extramural violence like rape. But in the Reaganite 1980s feminist consciousness raising about sexual violence hadn't led to a critique of the family; rather, it had encouraged moralism against evil people and narrowly legalistic remedies.[42]

Family life was in the midst of a transformation, Nathan wrote, evolving and rearranging in response to consumerism, reproductive technology, and women's migration into the workplace. "But it seems that the weaker the family gets, the holier its image." Day care made a perfect scapegoat: "If the private family is sacred, the public child-care center is profane. If stay-at-home mothers are holy, then the people they pay to take care of their kids when they escape from the house are witches."[43]

It would be hard to say that Nathan's article directly helped Noble and Dove. There are whole sets of courtroom procedures devoted specifically to preventing journalists from influencing a trial's outcome, and in any case, both defendants had been convicted by the time the *Voice* published Nathan's article. These convictions were not the end of the story, however. In November 1987 an appeals court overturned Noble's conviction by ruling that the use of children's videotaped testimony violated her constitutional right to confront her accusers in court. The district attorney's office prepared to try her again. Dove's case was also thrown into chaos just six weeks after her conviction when a juror came forward to reveal that the jury had seen documents never admitted into evidence during the trial. They weren't incidental documents either—in an affidavit, juror Dorothy Gentleman said the notes, which were written by one of the children's mothers, played a decisive role in changing her verdict from not guilty to guilty. Also playing a role in Gentleman's reversal was the fact that, although she believed "there was no evidence except what the parents had said their child said," peer pressure from the other jurors turned out to be intense. "I was made to feel guilty for voting not guilty because I felt I would be branded as one who condones child abuse."[44] Noble was retried later that month, convicted a second time, and sentenced to twenty years in prison.

Nathan's reporting and analysis, commissioned by a radical feminist intellectual and published by the country's preeminent alternative weekly newspaper, came from the far-left wing of the political spectrum. But just as feminists and evangelicals had found common ground in their victim-centered opposition to pornography and abuse, ritual abuse skepticism attracted a politically diverse group of supporters as well. One of the earliest examples is Victims of Child Abuse Laws (VOCAL), a group that formed in Minneapolis in the wake of the Scott County sex ring investigations. The group was founded by a Lutheran minister and psychologist named Ralph Underwager, who, along with his wife, Hollida Wakefield, had been retained by attorneys for two of the Scott County defendants to analyze the child interviews. On Thanksgiving Day 1984, VOCAL held a service on the steps of the state capitol at which Underwager appeared in robes and led a group of parents and protesters in song and prayer. "Parents are being subjected to laws designed to place children's rights in an adversarial role against parents' rights," read VOCAL's press release. "The damage done by Child Protection people is often irreparable."[45] Underwager went on in the coming years to provide skeptical testimony in many child abuse trials, and he and Wakefield also began to publish their own journal, *Issues in Child Abuse Accusations*. Where Nathan saw the day care cases as proof of society's inability to come to terms with the family's complicity in child abuse, VOCAL saw the investigations as a hostile government attack on family life.

Two books soon followed in VOCAL's wake. Paul and Shirley Eberle, the married couple who attended much of the McMartin trial, published *The Politics of Child Abuse* in 1986. With the words, "What has America become if police and social workers can forcibly enter your home and take your children away without due process, without even probable cause, supported by nothing more than an anonymous phone call?" printed on the cover, the Eberles' book also saw the day care trials as government-sponsored attacks on the family. Shocking anecdotes from various trials alternated with long, seemingly unedited transcripts of interviews with people like Roland Summit and Peggy Ann Buckey. In one of these interviews, defense attorney Forrest Latiner pointed out that the Buckeys were themselves Republicans. "They voted for all those conservative, law-and-order initiatives," he said, "and they never in their wildest dreams suspected it would ever come back to haunt them."[46]

The Eberles themselves took conservatism a bit less ironically. In an interview with Lee Coleman, a psychiatrist who testified for the defense at many child abuse trials in the 1980s and 1990s, they brought up what they saw as the problem of anti-male bias among child protectionists. "There have been a number of books published in the past three years," they said, "written by radical feminists on child abuse—mostly incestuous—that are long, strident diatribes of hatred of the male."[47]

1986 also saw the publication of *The Child Abuse Industry: Outrageous Facts About Child Abuse & Everyday Rebellions Against a System That Threatens Every North American Family*, a book written by a home-schooling advocate named Mary Pride. "Was there anything in the current anti-family climate that could stop a social worker from lying in order to yank a child away from his natural parents?"[48] she asked in the book's introduction. According to Pride, the family was an institution that lacked any civil rights whatsoever, and the recent uproar about child abuse was simply a ploy by "those who dislike the traditional family" to further their own professional interests.[49] She wasn't entirely wrong about the dangers social workers posed to working-class and minority families. In the 1980s, as in the Victorian era, the specter of child abuse allowed upper-middle-class professionals to keep a wary eye on marginalized communities, and child protection workers were much more likely to remove children from poor or nonwhite homes than from their wealthier counterparts.[50] Pride's defense of minority communities was complemented, however, by a paranoid fear of government as well as a sexual politics that would have made James Dobson smile. She thought the "*real* roots of child abuse" were abortion, pornography, sexual infidelity, and no-fault divorce.[51] She also thought the government had instituted "compulsory 'death education' classes"[52] in public schools to promote teenage suicide, and she worried that state-mandated abortions were soon to come.[53]

Ritual abuse and mass molestation skepticism retained this political heterogeneity as it slowly proliferated in the late 1980s. A year after the publication of her El Paso report, Debbie Nathan returned to the *Voice* with an in-depth investigation of Kelly Michaels, a New Jersey day care teacher convicted in 1988 of abusing twenty small children at the Wee Care Day Nursery in Maplewood. Michaels had experimented sexually with women in college, a fact that compounded the difficulties she faced in court. Believing that jurors pulled from a community with such "small town attitudes" would be eager to associate homosexuality with other kinds of sexual deviance, Michaels's attorney decided he could not call character witnesses to testify for his defendant; the risks of exposing them to cross-examination that would reveal Michaels's sexual history were too great.[54] This was, to an extent, the focus of Nathan's piece: the way a community's mistaken ideas about pedophilia and child abusers could intersect with other sexual fears and anxieties. Two years later, however, when *Harper's* published its own article on the Michaels case by conservative pundit Dorothy Rabinowitz, these sexual dynamics were nowhere to be found. Rabinowitz didn't even mention Michaels's homosexual experiences, much less examine the crucial role they played in the case. Perhaps Rabinowitz worried, as Michaels's defense attorney had, about what people would think of an accused child molester who also turned out to be gay or at least not consistently, uniformly straight.

This political muddle notwithstanding, ritual abuse skepticism was on its way to mainstream respectability by the end of 1987. In Los Angeles the district attorney's office dropped six of its seven jailhouse informants from the witness list as a result of Kevin Cody's *Easy Reader* story, and George Freeman, the one who remained, did not reassure courtroom spectators about the reliability of jailhouse informants. Soon after he testified in the preliminary hearing, Freeman was arrested and charged with a number of crimes, including selling drugs, burglarizing his employer's property, driving under the influence, illegally possessing a gun, violating his parole, and stealing sheep. Then, before he was even allowed to say anything at trial about Ray Buckey's alleged confession, Freeman had to offer testimony about perjuries he had previously committed while testifying in other cases, in exchange for which Lael Rubin offered him immunity.[55] (He also admitted to having previously perjured himself about *those* perjuries.)[56] Freeman repeated his story about Ray Buckey on direct examination, but the following day's newspapers paid more attention to his exchanges with Danny Davis. "Tell us," Davis asked Freeman, "did you do something with some sheep?"

A: Yes, I did.

Q: And please tell us what did you do.

A: A friend of mine and I took four sheep from a guy I worked for, and I
   took them over to a friend of mine's house and sold to him, sold two
   of them. We was going to barbecue the other two.
Q: Did your boss, your employer, give you permission to take the sheep?
A: No, he didn't.
Q: And when you went—took the sheep, did you intend to borrow them,
   originally?
A: No, because he always talked about how nasty they were, and he was
   going to get rid of them and stuff.
Q: So you were doing him a favor?
A: Yeah, I figured I was. . . .
Q: When you took these sheep, I guess it was in the dark of night?
A: No. As a matter of fact, it was in the daytime in the fog. I had a hard
   time getting them.
Q: Running them down?
A: Excuse me, yes.

Judge Pounders momentarily broke off Davis's line of questioning.
"If this gets any funnier," he said, "we're going to have to take a break"—
Freeman's testimony was hard to hear over the laughter. Davis asked Free-
man what he did with the sheep once he managed to run them down.

A: Put them in the back of my boss's truck.
Q: Again, without his permission or knowledge?
A: Yeah. He was at the lake.
Q: Fishing?
A: No. He was recuperating from an automobile wreck where him and his
   two kids almost got killed.

It was at this point that Lael Rubin asked whether she might interrupt
the proceedings and approach the bench for a sidebar.[57]
    Every aspect of George Freeman's involvement in the case—every as-
pect of the DA's efforts to use jailhouse informants at all, in fact—was a
disaster for the prosecution. And yet Freeman was seen even at the time
as a relatively small episode in a case that had already run for four years
and that was expected to continue for another year at the very least. Judge
Pounders worried about the jury's ability to endure such a lengthy proceeding. Jurors continued to fall asleep, two had to be admonished for

passing notes back and forth, and one was excused from further service after suffering a stroke. In 1988 Pounders conferred with the attorneys on how to answer a juror's question about the trial's estimated length. "If we tell the jury 12 more months," he said, "they will get up en masse and attack us."[58] Lael Rubin suggested he fudge and say eight months, and everyone agreed. Kee MacFarlane testified. For the first time jurors watched videos of the interviews at CII. The Supreme Court ruled that testimony delivered via closed-circuit television violated a defendant's constitutional rights, parents pulled three children off the prosecution's witness list, and twenty-seven charges were subsequently dropped. Preparations for the future remained very much on everybody's mind. In the fall of 1987 Virginia McMartin spent a day testifying out of the jury's presence, in front of a video camera. She was eighty years old; the tape was stored away in case she died before being called to the stand.[59]

Sensing, perhaps, some new and really significant vulnerabilities in the prosecution's public opinion campaign, former defendants began to give interviews. In the summer of 1988 the *Los Angeles Times* published simultaneous profiles of Babette Spitler, Mary Ann Jackson, and Betty Raidor, McMartin teachers whose charges had not made it past the preliminary hearing. Raidor talked nostalgically about puttering around the garden and putting on dinners for friends at her house, which she and her husband had sold for $225,000 to help cover her legal expenses. She said she missed her two cats and two dogs, which weren't allowed in her new apartment complex. Mary Ann Jackson was the only defendant who didn't lose her home, but she said it was just recently that people stopped giving her suspicious looks and making remarks on the street when she went out with her grandchildren. To sustain herself after the arrest, she said, she read books by concentration camp survivors and turned to her religious faith.[60]

Babette Spitler had a harder time. After her arrest she and her husband tried to send their two children to live with relatives in San Diego under assumed names, but it only took the Manhattan Beach police a few weeks to learn where they had gone and bring them back to the South Bay. There the children were interviewed for six hours at the Children's Institute International and then sent to the county facility for neglected and "wayward" youth. They eventually returned to their relatives in San Diego, but Spitler later learned her children had felt guilty for months, terrified they said something at CII to make matters worse for their mother and the other teachers. After the charges were dropped and after Babette and her husband passed a battery of psychological tests, their children were finally returned—the family had been separated for two years. The Spitlers' house and savings were gone, and they tried hard to prevent their new neighbors from discovering their involvement in McMartin. Unlike Jackson and Raidor, Spitler was bitter. "I wanted a trial," she said. "When they dropped the charges, they said they didn't have enough evidence to convict me. They never said that Babs Spitler is innocent."[61]

Even more public than these profiles with their sympathetic photo illustrations was Peggy Ann Buckey's decision to try to win back her teaching credentials. Immediately after her arrest, the state's Commission on Teacher Credentialing had revoked Buckey's certification to teach communication-handicapped children and then waged a two-and-a-half-year battle to keep her out of the classroom for good. Buckey filed suit in superior court, and over the spring, summer, and fall of 1988 the commission held a hearing that resembled nothing so much as the McMartin trial in miniature. Two years after District Attorney Reiner dropped all charges against her, Buckey heard four children testify that she had molested them. Where criminal proceedings operate under a formal presumption of innocence, the credential hearing required that Buckey essentially prove she wasn't guilty. Abuse experts and alibi witnesses appeared on her behalf, and children rehashed their courtroom testimony about trips to a farm and a chopped-up pony.[62] The night before the commission announced its decision, Buckey drove through a snowstorm up Interstate 5 and through Kern County, breaking off to the west just before Bakersfield and arriving in Sacramento at three in the morning. She won her appeal and began teaching in the Anaheim Union High School District in February 1989.[63] She refused to go back to Manhattan Beach—she said she wouldn't even drive through town unless forced to by traffic.[64]

The everyday sense of panic around child abusers in day care centers was dissipating in greater Los Angeles. Newspapers began to discuss the panic's height as though the events of 1984 and 1985 lay in the more distant past. "Four years after the McMartin child molestation case burst over the South Bay's preschools, owners say that their nursery schools are filled to capacity and that time has eased most of the pressures generated by widespread sexual-abuse allegations," the Los Angeles Times reported in the spring of 1988.[65] Enrollment had plummeted in the months following Wayne Satz's first KABC report, but teachers believed that parents had regained their confidence in day care's safety. Allegations targeting other centers had failed to produce a single conviction, and when, in December of 1988, a sixteen-month-old was found strangled in a Lomita day care home, investigators were very vocal about wanting to avoid "sensational," McMartin-style speculation.[66] "The McMartin thing," said a spokeswoman for the state's preschool licensing agency, "is pretty much behind us."[67]

The effects of a panic, however, are not undone just because panicked people begin to calm down. Of the seven preschools closed by abuse allegations in 1984 and 1985, five never reopened, and in 1987 allegations of abuse emerged at the South Bay Center for Counseling, which had been established in 1984 specifically to care for children allegedly molested at other day care centers in Manhattan Beach, Hermosa Beach, and Torrance. (Colleen Mooney, the center's executive director and a witness for the McMartin prosecution, said of the allegations that "the important thing to remember is that the child was believed. [Child sexual abuse] can happen anywhere, any time.")[68]

Day care became more expensive as well, with schools that had reputations similar to McMartin's in 1983 charging $325 per month for daily service (adjusted for inflation today, that would be more than $750). One preschool instituted policies forbidding teachers from cleaning off children after bowel movements, and two teachers had to be present to deal with any child who complained about an "owie" on his or her genitals. These policies, like day care workers' increased reluctance to show physical affection to the children they cared for, sprang not from a belief that they protected children from abuse but from a desire to protect workers from false allegations. A similar desire was behind many preschools' decision to stop hiring men. Day care owners believed the sight of men caring for small kids was likely to make parents nervous.[69] Child care, then, was exclusively women's work, even when the women got paid for it.

A month after Peggy Ann Buckey learned her teaching credentials would be reinstated, Ray was released from the Los Angeles County Men's Central Jail on $1.5 million bail. He was thirty years old and had been incarcerated for nearly five years. His mother had been freed months earlier on $295,000 bail. He walked through a crowd of reporters to Danny Davis's car in complete silence. One condition of the release required Ray to surrender his passport. Another forbid him from having unaccompanied contact with anyone under the age of fourteen unless the child was a blood relative.[70]

Chapter 7

Two Families

The great yellow journalist Geraldo Rivera hosted the 1988 television special *Devil Worship: Exposing Satan's Underground* nine days before Halloween. The two-hour broadcast opened with a warning. "This program deals with devil worship and satanic beliefs," a narrator said. "Because of the program's theme and controversial subject matter, parental discretion should be exercised."[1]

Parents were at the center of *Exposing Satan's Underground* from start to finish. Cutting away to commercial breaks, Rivera repeatedly begged parents to get their young children out of the living room in anticipation of the next segment's gruesome content. (He encouraged teenagers, however, to watch along *with* their parents, as the program might help them recognize and avoid the attractions of Satanism.) After interviewing an eighteen-year-old serving a life sentence for an allegedly satanic murder, Rivera cut to the boy's mother and asked her to describe the months that preceded her son's crime. "Pete gradually withdrew from family life," she said. "That is probably one of the main things I noticed. He even got to where he avoided eating meals with us."

Parents also served as the program's voice of moral responsibility, with one father expressing his opinion on whether a practicing member of the Church of Satan should be allowed to serve in the military. "Well, I think in this election year we've heard a lot about values, Geraldo," he said. "We've heard a lot about our children, that little children should be saying the Pledge of Allegiance to the flag." He found it "inconceivable" that "we can have somebody in our army, as a colonel, leading our troops into battle who is opposed to the very concept of God, and whose whole purpose is to fight against God." The special cycled through interviews with therapists, detectives, Charles Manson, and a retired FBI officer, but Rivera never lost sight of his most important audience segment. "Coming up," he said before the final commercial, "we're going to have warning signs that you should watch for, parents."[2]

Rivera spent a lot of time on the day care cases, spelling out the link between Satanism and "the vilest crime of all: sexual abuse of children." Two-thirds of the way through he opened up a live satellite feed to a Manhattan Beach living room, where eleven McMartin parents sat facing the camera in two rows. "We know that the parents and children allege child abuse," Rivera said by way of introduction. "What is much less known is that they say it was ritual abuse as part of a satanic cult." These were the parents who had not been asked to provide testimony at the McMartin trial, whose children had not been included on the district attorney's official complaint. As though to compensate for their exclusion from the formal judicial proceeding, they had done more than any other group to pursue the satanic ritual abuse theory involving the McMartin Preschool. Geraldo asked the group's spokesman, Bob Currie, to explain why he believed the abuse had been satanic. Currie had an agitated affect on camera. He spoke a little too quickly and a little too loudly:

> Well the easiest reason to that question, Geraldo, is the fact that when the children started talking, they started talking about robes and candles. They described an Episcopal church. And once they started narrowing that down, you could see it had to be Satanic. It's very important in Satanic religions to have a priest, because they truly do believe in power. . . . The truth about Satanism is they truly do use blood, and they mix it with urine, and then they also use the real meat, the real flesh. This is what makes Satanism true, and this is what 1,200 molested kids in the city of Manhattan Beach have told the sheriff's department. And it's an outrage that we are where we are with this case, these poor, unprotected kids that have, uh, that's a third of the school system in the city of Manhattan Beach that's been molested. We have eight preschools closed here. This is the child molestation capital of the world. We have more preschools closed in this city than any city this side of Detroit, and I'm not picking on Detroit.[3]

Geraldo also broadcast a taped interview with four McMartin children. Seated outside on a sunny afternoon, he asked one girl what she meant when she said her teachers molested her. "Touching us in places we don't want," she replied. "They would scare us really much."[4]

A little more than a year later, many of these children returned to Geraldo's studio with their parents for an update on the trial. They were older now, some of them in adolescence, and when Peggy Ann Buckey appeared via satellite for an interview they visibly seethed with rage. Bob Currie's son said he and other kids had stayed up until three in the morning the night before the broadcast, telling stories about McMartin. When Peggy told Geraldo she was teaching again, someone in the audience yelled, "Don't send your kid to that teacher!" The children smiled as other audience members broke into loud cheers. When Peggy Ann Buckey called the whole case a witch hunt, a woman in the audience derisively yelled, "That's right! We're looking for witches, *aren't we*?"[5]

Most of the time parents were the only victims in full public view, speaking to reporters and founding activist groups while judges told journalists not to print the children's names. Watching the children on Geraldo tremble with such obviously authentic anger and fear, however, one begins to wonder just how much effort their parents put into stoking and encouraging that anger at home, how much the trials must have transformed their private lives. Some of the parents even managed to identify positive aspects of what would otherwise have been an unmitigated nightmare. "It was rather a lucky situation to have this happen in my family," Bob Currie said brightly during his second *Geraldo* appearance. "It allowed me the pleasure and the time to take full-time off work and develop this material."[6]

It is hard to know for sure, however, what effects Currie's mind-set, with its sadness, its rage, and its make-lemonade-out-of-lemons quality, had on his son. By the late 1980s research psychologists were beginning to comb through the child interviews therapists and detectives conducted in day care and sex ring cases, testing for the extent and limits of a child's suggestibility or the effects of a therapist telling a subject that all of his friends already told what happened.[7] These studies were possible because there were transcripts and videotapes of the interviews to study. But nobody transcribed the conversations that took place in the car going to or from Children's Institute International, nor did anybody set recording devices on mantelpieces around the South Bay as parents asked their children about McMartin in 1984. This makes it difficult to understand just what the ritual abuse cases did to the families they swept up or how the investigations changed their ways of talking and thinking.

By the second half of the 1980s, with Ronald Reagan in office and populist evangelical conservatism at its peak, profamily rhetoric was politically triumphant. A central element of the neoconservative surge that began in the 1970s, this rhetoric was such an effective instrument of the Republican social agenda that only the most radical leftists even bothered trying to challenge it. Feminists were one such radical group. "As our cultural myth would have it," Ellen Willis wrote, "the family is not only a haven in a heartless world but a benign Rumpelstiltskin spinning the straw of lust into the gold of love."[8] But critiques like these never became part of mainstream discourse, according to which the nuclear family was just as sacred to the American way of life as the Constitution. How people actually lived, however, suggested much more ambivalence about the benefits and costs of family life. The 1980s were also a decade in which the national marriage rate continued a steady decline that had begun in the sixties and seventies, and for those who stayed married, the single-income household with a male breadwinner in the workplace and a housewife preparing meals became a perpetually unattainable ideal. Americans had sex and raised children as they had in the past, but most of them no longer had those experiences in the context of a single marriage that would last for the rest of their lives. 40 percent of all Americans born in the 1970s spent at least some time living with a single parent, but politicians in the 1980s almost never recognized these experiences except to condemn them.[9]

The McMartin parents on *Geraldo*, with their angry paeans to child protection and harsh justice, said all of the things people expect nuclear families to say when speaking in public. But the private experiences of families involved in different day care and ritual abuse cases around the country were much less straightforward, and families' private reactions to those experiences were often colored by ambivalence and confusion. Feelings of anger, guilt, and victimization sometimes overlapped to such an extent that they could not be distinguished from one another. This is true of families with alleged child victims, families with alleged abusers, and families with both. Fortunately—and unfortunately, as it turned out—at least one of these families made extraordinarily detailed documents of their own.

Before he led chemistry classes as a Long Island schoolteacher, Arnold Friedman made a brief go at a career in music. He spent his twenties playing Latin jazz at resorts in the Catskills under the stage name "Arnito Rey," and for years afterward he gave piano lessons in his family's living room. In 1982 Arnold began to supplement these music lessons with computer classes conducted in his basement on 8-bit Commodore 64s. The desktop computer was still a new invention then, but Great Neck was an affluent town where people wanted the best for their children, and familiarity with this new technology would look good on college applications years down the line. Arnold soon had classes running almost every night of the week.

Arnold and his wife, Elaine, had three children of their own: David, Seth, and Jesse. The boys inherited their father's love of performance. Equipped with home video cameras, the brothers put on sketch comedy shows and musical performances for one another around the house, and they also took their act out on the town, using vegetables as pretend microphones while conducting man-on-the-street interviews at grocery stores. These videos were the connective tissue of their relationships with one another and with their father, who often joined in the fun by playing a role or providing musical accompaniment. Elaine was not involved; she was less outgoing than her husband and children, and she was sometimes made to feel bad about not keeping up with their endless stream of jokes. But she and Arnold believed their family was a happy one, more or less. In 1984, at the age of fifteen, Jesse began to help out with his father's basement computer classes. He was the youngest member of the family.

A pedophile is not the same thing as a child abuser. "Pedophile" refers to anyone who is sexually attracted to prepubescent children, whereas a child abuser is someone who actually acts on those desires. Whether Arnold Friedman was a child abuser became a very controversial topic in the late 1980s, but there is no question that he really was a pedophile. It is probably impossible to know for sure when and where Arnold's sexual troubles began. Maybe in childhood, maybe in adolescence; maybe it had something to do with his younger brother, Howard.[10] What is known is that his legal problems began in 1984, when postal inspectors intercepted a package containing child pornography, sent from the Netherlands and addressed to Arnold Friedman's home in Great Neck. On its own, simply receiving child porn in the mail did not constitute a crime. In order to make an arrest, the government needed Arnold to send something back. "What we would do then," a postal inspector said in an interview, "is initiate a correspondence with Arnold so that we can determine whether he is in fact willing to violate the statute."[11] It took three years of cajoling letters, but the government, posing as a fellow pedophile in search of magazines, finally got Arnold to send a package containing child porn (the enclosed note read, "Enjoy!"). Then the Feds arrived at the Friedman house one day in 1987 with a search warrant. They found a stack of magazines behind the piano in the basement.[12]

They also found a partial list of students who attended the computer classes. Once the police realized that Friedman had groups of children in his basement almost every night of the week, they decided they were dealing with a different kind of investigation. They brought in a detective named Fran Galasso, then working as the head of the Nassau County Police Department's Sex Crimes Unit, to organize a group of detectives to interview Friedman's current and former students.

In 2003 a director named Andrew Jarecki released his documentary film *Capturing the Friedmans*, in which he spoke with a number of those who were involved in the interviews that followed Arnold's arrest. The computer students were eight, nine, and ten years old. "They came in and they said, 'We know something happened to [your son],'" one father recalled. "They didn't say 'Believe.' They said, 'Know.'" Ron Georgalis, who attended the classes and insisted that nothing criminal took place, remembered listening in on police officers' initial conversations with his parents. "I remember actually eavesdropping on what they said [happened]. And what they said made my heart race." Other students experienced the kind of badgering and harassment that characterized other child care abuse investigations. "They told me repeatedly that other students in my class had already told them that they had been abused," one former student said, "and that they were certain that in fact I had also been abused and that I should tell them so."

Detective Galasso's substantial experience with child abuse investigations notwithstanding, the officers who made up her team were not experts of any kind. One, perhaps taking inspiration from film noir or police procedurals, referred to a reluctant child interviewee as a "wise guy," and the questionnaire used by another contained the query, "Have you ever been touched by anyone?"[13] One child went through fourteen police interviews without describing any wrongdoing in the basement. When police arrived for the fifteenth and final visit, they assured the child's mother that they were going to stay for "as long as it takes." Anthony Squeglia, one of the detectives who worked on the case as part of Fran Galasso's team, all but confirmed this child's account in his interview with Jarecki: "If you talk to a lot of children you don't give them an option really. You just be pretty honest with them. You have to tell them pretty honestly that we know you went to Mr. Friedman's class. We know how many times you been to the class. We—you know, we go through the whole routine. We know that there was a good chance that he touched you."

As in other cases, children eventually figured out what it would take to end the interviews. "I remember telling myself, 'It's not true—just say this to them in order to get them off your back,'" one student said. His testimony led to sixteen counts of sodomy.[14]

Over the course of these interviews children said that Arnold had patted them on the back and left his arm lingering around their shoulders. They said that he had shown them pornographic computer games and magazines, and that Arnold, along with Jesse, had also made them take off their clothes. Police believed Jesse had sometimes taken a single student off to another room and that other children then heard sobs and screams coming through the wall. Children said they were made to line up in a row on the floor so that Arnold and Jesse could play "leapfrog," hopping over and sodomizing each student in turn. In addition to the indictment filed against Arnold, the district attorney's office charged Jesse with 243 counts of sexual abuse.

The Friedman family thus took on all of the different roles available to families involved the mass abuse investigations of the 1980s. They were perpetrators, or at least Arnold was—nobody denied he had actively sought out the stack of magazines in his basement. They were also outraged defendants, wrongfully charged with bizarre crimes they never committed. Finally, they were victims, not only of a prosecutor's efforts to send two of them away to prison for decades but also of Arnold's pedophilia, which destroyed their long-held belief that they were a normal, contented family. The boys' response to this experience is both easy and absolutely impossible to understand: in the weeks between the arrests and the trial, as Arnold and Jesse tried to figure out what to do, oldest son and brother David kept his home-video camera rolling.

David made twenty-five hours' worth of footage, which sat untouched in his closet until Andrew Jarecki got hold of the story.[15] He filmed trial strategy sessions, angry outbursts, private monologues—every aspect of the family's disintegration and collapse. The camera follows Elaine as she retreats down hallways, with David and his brothers screaming from behind. It sits on the mantle over the course of a long dinner celebrating Arnold's birthday and watches everyone fight. "Do you honor and respect your husband?" David asks his mother. "That's why I don't talk to you."

"Things are getting a little out of hand," Arnold says, trying to defuse the situation, but most of his time is spent sitting in silence at the head of the table, all but invisible. These scenes alternate with moments of sad levity: a birthday cake, Arnold playing standards on his piano. In the midst of the investigation, as Arnold tried to figure out whether a guilty plea would improve or harm Jesse's chances of acquittal, David videotaped as his brothers cheered up their dad by outfitting him in a balloon animal costume. They've made him look like a pterodactyl, and then Arnold says, "It's a *Jewish* pterodactyl," and then he ingeniously elaborates the joke by squawking out, "Schmuck! Schmuck! Schmuck!" while flapping his wings. His sons dissolve into laughter.[16] These home movies are almost impossible to watch. They should have been destroyed once the investigation ended. They should never have been made at all.

Elaine Friedman could not completely understand her sons or her husband, and in turn she was not understood by them. Along with his recordings of family quarrels, David kept a private video diary, and in one entry he makes the family alliances, and the speed with which they are falling apart, clear. "I don't care about my parents," he says. He is sitting alone on a bed, and he is wearing a white T-shirt. "I wish it was just my brothers. Oh fuck, I don't care about my mother, that's for sure. My brothers were OK and my mother can go to fucking hell. . . . When the guilty verdict comes in on Jesse, my father is gonna kill himself, Jesse's gonna go away to jail for the rest of his life, Seth is gonna move West."

Although David and his brothers had all the normal filial reasons to resent and criticize their mother, their specific grievance during this period had to do with Elaine's persistent belief that Arnold should plead guilty. She thought it would help Jesse, who could then stand trial without his pedophile father standing there next to him, making the jury wonder about the "cycle of abuse." But the home movies suggest that she also wanted Arnold to plead guilty because she was justifiably furious at him, and her sons hated what they perceived as the influence Elaine's anger exercised over their father. "He's my husband! He doesn't belong to you," Elaine yells at Jesse in a home audio recording, and Jesse yells back, "He's my father, he doesn't belong to you!" Then Elaine pauses and says, her voice falling and softening, "Well, he doesn't belong to anybody now." This, very simply, is the truth—he belongs to the state. But by this point the sons' idolization of their father has linked up with their belief in his legal innocence, and Elaine cannot reach them at all. "You're so *fucking stupid*," Seth says.[17]

Arnold Friedman did plead guilty. He thought it was Jesse's only hope, and there is also evidence that something really was amiss in his computer classes, though nothing like the crimes with which he was charged. In the run-up to his guilty plea, Arnold's defense attorney called other former students not listed on the official complaint and asked whether they would testify that Arnold had done nothing inappropriate. They wouldn't. The atmosphere in Great Neck may have had something to do with this reluctance, but one former student also said that although he was never abused in computer class, he did remember Arnold patting boys on the legs through their jeans or putting his arm around their shoulders and letting the embrace linger. A mother also removed her child from class after he revealed that Arnold sometimes asked students to sit on his lap.[18] Years before his arrest, Arnold said, he told a therapist about his pedophilia, and the therapist suggested he go to Times Square and buy porn to sublimate with.[19] Even David Friedman, in an interview with the *Village Voice*, said that he and his brothers found their father's magazines when they were young and rummaging around in the basement one day.[20] In other cases, the fact that the defendants maintained a stance of outraged innocence helped them during the trial and the appeals process. But "not guilty" won't generate as much outrage as "innocent," and the Friedmans directed a substantial amount of the outrage they did have at one another.

The last night Arnold spent at home, he and his sons did what they loved to do best: they improvised and recorded a little performance. The clip appears in *Capturing the Friedmans*, and it is extraordinarily tender and brief. The scene is made up of about two dozen shots, each less than half a second long. It begins with Arnold and Jesse in profile, standing still and facing each other from across the living room. In the next shot each one, still stationary, has moved in by about six inches. This repeats until they are just slightly apart, nose to nose, and then they circle one another, smiling gently and locking eyes. Once they have rotated 180 degrees, changing positions as though in a stop-motion animation, they begin to back away from the center of the room until they back out of the frame entirely. The symmetry is a little awful to look at. The scene that Arnold and his sons have dreamed up expresses their situation so elegantly. They had been working together for years on these videos, and they were very good at them.

Soon after he went to prison Arnold received a telegram from David: "HI DAD, HANG IN THERE, EVERYTHING WILL BE BETTER SOON, REMEMBER HOW GOOD IT CAN BE, DON'T WORRY ABOUT MOMMY, NO MATTER WHAT MOMMY SAYS, JESSE WILL NOT TAKE THE PLEA, I PROMISE. I LOVE YOU VERY MUCH. LOVE DAVID."[21]

The older sons were anxious to curtail their mother's influence over Jesse's decision, but David could not make good on his promise: Jesse eventually replicated his father's mistake and pled guilty too. Given the judicial atmosphere that prevailed in Nassau County at the time, it is hard to blame him. Even before hearing any evidence, a judge told defense attorney Peter Panaro that she would sentence Jesse consecutively on every count against him should he decide to go to trial, and she also later admitted that "there was never a doubt in [her] mind" as to Jesse's guilt.[22] Once Arnold went away to a federal prison in Wisconsin, the brothers seem to have drawn one another close in a rather manic way—they had the camera rolling even as they drove over to the courthouse so Jesse could enter his plea. "Are you a child molester, Jesse?," David says from the passenger seat, in a melodramatic voice. "Did you do what they said you did?"

"I never touched a kid," Jesse replies. "I never saw my father touch a kid."

One brother says, "Good," in an affectionate tone of voice, and then there is a little pause. "Yeah, but still, you must have done it," David says, and then all three of them burst out laughing.

The brothers would give their last public performance on the steps of the courthouse later that day, after Jesse entered his guilty plea and after he tried to win the judge's sympathy by making the argument that he too was a victim of Arnold Friedman's abuse. "My father raised me confused about what was right and what was wrong," Jesse told the court, "and I realize now how terribly wrong it all was. I wish I could have done something to stop it sooner." He sobbed as Panaro reiterated the point, identifying Arnold Friedman as a "monster" and begging the court to take Jesse's history of abuse into consideration. "This *can't* be overlooked," Panaro said. "I can't believe we live in such a cold society that no one could look at this man and understand that." After the hearing, Jesse went outside with his brothers and put on a bizarre and reckless performance, which many people around the courthouse witnessed and remembered years later. They did a Monty Python bit, an unhinged sketch in which a man complains to a doctor, played by John Cleese, that his brain hurts. The joke is that everybody yells everything in stupid voices. "My brain hurts!" Jesse yells in the brothers' video. "Nurse! Nurse!" There is only one line in his performance that isn't also in the original sketch, and it happens right after one of the brothers says to Jesse that his brain will "have to come out." Jesse says, "But I'm using it!"[23]

Jesse wasn't using his brain very well during this period, though. Before he decided to enter his guilty plea he regularly speculated at home about trying the case "in the media." Once he determined that he could not possibly come out of a trial with an acquittal, he decided to play the media in a different way, and in the months after his guilty plea he sank deeper into his adopted role of traumatized abuse victim turned abuser. His worst decision during this period was to appear on a Geraldo Rivera special, *Busting the Kiddy Porn Underground*, which aired in February 1989. In between speculative reporting about the child pornography industry, Geraldo asked Jesse to describe his crimes. In the interview Jesse's voice is small and soft, and he glances around in a dazed way that appears nowhere in any of David's home movies:

> I fondled them. I was . . . forced to . . . pose in hundreds of photos for my father in all sorts of sexual positions with the kids. And the kids likewise with myself. Oral sex going both ways. I was forced to pose with my penis against their anus. . . . I . . . I know my . . . my father had made vicious threats to the kids about . . . about burning down their homes and things like that and . . . I . . . reestablished that with the kids that I . . . I thought it was completely possible that my father would actually burn down their homes.[24]

The claims Jesse made in this interview are ridiculous—no homemade pornography produced by Arnold or Jesse Friedman was ever found anywhere. His decision to incorporate his family pastime of character acting into his public defense was very ill-advised. The jokes were not as funny on the courthouse steps as they had been in the living room, and the personas did not have a sympathetic audience. Jesse's attempts to apply the dynamics of his family life to the news media placed him in an apparently intractable situation.

Pedophilia and hysteria about pedophilia are not mutually exclusive. The reality of pedophilia in the Friedman family is that Arnold experienced sexual attraction to children from a young age and tried to keep those feelings at bay with child porn, especially during stressful periods of his life, when the feelings intensified. While struggling with these feelings he also became a beloved and award-winning teacher whose conduct outside the computer class—at school and in the privacy of his own living room, where he gave piano lessons—was never criticized. If Arnold did show magazines to his students, if he provided or tolerated the pornographic computer games, if he was figuring out just how long he could leave his hand on a child's shoulder or back before anybody noticed, then clearly something needed to be done. But in Great Neck the final truth of Arnold's actions was swallowed up by a hysterical narrative of pedophilia that combined the police department's sprawling, violent fantasy and the community's eagerness to believe it. When Jesse appeared on *Geraldo* and talked about the shadowy "friends" to whom Arnold would send his nonexistent homemade porn, he was trying to give an account of himself that squared with this hysterical narrative. His mistake was based on a real insight, which is that the real story was not one people were interested in or willing to hear.

Elaine filed for divorce after Arnold went to prison. Even if he were to come home one day, she said, "I would have to stare at Arnie across the dinner table with just the two of us. There was really nothing between us except these children that we yelled at." She found a measure of peace in the wake of her son's conviction. "I know my friends said to me, 'Don't you feel, like, terrible being alone in such a big house?'" she says in *Capturing the Friedmans*. "I said, 'No, I feel calm.' That's when I really started becoming a person."[25]

What did Elaine feel like just before she started becoming a person? The footage in *Capturing the Friedmans* suggests that she, along with Arnold, David, Seth, and Jesse, felt like a family. Jarecki's film documents the process by which the investigation and trial steadily and unbearably intensified the dynamics that had always characterized the Friedmans' lives with one another. So over the course of the documentary's 107 minutes, the boys' shared affection for their father becomes a more desperate and lacerating kind of love, and Elaine's bemused distance from her husband and sons' antics turns into real bitterness. The case bound the Friedmans closer and closer together right up until the guilty pleas sent them irrevocably on their separate ways.

This destructive intensification of the dynamics of family life wasn't only present in the private experiences of those involved with the day care and sex abuse investigations; it also appeared, on a larger scale, in the social and cultural shifts that made those investigations possible and changed how people talked and thought about families and the dangers they faced. This shift and its link to a resurgent cultural conservatism was perhaps most powerfully articulated just as it began to gather steam in 1972, when Richard Nixon gave an interview to the *Washington Star-News*. It was just two days since Nixon had won a second term as president, defeating liberal icon George McGovern in forty-nine out of fifty states. In the interview Nixon spoke expansively about the national character. With the country's long countercultural moment beginning to wane, Nixon stood at the beginning of a conservative revival that would continue for the next three decades, and he talked like someone who knew it. The sixties were fading into history, and it was time to restore a little discipline to American life:

> The average American is just like the child in the family. You give him some responsibility and he is going to amount to something. He is going to do something. If, on the other hand, you make him completely dependent and pamper him and cater to him too much, you are going to make him soft, spoiled and eventually a very weak individual.[26]

Nixon's remarks were aimed at hippies, activists, and others who had spent some portion of the previous decade experimenting with hallucinogenic drugs or making liberationist political demands, and the reelected president appealed to the family as a model for civic life not because of the care families provide but because of the authority fathers wield. The federal government, law enforcement, Christianity, and the military collectively represented for Nixon a kind of national father figure. The country's future depended on people's willingness to relearn their respect for traditional authority and to understand that being a citizen was much like being a child.

Paul Ingram was a man who lived out Nixon's ideal at home, where he was the church-going figurehead of a large, close-knit family, and at work, where he was a cop. He lived in Olympia, Washington, with his wife, Sandy, and five children, and he was forty-three years old in 1988. He was chairman of the local Republican Party. With his family, Ingram's authority was nearly absolute, both as a disciplinarian and as the final word on group decisions, which Sandy claimed not to mind, as she almost always agreed with him. Residents of Olympia and the surrounding communities had a pronounced streak of enthusiasm for self-sufficiency. Paul and Sandy built, painted, and wired their home from the ground up, and they raised all kinds of animals on their ten acres of land. Sandy made stews and roasts out of some of these animals, rounding out big meals with produce from the large vegetable garden she kept.[27] She also tended to small children, running a day care out of the house to supplement her husband's income.

The day care kids would become objects of resentment for the Ingrams's biological children, who felt their mother and father were distant and withholding of affection. Paul knew this was a problem, and he worried about it. His own parents, especially his father, had been similarly distant. It frustrated Paul to be visiting the same emotional difficulties on his own children, but he had trouble softening his authoritarianism. Things got worse after he and Sandy underwent a religious transformation in the 1970s. Though devout Catholics when they met and married, the Ingrams converted to evangelical Protestantism after a few months of attending services at a local Pentecostal congregation. The church emphasized the importance of family life, and people spoke in tongues at its services. Paul stopped allowing the boys to participate in sports at school, and this was especially upsetting to his athletic son, Chad. Rock music was also banned. "The old man didn't give a shit about anybody as long as you did your chores," his oldest son said.[28]

Paul also loved authority at work, but in a different way—conforming to the codes and procedures of a career in law enforcement gave his life meaning. After a long tour of unsatisfying jobs in his youth, Paul began working traffic and domestic disputes with a small-town police department in 1969. By the 1980s he was third in command at the Thurston County Sheriff's Department. Police work suited him tremendously. He wore the mustache that appears in caricatures of police officers, and he relished traffic patrol even as he rose through the professional ranks. Social life revolved around work too. He talked about religion with a colleague named Neil McClanahan as the pair cruised around in a squad car.[29] He joined a poker game that took place in a different cop's basement or living room every week. It was a close-knit department.

A complicated and murky set of circumstances preceded what happened to Paul and Sandy's family in 1988. Others saw the Ingrams as such an attractive model of domestic happiness that friends and acquaintances from church consciously imitated them, but like the families in mid-twentieth-century American novels, the idealized exterior concealed different kinds of unhappiness. The oldest son, Paul Ross, had a difficult late adolescence. He wrecked his car a few times, bucked college plans his father had laid out for him, and left home one day in 1984 at the age of eighteen, leaving behind a note explaining that he would soon be in South America with his friends—his parents had no idea who these friends were. Chad also moved into an apartment of his own as a teenager, then moved back home. Then he went to Bible school, dropped out, and came home again. These are familiar if somewhat extreme teenage responses to a strict upbringing. Both boys remembered an incident in which their father, standing on a deck that looked down over the yard, became angry that the brothers had allowed the blade of an axe to become dull. Paul later said he only meant to toss the axe down to his sons, but he put too much muscle behind the throw, and if Paul Ross hadn't stepped to the side, the axe would have hit him. Paul regretted the incident. His oldest son, at least, did not forgive him for it.[30]

Ericka Ingram was four years older than her sister, Julie, but the two shared a room growing up and spent much of their time together. Though introspective and moody, Ericka was the dominant sibling, her stylishness marking a sharp contrast with Julie's deference and plain clothes, similar to those her mother wore. In 1983, when she was seventeen, Ericka attended one of her church's annual Heart to Heart retreats for girls and told a counselor that a married man had tried to rape her. One of Paul's colleagues investigated the allegation and concluded that the man had put his hand on Ericka's knee while giving her a ride—harassment, perhaps, or quite plausibly a prelude to something else the man was hoping for, but not attempted rape in itself.[31] That was that for the investigation. Then, two years later, Julie attended the same retreat and said a neighbor had sexually abused her; Ericka alleged abuse by the same person. Paul helped his younger daughter file a complaint with the prosecutor's office, but Julie became reluctant and then unable to talk about what happened. Investigators began to find inconsistencies in her account, and charges were not pursued. In 1987 Ericka had to be hospitalized on the way to California with a friend named Paula. A doctor diagnosed her with pelvic inflammatory disease, and when Ericka asked how one gets pelvic inflammatory disease, the doctor said through sexual intercourse. But this explanation made no sense to Ericka, who said she was a virgin. What the doctor didn't say was that the disease can also be caused by an ovarian cyst, which Ericka had.[32] The hospitalization shook her.

Sexual abuse often came up at Heart to Heart. The retreat undoubtedly provided an environment in which kids and adolescents could ask questions and talk about experiences they couldn't bring up at home, but adult organizers also raised the topic of abuse whether children asked them to or not. In 1988 a charismatic Christian speaker named Karla Franko addressed the retreat's girl attendees. A kind of motivational speaker slash performing psychic, Franko believed she was endowed with special biblical capabilities, that the Lord provided her with insight into the lives of those in her audience. Standing in front of a rapt audience, Franko said she had a vision of a little girl hiding in a closet while heavy male footsteps drew near. A girl in the audience called out that she had been that girl, and then she rushed out. By the end of the weekend, other girls also came forward to say they had been abused. The emotional atmosphere was extraordinarily charged.

That fascination with abuse—especially the sexual abuse of girls—was characteristic of fundamentalism as a whole. Ericka Ingram was at the 1988 Heart to Heart, interpreting Franko's talk for the deaf girls in attendance. Already that summer she had read *Satan's Underground*, Lauren Stratford's purported memoir of her upbringing among and subsequent escape from abusive Satanists. The book was eventually discredited by a Christian magazine and withdrawn from publication, but evangelical readers in 1988 were drawn to its vivid depictions of hidden depravity and redemption through Christ.[33] The book's opening pages described a façade of domestic perfection that Ericka may well have recognized: "My adoptive parents were both professionals. We lived in an upper-class neighborhood. I was always dressed well. The house was beautifully decorated, and the kitchen looked like it was right out of *Good Housekeeping* magazine. By all outward appearances I had every advantage that a kid could want. Why, I was even taken to church!"[34]

Beneath the surface, of course, lay a hell of parental abuse, child pornography, and infant sacrifice, all orchestrated by a shadowy cult leader named Victor. "To keep her from even thinking about telling the police or anyone else," Stratford wrote, "the high priest calls upon demonic spirits to do something of such a diabolical nature that she will be frightened into silence. . . . And well might she take that threat to heart, for it is not just an empty threat. Those spirits are real!"[35]

That was one of the things in Ericka Ingram's mental atmosphere as the Heart to Heart kids boarded the bus back home at the end of the retreat's final day. What she was thinking about specifically as she sat down on the stage and began to sob uncontrollably is impossible to know. Counselors gathered around the twenty-one-year-old and offered consoling pats on the shoulder, and then one of them went to find Franko and asked whether she would pray over Ericka. According to a report subsequently filed by police, Ericka then announced that her father had sexually abused her. But this is not what Franko said happened when she spoke to a journalist later. She said she began to pray over Ericka's huddled body, and then she thought, "molestation," and then she spoke. "You have been abused as a child, sexually abused," Franko said. "It's by her father, and it's been happening for years."[36] Ericka continued to sob, unable to speak; Franko specified that at no time did Ericka utter a word confirming or disputing the allegations of abuse. A few weeks later, in September 1988, Ericka moved out of her parents' house, and Julie followed six weeks after that. Ericka was twenty-two and Julie was eighteen.

Paul and Sandy were initially bewildered by their daughters' sudden departure, but not for long. Ericka met with her mother at a Denny's to relay her allegations, also accusing her brothers, Chad and Paul Ross, of molesting her. Julie also accused her father of abuse in a letter she wrote to a teacher. "I can remember when I was 4 yr old he would have poker game at our house," she wrote, "and a lot of men would come over and play poker w/ my dad, and they would all get drunk and one or two at a time would come in to my room and have sex with me they would be in and out all night laughing and cursing."[37] Word got around to friends at the Church of Living Water. Paul denied everything. The sisters' stories began to change almost as soon as they began to tell them—the abuse had stopped five years ago, one said, and then that changed to three years. Eventually both would claim that the rapes had continued through the end of September, after Heart to Heart and after Ericka moved out. Each also insisted their father had mostly left the other sister alone, competing claims that were hard to reconcile with the fact of their shared bedroom. In October, shortly before Halloween, the Ingram family watched Geraldo's Satanism special. Then Paul was arrested by his coworkers and brought in for an interview.

The allegations trapped Paul between the two systems of authority he loved best. Ingram often talked about wanting to be a good father, and surely one part of being a good father involved not subjecting your children to years of abuse. Sitting in the police station's interrogation room, though, Ingram also wanted to be a good cop. Even though he was the one being interrogated, his friends across the table were just doing a job he loved, and he wanted to help them. "If this did happen, we need to take care of it," Ingram said. "I can't see myself doing this."[38]

"If this did happen." In 1988 Ingram and his colleagues all subscribed to what was then common wisdom among many police officers about child sexual abuse: victims could repress and forget their trauma for long periods of time and, crucially, so could perpetrators.[39] Ingram himself had attended a statewide crime prevention meeting focused almost entirely on repressed memories, and he thought the presentation he heard there was very convincing.[40] Ingram was interviewed for two hours in the police station before detectives turned on a recording device, and by the time they did start recording, Ingram was willing to believe in a guilt he could not recall:

INGRAM: I really believe that the allegations did occur and that I did violate them and abuse them and probably for a long period of time. I've repressed it, probably very successfully from myself, and now I'm trying to bring it all out. I know from what they're saying that the incidents had to occur, that I had to have done these things.

Q: And why do you say you had to have done these things?

A: Well, number one, my girls know me. They wouldn't lie about something like this, and there's other evidence that would point out to me that these things occurred.

Q: And what in your mind would that evidence be?

A: Well, the way they've been acting for the last couple of years and the fact that I've not been able to be affectionate with them even though I want to be. I have a hard time hugging them or even telling them that I love them, and I just know that's not natural. . . .

Q: You don't remember going into that room and touching Ericka?

A: No.[41]

Ingram's affect began to change as the detectives encouraged him to dredge his memories up out of the depths. While maintaining his weird solicitousness, he closed his eyes, lowered his head, and slowed his breathing. He punctuated his utterances with long, frustrating silences that sometimes ran to ten minutes. He appeared to be hypnotized or at least in some kind of trance. Among psychologists working on child sexual abuse, hypnosis was becoming a popular therapeutic technique. Hypnotizing their adult patients, these therapists believed, allowed them to access repressed memories of childhood trauma. Ingram already believed in traumatic repression, and his susceptibility to hypnosis—by definition, a state of heightened suggestibility—was high. He discovered recovered memory techniques on his own, by accident, and he administered the therapy himself.

He began to narrate. On November 28 he described abusing Ericka when she was as young as five years old. The next day, speaking out of the same trance-like state, he described abusing Julie, and he also recounted scenes confirming the allegations about poker games and late-night group abuse, implicating two of his colleagues in the department. During that same interview Ingram was asked whether he had been involved in black magic—"the Satan cult kind of thing"—before his conversion to evangelical Christianity. For a time all Ingram could recall was having occasionally read his horoscope in the paper, but further reflection produced visions of shadows and tombstones. Within a week Ingram was worried that he was possessed by a demon, and he invited his pastor to join his interview sessions with the detectives. The pastor assured Ingram that God would only allow him to recall memories and scenes that had actually taken place. "Boy, it's almost like I'm making it up," Ingram interrupted himself to say at one point. "But I'm not."

Detectives found the style of Ingram's confessions almost as unnerving as their content. Paul didn't talk in the past tense about acts he remembered committing. He seemed instead to be narrating events as though seeing them for the first time, and he used the conditional to an alarming extent, talking about what he "would have" done or where Ericka "would have" been when he found her. "I can kinda see the girls running when they saw what was happening," Ingram said of a memory in which a police colleague raped Sandy, "when they saw the viciousness with which Jim grabbed Sandy by the hair and started screaming at her. They ran into the living room and hid. I believe I was kind of outside the room when all this was going on, and I don't know what the boys did."[42]

Ingram's way with detail also frustrated detectives. Though perfectly willing to supply memories that conformed to his daughters' allegations, he could not—or, as the detectives sometimes believed, would not—elaborate. "You just keep copping out!" one interviewer eventually said. "It's kinda like you're saying, 'I'll agree to whatever my daughters say and I'll give you that information, but I'm not gonna tell you anything more.'"[43] The details Ingram did manage to provide should not have been reassuring to his interrogators. In one interview Paul described seeing another man abusing one of his daughters, and a detective asked whether the man had any jewelry on. "May have a watch on his right hand," Ingram said. "A gold watch." The detective asked him to read the time off the man's watch. "Uh, two o' clock," he said.[44] This was not, for Ingram, a Proustian recollection of the sensory detail that animates a chain of associated memories; rather, the scenes he produced had a cinematic quality. Ingram did not "know" the time on the watch until he read it off of the screen playing across his mind. The alleged scene from which Ingram drew this extraordinarily fine and specific detail had taken place seventeen years earlier.

The detectives continued to solicit information from Ericka and Julie, with Ericka usually leading the way. (Julie, who may not have expected that her allegations would lead as far as they did, eventually became almost completely unable to talk during interviews.) One of the investigators became so emotionally invested in Ericka's plight—so enamored of her vulnerability and so disgusted by what Paul had done to her—that other officers in the department began to joke that he was in love with her.[45] The information gathered at these interviews with the daughters was then taken back to Paul and used to fuel his imaginative trances. Unable to recall a particular allegation, he would go back to his cell, pray on it, and return to the interrogation room the next day with a written confession, of which he always seemed to be proud.

Detectives encouraged Paul in person as well, overlapping his prayers to Christ with exhortations to admit his guilt. These encouragements gave the interrogation room some of the atmosphere of Living Water, where parishioners often spoke in tongues. "It's your responsibility as a father," they said to him in one interview. "It's important. It's got to come out." Paul felt he needed to be berated in this way. When his interrogators stopped he said, "Just keep talking. Just keep talking, please."[46] Paul's stories transitioned from the bizarre to the completely implausible— at one point he tried to implicate himself in the unsolved murders of dozens of prostitutes near Seattle and Tacoma, known as the "Green River Killings," but the investigators were too energized to notice. Two attended a law enforcement conference on satanic cults in Canada and were delighted to find other cops asking them for advice. In their excitement they called up Ken Lanning at the FBI. They told him they were working on the first verifiable satanic ritual abuse investigation in the country's history.

In February 1989 Thurston County police invited Richard Ofshe, a social psychologist at the University of California at Berkeley, to visit Olympia and have a look at Ingram's case. During the first two decades of his successful academic career, Ofshe had spent a lot of time researching groups referred to by many people as cults: the Church of Scientology, the Unification Church, and the Santa Monica–based Synanon organization, a drug rehabilitation program that developed into a religious movement.[47] Among other things, Ofshe was interested in mind control. He wrote about thought-reform techniques used in Soviet Russia and North Korea, and he argued that the more dangerous groups among the post-1960s explosion of new American religious movements had adopted these techniques as their own.[48] The Ingram investigators wanted to talk to Ofshe because they were still worried about Paul's trances and because Sandy and some of the Ingram children had also behaved strangely in police interviews. Maybe the satanic cult to which Paul had belonged subjected its members to some kind of psychic programming.

Ofshe met Paul Ingram with the two lead investigators in the room. He asked Paul about his life—where he lived, what his childhood was like.

Ofshe had been briefed about the vaguely cinematic qualities of Ingram's abuse recollections, but he found that Paul's memory seemed to function with no irregularities so long as the conversation was confined to everyday subjects. Though brought in for his cult expertise, Ofshe had also done work on false confessions in police interrogations, and he knew it was not uncommon for suspects to "admit" to crimes they could not remember so long as their interrogators provided assurances that the evidence against them was overwhelming. That Ingram was himself a cop doing everything he could to help his questioners could only have made this dynamic more powerful. Ofshe decided on the spot that Ingram, maliciously or not, was not telling the truth, and he tested his theory in the interrogation room with an improvised experiment.

Without warning the other detectives, Ofshe told Paul that he had already spoken with Ericka and Paul Ross—which he had not—and that they had told him about an incident in which Paul made the pair have sex with each other so he could watch. Ingram said he could not remember any such incident, but Ofshe insisted, and the other detectives soon caught on and began to play along, specifying for Ingram the place in which the episode had occurred. Ingram assumed his meditative pose: head lowered, eyes closed. "I can kind of see Ericka and Paul Ross," he said.[49] Ofshe told Ingram to return to his cell for further reflection. The next day Ofshe visited Ingram again. Paul said he now had some clear memories, and Ofshe told him to keep thinking in his cell. When Ofshe visited for a third time Ingram handed him a written confession:

> Daytime: Probably Saturday or Sunday Afternoon. In Ericka's Bedroom on Fir Tree. Bunk Beds set up. Ericka & Julie are sharing the room. I ask or tell Paul Jr. & Ericka to come upstairs & then we go into Ericka's room. I close the door and tell them we are going to play (a game?).
>
> I tell them to undress. Ericka says "But Dad," I say "Just get undressed and don't argue." From my tone or the way I say it, neither objects and they undress themselves. I'm probably blocking the door so they could not get out.

What followed was a detached, pornographic description of Ingram's children having sex with each other and with him, a father's incest fantasy. Despite the rapid development of Paul's memories, some details remained blurry. "I may have had anal sex with Paul," he wrote. "Not real clear." At the end of his confession Ingram described vague memories of a power dynamic that conformed to the cult-based theories of the investigation: "I believe that when I tell Paul & Ericka to come upstairs, those on the main floor who heard me and Paul & Ericka, knew what was going on and not to interrupt us. The ability to control Paul & Ericka may not come entirely from me. It seems there is a real fear of Jim or someone else. Someone may have told me to do this with the kids. This is a feeling I have."[50]

Ofshe was now almost sure that Paul's confessions were false, and interviews with Ericka and Julie persuaded him that the girls' satanic allegations were frantic attempts to resolve inconsistencies in a story and a situation that had gotten completely out of hand. He would have done well, though, to spend more time—which is to say, any time at all—on the planning stage of his experiment. As detectives noted at the time and as appeals courts and other critics would note later on, the scenario Ofshe proposed was not all that different from the scenes Paul had already been producing for months.[51] With incest and group sex already on the table, brother-sister intercourse plus paternal voyeurism wasn't exactly coming out of nowhere. Why couldn't Ofshe have picked a wilder story or, better yet, a story involving some easily falsifiable element, like airline travel? Although the experiment certainly contributed to the mountain of evidence suggesting that Ingram's claims were not actual memories but anguished fantasies produced under intense pressure, it did not discredit the prosecution's case as swiftly or decisively as it probably should have.

After reading over Ingram's confession, Ofshe confronted him with the truth. Ingram wouldn't budge. Again and again Ofshe tried to explain that he had made up the scene on the fly, but Ingram countered that the memories he had recovered during his two days of jail cell reflection and prayer were "just as real to [him] as anything else," a claim that makes perfect sense. Ingram built the memory-generating machine inside himself at great personal cost, and it is not surprising that he would have been so reluctant to relinquish its benefits. It allowed him to say and believe that his daughters always told the truth no matter how crazy their stories became—by confessing his crimes, Ingram was now protecting his children, even if he had betrayed them for years. Ingram's memories also provided him with an elegant solution to the problem of how to be a good cop while being interrogated by cops. That his family and his workplace somehow accidentally conspired to incarcerate him for decades did not weaken Ingram's identification with either institution. He pled guilty and was sentenced to twenty years in prison.

Ingram was well suited to prison, itself an environment structured around deference to authority. He managed the inmates' library, and as the time separating him from his sessions in the interrogation room grew, he found himself becoming less certain of the memories he had produced in Olympia. He became sufficiently certain of his innocence that he tried to appeal his conviction. In 1993, still in prison, he told the journalist Lawrence Wright, whose book *Remembering Satan* remains the definitive account of the case, that feelings of guilt about his parenting made his confessions possible. He had slapped Julie once when she ran a hot bath that scalded her brother, and there was also an instance when he hit Paul Ross on the back of the head. "I wasn't there for the kids," he said. "I wasn't able to communicate with them as I should have. I never sexually abused anybody. But emotional abuse—you don't like to admit it, but somebody has to."[52]

"Is that all?" Lawrence Wright wrote at the end of his book on the Ingram case. "Certainly that would be the most frightening conclusion of the Ingram case, that the bonds of family life are so intricately framed that such appalling perversions of memory can arise from ordinary rotten behavior."[53] Working to at least partially resolve some of the many open questions that remained after Paul went to prison, Wright noted that both of the Ingram daughters had talked about having sex with their brothers from the investigation's earliest days. He also noted that investigators had not pursued this line of inquiry at all, presumably because of their assumption that any sexual activity among the siblings "must have been learned" from the abusive parents. Of course, by the time Wright began the reporting for his book, the Ingrams's stories had changed so many times and for so many reasons that pinning down the final truth of what happened to their family seemed hopeless.

In 1990 Paul Ingram was moved to a prison in Delaware, and he found conditions there to be "relatively easy."[54] While Ingram served out his time, two other members of his family appeared on television. Ericka appeared on *Sally Jessy Raphael* and said she had been given a ritual abortion. "The baby was still alive when they took it out," she said, "and they put it on top of me and then they cut it up."[55] The broadcast actually helped Paul. Many of his fellow inmates watched the show, and the consensus among them was that Ericka was lying. Another news program tracked down a relative whose involvement in the case was otherwise very limited: Paul Ingram's father, Ross. When asked about his son's susceptibility to hypnosis, Ross said that it had been evident from a very early age. He also said that he had been the one doing the hypnotizing:

> When Paul was probably 10, 12 years old, I'd learned hypnotism. And so I would hypnotize the children to get better grades in school, be kind and courteous, and to listen to what other people had to say, and always be helpful. Paul was real easy to hypnotize. I would tell the kids to set back and relax, get comfortable, close their eyes, and just imagine that it would be a nice white cloud floating overhead. Just to imagine they were riding on that cloud without a worry in the world.[56]

As a child and as a young man, Paul had been tormented by his father's emotional distance, and as an adult and father he had maintained a similar emotional distance from his own children. But Paul's experiences with the pastor and the police detectives in the interrogation room suggest that he took his father's lessons about helpfulness and listening to what other people had to say very much to heart. When he tried to live up to his familial and professional obligations in his jail cell by closing his eyes, taking a deep breath, and—in his own words, and his father's—floating off "on a white cloud," Paul may have simply been trying to be a good boy.

Or maybe not. Today Ingram has no recollection of ever being hypnotized by his father. "I remember reading about it, and after that my father did state he did it, but I don't recall it ever happening," he wrote after being released from prison. "I do recall that my father tried a hypnotizing treatment to stop his smoking addiction, but it never worked for him."[57]

Chapter 8

McMartin—The Verdict

Danny Davis spent several thousand dollars to spruce up the McMartin Preschool in the spring of 1989. Defense staff and Peggy McMartin Buckey's husband, Chuck, applied fresh coats of paint inside and out, restoring the building to its original pea-green color and brightening the school's handmade clown cabinets, giraffe chairs, and other furniture. Davis owned the building now. The McMartin-Buckeys had signed it over as partial payment for their legal fees. After the restoration Davis asked a staff member with a video camera to walk through the building and document the changes.[1] Except for the absent teachers and children, it looked much the same as in the fall of 1983. In the video the cameraman wanders from room to room. There is a stack of green cots pushed up against the wall. Everything seems to be in order. Only the broken climbing toy outside in the yard suggests the school's more recent history of vandalism and arson, which damaged the property's shrubs and trees in addition to the building itself. Davis restored those too, hiring a plant rental nursery that usually did work for television and film productions. Workers installed potted plants, wired fake branches onto those trees that had survived, and planted artificial junipers, oaks, and Chinese elms in the ground.[2] Judge Pounders's subsequent tour of the property convinced him that Davis had produced an accurate facsimile of the school as it appeared in the early 1980s. He granted Davis's request to allow the jury to see it for themselves.

Davis believed jurors needed to see just how small the building was to understand the implausibility of the stories that had been told about the defendants, so the City of Los Angeles bused them down to Manhattan Beach on a sunny Wednesday morning in April. Reporters were told to keep their distance, so they photographed the event from the other side of busy Manhattan Beach Boulevard while jurors toured the school in silence. Anyone who wanted to ask a question had to make a hand signal first so that Judge Pounders and the attorneys could scurry over, supervise, and raise objections if necessary. A few jurors timed the walk from the playground entrance to the building itself. Others got approval to shout from one room to another so that they could hear how noise carried. They looked into the school's closets and bathrooms, and they also looked at the property from the balcony of an apartment building across the street. They left a little more than an hour after they had arrived, and then the reporters were allowed to tour the school. One journalist climbed onto a piece of playground equipment that said FORT ISSIMO on the side, testing whether a child could have served as a "lookout" from the perch. Others looked around for the "secret room" to which one child said he had been taken.[3] The following day McMartin surpassed the Hillside Strangler case to become the longest criminal trial in American history.

The McMartin children and their parents had already testified. So had Kee MacFarlane, Astrid Heger, Bruce Woodling, and a host of medical experts. The summer was given over largely to testimony from those who had actually worked at the school. Betty Raidor took the stand for eight days. A sixty-nine-year-old disciplinarian, she criticized Ray as an "incompetent" teacher who let the children run around noisily when he should have been organizing activities instead. She said she never saw anything at McMartin that suggested sexual abuse. Charles Buckey took the stand and fielded humorous softball questions from Danny Davis about his family's alleged involvement in child porn. "During the time that you and your wife operated the preschool," Davis asked, "did you receive large sums of money from the worldwide sale of child pornography?"

"No," Buckey said.

"From 1979 to 1983 did you and your wife come into huge amounts of money from unknown sources?"

"No."[4]

Babette Spitler took the stand and talked about the two years she spent trying to recover her own children from Los Angeles County's child protective services following her arrest. In May, Peggy McMartin Buckey testified that she had been molested as a child (a neighbor put his hand up her shirt), but she disputed the prosecution's claim that she had told McMartin parents the molestation was not a "big deal."[5] So much attention had been focused on the preschool's lone male teacher for so long that it was sometimes possible to forget that Peggy still faced charges herself. She sat quietly at the defense table, and she gave few interviews. Prosecutors questioned Peggy about her impressions of Ray. She said he was a shy and somewhat aimless young man, and she talked about his problems with alcohol and occasional marijuana use. She had once asked her son to speak with a church counselor about his lack of direction. Prosecutors stated that Ray had sought counseling for his problems with molesting children, but the minister who actually provided the counseling said there was "not a word of truth" to the allegation.[6]

The month she first testified, Peggy put two smiling bear stickers on a small memo pad and began to write. During recess breaks, sidebar conversations among the attorneys, and the other stretches of idle time that are a regular feature of any trial, she was writing. Raised a Christian Scientist by her mother, Virginia, Peggy's faith had intensified in the years following her arrest. She once told her attorney, Dean Gits, that she believed God had brought him to her in jail, and in the spring of 1989 she wrote down short prayers and bits of Scripture in her memo pad.[7] "Lord remind me that nothing is going to happen to me today that you & I can't handle together," the first one read. "God doesn't take you half the way, he takes you all the way," was the second. She encouraged herself to "be gentle, be loving." When encouragement wasn't enough, her notes took the form of mild admonishments—she once simply wrote "golden rule" in the corner of a page. Peggy had a harder time in jail and in court than did her son. She was constantly preoccupied by her plight, and she became somewhat paranoid. She wrote down lines from Psalm 19, and she focused on different words and phrases from day to day. One page includes various meditations on gratitude, and another deals with love: "<u>Love</u> is the liberator," "<u>Love</u> never loses sight of loveliness," and "<u>Love</u> must triumph over hate."[8] She used the notepad to keep on an even keel.

When Peggy took the witness stand she began to write out a list with the heading "Grateful For." She started out by listing standard virtues, each on its own line. First came "God," then "Life," then "Truth," "Love," and "Joy." But Peggy was on the stand for a long time, and the list grew. In items 32 through 101 she wrote out the first names of people she knew. Then she listed features of the natural world: "112. Sand, 113. Dirt, 114. Seeds, 115. Fog." Entries indicating gratitude for "Surf boards" and "Trucks" followed, and so did "Motels" and "Hospitals." She made it through "437. Freedom of speech," "568. Legs," and "588. Watering Can," before she ended the list at item number 598, "Beauty Shop." When her testimony ended, she set the notepad aside for the time being.

Ray Buckey spoke in front of a jury for the first time in July. Prosecutors spent much of his time there trying to determine, all the other evidence notwithstanding, whether he was the kind of weirdo who *would* molest children, given the chance. He spent hours answering questions about his habit of not wearing anything underneath his board shorts, and attorneys for both sides wanted to know why he had been spotted wearing a wire pyramid on his head while driving around Manhattan Beach in the early eighties. As it turned out, Ray had a good explanation for that, if also an odd one. In 1976 two writers, one of them an astrologer, claimed in their book *Pyramid Power* that ancient Egyptians had used the structures to store mystical energy that improved health and preserved food. Some people who felt this energy for themselves, the authors wrote, "were so energized that they could not cope with the dynamo effects they experienced."[9] Ray only wore the pyramid hat in his car when he felt he needed an extra boost for the day; normally he just slept beneath the pyramid that hung over his bed. "It was supposedly to help me sleep," he told Danny Davis on the stand. "Just the effect of a pyramid supposedly from what I had read and experimented with it, it either helped me sleep or was a great placebo."[10]

Feeding off the momentum of the new religious movements that proliferated around the country after the 1960s, pseudo-scientific health and self-improvement fads claiming links to ancient civilizations and means of tapping into different currents of energy had become popular. Pyramid power was one of them, and Ray seemed at least slightly embarrassed about having to discuss his youthful experiments in public. Davis kept the mood light. "Is it possible, Mr. Buckey, that pyramid power drove you to molest children?" he asked.

"No."

"Is it possible that pyramid power blanked your mind out so that you forgot horrible events like molesting children?"

"No."[11]

Ray also had a special kind of pyramid, amusingly called a "raydome," that was supposed to be more powerful than the normal kind. When Danny Davis asked Buckey to specify the extent of the raydome's capabilities, Dean Gits tried to raise an objection, but he broke down laughing after a second or two. "Laughter is not an objection," Judge Pounders said. "I'm glad you can still laugh."[12]

Buckey also testified about a weekend he spent selling pyramids at a healthy eating/UFO convention in the fall of 1982. Prosecutors wanted to poke holes in Buckey's claim that as a result of attending this conference, he had had sex with an adult woman. Working the pyramid booth in a Reno, Nevada, convention center, Buckey met Barbara Dusky, who was thirty years old and divorced. The pair hit it off, and the next day they set out together for Pyramid Lake, a body of water formed from headwaters that drain off Lake Tahoe. They stopped at a motel called the Fantasy Inn on the way, and the manager there gave them a room with a round bed, a heart-shaped bathtub, and red velour on the walls. They took a bath together. "And is it fair to say," Lael Rubin asked on cross-examination, "when the two of you took a bubble bath together, that neither of you had your clothes on?"

A: Neither one of us had our clothes on.

Q: Is it fair to say that during the time that you and Barbara were taking a bubble bath together in this heart-shaped tub, that you didn't have an erection?

A: I don't remember if I had an erection at that time.

Q: Is it fair to say that being in this heart-shaped tub, this bubble bath with Barbara did not sexually arouse you?

A: I think it did.

Q: Now, is it fair to say, Mr. Buckey, that after the two of you took this bubble bath together, you did not have any sexual relationship with her?

A: Oh, Miss Rubin, we had a sexual relationship.[13]

This was Ray's first sexual relationship, actually. He told Lael Rubin that he was "on cloud nine" with Barbara, around whom he felt "just like a puppy dog."[14] The following day the couple completed their trip down to Pyramid Lake, where they were baptized in the nude by a traveling minister. They saw each other a few more times in Manhattan Beach before going their separate ways.

Ray didn't want to ask Barbara Dusky to offer sworn testimony about a sexual encounter that had taken place eight years earlier, but Lael Rubin did. Dusky spoke warmly and affectionately about Ray, whom she described as an "inexperienced" lover. "[She's] straight out of central casting," Rubin said to reporters after Dusky's testimony. "The soaps ought to sweep her up while she's still in California. She's lying about everything."[15] Although Dusky's testimony probably did more to humanize Ray, at least from a sexual standpoint, than anything else in the case, it is hard to fault the district attorney's office for thinking to call her as a witness. Buckey often struck those around him as a little odd romantically, which is to say that some of his mother's friends worried he was gay. One family friend who shared this worry believed that Ray's repressed homosexuality would make him vulnerable during his time in jail, and when McMartin parents first received word of the allegations, one of them tried to console Peggy McMartin Buckey by saying that anybody could have a gay son.[16] Prosecutors never openly expressed a belief that Buckey was gay, but the idea was obviously implied by Rubin's incredulous reactions to the notion that Ray had once slept with a woman. The district attorney's office also put three investigators on the stand to testify that when Ray once spent an afternoon relaxing on the lawn of a local college, he rather suspiciously had *not* stared and gawked at the female students; instead, he spent time watching children run on the playground.[17]

Ray's imagined homosexuality had the potential to make a significant impact on the trial's outcome, as actual homosexuality helped send day care workers to prison in a number of other cases. In Maplewood, New Jersey, Kelly Michaels's attorney believed it was absolutely necessary to conceal her same-sex romance from the jury, and this made her defense much more difficult.[18] Michaels could not, for example, discuss the details of a doctor's visit she once made, the reason being that a lesbian friend had accompanied her to the appointment. Michaels believed that discussing the visit in court risked revealing her friend's homosexuality and, by extension, her own sexual history. That Michaels seemed unwilling to testify about the details of this visit was and still is regarded as suspicious by some of her critics.[19] In Pittsfield, Massachusetts, Bernard Baran was accused and prosecuted specifically because a mother's boyfriend, accused of abusing a small boy, redirected suspicion toward the gay nineteen-year-old. A number of people recalled the man expressing disgust at the idea of a gay man supervising his girlfriend's son in the weeks preceding his allegations, and Baran was sentenced to three life terms after his conviction.[20] This was another element of the day care and ritual abuse hysteria's political conservatism. The idea that gay sexuality necessarily included the desire to abuse children had been a founding myth of homophobic sex panics going back to World War II. By implying he was gay, Ray Buckey's prosecutors were simply pursuing a tactic with a proven record of success.

McMartin's slow pace had always been a curiosity and an annoyance, but as spring gave way to summer, the trial's length became a phenomenon in its own right. Journalists wrote about its duration and cost in almost unbelieving tones, and jurors progressing through their third year of civic service developed elaborate inside jokes and small ways of expressing frustration, such as bringing a birthday cake into their waiting room on the trial's anniversary. They did crossword puzzles to kill time during the many long bench conferences and breaks in testimony, and then they switched over to Uno. Having mastered and grown tired of Uno, they learned to play chess. One juror lost his wife and then remarried during the trial, and other jurors attended the wedding. Judge Pounders nervously monitored the jury for signs of discontentment and psychological stress. One member announced on a winter morning that she was buying a new car, and she asked her fellow jurors to help her come up with a personalized license plate relating to the trial. They wrote their suggestions on a chalkboard: $10ADAY (a juror's wage), JURY PRO, HUNGJRY, and ITEM352 were among them, the last referring to legal code for an objection to a prejudicial question. Pounders was so unnerved by this that he conducted a day-long inquiry into the license plates' meaning, interviewing jurors one by one.[21] When one juror said he needed to leave or else lose his job in tech support, Pounders hired him to fix computers for Los Angeles County.

Four of the original eighteen jurors (twelve primary members and six alternates) had been dismissed by the summer of 1989. In July a fifth juror learned she needed a gallbladder operation that entailed at least a month-long recovery. Pounders was frantic. With only one alternate remaining, two more jurors gone would mean the end, and Pounders had developed a deep pessimism about the trial's effects on those who surrounded it. "This case, in my view, has poisoned everyone who had contact with it," he said. "By that I mean every witness, every litigant, and every judicial officer."[22] He noted Judy Johnson's descent into alcoholism and death. There was also the defense investigator who committed suicide one day before he was to begin testimony in 1987. Pounders had a grim interpretation of the fact that so many jurors had dropped out for medical reasons: "I think it's due in part to the pressure," he said.[23] "There is a strong possibility that we're going to lose [another] juror before very long. In my view, it is a probability that this case will end in a mistrial."[24]

Spooked by his premonitions of judicial collapse, Pounders tried to get through the trial's final months as quickly as possible. Refusing to hear witnesses was the most effective way to hurry things along, and as the prosecution had rested its case some months ago, this meant refusing to hear defense witnesses. Pounders prevented more than two dozen people from taking the stand, among them two physicians ready to testify that one of the McMartin children had originally accused his father of molesting him, not Ray Buckey.[25] Danny Davis and Dean Gits were incensed at Pounders and much less worried than he about the prospect of further jury dropouts. "They look healthy to me," Davis said, "and the attrition rate over a long haul indicates that we'll have plenty of jurors and extras when it's over. I don't join in this kind of karmic doom that emanates from the judge."[26]

That their irritation had at least some justification can be seen in the fact that the defense was only allowed to present one medical expert in response to the six expert witnesses the prosecution presented. The most important of these excluded medical experts was John J. McCann. In the late 1980s, McCann and his colleagues became the first to conduct and present studies on what the genitals of nonabused children looked like. Ever since the passage of mandatory reporting laws in the 1970s, physicians and researchers had repeatedly photographed and described the genitalia of child sex abuse victims. In their haste to bring their diagnostic powers in line with their new professional duties, however, the researchers neglected to examine a control group. When they saw skin tags, dilation of the anus (Woodling's "wink response" test), and variations in the dimensions and shape of girls' hymens, they assumed they were looking at medical evidence of past abuse. McCann found all of these variations, however, in hundreds of nonabused children. In one presentation he said that he and his colleagues had to go through many slides of nonabused children before finding even *one* whose appearance perfectly matched the conventional understanding of what was normal.[27] Bands of redness, skin tags, and uneven pigmentation were found on many children's anuses.[28] Even more significantly, McCann found that the anal wink was also common in nonabused children, suggesting that Woodling's most widely publicized discovery had been completely in error. In examining prepubescent girls the researchers found that hymens also varied widely in size and shape.[29] The rounded or flattened edges that were often cited as evidence of abuse by Astrid Heger and other doctors appeared frequently in Mc-Cann's nonabused subject population. What this work highlighted, aside from a previously undocumented range of biological variety, were the severe diagnostic limitations of a field of medical knowledge that spent the seventies and eighties scrambling to catch up with the rising social and political importance of child abuse.

Though major injuries, still-healing wounds, the presence of bodily fluids, and sexually transmitted infections obviously could be diagnostic of abuse, there was no medical consensus at all on what to make of minor scars, abrasions, or areas of redness. Although such scars may provide useful corroborative evidence when a child patient describes abuse or when an adult caretaker has strong reasons to suspect that abuse occurred, pediatricians today caution against assigning too much significance to such phenomena on their own. At the very least, such physical findings should be cross-checked by an expert specialist.[30] This means that the responsible retrieval of a patient history is often the single-most important step toward accurately diagnosing sexual abuse, and "responsible" obviously is not the best word for the way in which the McMartin students' patient histories were retrieved. Though Heger was asked to discuss McCann's findings during her cross-examination, that is not the same thing as hearing from the expert in person, in his own words, which the jury never did. Instead, Virginia McMartin took the stand as the trial's final witness. Like everyone else, she was fed up. She replied to prosecutors' questions with long harangues and angry questions of her own. When Judge Pounders told her to answer the questions, Virginia exploded. "I just want to let all of you know that I'm a great believer in the Constitution," she said. "The Constitution says I have the right to talk all I want and to criticize public officials."[31] Pounders threatened to send her to jail until crying family members intervened to settle her down.

Closing arguments began on October 12, 1989. Peggy McMartin Buckey returned to her memo pad with another "What to be grateful for" list. God, life, truth, love, and joy occupied the top five once again. Lael Rubin's assistant prosecutor, Roger Gunson, was the first to speak. He said the children's most bizarre stories were confused but true accounts of strange events actually staged by Ray Buckey. He said the purpose of Buckey's pretending to beat a horse to death was specifically to damage the children's credibility later on—the jury must not be taken in.[32] Number 63 on Peggy's list was "creative." Myra and Abby Mann were numbers 81 and 82, and number 140 was "good reporters." Her attorney, Dean Gits, gave the second closing. He told the jury that although CII had initially drawn false allegations out of the McMartin children, it was the parents who did the crucial work of reinforcing those allegations in their well-intentioned efforts to be supportive. Item number 161 was "snow." Danny Davis spoke third. The first two attorneys' arguments had been brief, at least by the trial's standards, but when Davis began his presentation, he pointed to two enormous briefcases and said, "They're not full of lunch." His closing chugged along for six days. It included lectures on the progress of history and a surrealist painting. In a subsequent interview Davis recalled winning a moot court judgment during his first year in law school at the University of Texas. "There's something wrong with you," Davis remembered the judge telling him after his victory. "You won, but we don't like you. And when you go out into the real world, other judges aren't going to like you, either."[33]

Peggy started her list from scratch yet again when Lael Rubin rose to give the trial's final set of closing arguments on October 27. The prosecutor probably had more of her professional future riding on the jury's verdict than anybody else involved with the trial. She wrote the words "Don't Be Fooled" in block letters on a chalkboard near the jury box, and then she started to talk. She referred to a torn half-page that had gone missing from Virginia McMartin's diary, implying there was additional evidence the jurors should be thinking about, even if they hadn't seen it. "It reminds me of Watergate and the 18 minutes missing on the crucial tape," she said. "If there was nothing on the page, the person who cut it out would have been in here. . . . You have to keep asking yourself who is fooling with the evidence."[34] Peggy kept writing: "366. Toaster . . . 401. Banjo . . . 467. Air conditioning." On the final day of her closing argument, Rubin talked about medical evidence, recalling that Astrid Heger said she had found scarring on the genitals of all six girls listed as official complainants. Rubin also quoted the first parent who testified in the trial. She would have liked to believe that nothing happened, the parent said. "But I can't, because I talked to my daughter."[35] The final item on Peggy's list—number 712, after "jurors" and "bees"—was "children."[36]

The jurors deliberated for about a month, not counting a much-needed Christmas vacation. On January 18, 1990, their verdicts were read out in court.

As he flipped through the verdicts before having them announced, Judge Pounders's face turned red, then white.[37] The jury deadlocked on thirteen counts against Ray. The verdict on the other fifty-two counts against him and his mother was "not guilty." A single scream rang out in the gallery, and then people rushed out into the hallway and told reporters what they thought. Peggy finally expressed the anger she had sublimated for weeks with her silent list-making. "My concern was for my son and what they've done to him," she said. "I've gone through hell, and now I've lost everything." The parents were furious too. Some of them had grumbled for months that Lael Rubin and her colleagues were botching the prosecution, and the verdict validated all of their worst suspicions. "The system doesn't allow us to protect kids," said the father of two McMartin children. "I have no doubt these children were abused."[38] Some of the parents were photographed hugging and consoling their children, many of whom were now adolescents. Ray refused to talk to the press. He left the courthouse, stepped into his attorney's car, and drove off to some unknown location.

Anger and relief swirled around the courthouse, but the news also set off a frenzy of anxious retrospection. The day after the verdict, as the city's newspapers and TV stations provided saturation coverage of the trial, the *Los Angeles Times* published the first in a series of four columns by staff reporter David Shaw. Based on a three-month review of nearly two thousand print and television news pieces, Shaw argued that, especially in the early months of the investigation, the media "frequently plunged into hysteria, sensationalism, and what one editor calls 'a lynch mob syndrome.'"[39] He devoted one of these columns to Wayne Satz, the KABC reporter who first broke the story, and another to his own employer, the *Los Angeles Times*. "The *Times*," he wrote, "is the largest and most influential news organization in the area," and he found that the paper "did seem to ignore, minimize or cover late various developments that tended to raise questions about the prosecution's case." Shaw concluded that the paper's coverage was biased, and in 1991 he was rewarded for his willingness to criticize the paper that employed him with the Pulitzer Prize in Criticism (this less than a decade removed from a climate in which major papers had been totally unwilling to publish skeptical reporting on day care and ritual abuse).[40]

Satz did not take kindly to Shaw's analysis, which characterized his early McMartin reports as a "daily drumbeat of charges and disclosures."

But even as he wrote an amusing and mildly indignant letter to the editor, Satz gave an interview in which he agreed with Shaw's larger thesis. "I found the coverage to be pack journalism—relatively mindless, as if reporters didn't trust [their] own perceptions," Satz said. "I don't have a whole lot of respect for the news media today." By this point Satz had left KABC. He said he was planning a funny cable show that would satirize the media and the role it played in manipulating people's opinions.[41]

To most of those who followed the trial during its six-year run, these arguments about media bias would have been familiar to the point of exhaustion or boredom. But they were completely new to the McMartin jurors. Having spent three years in a closely monitored state of information isolation, jurors could now return to their jobs, watch the local news, and read the morning paper. Many of them took advantage of their first opportunity to speak to the media—or to anyone at all, technically—about the case. An interviewer sat down with seven jury members and asked whether they thought that at least some of the children had been molested. All seven said yes—with qualifications. One juror said that although children "may" have been abused, he thought the prosecution failed to prove it. Another felt a little more confident that molestation had occurred *somewhere*, but she saw no really convincing evidence that abuse took place at the preschool. None of the jurors thought that any of the children intentionally lied on the stand, but they thought the CII interviews made it impossible to draw clear distinctions between obvious fantasies and more plausible allegations.

More than anything else, the jurors said—more than the stories of satanic ritual abuse, more than the child witnesses' shifting accounts of what happened—it was viewing the CII videotapes that compelled them to acquit Peggy on all charges and Ray on most of them. "I could not tell from watching the tape," one juror said, "that the children were telling what actually happened to them, or if they were repeating what their parents told them." Another said, "We never got the children's story in their own words." Overall, the group took a melancholy view of the trial. "I think everybody was a victim," one said. "I don't think anybody came out of this case better off than they were before."[42]

Jurors worried about readjusting to normal life after such a long time in court, but they were proud of their work and believed they had delivered a responsible verdict. The consensus around Los Angeles, however, and especially around Manhattan Beach, was rather different. Jurors fielded constant questions from relatives at home, friends at work, and even strangers in restaurants and cafés—how could they possibly have let the McMartin teachers go? Some of the conversations that ensued produced an understanding, but others ended angrily. Many people were still convinced of the Buckeys' guilt. When one television station organized a call-in poll to gauge the public's reaction, viewers asserted by a margin of seven-to-one that "justice was not served."

This anger reached one kind of apotheosis on a Saturday evening in late January when people began to gather outside the Manhattan Beach police station. The crowd included McMartin parents, new mothers pushing strollers, and local teenagers, and it had grown to more than five hundred people by the time it started marching through town. They carried signs and bumper stickers with various slogans about children on them. If anything, the verdicts strengthened the protesters' sense of the horrors that had visited Manhattan Beach. "We have 1,400 disclosing children in this community," one woman told a reporter from *60 Minutes*. "1,400 children in this community have been ritualistically abused. Eight schools have been shut down. 1,400 children! I mean does that— doesn't that hit you?"[43]

Cyclists and people eating dinner at outdoor cafés and restaurants shouted words of support as the protesters worked their way down the Strand. One photograph shows marchers in short sleeves with the Pacific Ocean in the background. It looks like a beautiful evening. Aside from mobilizing and expressing the community's free-floating anger, the march's purpose was to cap off a letter-writing campaign designed to pressure Ira Reiner's office into retrying Ray on the remaining thirteen undecided counts, but one speech given at the end of the march suggested that the parents' relationship with the DA was beyond all saving. "The crime outside the courtroom," one McMartin parent said, "was almost equaled by the crime inside the courtroom."[44]

Many people agreed that the system's betrayal of those it was meant to protect was obvious. The jury's failure to reach a guilty verdict on any of the sixty-five counts was, of course, painful enough on its own, but it was the trial's extraordinary duration and expense that really made the acquittal sting. Had $15 million and more than six years of work really produced *nothing* of value or use? Developments elsewhere in the country began to give parents and prosecutors the impression that the trial's net effect might actually have been counterproductive, at least in terms of society's willingness to recognize and deal with instances of mass abuse in child care. The increased scrutiny now being directed toward ritual abuse investigations cast earlier convictions in a new light. In Kern County, California, six children recanted testimony they gave in the "Pitts ring" investigation and trial.[45] An appeals court overturned seven convictions and threw out the more than twenty-five hundred years' worth of prison sentences that went along with them on the grounds of serious prosecutorial misconduct. In El Paso, Michelle Noble and Gayle Dove had their guilty verdicts overturned. At conferences, therapists and detectives began to refer to their critics, who seemed to be gaining ground, as "the backlash." They worried McMartin would come to be known as little more than a wasteful embarrassment.

This assessment was too pessimistic by half. Caught up in their anxiety over a handful of judicial reversals in a handful of states, parents and their allies failed to recognize the continued influence of the powerful fears that made the trials possible to begin with. By 1990 the panic's psychological roots ran deep, and their effects were still unfolding in Sacramento. In June state legislators put Proposition 115, the Crime Victims Justice Reform Act, to a statewide vote. The measure was approved by a fourteen-point margin, and it was a windfall for prosecutors, radically shifting the balance of power in California's criminal justice system. Hearsay evidence became admissible under certain circumstances. Under this change the McMartin students would never have been compelled to testify nor, in all probability, would the jury have seen the CII videotapes; testimony from parents and therapists, relaying what they remembered the children saying to them, would have sufficed. The proposition also removed clauses from the state constitution that provided defendants indicted under a grand jury with the right to a preliminary hearing.

After the verdict people had often cited McMartin's eighteen-month preliminary hearing as evidence of the need for reform. But it is not at all clear that people other than prosecutors and their allies saw the McMartin hearing as a waste: it decreased the size of the case, both in terms of the number of defendants and the number of charges against them, by more than two-thirds. Had seven teachers gone to trial, the whole process may well have taken even longer, and it is also fair to say that without the preliminary hearing, guilty verdicts would have been more likely (certainly, at least, for Ray and his mother). The possibly unconscious assumption pushing these reforms into law was that the McMartin jury had come to the wrong verdict. The jurors themselves saw this very clearly, and they resented it. "Now that we found them not guilty, everyone wants to change the system," one said. "If we had found them guilty, no one would have wanted to change anything."[46]

The same assumption lay at the bottom of an article Lois Timnick wrote for the *Los Angeles Times* about how McMartin prompted reforms within day care. Despite the "initial hysteria" that ripped through the South Bay, Timnick argued, the case had ultimately brought positive change to the child care industry. Whereas pre-McMartin facilities had been largely unregulated, most centers now subjected job applicants to criminal background checks, and some analyzed prospective teachers for personality traits thought by law enforcement to correspond with pedophilia. Other centers instituted policies ensuring that no adult teacher was ever left alone with a single child—a second teacher had to be in the room as well. "Good schools," Timnick wrote, might also allow parents to secretly observe their children at day care via windows or one-way mirrors. The piece acknowledged studies demonstrating that children actually faced a far greater risk of abuse in the home than at day care, but all of the reforms it praised were aimed, first, at easing parents' largely unjustified anxieties and, second, at shielding day care workers from Ray Buckey's fate. "We want to provide safeguards," one Kentucky child care coordinator said, "and we don't want to leave ourselves open to being accused."[47] Day care was being reformed as though the Buckeys had been found guilty.

In any case, it turned out that the judiciary wasn't quite done with Ray Buckey. Civil suits of all kinds threatened to keep courts occupied with the preschool for years, and two weeks after the verdict prosecutors announced that they would retry Buckey on the thirteen remaining counts. Buckey faced thirty-two years in prison. Jury selection began almost immediately.

Speculation swirled about the political arithmetic behind the decision to stage another trial; Ira Reiner was engaged in a tough primary campaign for state attorney general, and the first McMartin verdict was just one in a series of recent high-profile courtroom defeats for the sitting city attorney. Everyone was angry. Ray Buckey went on *Larry King* and *60 Minutes*, vowing to fight the charges to his dying breath.[48] Judge Pounders appeared on *Oprah* to discuss the case, prompting defense attorneys to file motions asking that he not be allowed to preside over the retrial. And parents, still feeling disenchanted with the district attorney's office and suspicious of its motives, decided to mount one last independent investigation.

In the spring Danny Davis sold the McMartin Preschool building to a Manhattan Beach realtor named Arnold Goldstein, who planned to knock it down and put an office building in its place. A month or so before the demolition crew was scheduled to arrive, parents asked Goldstein for permission to excavate the grounds for a second time, which he granted. "I'm permitting these people to go on the property to find whatever they want and get it out of their system," Goldstein said. "It would be nice if this would all die down."[49] Parents began by using a concrete saw to cut a rectangular hole in a classroom floor.

The dig did not get McMartin out of the parents' system; it just provided them with another opportunity to stage the anger that had been concentrated and re-energized by the twilight march through the streets of Manhattan Beach. Whereas their 1985 dig had been essentially haphazard and impulsive, they made what were at least cosmetic efforts to do things responsibly this time around. They hired a geologist and a photographer to document whatever they were to find, and they also brought in a professional to lead and supervise the whole endeavor. With a major judicial defeat on the books, though, the parents' cause was perhaps a bit less respectable than it had previously been, and this seems to have nudged them toward extremism.

Leading the dig was Ted Gunderson, a private investigator who had formerly been the Los Angeles Bureau Chief for the FBI. He grew distant from and then left the Bureau in the late eighties while cultivating an interest in the satanic menace (he appeared on the 1988 *Geraldo* Satanism special and talked about the devil worshippers' supposedly sophisticated communication networks). By the time he came to Manhattan Beach he was an enthusiastic conspiracy theorist who gave lectures all across the United States. (Later he did a lot to publicize the "chemtrails" conspiracy theory, which holds that the government makes use of commercial airplanes to lace the atmosphere with harmful biological agents.) All indications are that he had a great time excavating McMartin. He posed for photographs displaying the haul of allegedly satanic artifacts retrieved from the site, and he struck up a romance with one of the McMartin mothers.[50] That relationship was sadly not built to last—the woman later accused Gunderson of embezzling $30,000 from her.[51]

An archaeologist named Gary Stickel produced a report on the dig's results. (Reflecting the endlessly tangled politics of the ritual abuse panic, the publication of this report was funded in part by what Stickel described as "a generous donation from Gloria Steinem.")[52] The main lot measured approximately 115 by 35 feet, and the team also explored an adjacent lot of similar size. The hole carved out of the floor in the classroom produced wood chips, charcoal, ribbons, and some pieces of glass, concrete, and ceramic. When a professional mineral miner dug some two feet further down, he found large roots, fragments of wood, and what was catalogued as a "prehistoric Native American chert scraper."[53] On May 2 a backhoe rolled in and excavated a trench along the building's west wall, uncovering what appeared to be garbage from the 1940s.

Objects of more recent provenance were also discovered. Stickel saw two of these finds as particularly crucial. The first was a plastic bag with images of cartoon Disney characters on it, bearing the copyright date 1983. The second was a pair of metal clamps, whose manufacture could be dated to after the school's construction, attached to some plumbing a couple of feet below ground near the outer wall. Unless there were tunnels providing some means of access, Stickel did not see a way for these objects to have ended up in the dirt. The entire building sat on a thick concrete slab, making it impossible to get at the school's underground plumbing by going through the floor. (Stickel did not consider what this slab meant for the children's stories of trap doors leading underground.) But Stickel also firmly believed the crew *had* discovered tunnels. Underneath two of the classrooms, excavators located what appeared to be filled-in areas leading out beyond the school's walls. Remove the fill, Stickel wrote, and you had a tunnel large enough to accommodate adults with ease.

Time constraints cut the dig short. Goldstein wasn't willing to postpone the school's demolition any further, so Stickel had to mark down some of his findings as inconclusive. But for the parents who cheered as bulldozers finally tore down the McMartin Preschool in late May, there was no doubt that tunnels had been there all along, waiting for someone committed enough to find them. That Memorial Day weekend was filled with news reports of the team's discoveries, as Ted Gunderson gave interviews describing the dig.

One of the few skeptical voices in the media was that of Paul Barron, a private investigator working for Danny Davis. He said bluntly that the

"tunnels" were more likely a collection of old "shitholes." Although he may
have selected his words primarily for effect, they were also probably accurate. Property records show that a private home and garage sat on the preschool's adjacent lot as early as 1928. Manhattan Beach was a rural area at
the time, far from the center of Los Angeles and lacking city services. The
absence of trash collection would be especially relevant here. The filled-in
depressions were most likely old trash pits, a hypothesis strengthened by
all the old rubbish found on the site. The presence of the two objects that
postdated the school's construction also has a benign explanation. The
Disney bag found two feet underground near the school's edge was probably brought there by some burrowing animal. As for the plumbing clamps,
located at a similar shallow depth near the school's edge, a plumber could
have easily installed them by digging down from outside the building.[54]
None of these possibilities are considered in Stickel's report, and well into
the 1990s the existence of real tunnels underneath McMartin would remain an article of faith among a small, dedicated group.[55]

The second McMartin trial began on May 7, and it was a miniaturized
version of the original; everybody knew that nobody was going to tolerate
another long proceeding. Because of two parents' unwillingness to have
their child testify for a second time, the number of charges against Ray
had dropped to eight. A new judge, Stanley Weisberg, oversaw the case—
Pounders had been let off following his *Oprah* appearance—and a new
prosecutor was on hand to try it. Only three children testified, and the
years separating them from the case's origins had done their memories
no favors. An eleven-year-old girl said that Ray took pictures of her in
the nude, but she faltered when asked about the specific content of the
charges against Ray. Did Ray put anything inside her vagina? "Not that I
can remember," she said, and she provided the same answer when asked
about anal penetration.[56] Astrid Heger testified again about the results
of her medical examinations, but Kee MacFarlane's role was very diminished. The prosecution wrapped up its case and handed things over to the
defense after only three weeks.

From a distance, it looked very much like an ordinary criminal proceeding working to resolve an unusual but not outrageous set of allegations. It was only on the periphery that little events recalled the case's
colorful past. The old anxiety about a possible mistrial rose up again when
Judge Weisberg had to excuse a juror after half an hour on the first day.
The woman's boat had caught fire over the weekend, and she could not

stop coughing in the jury box. In Hermosa Beach the head minister at St. Cross Episcopal Church, the formerly alleged site of Ray Buckey's black mass, announced he would seek disability retirement. He could no longer withstand the "extreme stress" caused by repeated episodes of vandalism and harassment. When Virginia McMartin took the stand, the new judge eventually had to ask her to refrain from embellishing answers with long harangues. She responded as she had in the past: "Oh, you're not allowed freedom of speech in *this* court, either!"[57]

There were many elements of the investigation that did not make an appearance at the second trial. Perhaps the most remarkable exclusion was that of the woman who started everything. Prosecutors, of course, had no desire to bring up Judy Johnson, whose alcoholism and mental illness were certain to work against the story they wanted to tell. Danny Davis did want to include Johnson as part of his arguments, but her son was not listed as a complainant on any of the remaining eight charges. The presiding judge refused to compel Matthew to testify, and so McMartin attained the further distinction of having lasted long enough to officially forget its origins. The McMartin II jury heard nothing about Judy Johnson. These and other constraints brought the defense's presentation to a quick end. Courtroom officials originally promised a six-month trial, but the case was handed over to the jury on July 3, just three months after opening arguments. The jury deliberated for six hours a day. On July 15 the foreman informed Judge Weisberg that they were hopelessly deadlocked, favoring acquittal on six of the eight counts but completely unable to make further progress. Weisberg summoned jurors to the courtroom and asked each one whether he or she agreed with their foreman's assessment. They did. "I don't think you could ever get 12 people together who could make a unanimous decision on this," said one jury member.[58] Weisberg declared a mistrial, and one week later he presided over the McMartin case's final criminal hearing. "The case of the People vs. Raymond Buckey is hereby dismissed, and the defendant is discharged," he said. "All right, that's it. That completes this case."[59]

Chapter 9

Therapists and Survivors

The final collapse of the McMartin trial dealt a serious blow to the day care and ritual abuse panic's legal and political fortunes. In 1983 prosecutors and reporters had quite reasonably seen McMartin as the kind of case that could launch a whole career; now it stood as one of the great judicial debacles in California history. District attorneys slowly began to shy away from similar cases, or at least to pursue them with slightly less enthusiasm—the risks they presented often seemed to outweigh the potential benefits. However, a social panic doesn't only reside in a society's legal and political institutions; it also lives in the private mental experiences of individuals and the tools people use to make sense of those experiences, which is to say that a panic is also a matter of psychology. As day care prosecutions receded into the middle distance, Multiple Personality Disorder (MPD) and the recovered memory therapists who championed it came fully into their own. These therapists' successes made what had been a rare and fantastic diagnosis into a kind of national shorthand for the effects of childhood sexual trauma on people's adult lives.

Ellen Bass, a poet by training who studied with Anne Sexton at Boston University, was one of the most important advocates for recovered memory therapy and MPD. She first became aware of child abuse in 1974, when a student in her creative writing workshop submitted a thinly veiled autobiographical account of her childhood experiences of incest. Over the next few years Bass encountered many women with similar stories, and she guided them as they tried to turn their experiences into poetry and prose. In time she began to collect these accounts. She had in mind a book that would bring them together and demonstrate to survivors that they were not alone.

In 1983 Bass published an anthology called *I Never Told Anyone: Writings by Women Survivors of Child Sexual Abuse*.[1] By this point she was also working as a counselor to groups and individuals, and she wanted to provide survivors with a practical guide to the healing process. Again she solicited stories and poems, and she took on Laura Davis, one of her clients, as a coauthor. Together the pair produced a handbook for adult women who wanted to acknowledge, work through, and repair the psychological damage done to them in childhood. *The Courage to Heal: A Guide for Women Survivors of Child Sexual Abuse*, was published in 1988.[2] In the preface, Bass admitted and even emphasized her lack of formal training. "None of what is presented here," she wrote, "is based on psychological theories." The book would go on to sell more than a million copies and is currently available in its fourth edition.

The Courage to Heal became the recovered memory movement's indispensable text, and Bass's disclaimer notwithstanding, it was obviously based on the same psychological theories that had begun to circulate at MPD conferences earlier in the decade. Assuming a vulgarized Freudian model that replaced the psychic repression of unwanted thoughts and desires with the total repression of events that actually occurred, Bass and Davis addressed long passages directly to women who didn't yet know they were victims. "You may have forgotten large chunks of your childhood," they wrote. "Yet there are things you do remember. When you are touched in a certain way, you feel nauseated. Certain words or facial expressions scare you. . . . You were taken to the doctor repeatedly for vaginal infections."[3] Odd revulsions, reluctance to spend time with a certain family member, fear of basements, and similar experiences made it likely that buried memories were waiting to be drawn to the surface. Although these memories might be hazy, dreamlike, or fragmentary, the authors wrote, that was no reason to discount their authenticity: "If you . . . have a feeling that something happened to you, it probably did."[4] And if a long course of therapy failed to stitch these memory bits into a coherent narrative whole, that still shouldn't dissuade you from confronting those who may have abused you. "To say 'I was abused,'" they wrote, "you don't need the kind of recall that would stand up in a court of law."[5]

On the surface, the popularity of such a book is baffling. It is hard to imagine a group of people who would welcome the revelation that such awful traumas had disfigured their childhoods and, as a consequence, their adult lives. But like no previous book, *The Courage to Heal* outfitted victimization with a redemption narrative, and in recasting victims as survivors, it made victimization into an identity with its own kind of bleak attractiveness. Though it warned that any kind or degree of abuse, from violent rape all the way down to being made to "listen to sexual talk," would inevitably have severe, long-term psychological effects, it also provided constant reassurances that things would improve in time, and it mapped out recovery's "stages" in detail. Other affirmations included the injunction to honor the things one did to survive the abuse by regarding coping mechanisms—including split personalities and memory repression—as signs of the survivor's ingenuity and strength.

The book also advocated a regimen of self-care directed in particular at the survivor's "inner child," a part of the psyche paralyzed in a state of arrested development by the abuse. "Your job is to give that child pleasure and to listen to the stories she has to tell," Bass and Davis wrote. One survivor described caring for her inner child by throwing herself a birthday party as though she were three years old. She planned to gather her friends together, make a fort out of sheets, and spend the night inside, reading stories by flashlight. "Oh, I love being little!" she wrote.[6]

Different kinds of pleasure took on an oddly prominent place in *The Courage to Heal*. In addition to giving survivors permission simply to spend time doing activities they liked, with inner-child care as the cover story, Bass and Davis described the healing process as intellectually fascinating, with memory retrieval as the highlight. If McMartin turned many parents into rogue investigators, monitoring their children's behavior and the school's grounds for evidence, *The Courage to Heal* made survivors into amateur detectives of the unconscious. On their own the memories and flashbacks, coming in dreamlike fragments, would not provide an intelligible picture of the abuse's chronology or substance. The survivor had to help, and Bass and Davis described the process as "like putting together a jigsaw puzzle." Solving the puzzle was important emotional work that was also interesting in its own right. "Part of me felt like I was on the trail of a murder mystery," one survivor wrote. "I really enjoyed following all the clues. 'Okay, I was looking at the clock. It was mid-afternoon. Why was it mid-afternoon? Where could my mother have been? Oh, I bet she was at . . .' Tracing down the clues to find out exactly what had happened was actually fun."[7]

It was also clear, however, that Bass and Davis expected the process of recovering abuse memories to be horribly upsetting, even debilitating. The second step in their recovery schema, right after making the "decision to heal," was "the emergency stage," which they described as follows:

> The emergency stage feels like this: You walk out the door to go to work, and you fall on the steps and break your leg. Your spouse tries to drive you to the hospital, but the engine of your car blows up. You go back to the house to call an ambulance, only to find you've locked yourself out. Just as a police car pulls over to give you some help, the big earthquake hits, and your home, your spouse, your broken leg, and the police car all disappear into a yawning chasm.[8]

Many of the women interviewed for *The Courage to Heal* described personal, social, and professional breakdowns. "I just lost it completely," one said. "I would go out in the middle of the night and hide somewhere, behind a Dipsy dumpster or something."[9] Bass and Davis wrote that the emergency stage could be especially crippling for people who repressed their abuse. Davis knew from experience. When she recovered her first memories it made her entire life seem a falsehood. "If this could have happened and I could have forgotten it," she wrote, "then every assumption I had about life and my place in it was thrown up for question." Survivors quit jobs, cut off communication with everyone other than their therapists, and spent long periods of time alone in the outdoors. "I dropped everything else in my life," one wrote. "It was like there were large six-foot-high letters in my living room every day when I woke up: *INCEST!*"[10]

Things supposedly calmed down to a certain extent after the emergency stage, but it seemed that no part of the healing process was without its attendant crises. And although *The Courage to Heal* always kept its readers oriented toward recovery, at least on the surface, the testimony of some survivors suggested that much of what made the process appealing were the crises themselves. This fact slipped out in asides and stray bits of observation, as when the authors introduced a survivor who had been recovering abuse memories for the past *ten years*. Although this constituted more than a quarter of the woman's life, she said the passage of time had made memory retrieval more difficult, not less. "I believe [the memories] now," she said. "It hurts more. I have the emotions to feel the impact."[11] The memory retrieval process also echoed the day care abuse investigations in that the initial discovery of abuse often led not to resolution and healing but to the repeated discovery of more and increasingly bizarre abuse. "The more I worked on the abuse, the more I remembered," one woman said. "First I remembered my brother, and then my grandfather. About six months after that I remembered my father. And then about a year later, I remembered my mother." Retrieving these memories was traumatic, but she ultimately found the revelation that everyone in her family had abused her for years to be reassuring. "My life suddenly made sense."[12]

The memories did not make sense of everybody's life, though. A section titled "Believing It Happened" quoted a number of survivors who clearly remained skeptical of their memories long after recovering them. "Up until three months ago," one said, "I didn't *really* believe it happened: 'It was hypnosis.' 'I only imagined it.' I was acting as if it really happened. I'd go to an incest survivor's group. I'd freely tell people. But when I was alone, I'd say, 'Of course it didn't *really* happen.'"[13] Like Freud's early patients, who reluctantly assented to his belief in their histories of childhood abuse even as they lacked any "feeling of remembering the scenes," this survivor identified as a victim despite the intuition that her abuse memories were somehow fundamentally not like her other memories of normal life.[14] "It's natural that you have periodic doubts," Bass and Davis wrote, breezily dismissing all the things their readers actually knew of their own experience. "But that's because accepting memories is painful, not because you weren't abused."[15] One of the book's final sections, "For Counselors," drove home similar points to the psychologists, family therapists, and social workers who made up another key chunk of the intended audience. "No one fantasizes abuse," it read. "Believe the survivor. You must believe that your client was sexually abused, even if she sometimes doubts it herself." And, "Be willing to believe the unbelievable. Working with survivors puts you face to face with the sickest, most twisted things human beings do to each other."[16]

Recovered memory therapists believed their breakthroughs were possible because they were able to acknowledge and confront what Freud and his Victorian contemporaries could not. In rehabilitating the seduction theory almost a century after its initial proposal, they saw themselves as heirs and successors to Freud's only truly revolutionary work, work that had been carried out in the white heat of passionate commitment and then abandoned out of careerism, in response to social denial. "Freud's new theory," Bass and Davis wrote, referring to the system of Oedipal complexes that replaced the seduction theory, "was obviously more palatable to society and to the patriarchal profession in which he worked."[17]

What these vulgar Freudians miss, however, is the fact that the seduction theory was not revolutionary for its time, nor did it provoke a storm of criticism within the psychiatric community. It only added a new wrinkle—the idea that the repressed traumatic events *must* have taken place before puberty—to a line of thought that had been developing, step by step, for more than a century. In 1864 the physician Moritz Benedikt began to publish a series of papers arguing that a secret, usually having to do with sex, lay at the root of many cases of hysteria.[18] Further back in the history of dynamic psychotherapy was the German physician Franz Anton Mesmer, who theorized in 1779 that the key to treating disease lay in provoking "crises" within the patient. Only by inducing successive attacks of asthma in an asthmatic person, for example, would the symptoms eventually disappear. This was a key predecessor to Freud's emphasis on the need to "reproduce" traumatic scenes and, in turn, to Bass and Davis's emergency stage.[19] Preceding Mesmer was Father Johann Joseph Gassner, known during his life as one of Germany's most brilliant healers. Gassner also ascribed great therapeutic significance to the crisis, but he was an exorcist, not a physician, and he believed the crisis was evidence of possession. When the Enlightenment drove the exorcist and demonic possession out of good standing, the physician and multiple personality replaced them, accounting for at least some of the ease with which MPD and recovered memory therapy in the 1980s often produced stories of satanic abuse.[20]

Well before Freud ever got involved, the nineteenth century also saw prolonged debates about split personalities, forgotten trauma, and the efficacy of hypnosis as a treatment for hysteria. In the 1880s the French psychologist and psychotherapist Pierre Janet (who coined the term "subconscious") conducted experiments on a nineteen-year-old woman named Lucie, who suffered from sudden attacks of crippling terror that she could not explain. He hypnotized Lucie and discovered a second personality hidden inside her. This second personality, Adrienne, constantly relived an experience from early in Lucie's life in which two men jumped out at her from behind a curtain as a practical joke—that was the cause of Lucie's attacks of fear. Janet went on to theorize more generally that hysterical symptoms were caused by split parts of the patient's personality. These personalities could be brought into the open and treated via hypnosis, at which point the therapist could guide the patient through age regression to recover the original trauma. Janet believed it was necessary to heighten psychological tension within the patient in order to make the symptoms disappear for good.[21]

Janet and Freud both studied at the famous Salpêtrière hospital in Paris, working at the clinic established there in 1882 by the neurologist Jean-Martin Charcot. With forty-five buildings, streets, gardens, and even its own church, the Salpêtrière was less a hospital than a small independent city, and Charcot was its philosopher-king. He was one of the most famous scientists in Europe, a status he achieved in part thanks to his flair for the dramatic. Charcot was believed to have discovered hysteria, hypnotism, and split personalities, achievements for which he was bestowed the nickname "Napoleon of Neuroses." He published selections from his collection of rare works on witchcraft and possession under the title *The Diabolical Library*. He charged enormously high fees in his private practice, and he put on public demonstrations of the effects his hypnotic treatments had on the young hysterics (mostly women) who lived at the Salpêtrière.

These demonstrations attracted intensely interested crowds of fellow scientists (all, naturally, men), and Charcot's own photographs of his patients in the midst of hysterical fits make it easy to understand why.[22] The women's poses are extraordinarily varied and interesting: sometimes playful and childlike, sometimes prone and vulnerable. They lie in beds and wear loose garments that fall away at the shoulders. Sometimes, in these beds and in these clothes, their bodies and faces contort and strain in what is unmistakably a pose of sexual arousal. Audience members could enjoy these displays while simultaneously condescending to the women who put them on. Charcot's assistant, assenting to the widely held belief that hysterics were vain, dramatic, and often dishonest, thought these traits were just exaggerated manifestations of normal female character. "One might even say that hysterics are more womanly than other women," he said.[23] A strange atmosphere of mutual suggestion seemed to circulate among the Salpêtrière's physicians and patients.

Charcot made a big impression on the young Freud. In an obituary he wrote for the great neurologist in 1893, Freud said of Charcot's lectures that "each . . . was a little work of art in construction and composition; it was perfect in form and made such an impression that for the rest of the day one could not get the sound of what he had said out of one's ears."[24] In addition to the time he spent watching Charcot stage his demonstrations with the appealingly feminine hysterics, Freud also explored the contemporary scientific literature on incest, which was the subject of lively professional debate and study. Freud owned copies of works on child abuse by Paul Brouardel, chair of legal medicine at the University of Paris, and Paul Bernard, who taught at the University of Lyon. Bernard's *Sexual Assaults on Young Girls* documented more than thirty-five thousand reported attacks in France between 1827 and 1870, and Bernard wrote that he was particularly "struck by the large number of cases of incest."[25] Brouardel was more reluctant to specifically assign blame to fathers, but he did remark that "sexual assaults are crimes of the home."[26] The seduction theory as eventually articulated by Freud, then, simply took up work being carried out by many European physicians and applied it to the problem of hysteria in a new way. With its belief that repressed traumas caused hysterical symptoms, its rhetorical habit of regarding women and children as interchangeably helpless, and its faith in hypnosis as a means of accessing and treating the buried memories, the seduction theory may well be the most conventionally Victorian of Freud's ideas.

It was not until his abandonment of the Seduction Theory, which led directly to the invention of the Oedipus complex and mature psychoanalytic thought, that Freud decisively broke with Victorian notions about the psychology of trauma. Although it is true that part of this shift involved Freud's realization that much of what he had previously taken for accurate memories were actually fantasies of events that never occurred, it would be more truthful, as a matter of emphasis, to say that Freud discovered that his patients' *fantasies* were *real*. Dreams, unwanted sexual or violent desires, memories that turned out to be false—Freudian psychoanalysis recognized that all of these could affect people's interior lives in ways that were just as tangible and consequential as those exercised by external events. Casting the distinction between fantasies and memories of real events as, in a sense, unimportant of course made psychoanalysis useless in forensic terms, but that was part of the point. In ascribing so much power to mental life in its own right, psychoanalysis rebuked those theorists and physicians who insisted that symptoms of hysterical illness must have their source in some obviously traumatic life event. These physicians,

Freud argued, had insufficiently credited both the complexity and the force of the mind's responses to what happened around it. This proposition was still provoking angry objections in the late 1980s.

Recovered memory therapists paid constant homage to the seduction theory–era Freud, but in practice they more often appeared to see themselves as latter-day Charcots. The technical signature of Freudian psychoanalysis is the therapist's impassivity, his prohibition against endorsing or condemning his patients' thoughts and feelings. Even the arrangement of the analyst's office, no longer much in use but still familiar to many people via decades of *New Yorker* cartoons, enforced this distance, with the patient prone on a couch and the analyst seated out of the patient's view. Recovered memory therapists, however, cultivated intimacy. This was true in the early days of "Sybil's" dependence on Cornelia Wilbur and Michelle Smith's marriage to her therapist, Lawrence Pazder, and it was true as recovered memory reached its peak in the late eighties and early nineties. Therapists made themselves available for frequent phone calls. The establishment of dedicated recovered memory and MPD clinics in St. Paul, Dallas, Chicago, and elsewhere—little Salpêtrières scattered across the country—ensured that doctors were in constant contact with their patients and, crucially, that patients were in constant contact with one another. The contents of the recovered memories also furthered this sense of closeness. As patients discovered they had been betrayed by their fathers, then their brothers, then their uncles and also their mothers and grandparents, the therapist began to seem the only trustworthy person left.

Patients saw their therapists and fellow MPD sufferers as making up a kind of surrogate family, and as in most families, that involved a clear hierarchy to go along with the nurturing care. The men who ran these clinics (and it was, in fact, usually men) were patriarchs surrounded by patients who, because they invested so much energy in cultivating and communicating with their inner children, were predisposed to thinking of themselves as infantile.

This dynamic was not subtle. Colin Ross, one of the most prominent figures in the treatment of MPD, wrote in one of his books that the disorder could best be described as "a little girl imagining that the abuse is happening to someone else," and he liked the line so much that he used it again in a completely different passage.[27] In group therapy, patients were asked to vent their anger by striking at mattresses with rubber hoses and yelling at their absent childhood tormentors. These outbursts alternated with periods spent in tears, as patients held teddy bears and curled up in the therapist's arms. The emotionally grueling quality of these sessions sometimes ran alongside or on top of a thinly veiled and repressed eroticism that also seemed drawn from the intimacy of family life.

The recovered memory therapist Richard Kluft, one of the founders of the International Society for the Study of Multiple Personality and Dissociation, described the experience of treatment as "exquisitely uncomfortable" for the patient."[28] And if patients expressed too many doubts about their memories, if they stepped back to wonder at the enormous gulf separating their new abuse narratives from everything they had previously known of their lives, the therapist, whether male or female, could fully inhabit the role of dad at the head of the table. One journalist attended a group therapy retreat at which a woman named Andrea wrestled with having recovered memories of her mother in a satanic cult. "I don't know if what I'm remembering is really true!" she said. "I don't want the memories to be true." Her therapist, Beth, replied, "Andrea, all the wants in the world can't change what you know. You really know inside what happened, but you spend all your energy saying, 'No, it didn't.' You need to face those memories, that rage. I want you to get onto a mattress. Now."[29]

Although the popular literature on MPD tended to repeat simple versions of Freud's ideas about trauma and the unconscious, more academic recovered memory researchers proposed an entirely different psychological mechanism by which abuse memories were pushed out of view. Whereas repression, in the classic view, involved a mind divided in the manner of an office building's floors, with traumatic memories pushed down into the basement, these researchers favored a concept of *dissociation*, in which different parts of the conscious mind were sequestered off from one another like jail cells along a single corridor. The split personalities exhibited by MPD patients, in this view, were not manifestations of unconscious conflict but simply different segments of the conscious mind that would need to be integrated in order for the patient to recover. "For me," Colin Ross wrote, "MPD demonstrates that the so-called unconscious is not unconscious at all—it is wide-awake and cognitive in nature, but dissociated."[30] Different researchers took different views on how this worked exactly. For some, dissociation and repression were distinct phenomena, only one of which could be seen at work in MPD.[31] Though repression might occur in response to certain internal or external events, they argued, dissociation was the psyche's privileged response to certain kinds of trauma.[32] Others used the terms interchangeably to a certain degree, perhaps favoring one over the other most of the time.[33]

These variations in the use and meaning of the terms "dissociation" and "repression" made things tricky for those trying to determine the scientific validity of the MPD therapists' claims, but so did the history of one of the terms. Many of the last century's most prominent psychoanalytic thinkers have claimed that repression specifically refers to forgetting that happens *involuntarily*, using the term "suppression" to describe situations in which a person makes a conscious effort to avoid thinking about an idea or event. But this was not Freud's contention. He argued in one paper that *"the essence of repression lies simply in turning something away, and keeping it at a distance, from the conscious,"* and elsewhere he wrote that in order for hysterical symptoms to emerge, "an idea must be *intentionally re-pressed from consciousness."*[34] Of course, subsequent decades during which disciples and critics layered hundreds of new theories and objections on top of Freud's originals significantly muddied the waters, and so it could occasionally be difficult to determine exactly what MPD researchers were claiming when the word "repression" appeared in their work. But taken as a whole, the MPD literature does make one clear and fundamental claim, which is that people sometimes respond to the experience of trauma by instantly and completely excluding those experiences from the parts of consciousness to which they normally have access. This forgetting is a reflexive, automatic event that happens involuntarily.

So this became an important question for researchers working on cognition and memory: Did people actually forget trauma in the ways the MPD champions claimed? Some parts of this question were easier to answer than others. In cases in which people were abused, whether physically or sexually, at a very young age, forgetting does occur, although not because of psychological trauma. Scientists still disagree about the mechanism behind it, but childhood amnesia, or the inability to remember almost anything at all before the ages of three or four, is one of the most well-documented phenomena in all of developmental psychology. Young children are actually very good at remembering events that occurred up to about a year in the past, but these memories almost invariably fade as children age, and many adults have no memories at all until the age of seven.[35] In the hypothetical case of an adult who knows (because of adult witnesses or the preservation of documentary evidence) that he or she was abused as a two-year-old but cannot remember it, there would be no reason to cite repression as the cause.

Cognitive psychologists have had no more success turning up evidence of traumatic repression in adults. If anything, as the research psychologist Richard McNally wrote in his book *Remembering Trauma*, "people remember horrific experiences all too well." Although the kinds of stress associated with trauma can make it more difficult to remember peripheral aspects of an event (e.g., the kind of shoes worn by a mugger brandishing a gun), that is only because the victim's attention is more intensely focused on the event's central components (the mugger, the gun).[36] Of course, such studies have built-in limitations when conducted in the laboratory, as researchers cannot ethically subject test subjects to levels of stress that would cause actual trauma.

But field studies confirm the laboratory results. Some months after a fatal shooting, two researchers interviewed more than a dozen people who had witnessed the crime in person. Their accounts, when compared to the official version set down in police reports, turned out to be remarkably accurate, and those witnesses who were most upset by their experiences provided the most accurate accounts of all.[37] Even some of the earlier feminist research on sexual abuse supported the idea that trauma did not have a negative impact on victims' ability to remember. In 1981 the feminist psychiatrist Judith Herman published her classic work *Father-Daughter Incest*. The book featured interviews with forty adult victims of childhood incest, and its publication date meant that it preceded the popularization of ritual abuse and recovered memory. None of Herman's interview subjects mentioned torture at the hands of satanic cults, and none mentioned ever forgetting what they had endured as children.[38]

The child psychiatrist Lenore Terr tried to find a way around this problem. She argued that children exhibited two distinct responses to different kinds of trauma. Type I syndrome, as she called it, involved children exposed to isolated episodes of terror or violence such as shootings, robberies, and car crashes. Terr argued that children remember Type I traumas very well, and in fact they do. But Terr argued that children dealt very differently with Type II traumas like repeated abuse at the hands of a family member or teacher. These traumas occurred regularly as part of a child's daily life, and Terr believed it was this very regularity that caused the child to begin to respond to his or her experiences with self-hypnosis, denial, and other techniques that pushed memories out of consciousness.

Of the two types, it was the second that constituted Terr's original contribution to the field, but the scientific literature does not offer much supporting evidence for its existence. She interviewed twenty children who had been abused before the age of five and concluded that those exposed to Type II trauma had a harder time remembering what happened to them. However, the three children who were completely unable to articulate abuse memories were all victims of abuse that ended before they were two and a half years old, falling well within the window of normal childhood amnesia.[39] Studies have also failed to turn up Type II syndrome in the field. Child soldiers, Holocaust victims, and children raised in conditions of extreme neglect or violence all remember their experiences very well.

It does sometimes happen that a person molested at a young age will not think about the event for many years, only to find his or her memory rushing back in response to some stimulus—say, a scene in a TV crime drama. In 1993 the child abuse and trauma researchers John Briere and Jon Conte published the results of a study in which they asked 450 people, all of whom said they had been sexually abused as children, whether they had experienced periods of time during which they were unable to remember the abuse. More than half of Briere and Conte's subjects said yes, and their study became a touchstone for advocates of recovered memory therapy.[40] As Richard McNally pointed out, however, the question at the paper's heart—"Was there ever a time when you could not remember the forced sexual experience?"—makes no sense. "An affirmative answer," McNally wrote, "implies that the subject has spent a period of time unsuccessfully trying to remember having been abused. But if a person has repressed all memories of abuse, on what basis would he or she attempt to remember it in the first place?"[41]

It is more likely that those who answered the researchers' question affirmatively meant that there had been periods of time during which they simply did not think about their abuse, and as a number of subsequent studies have clarified, that is perfectly normal. A team of researchers that included Elizabeth Loftus—an important figure in the study of child suggestibility in forensic interviewing—found that periods during which adults did not remember or think about their childhood abuse can largely be explained by the children not finding their molestation to be traumatic at the time.[42] Lacking an understanding of sexuality and its implications, these young victims of nonviolent sexual abuse, mostly involving fondling and other kinds of touching, tended to see their experiences as having either a slightly negative emotional impact or none at all. Only in adulthood, when those victims recalled their experiences and came to understand them as abusive, did the memories become a regular matter of conscious thought. This coming to awareness of the abusive nature of one's own childhood can be a traumatic experience in its own right. Family dynamics that once seemed benign or a relative's habit of avoiding certain visits might take on ominous new undertones, and such delayed trauma, were it to set in, would obviously merit treatment. But the long effort to find evidence that the emergence of such an awareness implies the years-long repression of earlier wounds came up empty. The most sensible conclusion remains that it was not the psychological effects of trauma occurring at the time but the very absence of those effects that made it possible to forget that the abuse had taken place.

Proponents of recovered memory ceded no ground in response to this body of work, citing dozens of studies allegedly providing strong evidence for their account of traumatic amnesia. A close look at many of these studies, however, makes it clear that they do not say what recovered memory advocates think they do. Some of these misreadings were made possible by a single clause in the DSM-III. In the fourth subsection of the diagnostic criteria for Post-Traumatic Stress Disorder, the authors list "memory impairment or trouble concentrating" as a symptom. As its pairing with "trouble concentrating" suggests, "memory impairment" refers not only to the possibility of traumatic amnesia but also to the more prosaic kinds of memory disturbance that can follow a traumatic experience: missing appointments or forgetting friends' birthdays. These problems are caused precisely by victims' preoccupation with what has happened to them, not their inability to remember it. But when Cory Hammond and other recovered memory researchers came across a study in which a group of disaster witnesses reported memory impairment, they cited it as evidence of amnesia.[43] In reality the study subjects, who had seen a series of skywalk collapses at a hotel in Kansas City, had no trouble remembering what they saw; some had made "efforts at repression," but those efforts had failed.[44]

Freud developed the seduction theory out of an earlier theory's failure. The work he conducted on hysteria with Josef Breuer convinced Freud that hysterical symptoms were caused by repressed memories of sexual trauma that took place *after* the onset of puberty, and that hypnotic abreaction of these memories would alleviate the patient's symptoms. Again and again, however, Freud's patients failed to improve after recovering their memories, or Freud would determine that the memories lacked sufficient traumatic force to produce the kinds of hysterical symptoms he encountered. Freud could have abandoned traumatic repression in the face of these results, but he was at a crucial early stage in his intellectual career, when it is sometimes common to believe that a setback is best overcome with even more ambitious flights of intellectual daring. So he said the repressed trauma must really lay further back in the patient's past, not during adolescence but rather before it.

A similar impulse appears in the recovered memory researchers' tortured attempts to prove that the available scientific evidence provided them with more support than it actually did. Of the many flawed and inaccurate interpretations put forward, one stands out as a gross misrepresentation of the source material. In 1985 a researcher named Stephen Dollinger studied thirty-eight children who were playing a soccer game when lightning struck and killed one of their teammates. He found that although many of the children exhibited mild to moderate emotional effects in the wake of the disaster, including sleep disturbances and separation anxiety, particularly during storms, two of the thirty-eight had no memory of the event whatsoever. The research group that included Cory Hammond cited this fact as evidence that traumatic amnesia was more common than mainstream psychiatry was willing to admit.[45] What they did not mention was that the two children in question had also been struck by the bolt, which knocked them both completely unconscious.[46] None of the other children reported any memory issues, though some became reluctant to play soccer.

Like their patients, therapists found the high drama of recovered memory work intoxicating. "Like a play, novel, or movie," Colin Ross wrote, "there is a rise and fall in the action of therapy, and interludes of different intensity are required."[47] The outlaw status of their project, held at a wary arm's length by mainstream psychiatry until, all of a sudden, it wasn't, also made it easy for therapists to think of themselves along the lines of nineteenth-century psychiatric pioneers whose genius would eventually induce an awed respect in society at large. "Like Janet," Ross wrote, describing the power plays in which he engaged a patient's alter personalities, "I am willing to exploit the vanity of the demons."[48] Ross had such confidence in his therapeutic powers that he even unleashed them on unsuspecting readers of his academic MPD monograph. After describing therapy as a "mysterious ritual" and outlining his methods for preparing a patient to undergo hypnosis, Ross set down the following paragraph:[49]

> And now as you sit reading this book you begin to notice that your body is a little more relaxed and warm and comfortable than usual, as you listen to the sound of my voice. You aren't disturbed by any other thoughts or sensations, you're able just to focus on the words, understand their meaning, and feel yourself calm and comfortable and relaxed. And the more you read, the deeper and deeper you go into this pleasant, relaxed, natural state of calmness and tiredness, as you listen to the sound of my voice. This feeling of calmness and relaxation becomes stronger and stronger with every word you read, until, at the beginning of the next paragraph you will be in a deep hypnotic state, perfectly relaxed and calm. This will last for 30 seconds or until you read to the end of the paragraph, whichever comes first. Then you will be wide awake, fresh, and alert, feeling calm and confident and ready to continue reading.[50]

Two paragraphs later Ross acknowledged that readers might "have reservations about the ethics of including such a hypnotic induction in a book," which he brushed aside with the assertion that reading is by definition a hypnotic practice. "For me," he wrote, "writing induces an even deeper trance state than reading."[51]

Recovered memory therapists judged the magnitude of their achievements by the extremity and complexity of the cases they uncovered. The line of thinking seemed to be that although a patient with three or four alters and a history of harsh physical punishment could be detected by any reasonably skilled practitioner, only a therapist with real vision and courage would be able to suss out the hundreds of alters produced by a childhood of satanic ritual abuse. Accordingly the number and variety of alters discovered in treatment increased, as did the extent of the abuse that supposedly brought them into being. Therapists discovered animal alters, alien alters, dead alters, plant alters (trees), and angel alters. The abuse narratives began to include cult rituals, forced abortions, murders, rape, and cannibalism. Whether therapists really believed, deep down, in the reality of these stories is a tricky issue. One group of psychiatrists that included the prominent recovered memory advocates Roberta Sachs and Bennett Braun published a paper in which they certainly appeared to take patients' allegations of ritual abuse at face value, but they later claimed to have been simply documenting these stories, not endorsing them.[52] The latter claim looks like a cover for the mistake of having made the former, but the former was also a cover that justified recovered memory's extreme therapeutic techniques, which included administering huge doses of Sodium Pentothal and other barbiturates. It was certainly in these therapists' interest to behave as though there really were groups of Satanists out in the world splitting children's minds apart. It justified their exercising extraordinary amounts of control over their patients' lives. One Texas institute for dissociative disorders censored patients' mail for the ostensible purpose of screening out coded messages from the cult. That institute also told a patient she would have to prove the cult no longer presented a safety risk before they would grant her discharge request.[53]

Popular books on recovered memory often included lengthy symptom checklists that readers could use to determine whether they were likely to be harboring a repressed history of abuse. Taken as a whole, these checklists encompassed an impressively wide range of unpleasant and upsetting experiences. An interest in religions or a preference for baggy clothes suggested childhood abuse, as did promiscuity, celibacy, workaholism, breast lumps, trouble sleeping, fear of closets, fear of coffins, alertness, vagueness, gambling, and dozens of other troubles. Although the wide symptomatic net cast by recovered memory obviously helped therapists to grow their practices, it may be more important to consider what these checklists told patients about themselves and the society they inhabited.

In 1992 Debbie Nathan attended and reported on a four-day retreat organized by the group Incest Survivors Anonymous (ISA). She sat through group sessions, listening to the three dozen women in attendance, and she noticed interesting currents of guilt and doubt running underneath the tales of ritual abuse. "Ritual-abuse survivor Cathy," Nathan wrote, "fingered a crucifix as she recited, in rote tone, details of eating the livers of newborn babies." But Nathan heard real emotion flood Cathy's voice when she described an affair undertaken with a married man more than two decades earlier, when she was a student. "I was a virgin then," Cathy said, "at least I thought I was until I remembered the cult stuff recently."

Cathy fell in love, had sex, and became pregnant. The man refused to divorce his wife. "So I had an abortion. I killed my own baby! My own baby. The worst thing I've ever done." The ritual abuse story that came much later amplified Cathy's sense of guilt about what happened (by replacing a single aborted fetus with multiple cannibalized newborns) and mitigated the extent to which she was to blame—she had not chosen to give up her virginity; the cult had taken it from her.

Some women clearly did need some version of the help ISA provided. Nathan listened as one survivor described how her father began to climb into bed and fondle her while her mother was in the hospital. When she finally told the family what happened, her father said she had wanted it, and then her brothers beat her up. Another woman talked about her army colonel father who beat her and her sisters for saying it was wrong for President Nixon to bomb Cambodia. The beatings stopped when the sisters said they supported the president. These stories, Nathan wrote, "were so prosaic in their detail that they could be nothing but real." But then there was Donna, a thirty-something woman with a good job and a happy social life. The issues she described sounded like the kind of thing that would send any reasonable adult to a psychotherapist. "She suffered from 'relationship' problems," Nathan wrote. "She was supercompetitive and a control freak." Donna's therapist assured her, despite her complete lack of memories, that these problems stemmed from incest, and now, at the retreat, Donna was tentatively trying to live up to her therapist's expectations. One time she had walked in on her father having sex with his secretary; she told Nathan her father had probably done the same to her.[54]

What was the source of this pressure that asked women to shoehorn all of their different experiences into a rigidly generic father-daughter incest narrative? Some part of the answer can be found in the legislation that extended the statute of limitations for adult survivors of childhood abuse only if the abuse had been sexual. Those laws did nothing to help adults who may have wanted to bring suit against their parents for physical abuse or neglect, and this created an incentive for women to talk about their childhood traumas in terms of sexual abuse regardless of their actual experience. Delayed discovery laws then created an additional incentive for plaintiffs to claim they had completely repressed memories of the abuse until recently. Plaintiffs who said they had always remembered what happened to them, that what they recently discovered was not the abuse itself but the psychological harm it caused them, had a harder time winning a favorable verdict. Finally, because there is no point in bringing a civil suit against someone who simply does not have much money, the suits that did wind up in front of a judge and in front of the media usually involved upper-middle-class families, who were also usually white. That this archetypal narrative of incest, trauma, repression, and recovery, all taking place in the context of middle-class family life, did not match the vast majority of abuse experiences that people actually had did very little to weaken its appeal. The narrative was a kind of key, and women who would or could not make use of this key found that the doors to social and legal recognition and aid remained closed.

The infantilization of adult women has long been one of patriarchy's most effective tools. The ostensible meaning of the classic Victorian expression "Women and children first" is that society values those groups in a special way, but it also lumps them together as helpless victims in need of saving by men, who hoist them into lifeboats as the ship goes down. Recovered memory therapy emerged in the midst of an intense, reactionary antifeminism that sought to undo many of the changes of the 1960s and early 1970s. Feminism's legislative momentum was halted entirely, as the long push to ratify the Equal Rights Amendment stalled in the early eighties, and the cultural climate reflected the revived prestige of domesticity and traditional family life. As the journalist Susan Faludi pointed out in her book *Backlash*, recovered memory guides shared space on bookstore shelves with a deluge of self-help titles designed to persuade women to reconcile themselves to the old sex roles: *Women Who Marry Down and End Up Having It All*; *No More Lonely Nights: Overcoming the Hidden Fears That Keep You from Getting Married*; and *If I'm So Wonderful, Why Am I Still Single?*[55] What made these titles such powerful instruments of the decade's reactionary politics was their recognition, first, that political change is partly a matter of psychology and, second, that it is frightening to be suddenly granted new freedoms. They played on the anxious underside of the realization that women no longer had to marry to achieve social respectability: a fear of dying childless and alone after a lifetime of empty individualistic hedonism. Multiple Personality also dramatized a kind of nightmare version of women's liberation. If feminism had won for at least some women—white and middle class, the same demographic in which MPD appeared—the power to choose from among different kinds of social roles, MPD recast that victory as a grave error. What is an MPD patient but a woman who cannot choose between the different roles available to her and whose struggle to do so ruins her life? Along with the self-help titles and magazine cover stories asking whether women could "have it all" (they couldn't), recovered memory reimagined the previous two decades of political change as brutal traumas from which women needed to heal. The goal was to make women too insecure and too anxious to make use of any of the freedoms they had won for themselves. (The first entry on a list of repressed memory symptoms from 1992: "Do you have trouble knowing what you want?")[56]

Of course, some recovered memory advocates saw their work as a feminist project, and there is a long line of conservative objection to such victimization-based appeals for political change, running from Janet down to the pundit George Will, that condescends to self-identified victims as vain attention seekers. But the women who entered into recovered memory were not frustrated hack actresses looking to use the psychiatrist's office as a stage; they were adults in distress who needed help with very normal adult problems: depression, divorce, isolation, job loss. Recovered memory therapy struck an unfair bargain with these women. It said, *Tell us that you are a victim and behave like a child, and you will be listened to—or if not listened to, then at least pitied. Refuse to play this role, refuse to identify yourself as mentally ill, or insist that your distress is a normal adult's response to the people around you or the conditions in which you live, and you will receive no assistance at all.*

So despite the feminist rhetoric of books like *The Courage to Heal*, recovered memory therapy rested on a chauvinistic vision of female weakness that was perfectly in keeping with the reactionary times. From the anticrime campaigns that began to fill the country's prisons to the day care cases that helped expand prosecutorial powers in state governments, victimization was turned to many conservative political ends in the 1980s. Recovered memory was part of this political shift. An earlier feminist analysis of incest and abuse had placed blame squarely on the nuclear family as an institution, as a way of distributing power among small groups that allowed fathers and husbands to exercise dangerous amounts of control over their children and wives. But recovered memory discarded this argument and replaced it with horror-movie plots and a parade of traumatized child-women. The isolation these women experienced in treatment, their dependence on the therapist as a surrogate parent figure, and the unprovability of their allegations rendered them completely nonthreatening from a political point of view.

For most of the really powerful figures in recovered memory, the majority of whom were men, this was not a problem. In his book of case studies on multiple personality, Colin Ross described treating a nineteen-year-old client named Loni. According to Ross, the young woman was "attractive, wholesome, relaxed, and casually dressed. Her blond hair and hazel eyes highlighted striking cheekbones."[57] Loni claimed to have a twelve-year-old inner child personality named Julie, and when "Julie" spoke, Loni pouted her lips and put her feet in a pigeon-toed position. The description of Julie's affect makes her sound more like a cartoon child than an actual twelve-year-old person. "Julie's eyes and facial expression were much more animated, childlike, spontaneous, and charming than Loni's," Ross wrote. "The host personality, Loni, was somewhat restricted in her emotion, and was more composed and adult. Julie was charming and engaging. One's natural response was to soothe and protect her, whereas Loni evoked a more neutral reaction."[58]

Ross embarked on a course of treatment that uncovered some fifty alter personalities (many of them also children) as well as a buried history of abuse that involved ongoing paternal rape, live spiders, a "contract rape" paid for by her father and carried out by a biker in a parking lot, and ritual abuse orchestrated by her mother. For nine months, Loni's "host" personality, which is to say her actual personality, disappeared entirely. "She became psychotic," Ross wrote, and she would sometimes "hold her head, hallucinate, rock, and be unable to carry on a conversation."[59] In order to protect her from further abuse as she tried to recover, Ross and Loni arranged for her to move to Montreal, where she could live in a woman's shelter for up to one year. Ross would stay behind. Loni planned to work with a former therapist while living in her temporary home.

But Ross perhaps did not anticipate the effect that Loni's time away from him would have on her mind-set. Six months after moving to Montreal, she began to talk about missing her parents, and within another month or two she decided that she did not have MPD at all. Ross advised her against coming back to Winnipeg and said that if she did, he would be unable to continue working with her. She moved back anyway, and over the following three years, up until the point when Ross wrote out his case study, he did not communicate with Loni at all. Ross describes the decision to terminate Loni's treatment as his own, and it is worth noting that he made this decision at the precise moment when Loni said she would no longer continue to present herself in therapy as a traumatized child.

But there is no indication that Loni expressed any particular eagerness to continue seeing him, and in the final pages of Ross's case study, a wounded tone begins to creep in. "The decision I made not to see Loni again was difficult," Ross writes, "and I was tempted to try to contact her many times." He blames part of their relationship's breakdown on "projective identification," which he describes as occurring "when the patient projects her feelings onto the therapist, then unconsciously engineers the situation so that the therapist actually feels the patient's projected feelings." Although this may have occurred, a simpler explanation is that once Loni realized she did not have MPD, she stopped wanting to see the therapist who was sure she did. Ross's case study ends on a melancholy note that also conveys a tinge of bitterness: "I feel sad when I think of Loni in her apartment, knowing that one of her inner children is still having intercourse with her father, probably on a weekly basis."[60]

Ellen Willis, who spent the 1980s railing against mainstream feminism's increasingly conservative focus on sexual violence and trauma, wrote, "The contradictions of contemporary American politics and culture are the product of a profound and largely unconscious psychic struggle: an ongoing clash of powerful desires for freedom and pleasure with guilt-ridden fear that such desires lead straight to license, chaos, and destruction."[61] To speak seriously of a social or cultural unconscious was as unfashionable then as it is now, and yet little else could account for the speed and eagerness with which evangelicals and disappointed feminists alike adopted MPD as a diagnosis and as a worldview, with all its attendant assumptions about the dangers of sex and the pervasiveness of trauma.

By the early 1990s MPD had fully entered the mainstream. Gloria Steinem's up-market self-help book *Revolution from Within* made caring for one's inner child a basic step toward achieving inner peace and also referred without skepticism to those women who had recovered memories of "ritual or cult abuse."[62] One year later *Ms.* magazine, the country's largest feminist publication, put out an issue with the cover headline: "BELIEVE IT! Cult Ritual Abuse Exists. One Woman's Story." Writing under a pseudonym so as to avoid further cult persecution, the author described the satanic activities of her mother's "otherwise ordinary middle-class family."[63] She claimed to have witnessed multiple murders, including the decapitation and cannibalization of her baby sister. Sidebars on MPD and various treatment recommendations accompanied the article, including a paragraph that warned about the effects ritual abuse might have on a victim's ideas about sexuality. "Some survivors may not know what 'normal' (nonviolent) sexual behavior is," the article said, and for this reason survivors should "never" engage in sadomasochistic sex—it would only repeat the abuse.[64] At the time of publication, the author was married with two children who had "never been exposed to cult activities." She said she was working on a novel about her experiences.

The article generated more mail than any other in the magazine's history.[65] Not all of it was supportive. "If you ask me to believe in a systematic network of fiends, then Goddamn it, I want facts and figures," one reader wrote. "And why, if these horrors are still going on, is the pseudonymous author writing a *novel* about it, instead of banging down the doors of every judicial office in the country?" Pamela Freyd, the executive director of the False Memory Syndrome Foundation (FMSF), also wrote in with objections to the story. "The article presented the existence of satanic ritual abuse conspiracies as real when there is no evidence," she wrote.

Freyd had founded the FMSF with her husband, Peter, in 1992 after the couple's adult daughter accused her father of sexually abusing her as a child. Although the process by which Jennifer Freyd came to confront her father did not conform to the standard recovered memory narrative—she was not hypnotized in therapy, for example—and although evidence supporting the existence of false memory syndrome as a verified medical phenomenon was thin, the FMSF was soon mailing out newsletters and fielding phone calls from accused parents. By the time Pamela Freyd wrote to *Ms.* she was speaking on behalf of a small but growing constituency. "Repressed memory therapy is incredibly lucrative for therapists," she wrote. "Families are being destroyed by this nonsense. Will your next article be on space alien abduction?"

The FMSF was an advocacy organization, not a research group or a think tank, and as such it devoted itself primarily to publicizing research that debunked recovered memory therapy—it actually coined the term "recovered memory therapy"—and steering legal resources toward accused parents. These were understandably felt to be urgent tasks; some therapists recommended that patients sue their abusive parents in court, and by the late nineties more than eight hundred civil suits, criminal cases, and restraining orders would be filed. (This number constitutes less than one-fifth of the number of cases in which adults recovered memories of childhood abuse.)[66] But although the FMSF's courtroom and media campaigns were ultimately effective, there are ways in which the group inadvertently deepened the confusion in which the issue was mired. Pamela Freyd's claim that therapists were primarily in it for the money was, of course, not designed to foster understanding—everyone who is engaged in a media relations war says their opponents are in it for the money. (This includes recovered memory advocates themselves, some of whom implied, when patients began to sue them for malpractice, that the lawsuits were primarily motivated by the possibility of a big payout.)[67] The FMSF also associated itself with conservative activists who believed the problems with child abuse law originated not in *Michelle Remembers* and recovered memory suits but with Walter Mondale. One FMSF member, when not organizing events to support victims of false accusations in Salem, Massachusetts, worked with a Republican senator to try to remove the statutory requirement from the Child Abuse Treatment and Prevention Act to report suspected abuse.[68] Combined with the group's failure to establish clear internal guidelines for distinguishing actual cases of false accusations from cases in which parents may have been using the syndrome as a cover for abuse that really took place, this left the FMSF vulnerable to criticism from those who were already inclined to see it as a cynical attempt to provide abusers with a cloak of outraged respectability.

In its newsletters and publicity materials the FMSF emphasized the damage done to families. But the real targets of recovered memory therapy were the women in whom treatment cultivated such a debilitating sense of vulnerability and helplessness. In previous decades, women who tried to tell somebody (whether a judge, a relative, or a friend) about abuse they had experienced (whether as a child or as an adult) often discovered that on this subject in particular they would not be permitted to give an account of what happened to them that others were willing to hear. Perhaps the central irony of recovered memory therapy is that in its efforts to bring the issue of child sexual abuse out into the open, it did the same thing to women, prioritizing reanimated zombie versions of Victorian-era psychological theories over anything that women might have actually had to say for themselves. As the therapy reached its media peak, it received what essentially amounted to celebrity endorsements, one of them from the producer and actress Roseanne Barr, who revealed that she had been diagnosed with MPD. Her therapist unearthed twenty-one separate personalities with names like Piggy, Fucker, and Bambi.[69] She appeared on *Oprah* to discuss her experiences with MPD. "When someone asks you, 'Were you sexually abused as a child?' there are only two answers," she said. "One of them is, 'Yes,' and one of them is, 'I don't know.' You can't say, 'No.'"

Chapter 10

Repression and Desire

"In 1983 and 1984," Kenneth Lanning wrote, "when I first began to hear stories of what sounded like satanic or occult activity in connection with allegations of sexual victimization of children (allegations that have come to be referred to most often as 'ritual' child abuse), I tended to believe them. I had been dealing with bizarre, deviant behavior for many years and had long since realized that almost anything is possible. Just when you think that you have heard it all, along comes another strange case."[1]

This paragraph appeared on the first page of Lanning's 1992 FBI report on ritual abuse, and the intervening years had modified the special agent's sense of what was possible. After some five years of investigative work that failed to uncover the country's clandestine satanic network, Lanning began to raise respectful but unmistakably skeptical questions at professional gatherings in the late eighties. In response, some of the jumpier conference attendees began to wonder aloud whether Lanning was himself a Satanist who had infiltrated the Bureau. Addressing these insinuations in his report, Lanning noted the difficulty and unfairness of being asked to prove that you are *not* working on behalf of a secret conspiracy. "All I can say to those who have made such allegations," he wrote, "is that they are wrong."

Lanning very much wanted to keep people on topic. He had spent eleven years researching and consulting on child abuse and its prevention, and he now believed that the specter of ritual abuse threatened to undo much of that work. "A satanic murder should be defined as one committed by two or more individuals who rationally plan the crime and whose primary motivation is to fulfill a prescribed satanic ritual calling for the murder," he wrote. "By this definition I have been unable to identify even one satanic murder in the United States." Lanning described the urge to believe in ritual abuse as an updated version of the 1950s "stranger danger" panic that swapped out the trench coat–wearing pedophile for the satanic cult. Such a conception of child abuse set out the problem in appealingly straightforward terms. "One of the oldest theories of crime is demonology," Lanning wrote. "The devil makes you do it."

Lanning's long and detailed report worked step-by-step through the tangle of confusion that surrounded ritual abuse. He described how police officers attended training conferences on Satanism and then seized on ritual abuse as an explanation for a dizzying range of real and imaginary social phenomena, including, but not limited to, heavy metal, teenage depression and suicide, fabricated "histories" of witchcraft in Europe, the New World Order conspiracy, and marijuana use. He also carefully and rather sensitively explained why parents who believed their children had been abused might have been drawn to the idea that the abuse was satanic: it helped them to assuage their own feelings of guilt. If the culprits were not mere child care workers but members of a global conspiracy, how could parents have been expected to know what was happening? But none of this matched the importance of Lanning's basic claim: satanic ritual abuse does not exist. One of the previous decade's most prominent ritual abuse proponents was now saying not that ritual abuse had been somewhat overblown, not that its reach had been exaggerated, but that it simply was not happening.

As a national phenomenon, the ritual abuse hysteria broke down for good with the end of the second McMartin trial in 1990. Its decline unfurled slowly, with various detours and reversals, over the course of the next quarter-century. For convicted defendants in the day care cases, getting out of prison was a much longer process than getting into it had been, but most of them did get out eventually. Release, however, did not by any means guarantee a return to normal life. Peggy McMartin Buckey had a lot of trouble after McMartin. She became fearful of other people and would often refuse to leave her house. She filed a lawsuit against Los Angeles County and the City of Manhattan Beach alleging civil rights violations, but a federal judge dismissed it. She had a new grandson, though. Peggy Ann married in 1987, and her son was almost two years old when Judge Weisberg declared the mistrial. She said that people who recognized her on the street now frequently offered support, and she wondered where these people had been years before.[2] Virginia and Peggy Ann appealed their lawsuit against Children's Institute International and the district attorney's office up to the federal level, but the Supreme Court refused to hear it.[3] The McMartin family also sued Bob Currie for slander. A superior court judge found in the McMartins' favor but essentially ruled that Currie could not have damaged their reputations beyond the extent to which two trials and seven years of public notoriety had already damaged them. He awarded each of the plaintiffs one dollar in damages.

Ileana Fuster, having served three of the ten years to which she had been sentenced in exchange for testifying against her husband, was released from prison in 1989 and immediately deported to her native Honduras. One year earlier, Richard Barkman, who taught at the Small World Preschool in Niles, Michigan, until being accused of ritualistic abuse in 1984, completed a successful effort to have his conviction overturned. That case began when Barkman reported a student's mother for neglect; in response the mother accused Barkman of molesting her child, and investigators eventually persuaded more than sixty Small World kids to do the same. Facing a second trial in 1990, Barkman entered a no-contest plea to one count of assault. He was sentenced to time served and five years probation. Betsy Kelly, a former teacher at the Little Rascals Day Care Center in Edenton, North Carolina, did the same after spending two years awaiting trial in jail. She pled no contest to the charges against her in January 1994, served an additional ten months, and was released. In 1993 a New Jersey appeals court also overturned Kelly Michaels's conviction, vacating her sentence and freeing her after five years in prison. After a chaotic hearing, Michaels rushed out of the courthouse and got in a car headed for New York City, where her family and friends were waiting. "Look at that beautiful skyline!" she said, crying, as the car approached Manhattan.[4] She still faced more than one hundred counts of child abuse, but in 1994 prosecutors announced they would not pursue a retrial.

Violet Amirault and Cheryl Amirault LeFave were released in 1995. They were, respectively, the mother and sister of Gerald Amirault, and together the trio worked at the prestigious Fells Acres Day Care Center in Malden, Massachusetts, until 1984, when Gerald was arrested and charged with abusing many children. The case expanded in the usual way. One investigator said that coaxing allegations out of the children was "like getting blood from a stone."[5] Violet and Cheryl were freed on appeal when a judge ruled the earlier trial had violated the women's constitutional rights, but then, in 1997, the state's highest court reinstated their convictions, arguing that "the mere fact that if the process were redone, there might be a different outcome, or that some lingering doubt about the first outcome may remain, cannot be a sufficient reason to reopen what society has a right to consider closed."[6] The word "finality" appeared five times in the opinion. Cheryl was returned to prison. Violet, who was in her seventies, only managed to avoid the same fate by dying of stomach cancer before her reinstated sentence was set to begin.

The media turned against recovered memory, ritual abuse, and the day care cases more quickly and more decisively than any other institution. The first skeptical article to appear in a major national magazine was published by *Harper's* in May 1990. The piece's author was Dorothy Rabinowitz, a reporter and editorialist for a New Jersey television station who had followed the Kelly Michaels trial from the outset. After Debbie Nathan's 1988 *Village Voice* story bolstered Rabinowitz's own growing doubts about the prosecution's case, she decided to file her own investigative report. She accused police, parents, and prosecutors of falling for "tales as fantastic as any fairy story ever told to them by the Brothers Grimm."[7] This article set the tone for the coming decade. In 1995 Violet Amirault, other day care defendants, and two professors appeared on a CNBC special devoted to the topic of wrongful child molestation convictions. Leading the panel and moderating the discussion was Geraldo Rivera, who interrupted proceedings at one point to announce that he had been "terribly wrong" to support "the 'Believe the Children' movement of the 1980s." He now believed that innocent people had been wrongly convicted and that recovered memory therapy was a "bunch of crap."[8]

Even TV movies changed their tune. The late eighties had seen a number of network-produced films along the lines of *Do You Know the Muffin Man?*, a CBS docu-drama in which a young Stephen Dorff played the older brother of a boy abused and then scared into silence by teachers at a community day care center (oddly, the film features no reference whatsoever to a "muffin man").[9] But in 1995 HBO finally aired Abby and Myra Mann's McMartin film, *Indictment.* James Woods played Danny Davis, emphasizing the lawyer's tenaciousness and downplaying his fondness for rambling courtroom monologues.[10]

Outside the media the panic occasionally resurfaced with surprising violence. In 1994 a police lieutenant named Robert Perez was placed in charge of all sex crime investigations in Wenatchee, Washington, a small city some 150 miles from Seattle. Though Perez took to the job enthusiastically, he said the reason for his appointment was "a mystery to him"—he did not have extensive training or relevant prior work experience.[11] That summer a fifteen-year-old girl tried to poison her foster father with iodine and then accused him of raping her. Perez arrested the foster father. The next day the girl's caseworker, Paul Glassen, reported that she had recanted her story entirely, and Perez arrested Glassen for alleged witness tampering.[12] Perez expanded his investigation in 1995 and became convinced he was uncovering a ring of abusers. He believed one of the victims was his own foster child, a nine-year-old girl named Donna, and one spring day he put Donna in his police car and took a long drive through Wenatchee, asking her to point out houses in which she and her friends might have been abused. In the midst of identifying twenty-two buildings, Donna also told Perez she had been abused by a taxi driver and a delivery man on his rounds, the beginnings of a group that would eventually include forty-three arrested adults and sixty alleged child victims. Perez's investigation resulted in the filing of more than twenty-nine thousand counts of child sex abuse, eighteen convictions, and a dozen no-contest or guilty pleas. These thousands of acts of abuse, molestation, and rape were all supposed to have taken place within a city of just twenty-two thousand people.

The Wenatchee sex ring was such an elaborate and outlandish construction that it is perhaps unsurprising that it should have fallen apart so quickly. In 1996 one of the accusing girls told a television reporter, an attorney, the Wenatchee County Commissioner, and her grandmother that Perez forced her to fabricate rape allegations.[13] She also said Perez had physically intimidated her, including throwing her to the floor on one occasion when she expressed reluctance to testify. By the end of the decade almost all of the Wenatchee convictions were overturned or set aside.

Also freed in the second half of the 1990s were Alvin and Debbie McCuan and Scott and Brenda Kniffen of Kern County, California. Each more than a decade into a combined prison sentence of exactly one thousand years, the two couples were released in 1996 after an appeals court ruled investigators had coerced their children into testifying against them—the Kniffens' sons, Brian and Brandon, said as much in television appearances.[14] The appeal was the first time in six years that Scott and Brenda had seen one another. "Oh god," Brenda said when she saw her husband. "Honey, you need Rogaine."[15] Thirty-four sex ring convictions were eventually overturned in Kern County. Alvin and Debbie's two daughters, whose initial allegations of incest at the hands of their step-grandfather and father launched the investigation, never recanted.

In 1995 the North Carolina Court of Appeals overturned the convictions of Robert Kelly and Dawn Wilson, who had worked at the Little Rascals Day Care Center in Edenton until the fall of 1989. The pair were serving thirteen life sentences between the two of them (twelve for Robert). Another Little Rascals defendant accepted a no-contest plea rather than face a trial. In 1999 Cheryl Amirault LeFave reached an agreement with the Middlesex County district attorney to serve ten years' probation in exchange for her release, with a number of additional stipulations. One was that she have no unsupervised contact with children to whom she was not related nor any contact whatsoever with the alleged victims' families. Another was that she not sit for television interviews or attempt to profit from her experience by writing a book about it. The following year the state's parole board began to investigate the possibility of commuting Gerald Amirault's sentence, and in 2001 it recommended by a 5–0 vote that he be released. Martha Coakley, the district attorney, organized press interviews for the alleged child victims—now adults—and encouraged the governor to keep Amirault in prison. In early 2002, Acting Governor Jane Swift denied Amirault's commutation.[16]

Given the number of convictions overturned in the century's final decade and the frequency with which judges and appeals courts attributed the wrongful convictions to clear instances of investigative and prosecutorial overreach, one might have expected more people to lose their jobs. Yet in Kern County, California, Ed Jagels remained at the head of the district attorney's office until 2009, when he announced he would not pursue an eighth term. Until the very end, his office's official web page noted with pride that under Jagels's watch "Kern County has had the highest per capita prison commitment rate of any major California County."[17] In Massachusetts Martha Coakley served as Middlesex County district attorney until winning an election that promoted her to attorney general in 2006. She won reelection four years later. Debra Kanof, the prosecutor who won convictions against Michelle Noble and Gayle Dove—both of which were overturned—currently works as an assistant US attorney, and Robert Perez retired on disability (he did, however, face a number of civil suits filed by defendants in Wenatchee).

Perhaps no prosecutor, therapist, or detective enjoyed as brilliant a posthysteria career as Janet Reno. In 1993, four years after Ileana Fuster was deported to Honduras, President Bill Clinton nominated Reno as the first woman candidate for US attorney general. Reno was confirmed and then famously became the center of controversy after ordering FBI forces to launch an assault on a compound held by a fringe religious group in Waco, Texas. The attack started a fire that consumed the compound and killed dozens of people, including twenty-two children. Though it went largely unnoticed at the time, there is evidence that Reno's experiences in Miami played a role in her decision to order the FBI attack. Reno was initially reluctant to send units into the compound—she wanted to give the hostage negotiators time to do their work. But then someone at the FBI—an official Justice Department investigation failed to determine who—relayed to Reno unsubstantiated allegations that children were being abused inside the compound. Reno then changed her mind about the wisdom of an assault because she thought "[the FBI] had learned that the Branch Davidians were beating babies." After the attack a doctor named Bruce Perry examined the twenty-one children who survived and determined that they had mild to moderate socialization problems but no signs of physical or sexual abuse. Of Reno's decision to order in the tear gas, he concluded, "The FBI maximized things they knew would ring a bell with her."[18]

Jesse Friedman left prison in 2001 as a registered "Level 3" sex offender, a designation reserved for those convicted of committing the most serious crimes. His efforts to have his conviction overturned and his sex offender status removed continue to this day.[19] Gerald Amirault was finally released in 2004, and in 2009 the Massachusetts Appeals Court threw out the conviction of Bernard Baran, whose consistent claims of innocence made him ineligible for parole for nearly a quarter-century. Baran died of an aneurysm in September 2014 at the age of forty-nine. He spent more years of his adult life in prison than out of it. In San Antonio, Anna Vasquez, one of four Hispanic lesbian women accused of aggravated sexual assault on a child in 1994, received parole in 2012. Elizabeth Ramirez, Cassandra Rivera, and Kristie Mayhugh followed in the fall of 2013.

This took place just one week after Fran Keller was released from prison on a personal bond, allowing her to return home for Thanksgiving, and one week before her ex-husband, Dan, with whom she remains close, was also released. The Kellers, who ran a day care from their home outside Austin until 1992, were freed in part because the doctor who testified against them in the early nineties recanted his testimony. The doctor's name was Michael Mouw, and he had been working at the emergency room at Brackenridge Hospital in downtown Austin shortly after a three-year-old girl first made allegations against the Kellers. At the time he noticed what he thought were irregularities in the shape of the girl's hymen, but several years later he heard a presentation that included slides depicting normal genital variations in children. That gave him pause, as did his memories of the emotional atmosphere that prevailed in the emergency room. "In the ER it is always guilty until proven innocent," he told a journalist in 2009. "I'm serious."[20] He said his own attitude had substantially evolved, and in the summer of 2013 he testified that his original diagnosis—the only physical evidence in the Keller case—had been wrong. "Sometimes it takes time to figure out what you don't know," he said. "I was mistaken."[21]

Scientific advances like these drove many of the exonerations appeals courts handed down in the last twenty-five years. In a judicial system that relies so heavily on the testimony of credentialed experts, even the most obviously coercive therapeutic interviews were often allowed to stand until research psychiatrists documented and quantified child suggestibility in controlled experiments. In 1995 the American Psychological Association published perhaps the most important volume of this work, *Jeopardy in the Courtroom: A Scientific Analysis of Children's Testimony.* After walking readers through a history of legal approaches to the problem of child suggestibility, the book's authors, Stephen J. Ceci and Maggie Bruck, looked at the ways different aspects of a forensic interview could affect a child's accuracy and reliability. Repeated interviews, they found, allowed children to describe what happened to them in more detail, but these descriptions also became less accurate with each successive session.[22] They also cited a large body of work indicating that in interviews with very young children, interviewer bias played an enormously important role. Although interviewers who were familiar with what actually happened going into the interview tended to elicit accurate accounts from children, interviewers starting out from incorrect hypotheses led children into providing inaccurate information of their own.[23]

Alongside Ceci and Bruck, the work of the research psychologist Elizabeth Loftus informed a number of appeal efforts that overturned abuse convictions.[24] Loftus conducted a famous study in 1995 in which she gave test subjects brief narratives, supposedly furnished by the test subjects' relatives, describing past events in their own lives. Included among a handful of true stories was a fabricated tale about getting lost in a shopping mall around the age of five. Loftus told her two-dozen participants that if they had no independent memories of any of the events, they should say so; nevertheless, a quarter of them claimed to recall their experience in the shopping mall, and some even embellished the story with unwittingly invented details of their own.[25] Though other researchers have since criticized the study for failing to take real psychological trauma into account—and of course it would be wildly unethical for researchers to try to implant false memories of rape or violence—the experiment's simplicity and elegance allowed it to function as a kind of shorthand for a whole field of research.

Today these scientific advances are cited and praised even by some of those whose work they criticize. "Nowadays, as opposed to back when McMartin took place," one CII official told the *New York Times* in 2013, "there's a very clear protocol about how to interview kids." Lael Rubin echoed his sentiment, arguing that investigators and therapists have spent the last twenty-five years working out "who should do it, who should be present, how all of that should occur and be videotaped . . . it really created a dialogue of examining the best way to talk to children who might be victims of crimes."[26]

With even Lael Rubin implicitly acknowledging that her investigators and therapists were out of their depth in 1983 and 1984, some people came to believe that the pendulum had swung too far toward skepticism. Political scientist Ross E. Cheit spent some fifteen years poring over police and court records from the day care and ritual abuse cases, and the results of his work were published in 2014. The central argument of *The Witch-Hunt Narrative: Politics, Psychology, and the Sexual Abuse of Children*, is that "there was not, by any reasonable measure, an epidemic of 'witch hunts' in the 1980s."[27] Cheit sometimes acknowledges prosecutorial excess and investigative mistakes, but he argues that with just one exception, every case commonly cited as part of the witch hunt probably originated in some real instance of sexual abuse. His analysis of the McMartin case concludes that although five or maybe six of the female teachers should never have been charged (he thinks Peggy McMartin Buckey's is a complicated case), the evidence against Ray Buckey was rather strong, and he believes the evidence against Kelly Michaels in Maplewood, New Jersey, was just as strong, if not stronger.[28] Of the Country Walk case, which sent Frank and Ileana Fuster to prison, he writes, "It takes significant distortion of the evidence to suggest this case was anything but a solid conviction."[29]

But Cheit's book features its own significant distortions of the evidence. In his chapter on the Country Walk case, for example, Cheit, like his pro-prosecution predecessors, cites Noel Fuster's positive test for gonorrhea of the throat as "the single most incriminating piece of evidence against Frank."[30] He refers to an article published in the *Journal of Clinical Microbiology* in 1983 as confirming the reliability of the test used on Noel's culture sample, but he totally misinterprets the paper's findings. "The positive predictive value of the RapID NH test was found to be 99.38 percent," he writes. The phrase "positive predictive value" refers to the chance that a person who tests positive for a particular disease or condition actually does have that disease or condition, so for Cheit to cite such a high positive predictive value for the RapID NH looks very damning. The problem is that the 99.38 figure appears nowhere in the paper Cheit cites, nor can it be extrapolated from any of its conclusions.

More recent research, much of which Cheit either discounts or fails to address, also suggests it would be unwise to place too much confidence in the positive test result. In 1988, the Centers for Disease Control (CDC) published a paper that specifically warned of the RapID NH test's potential inability to distinguish sexually transmitted strains of gonorrhea from other bacteria normally found in children's throats.[31] A 1999 affidavit by that paper's lead author reaffirmed the test's inadequacy for making forensic diagnoses. In another paper, published six years later in the *Journal of Medical Microbiology*, the authors stated, "the identification of this pathogen can be problematic, and as such no single method is currently recommended for a definitive identification."[32] In its current recommendations for the medicolegal diagnosis of gonorrhea, the CDC states that "because investigations of sexual abuse may be initiated on the basis of a laboratory diagnosis of gonorrhea, only definitive/confirmed identifications of *N. gonorrhoeae* should be accepted." The site notes that in order for an identification to qualify as definitive, the isolate must have been confirmed with at least two tests.[33] Although accounts vary, it appears that only one test, the problematic RapID NH, was used to diagnose Fuster's son with gonorrhea of the throat. By the current standards of medical forensics, that diagnosis is unreliable.

Cheit's errors go well beyond the particulars of a medical debate—his book offers a basic misunderstanding of the social realities that surrounded the day care cases. Unwilling to acknowledge that a society in which child abuse actually takes place could also be a society that stages panics over allegations of child abuse, Cheit spends more than sixty pages arguing that, whatever excesses and mistakes may have occurred, they did not constitute any kind of larger social phenomenon. Cheit seems to operate under the impression that one cannot describe a case as a witch hunt unless it entailed the arrest, trial, and conviction of someone who was really completely innocent of any wrongdoing whatsoever. By these criteria the sex ring investigations in Jordan, Minnesota, were not the product of a panic: James Rud, who really did abuse children, pled guilty, but none of the others accused of participating in the sex ring were actually convicted in court. Nor can the convictions of Dan and Fran Keller in Austin be said to have resulted from witch hunts. Though excessively interviewed children did make bizarre claims about satanic abuse, Cheit writes, those claims "were not part of the original criminal case against the Kellers, and they apparently involved only a small number of the parents and children who were interviewed in the case."[34] Again, by these criteria one would also accuse American historians of exaggerating the extent to which the Salem witch trials themselves constituted a witch hunt. A number of Salem residents, though suspected of witchcraft, were never formally charged—"What kind of witch hunt or 'justice denied' results in no charges whatsoever?" Cheit writes in his book—and more than two dozen of those people who were charged were found not guilty.[35] One servant was even tried for *falsely* accusing her mistress of practicing witchcraft.

Cheit argues that it is only by deliberately ignoring key differences among McMartin, Country Walk, and other cases that one can see them as all part of the same phenomenon. He is insistent about "the need to treat children as individuals and to take individual circumstances into account."[36] Yet only one kind of childhood experience is legitimized in his book, despite the fact that a number of people involved with the day care trials as children have since spoken out as adults. In 2005 the *Los Angeles Times* published an interview with Kyle Zirpolo, a then-thirty-year-old former McMartin student whose accusations resulted in some of the criminal charges that were eventually filed. The article was headlined "I'm Sorry." Zirpolo remembered CII therapists "almost giggling and laughing, saying, 'Oh, we know these things happened to you.'" He also remembered his mother asking whether he had ever played the naked movie star game. "After she asked me a hundred times," he said, "I probably said yeah, I did play that game." He said he knew his allegations were lies from the beginning, which forced him into a difficult balancing act: the encouragement he received from everybody for "remembering" what happened had to be weighed against the worry that he would eventually make a mistake. "At night in bed," he said, "I would think hard about things I had said in the past and try to repeat only the things I knew I'd said before." Zirpolo said that not everything about McMartin was clear to him even two decades on and that he didn't want to speak on behalf of any of the other students. "But I never forgot I was lying."[37]

Jennifer*, for many years, didn't have Zirpolo's confidence in her own memories, though she recalled the mundane aspects of her church basement day care rather clearly. "I remember baking," she said. "I remember going into the church's kitchen and baking as a group."[38] Then the day care moved to what she described as "kind of a Victorian house." She remembered its large rooms and its two floors.

She grew up in a small town of about ten thousand working-class people, and her parents both had full-time jobs, which meant that Jennifer spent mornings and afternoons at day care under the supervision of Chuck, his wife, Linda, and another woman named Janice. By the time Chuck was accused of sexually abusing children in 1984, Jennifer had graduated to elementary school. She was seven years old when her mother first took her to the police station for an interview. "A man—I can't remember if he was in uniform or not—had these anatomically correct dolls," Jennifer said. "And he asked me to show him stuff, and I didn't know what he was talking about." Much about the early days of the investigation was confusing, but the energy that surrounded that first police interview was palpable, and it persisted through the days that followed. "I remember it was, like, I could *tell* there was a buzz in my family," Jennifer said. "My mom was very drawn into it, and there were lots of phone conversations and meetings, and things happened. I remember my mom saying that a boy who I didn't know told his mom that something bad had happened, and she asked me what happened. I said nothing had happened."

---

* A pseudonym. The names of people and places associated with her case have been changed at her request, to protect her privacy.

It was the therapy sessions, which began soon after the first police interview and continued through Jennifer's adolescence, that had the biggest impact on her life. "What happened in therapy for me was the most—that was where all the trauma happened," she said. Jennifer went to regular one-on-one meetings with a therapist named Miriam, who also saw other children who had been allegedly abused at the day care. Miriam used dolls to demonstrate sex acts and then asked Jennifer to affirm that these things had happened to her. "I remember getting massive headaches," Jennifer said. "And I remember Miriam saying, 'Say this happened to you, it did, it did'—repeatedly—'it did, didn't it?' Over and over again." The questions made her "deeply uncomfortable" not only because of their subject matter but also because, like any seven-year-old, Jennifer's sense of the world and her place in it was delicate and unstable. Shortly before the therapy began, or maybe during its earliest weeks, a popular girl at school had teased Jennifer by saying that her father wasn't actually her father. This was actually true—Jennifer's stepfather had adopted her when she was three. There was an adoption party at some point, but Jennifer had forgotten, and she ran home to her mother, upset that the girl had insulted the man she thought of as her father. "But he's not your father!" her mother said. "He adopted you! Remember?" Therapy compounded the feelings of unease this episode brought about. "There was this sense like, what do you mean my dad's not my real dad?" Jennifer says. "What do you mean penises and vaginas do these things together? You think an adult did that to me? You want me to use these words?"

Jennifer remembers standing in front of a judge who asked whether she wanted to put all of this behind her. Jennifer understood the judge's phrase, "it all," as referring to therapy, and she badly wanted not to go to therapy anymore, so she "finally just started making stuff up." The trial passed. Chuck was convicted and sentenced to more than fifty years in prison. Therapy continued, though—there would be no putting it behind her. The parents' support group also continued, at least for a time. "I hated the mention of certain families' names," Jennifer says. "I hated when [my mom] talked about the Calvys. We'd go to their house, and the kids were supposed to hang out, and the parents were talking about the court case." After Miriam, Jennifer saw a therapist named Richard, who always had a plastic cup full of soda. It frightened her that Richard would lock the door at the start of their sessions, and one time she threw the soda cup, kicked him in the shins, and pounded on the door. Richard decided this meant Jennifer was afraid that Chuck would get out of jail and hurt her again. "So they took me in a state trooper's car with my parents—I was in the front, they sat in the back—to a jail. I had to get a tour of the jail to see how safe it was, the whole time freaking out, not wanting to be there."

Jennifer's mother was often physically abusive—"she would hit me all the time, would smack me on the face"—so as she entered adolescence, her therapy's focus began to shift. But day care was never far from the discussion, and her therapists' insistence that she really had been abused at day care complicated Jennifer's relationship to her own thoughts and memories:

> I felt like I had secret rooms in my brain. Like, I had rooms in my brain where I needed to think very clearly, and be honest with myself, and try really hard to remember if anything happened. And at the same time, I had to keep it completely hidden and protected from my mom and the therapists. . . . They would tell me, 'We have ways of finding out what you remember.' So my brain just didn't feel safe. I had to judge: If I thought really hard and remembered, could I also keep it hidden away from them? And they're also saying, in kid language, 'This could really backfire on you. You could end up an emotional wreck.' I had this fear that one day I would decompose or explode.

Civil suits meant that Jennifer and other children who attended the day care received money. This money went to the parents at first, but Jennifer gained control of it in her early twenties, and she will continue to receive payments at regular intervals, eventually totaling several hundred thousand dollars, until about the time she becomes eligible for social security. Like almost everything else about the case and its effects, the money was not openly discussed among Jennifer and her peers. She remembers a boy named Jake with whom she was close in high school. One day when they were seniors, Jake picked up Jennifer in a new red convertible he had recently bought. Then the pair drove to a nearby city, and Jake bought an expensive watch. A year later Jake came to visit Jennifer at college, and again he was talking about his money, and Jennifer asked him, "Where are you getting this money?" He said his parents told him they had invested in the stock market when he was young. Jennifer asked how much money he received and how often, and when he told her, Jennifer asked whether he had also attended the day care. He had. "I said, 'Your parents sued the day care, and that's where that money is from.' He had no idea what I was talking about."

Going to college was important, because Jennifer knew she would not be returning to her hometown. She came out as a lesbian, and she had a long, difficult relationship with a girlfriend. Sometimes she told people about the day care. "I would tell people, 'Nothing happened to me. I had all this crazy therapy that happened to me.' I would also say, 'It's fucked up that I'm getting all this money. I should not be getting this money. Nothing should happen to me.'" She started seeing a therapist during her junior year, after an older relative died, but things didn't get very far. "I was reticent to lay it all out there," Jennifer says. She graduated, moved, saw a new therapist, moved again, saw another therapist, stopped seeing that therapist. It wasn't until the early 2000s that Jennifer met a psychologist around whom she felt really comfortable. "From the very beginning," Jennifer says, "I had to say, 'You cannot get between me and the door, because if I feel in any way unsafe I am going to plow you over.' So there were real baseline kinds of things." Jennifer's therapist respected these needs, and the two saw each other almost every week for five years. Jennifer told her all about the day care case and the therapy to which she had been subjected throughout her childhood. "We've learned a lot since then," Jennifer says her therapist told her, "and you should not have been dealt with the way you were dealt with."

This therapy gave Jennifer a sufficiently secure grip on her childhood experiences for her to begin looking into them more deeply. Although her former lawyer had destroyed all of the files that pertained to her case, Jennifer was eventually able to track down a few dozen pages of documents. She was particularly interested to see the specific charges on which Chuck had been tried, in part because she wanted to know whether they matched two vivid memories she had of being abused at the day care. Although Jennifer knows the trauma she experienced took place in the therapy she was made to undergo, she cannot find a way to qualitatively distinguish her two day care abuse memories from memories of events she knows happened for sure, and she says they have not faded with the passage of time. In one memory, she is in the main room of the day care's big Victorian house, and she is facing Chuck, who sits in a chair. She is in a line with the other kids, waiting for her turn. When she gets to the front, Chuck lays her facedown across his lap and then pushes a thumbtack through the seat of her jeans, into her buttocks. He does this to each child.

"I don't remember it being a problem when it was happening," Jennifer says. "I was just like, 'Okay, there are three kids in front of me.' And then I remember anticipating the thumbtack going through the denim." In the other memory, Jennifer is taken from the day care to a gravel pit. She doesn't recall anything that happened there—just the gravel pit itself. She told her father about this once, and he drove her around outside of town looking for the gravel pit. "And as an adult, I've driven around trying to find it," she says. She never found it.

Jennifer eventually made a home for herself, her partner, and her child in a state hundreds of miles from her hometown. Her day care teacher's conviction was eventually overturned. Around the country people associated with the ritual abuse panic moved on and moderated—or even repudiated—their old beliefs, many of them in ways that made prosecutors look like defiant and unapologetic intransigents by comparison. In 1998 John Briere, one of the leading advocates of recovered memory therapy in the 1980s, told an audience at the 12th International Congress on Child Abuse and Neglect that efforts to "liposuction people's memories out of their brains" had been damaging. "It's not the therapist's job to help patients remember anything," he said.[39]

Some feminists in the incest survivors movement also expressed regrets and misgivings about their involvement with recovered memory. Diana Russell, the activist author of *The Secret Trauma*, wrote that although she had initially seen members of the False Memory Syndrome Foundation as "a bunch of perpetrators who were part of the backlash," reading personal accounts by women who retracted their ritual abuse memories changed her thinking. She came to see that it was the therapists who "pathologized and depoliticized incest" who did the greatest damage to incest survivors.[40] And, of course, there are the forensic interviewers who work to help child victims of abuse clearly and accurately describe their experiences in courtrooms. Professor Cheit's concerns about a new climate of skepticism notwithstanding, most professionals believe the field is much stronger today than it was thirty years ago.[41]

In other ways, however, the day care panic continued to paralyze scientific and intellectual debates on child abuse. In 1993, as satanic abusers were finally beginning to disappear from the front pages, psychology discovered yet another class of sexual predators: children themselves. The publication of *Sexualized Children: Assessment and Treatment of Sexualized Children and Children Who Molest* crystallized work that had initially been undertaken in the late 1980s. One of the book's authors, Toni Cavanagh Johnson, worked for a time at Children's Institute International, and although her tenure there postdated Kee MacFarlane's McMartin interviews, her writing on child sexual predators is imbued with the CII spirit. Although the preface to *Sexualized Children* states that it is just as important to avoid overreacting to normal sex play among children as to avoid underreacting to serious abusive behavior, the vast majority of the book's pages are devoted to addressing the latter concern.[42] With its treatment plans and multipage lists of "risk factors," *Sexualized Children* and similar books opened the door to the development of therapies that pathologized many normal kinds of childhood behavior, including masturbation and bodily exploration among peers. Within the judiciary, the specter of predators lurking even among the elementary school population eventually caused some states to begin including children on public sex offender registries. Today juveniles constitute more than a third of all people thought by police to have committed a sexual offense against a minor, with some 4 percent of the total offending population under the age of twelve.[43] In some states no law sets a minimum age for who can be placed on a public offender registry, and registration often lasts for life. By 2013 one such state, Texas, included nearly five thousand registered sexual offenders who were under the age of sixteen when they committed their crimes.[44]

As the residual effects of the day care and ritual abuse panic allowed these new fears to flourish in the 1990s, they also stymied attempts to roll back the old fears. In 1998 the prestigious journal *Psychological Bulletin* published a detailed meta-analysis of other scientific articles on the psychological consequences of abuse.[45] The paper's lead author was the Temple University psychologist Bruce Rind. In light of the prevailing beliefs about the irreparable long-term trauma caused by abuse, many of his findings should have been received as very good news. After reviewing fifty-nine studies in which adults who were sexually abused as children were asked to describe the effects the abuse had on their lives, the authors found that abuse victims were, on average, "slightly less well adjusted" than people who had not been abused. Looking more closely, they found that the probability of future psychological maladjustment was not meaningfully influenced by the victim's age or by the type of sex act that occurred but rather by the presence of some degree of coercion or force in the encounter. Even this insight, however, was complicated by the fact that many of the fifty-nine studies failed to distinguish the effects of abuse from the effects of a negative family environment in general. Once Rind and his colleagues controlled for family environment, the effects of abuse often became insignificant. "Basic beliefs about child sexual abuse in the general population were not supported," the authors wrote.

In many of the studies Rind and his team analyzed, people had been asked to reflect on their experiences of abuse and describe their reactions to them. Rind was struck by the fact that although a clear majority of women said the experience was a negative one, 25 percent reported neutral feelings, and the remaining 16 percent classified the experience as positive. For boys the results were even more surprising: 26 percent negative, 32 percent neutral, 42 percent positive.[46] The authors wrote that a number of factors might explain the diversity of the victims' responses, but first among these was the rather general scientific meaning of the terms "child" and "abuse." If preschoolers and sixteen-year-olds alike were classified as children, and if "abuse" referred to everything from repeated violent assault to incest to fondling to isolated incidents of exhibitionism, how could one reasonably expect to find uniformity in people's responses to child abuse?

The paper made two recommendations for future studies. First, for research purposes scientists should "focus on the young person's perception of his or her willingness to participate and his or her reactions to the experience."[47] And second, adolescent-adult encounters should be distinguished from encounters between adults and pre-adolescent children so as to take the developing sexuality of teenagers into account. Finally, Rind cautioned that "lack of harmfulness does not imply lack of wrongfulness"—in other words, that society could well have perfectly good reasons to forbid adult-child sexual encounters even if those reasons could not be grounded in "the presumption of psychological harm."[48]

That final caveat suggested that Rind and his colleagues had a fairly good idea that people might object to their findings, but it is hard to imagine that they could have anticipated the intensity of those objections. Several months after the article's publication, the National Association for Research and Therapy of Homosexuality (NARTH), an organization devoted to the idea that homosexuality was an emotional disorder that could be cured through psychotherapy, denounced the paper on its website.[49] Three months later a Catholic newspaper called *The Wanderer* called the paper "pseudo-professional" and "pseudo-academic."[50] That same month, having been alerted to the paper's existence by one of her listeners, Dr. Laura Schlessinger, host of a daily radio show that reached some 18 million people, spent nearly two days criticizing Rind's work. She said that meta-analysis was a worthless research technique (it is not), that as a "real scientist," she knew that scientific studies that contradicted "common sense" should be dismissed, and finally, that "the point of the article is to allow men to rape male children."[51] Then the conservative Family Research Council described the study as providing pedophiles with a "green flag." In April, Alaska became the first of six states to introduce resolutions condemning the article, and in June the American Psychological Association announced that it would ask an independent agency to review the scientific validity of the paper's findings, a stunning capitulation from the field's leading professional organization. On Capitol Hill, Republican Congressman Matt Salmon described the paper as "the Emancipation Proclamation of pedophiles," and on July 12 the House of Representatives passed Resolution 107, condemning the study and affirming that sexual encounters between adults and children are always harmful. The Senate followed suit on July 30. It was the first time in American history that Congress had condemned a scientific study of any kind.

As the feminist intellectual Carol Tavris pointed out a year after the passage of HRC Resolution 107, what made the study so incendiary was that it challenged three social assumptions about childhood sexuality. The first is that "any sexual experience that any child has is, by definition, 'abuse.'" This belief had allowed the set of experiences defined as "abusive" to expand during the 1980s and 1990s to the point at which it included not just unwanted sexual contact but also things like playing doctor, masturbation (in the day care cases this was often taken as a symptom of earlier abuse), and sex play among children and their peers. The second assumption, which follows directly from the first, is that "any sexual experience that any child has is, therefore, inherently traumatic, with long-lived emotional and psychological consequences." Finally, Tavris wrote, Rind's work had challenged a widely held belief about teenagers, who are thought "to have no sexual feeling of any kind until they are 16 (at which time they magically become mature adults) [and] are incapable of wishing to have sexual relations."[52] Congress's insistence that these experiences were always abusive and inherently traumatic was rooted in one of the key tenets of the conservative sexual backlash that had rolled through the culture during the same period as the ritual abuse panic: that people were completely nonsexual beings until they reached the age of majority.

Tavris and other writers also noted that it is not necessary to maintain a bogus vision of sexual psychology in order to justify laws that prohibit sexual contact between adults and children. What makes an affair between a sixteen-year-old and her teacher abusive isn't some inherent difference between adult and adolescent sexuality but rather the lopsided distribution of power that inevitably structures their relationship. That's what abuse is, by definition: an abuse *of power*. That abusive relationships are primarily defined by power imbalances becomes easier to see when child sexual abuse is considered alongside physical abuse, neglect, domestic violence, and assault. It is the battered housewife's economic dependence on her alcoholic husband and his full-time job that makes it impossible for her to leave, the predatory coach's ability to kick players off the team that leaves the student athlete unable to alert the administration, the child's total dependence on her father that maintains silence.

Extrapolating out from these intimate power structures of domesticity and personal relationships, the larger social causes of abuse come into view: the sex education curricula that prevent teens from knowing even the first thing about their sexuality, the poverty that always hits women and children harder than men, the social norms that continue to see single mothers as less worthy of aid than their married counterparts. It was exactly this type of analysis, moving from the particulars of individual experience to an analysis of the larger social structure, that characterized the work of the feminist movement in the late sixties and seventies, gave feminism's most famous slogan, "The personal is political," its meaning, and made the movement such a potent force. You will never end these abuses, the argument went, by adding new diagnoses to the DSM or putting abusers in jail for longer periods of time. You will actually have to democratize family life, change relations between the sexes, and work toward a more equitable economy. But beginning with Walter Mondale's insistence in 1974 that abuse was not a "poverty problem" but a "national problem," continuing through the day care trials with their relentless focus on deviant perpetrator cults and mostly middle-class, mostly white, often blond victims, and concluding with the horror shows of recovered memory and MPD, these more radical analyses of abuse were systematically forgotten.

Not everyone reacted enthusiastically to Congress's unanimous condemnation of science. In September 1999, after being asked by the APA to conduct an independent review of Rind's findings, the American Association for the Advancement of Science (AAAS) unexpectedly said it would do no such thing. "We see no reason to second-guess the process of peer review used by the APA journal in its decision to publish the article in question," AAAS Chair Irving Lerch wrote. He went on to express "grave concerns with the politicization of the debate over the article's methods and findings," and the APA would eventually receive many letters from other researchers angered by the way the organization handled the controversy.[53]

Complaints about the politicization of scientific debate, however, did little to defuse the larger debates about abuse and childhood sexuality, and so when the University of Minnesota published *Harmful to Minors: The Perils of Protecting Children from Sex* by the journalist and abortion rights activist Judith Levine in 2002, the controversy was ready to replay itself. "At the turn of the twenty-first century," Levine wrote, "America is being inundated by censorship in the name of protecting 'children' from 'sex,' both terms capaciously defined."[54] She argued that after a period of sexual optimism in the 1960s and 1970s, American culture had spent more than twenty years focusing on the moral and medical dangers of sex: disease, unwanted pregnancy, strangers with candy, porn. This shift had been particularly pronounced in discussions of childhood sexuality. Although earlier decades had seen the publication of a number of books designed to explain various aspects of sex to children with straightforward friendliness (one described an orgasm as like "climbing up the ladder of a long slide and then whooshing down"), recent guides spent more time dramatizing all that could go wrong. Levine noted that almost every sex-ed curriculum includes a list of reasons why someone might want to have sex, which students are often asked to brainstorm. She cited one list's collection of possible answers, which included "to hold onto a relationship," "to get affection," "to show that they are 'grown up,'" and so forth. Levine noted one reason not included on this list "or almost any other": because it feels good.[55]

The practical and lighthearted tone in which Levine delivered her various recommendations and reassurances was clearly designed to serve the book's larger goal: to dispel the climate of fear that surrounded all public discussions of children and sex. Following naturally from this goal was a belief that in order for society to approach adolescent sexuality with less anxiety, it would be necessary to entrust adolescents themselves with some measure of freedom to make their own decisions about sex. Levine suggested that age of consent laws be recast in a Dutch mold. This meant providing people between the ages of twelve and fifteen with the right to consent to sex while also allowing them to "employ a statutory consent age of sixteen if they felt they were being coerced or exploited." In addition, parents could step in and forbid a child's relationship with an adult, but only if they were able to persuade a special council that it really was in the child's best interest. Such a system, Levine wrote, would "balance the subjective experience and the rights of young people against the responsibility and prerogative of adults to look after their best interests."[56]

One can imagine how this suggestion went over. The University of Minnesota Press was deluged with more than eight hundred angry phone calls and e-mails even before *Harmful to Minors* had been shipped to retail outlets, meaning that the letters were written by people who could not possibly have read the book. The conservative state legislature also threatened to revoke funding from the publisher's parent university. Levine became the object of heated personal attacks. Robert Knight, a conservative activist affiliated with the group Concerned Women for America, described Levine's book as "every child molester's dream and every parent's nightmare."[57]

Although a George W. Bush–era debate about the sexual rights of teenagers and 1980s arguments about the existence of satanic pedophile cults might appear to be related to one other in only a distant way, it was not a coincidence that they attracted some of the same participants. One group involved in the attacks on *Harmful to Minors* was the Leadership Council for Mental Health, Justice, and the Media, an organization of therapists and other professionals that formed as recovered memory patients began to file malpractice lawsuits in the 1990s. Richard Kluft, Frank Putnam, Bessel van der Kolk, and other high-profile proponents of MPD—which had since been rebranded as Dissociative Identity Disorder—served on its advisory board, and one Leadership Council researcher told a reporter that Levine's book was a sign that a movement to promote adult-child sex was "gathering steam."[58] What drew these people to both debates was the fact that in each case the argument had less to do with any children in actual need of protection than with the adults who imagined themselves to be doing the protecting. A close look at the substance of their arguments suggests that the alleged need to protect functioned as a euphemistic substitute for the desire to control. "If Americans understood the radical roots of the sex education courses in their schools," Robert Knight said at a press conference on Levine's book, "they would be reaching for abstinence-based curricula as a literal life preserver even faster than they are now."[59] For many conservative activists, objections to comprehensive sex education have often been grounded in the notion that such programs usurp parents' natural authority to determine whether their children are allowed to learn about sex.

Today, however, the law can easily be turned against parents—specifically mothers—who choose not to wield every bit of their authority. The 1980s drastically altered people's views on the wisdom of ever allowing children to go unsupervised, whether walking to school on their own or hanging out on a playground a few blocks away from home. The country's op-ed pages regularly feature pieces in which middle-aged pundits bemoan the rise of "helicopter parenting," lament the endless succession of organized activities to which children are subjected in the name of college preparation, and eulogize the carefree childhood afternoons they spent running around in the woods. But the helicopter parenting debate is a debate about upper-middle-class people who choose to involve themselves in every moment of their children's lives despite having the resources to do otherwise. The consequences of these choices are described primarily as a matter of a family's psychological health.

But for parents with fewer resources, parents working multiple jobs, and single parents, the consequences of allowing children to roam free, even for a moment, can be much more tangible and destructive. In March 2014 a woman living in Scottsdale, Arizona, was arrested after leaving her young children alone in a car while she went to interview for a job with Farmers Insurance. She had arranged for a babysitter to watch the kids, but the babysitter never showed up, and she needed the job very badly. It was 71 degrees outside, and the children spent sixty-nine minutes alone in the car. Shanesha Taylor lost custody of her children, spent ten days in jail, and was charged with two counts of felony child abuse.[60] Later that year an African American woman from South Carolina left her nine-year-old daughter at a park while she went to her job at a McDonalds one and a half miles away. She was arrested and charged with unlawful conduct toward a child. "This day and time, you never know who's around," said one woman interviewed about the incident. "Good, bad, it's just not safe."[61] Around the same time, the police officer who arrested Nicole Gainey in Port St. Lucie, Florida, for allowing her seven-year-old son to play alone in a public park wrote in his report that "numerous sex offenders reside in the vicinity." "He just basically kept going over that there's pedophiles and this and that," Gainey said, "and basically the park wasn't safe and he shouldn't be there alone."[62]

Here, then, are cases in which the fear that violent pedophiles might abduct children from public places—a vanishingly rare occurrence—was used to justify the punishment of women who were looking for work, women who were at work, or women who simply thought that she and her child might both benefit from the child being allowed some time to play on his own—in other words, women whose failure to devote every moment to their role as mothers was viewed as literally criminal. There is a direct link between child abuse hysteria and antifeminism, and the fact that such punitive measures, when criticized, are invariably described as "well intentioned" only makes them more effective and harder to roll back. Although all of these cases were widely criticized in the media, most people support the general principles that justified them: 68 percent of Americans believe that parents should be legally prohibited from allowing children under the age of ten to play in public parks without adult supervision, and 43 percent think that prohibition should extend to children *up to the age of twelve*.[63] Of course, making affordable day care available to all parents would help working mothers to avoid situations in which they felt compelled to leave their children alone even when they did not want to, but the ritual abuse panic made sure that day care came under suspicion as well.

Who wields authority within the family? How much authority does the family, as an institution, wield in society? To a large extent these are the questions on which the ritual abuse hysteria was founded, and they run from at least the early 1980s up to the present day. That they provoked not just argument and conflict but specifically *hysteria* can paradoxically be credited to the fact that they had already been answered when the panic began.

In does not quite go far enough to say that the patriarchal nuclear family changed during the second half of the twentieth century; it became incoherent. For nearly two centuries, ever since the appearance of industrialization, life in the West had been organized around the idea that the best way for people to live was in private, single-family households. As men were expected to support the rest of the family through their work, these households determined much of the shape and structure of economic life. As sex was not to occur outside the confines of a monogamous marriage, and as the purpose of a marriage was to produce children, the family also bolstered prohibitions on homosexuality and determined the course of people's erotic experience. And as the family became the site of people's most intimate emotional relationships with others, from the very beginning of life to its end, it shaped psychology (the description of the psychology of family life was Freud's whole project).

All of this broke down with the sexual revolution and especially with the second wave of the feminist movement. But it didn't break down all at once in practice. In addition to the family's persistent psychological power, many areas of government policy are still biased toward the family as a kind of social ideal, with tax law being perhaps the most obvious. Women continue to perform more domestic and care-based work than men. And many people continue to live in single-breadwinner nuclear families, though not a majority of Americans by any means.

Theory is just as important as practice, however, and in theory the 1960s and feminism successfully did away with the idea that there could be no justifiable or desirable alternatives to family life. California became the first state to legalize no-fault divorce in 1969, and since then the social expectation that people get married and that marriage last until one spouse's death has steadily declined. As divorce rates increased, the fact of having been divorced became less of a social liability for women and even, in some cases, a mark of independence. As lifelong marriage and full-time care of children became less essential to women's social and economic security, women began to demand increased and fair access to work outside the home. And as the presence of women in offices and other professional environments became less of a curiosity and more of an accepted fact of life, new possibilities for the organization of life back at home proliferated: single parents, second and third marriages, cohabitation, second and third marriages to people with children from previous marriages, same-sex marriages.

Every stage of this diversification of private life has been accompanied by anxious predictions of moral decay, social breakdown, and sexual anarchy. Legislators have responded to and fueled these anxieties by passing laws designed to shore up the nuclear family's crumbling walls. But the legislation has had no effect—the percentage of Americans who are married continues its steady decline.[64] And the repeated expressions of anxiety are more likely to indicate simply that freedoms can be frightening when they are new, not that the new freedoms are bad or that people don't want them. In light of the obstacles thrown in its path, it is clear that the transformation of family life would not have happened except that people very much wanted it to happen. "Marriage as a social institution (an economic partnership, a secure context for child-rearing) only works when it's more or less compulsory," Ellen Willis wrote in the late 1980s.[65] By the time she made her observation, many people had decided that what they most wanted from marriage and the nuclear family, in spite of the difficulties involved, was to get out.

This was all well under way by the time Judy Johnson made her initial phone call to the Manhattan Beach police. That something fundamental about the family's place in society had shifted, that the shift was permanent, and that it was only gaining momentum had all become obvious by the end of the 1970s—at least it had to conservatives, who were by then a few years into their campaign of cultural resistance. The trouble since then has been to acknowledge this shift, to accommodate it, and to help people acclimate to its effects. This difficulty became especially acute in the 1980s, and it is worth considering that the psychoanalytic theory of repression, so maligned by Roland Summit, Jeffrey Masson, and the recovered memory therapists, provides a detailed description of what happens when people are unable to acknowledge what they already know and want. Repression is not so much an act of passive forgetting but of active mental avoidance, and it isn't so much events or memories that are repressed but rather ideas and desires. We repress that which we do not want to think about. One of Freud's most important intellectual leaps was the insight that repression occurs because of a particular desire's "sharp contrast to the subject's other wishes" and its incompatibility with "the ethical and aesthetic standards of [the subject's] personality."[66] On a social scale, the idea of the nuclear family's decline emerged with an alarming speed and force, and for many people it seemed to be alarmingly incompatible with the rest of society's ethical and aesthetic standards—its culture, its rhetoric, its view of what made for a good life. The family's decline was repressed almost from the very moment it began.

Freud also understood that repression doesn't actually make an idea go away. Excluded from consciousness by a mental process that Freud called resistance, the repressed idea finds other ways of making its presence known. It may appear in Freud's famous slips of the tongue, transforming an innocuous remark into a revealing gaffe, or it might shape the contents of dreams. It can manifest as a personality quirk, a tic, a phobia, a habit of speech, or a minor compulsion. A repressed idea can also inflect a person's emotional life, furnishing him with strong opinions he cannot explain or making him vulnerable to certain kinds of confrontation. Freud's case studies and clinical reports are also filled, however, with descriptions of the more outlandish consequences of repression: unexplained bouts of coughing that last for weeks at a time, mysterious illnesses for which a physician can find no somatic explanation, paralysis, temporary blindness, sleep disturbances. These are the mind's attempts to protect itself from some idea it does not want to confront, to release some of the psychic stress produced by repression. They are symptoms of hysteria.

Recovered memory and the day care and ritual abuse hysteria drove the social repression of two ideas. First, the nuclear family was dying. Second, people mostly did not want to save it.

Kee MacFarlane's interviews told the well-off, professional parents of Manhattan Beach that the potential freedoms afforded by day care could not justify depriving children of constant access to their mothers' love and attention. In Kern County, Jordan, and Wenatchee, prosecutors arrested and charged primarily poor and lower-middle-class defendants, people among whom mixed families were more common than among the upper-middle class. The moral of these three cases was that mixed families led to predatory sex rings. The trials in Pittsfield, Massachusetts, and San Antonio, Texas, which resulted in the conviction of gay and lesbian defendants, dramatized the long-held idea that homosexuality as such constituted a threat to normal family life. Multiple personality disorder said that women would inevitably be traumatized by the new roles that had become available to them, that in fact the availability of multiple roles itself was a form of mass mental illness.

Hysteria is a loaded term, one cocooned in sedimentary layers of psychological history, discredited theories, failed treatments, misunderstandings, and misdiagnoses. Many feminists also consider it to be a politically suspicious term for the simple reason that hysteria has long been thought of as a specifically feminine malady. To describe a man or his behavior as "hysterical" is in part to make him seem more like a woman, and to describe a woman in the same way is to dredge up a host of stereotypes about the female sex and its supposedly inherent weaknesses: its irrationality, its capriciousness, its emotionalism. Given the word's history and its long-running associations with these sexist ideas and therapeutic practices, and given the sexist fears that motivated the day care cases and the recovered memory movement, it can be tempting to discard "hysteria" altogether in favor of "panic" or some other more neutral term.

The problem is that no other word accounts for the way these cases simultaneously horrified and fascinated those who were involved in them, the way parents' feelings of repulsion flourished alongside an excitement born of the idea that conspiracies were unfolding in ostensibly idyllic communities. Some ritual abuse skeptics have explained the panic as a simple failure of reason, a sudden and violent collapse of the country's ability to distinguish fact from fiction. Those failures were real, and it is important, from a forensic and judicial perspective, to identify and remedy them. However, it hardly *explains* anything at all to point out that people got their facts wrong. The more pressing question has to do with the source and cause of this eagerness to mistake a decade-long waking nightmare for the truth. Of course, the hysteria played on people's fears about the social changes that began to work their way through American society at the end of the twentieth century: the reorganization of private life and the slow but still probably—hopefully—inexorable breakdown of the country's sexual hierarchy. But people also actively wanted these social changes to take place, even if they often found this was a desire they could not bring themselves to acknowledge, whether in public or in the privacy of their own homes or heads. The hysteria drew its special character in the 1980s and 1990s from the difficulty people had recognizing this desire and acknowledging that many areas of life were already being transformed to accommodate it. This difficulty persists today, and as a result, so do the hysteria's effects. But the middle-class nuclear family will not be restored to its former place, nor do most people want it to be. To imagine otherwise can only perpetuate this series of costly and destructive fantasies.

ACKNOWLEDGMENTS

My work on this book began in fall 2011 and continues up to the present, as I sit at a desk writing acknowledgments. The people listed here helped me with many aspects of research, writing, and editing. They all have my gratitude.

Thank you to the members of the *n+1* Research Collective: Christopher Glazek, Mark Greif, Elizabeth Gumport, Simone Landon, Nika Mavrody, Kathleen Ross, Erin Sheehy, Astra Taylor, and Dayna Tortorici. This book comes directly out of the work we did together and would not exist without it.

The following people and institutions provided me with access to many of the research materials on which this book is based: Ross E. Cheit, Kevin Cody, Danny Davis, Debbie Nathan, Michael Snedeker, Hollida Wakefield, James Michael Wood, the Lynn and Louis Wolfson II Florida Moving Image Archives at Miami Dade College, the Bodleian Library at Oxford University, and the Scott County Historical Society. Archival research was also made possible by a Research Support Grant from the Schlesinger Library at the Radcliffe Institute for Advanced Study, Harvard University.

Book research requires money, but book advances are small, and fellowship applications sometimes do not bear fruit. I want to emphasize the positive feelings I have for the people who gave me places to stay, often for free. They are Jake Galgon, Laura Jereski, Susan Laxton, Johanna Ojeda, James Pogue, Robert Andrew Powell, and Peter Valelly.

Thank you to everyone who read drafts of the manuscript and offered comments, advice, edits, and encouragement, especially Jesse Barron, Lois Beckett, Keith Gessen, Benjamin Kunkel, Rachel Riederer, and my editor, Brandon Proia.

I am grateful to Madeleine Schwartz for all kinds of things.

Jim Rutman, of Sterling Lord Literistic, is a terrific agent. Clive Priddle and everyone else at PublicAffairs have been a pleasure to work with, and the staff and writers of *n+1* are a source of constant support and delight. Thanks also to my family and friends for everything.

—RB, March 5, 2015

NOTES

Introduction

1. Wayne Satz, *Eyewitness News*, KABC, Los Angeles, February 2, 1984.

2. Wayne Satz, *Eyewitness News*, KABC, Los Angeles, Videotape "#1—Satz 1 and 2," in the possession of Danny Davis.

3. John Crewdson, *By Silence Betrayed: Sexual Abuse of Children in America* (Boston: Little Brown & Company, 1988), 140.

4. Laura M. Betancourt et al., "Adolescents with and without Gestational Cocaine Exposure: Longitudinal Analysis of Inhibitory Control, Memory and Receptive Language," *Neurotoxicology and Teratology* 33, no. 1 (January–February 2011): 36–46.

5. Statement of Hon. Arlen Specter, Chair, Subcommittee on Juvenile Justice, *Child Sexual Abuse Victims in the Courts: Hearing Before the Subcommittee on Juvenile Justice, Committee on the Judiciary*, US Senate, May 22, 1984.

6. Paul McEnroe and David Peterson, "Jordan," *Minneapolis Star and Tribune*, October 21, 1984, 18A.

7. Statement of Kee MacFarlane, *Child Sexual Abuse Victims in the Courts*, US Senate.

8. "Fuster, Frank" [video recording], Lynn and Louis Wolfson II Florida Moving Image Archives, Accession/Request No. 1194-005, 1985.

9. Jan Hollingsworth, *Unspeakable Acts* (New York and Chicago: Congdon and Weed, 1986), 544.

10. "The Best Kept Secret," *20/20*, ABC, June 14, 1984.

11. Peter W. Kunhardt and Kenneth Wooden, producers, "Why the Silence?" *20/20*, ABC, January 3, 1985.

12. "The Best Kept Secret."

13. Stephen J. Ceci and Maggie Bruck, *Jeopardy in the Courtroom: A Scientific Analysis of Children's Testimony* (Washington, DC: American Psychological Association, 1999), 10.

14. Kevin Cody, "Boy Testifies to Complex Abusive Acts at McMartin," *Easy Reader*, April 21, 1988, 11.

15. Interview with Jason Cramer (pseud.), August 28, 1984, Interviewers Laurie Braga and Joe Braga, transcribed by Laurie Alvarado on September 17, 1984.

16. Roland Summit, "Caring for Child Molestation Victims," *National Symposium on Child Molestation* (Washington, DC: US Department of Justice, 1984), 242.

17. "Wee Care Interview," June 28, 1985, transcript, Office of the Prosecutor of Essex County, Interviewer Lou Fonolleras, 134.

18. Ibid., 136.

19. Ibid., 142.

20. Gilbert Cates, director, *Do You Know the Muffin Man?*, produced by Daniel Freudenberger, Avnet/Kerner Company Productions, 1989.

21. CII interview with Jessie Lipton (pseud.), August 16, 1984, Interviewer Laurie Braga, transcribed by Cristina Bejarano, April 1, 1996, 14.

22. CII interview with Otis Lawton (pseud.), November 1983, transcript, interviewer Kee MacFarlane, 53.

23. Ibid., 71.

24. CII interview with Keith Doherty (pseud.), January 24, 1984, transcript, interviewers Kee MacFarlane and Sandra Krebs, 35.

25. Paul McEnroe, Dan Oberdorfer, and Cheryl Johnson, "Sources Suggest Link to Stories of Child Slayings," *Minneapolis Star and Tribune*, October 16, 1984, 15A.

26. Letter from We the Jurors, *State of Florida vs. Bobby Fijnje*, to Janet Reno, May 9, 1991, on *"Frontline*: The Child Terror," www.pbs.org/wgbh/pages/frontline/shows/terror/cases/fijnjeletter.html.

27. John A. Jackson, "McMartin Watch," *Easy Reader*, May 2, 1985, 5.

28. Advertisement placed by "The Friends of The McMartin Pre-School Defendants," *Easy Reader*, August 15, 1985, 13.

29. Ceci and Bruck, *Jeopardy in the Courtroom*, 8.

30. Paul Boyer and Stephen Nissenbaum, *Salem Possessed: The Social Origins of Witchcraft* (Cambridge, MA: Harvard University Press, 1974), 30.

31. Ibid., 24.

32. Ibid., 13.

33. Ibid., 5.

34. Richard Francis, *Judge Sewall's Apology: The Salem Witch Trials and the Forming of an American Conscience* (New York: Harper Perennial, 2006), 181–182.

35. Menachem Kaiser, "Panic in Jerusalem," *Tablet*, November 29, 2012, www.tabletmag.com/jewish-news-and-politics/117839/panic-in -jerusalem.

36. M. S. Denov, "The Myth of Innocence: Sexual Scripts and the Recognition of Child Sexual Abuse by Female Perpetrators," *Journal of Sex Research* 40, no. 3 (2003): 303–314.

37. Greg Allen, "Sex Offenders Forced to Live Under Miami Bridge," *NPR.org*, May 20, 2009, www.npr.org/templates/story/story.php?storyId =104150499.

38. Minnesota Department of Corrections, "Residential Proximity and Sex Offense Recidivism in Minnesota," April 2007, www.csom.org /pubs/MN%20Residence%20Restrictions_04-07SexOffenderReport -Proximity%20MN.pdf.

39. Human Rights Watch, "No Easy Answers: Sex Offender Laws in the US," vol. 19, no. 4(G) (September 2007), 28, www.hrw.org/reports /2007/09/11/no-easy-answers.

CHAPTER 1

1. Judith Sealander, *The Failed Century of the Child: Governing America's Young in the Twentieth Century* (Cambridge, New York: Cambridge University Press, 2003), 56.

2. Lela B. Costin, *The Politics of Child Abuse in America* (New York: Oxford University Press, 1996), 67.

3. Sealander, *The Failed Century of the Child*, 56.

4. Ibid., 60.

5. John Caffey, "Multiple Fractures in the Long Bones of Infants Suffering from Chronic Subdural Hematoma," *American Journal of Roentgenology* 56 (1946): 163–173.

6. John Caffey, "Infantile Cortical Hyperostoses," *Journal of Pediatrics* 29, no. 5 (November 1946): 541–559.

7. Caffey, "Multiple Fractures in the Long Bones of Infants Suffering from Chronic Subdural Hematoma."

8. F. N. Silverman, "The Roentgen Manifestations of Unrecognized Skeletal Trauma in Infants," *American Journal of Roentgenology, Radium Therapy and Nuclear Medicine* 69 (1953): 413–427.

9. V. Woolley and W. A. Evans, "Significance of Skeletal Lesions in Infants Resembling Those of Traumatic Origin," *Journal of the American Medical Association* 158 (1955): 539–543.

10. John Caffey, "Some Traumatic Lesions in Growing Bones Other Than Fractures and Dislocations—Clinical and Radiological Features," *British Journal of Radiology* 30 (1957): 225–238.

11. C. Henry Kempe et al., "The Battered-Child Syndrome," *Journal of the American Medical Association* 181, no. 1 (July 7, 1962): 17–24.

12. C. Henry Kempe et al., "Editorial," *Journal of the American Medical Association* 181, no. 1 (July 7, 1962): 42.

13. Barbara Nelson, *Making an Issue of Child Abuse: Political Agenda Setting for Social Problems* (Chicago and London: University of Chicago Press, 1984), 59.

14. Sealander, *The Failed Century of the Child*, 62.

15. Nelson, *Making an Issue of Child Abuse*, 56.

16. Marjorie Hunter, "U.S. to Press Ban on Child-Beating; Health Unit Drafts 'Model' Act for States to Use," *New York Times*, May 26, 1963, 95.

17. Charles Flato, "Parents Who Beat Children: A Tragic Increase in Cases of Child Abuse Is Prompting a Hunt for Ways to Select Sick Adults Who Commit Such Crimes," *Saturday Evening Post*, October 6, 1962, 32–35.

18. Nelson, *Making an Issue of Child Abuse,* 4.

19. Sealander, *The Failed Century of the Child*, 66.

20. Susan Brownmiller, *In Our Time: Memoir of a Revolution* (New York: Dial Press, 2000), 202.

21. Florence Rush, *The Best-Kept Secret: Sexual Abuse of Children* (Blue Ridge Summit, PA: Tab Books, 1980), 14.

22. Nelson, *Making an Issue of Child Abuse,* 102–103.

23. Text of President Nixon's veto message of the Child Development Act of 1971, *Congressional Record*, 10 December 1971, 46059.

24. David G. Gil, *Violence Against Children: Physical Child Abuse in the United States* (Cambridge, MA: Harvard University Press, 1970).

25. Testimony of David Gil, *Child Abuse Prevention Act, 1973—Hearings Before the Subcommittee on Labor and Public Welfare, United States Senate.* Ninety-Third Congress, First Session, March 26, 27, 31, and April 24, 1973, 17.

26. Ibid.

27. Testimony of Jolly K., *Child Abuse Prevention Act, 1973, Hearings*, 49.

28. Ibid., 51.

29. Ibid., 55.

30. Ibid., 57.

31. Betty Friedan, *The Feminine Mystique* (New York: W. W. Norton & Company, 1963), 22.

32. Ibid., 103.

33. Ibid., 104.

34. Ibid., 105.

35. Anne Koedt, "The Myth of the Vaginal Orgasm," in *Notes from the First Year* (New York: New York Radical Women, 1968).

36. Kate Millett, *Sexual Politics* (Urbana: Illinois University Press, 2000), 184; Shulamith Firestone, *The Dialectic of Sex: The Case for Feminist Revolution* (New York: Bantam Books, 1970), 46.

37. Germaine Greer, *The Female Eunuch* (New York: Bantam, 1972 [1971]), 104.

38. Ibid., 103.

39. Mari Jo Buhle, *Feminism and Its Discontents: A Century of Struggle with Psychoanalysis* (Cambridge, MA: Harvard University Press, 1998), 210.

40. Paul Roazen, *Freud and His Followers* (New York: Knopf, 1975), 45; Mari Jo Buhle, *Feminism and Its Discontents*, 236.

41. Sigmund Freud, "The Aetiology of Hysteria," in *Standard Edition of the Complete Psychological Works of Sigmund Freud*, vol. 3 (London: Vintage, 1962).

42. Sigmund Freud, *The Complete Letters of Sigmund Freud to Wilhelm Fliess, 1887–1904*, trans. and ed. Jeffrey Moussaieff Masson (Cambridge, MA: Harvard University Press, 1985), 289.

43. Ibid., 144.

44. Ibid., 141.

45. Ibid., 264.

46. Jeffrey Moussaieff Masson, *The Assault on Truth: Freud's Suppression of the Seduction Theory* (New York: Farrar, Straus and Giroux, 1984), 134.

47. Ralph Blumenthal, "Freud Archives Research Chief Removed in Dispute Over Yale Talk," *New York Times*, November 9, 1981, www.nytimes.com/1981/11/09/nyregion/freud-archives-research-chief-removed-in-dispute-over-yale-talk.html.

48. Masson, *The Assault on Truth*, xiii.

49. Ibid., 144.

50. Flora Rheta Schreiber, *Sybil* (New York: Warner Paperback Library, 1974 [1973]), 13.

51. Debbie Nathan, *Sybil Exposed* (New York: Free Press, 2011), 17.

52. Ibid., 50.

53. Ibid., 89–90.

54. Schreiber, *Sybil*, 110.

55. Ibid., 11.

56. Ibid., 123.

57. Ibid., 173.

58. Ibid., 203.

59. Ibid., 183.

60. Ibid., 205.

61. Irving Bieber et al., *Homosexuality: A Psychoanalytic Study of Male Homosexuals* (New York: Basic Books, 1962).

62. Schreiber, *Sybil*, 209.

63. Ibid., 210.

64. Shirley Ann Mason therapy diary, Flora Rheta Schreiber papers (1916–1988), Lloyd Sealy Library, John Jay College of Criminal Justice, box 37, folder 1085, May 2, 1958.

65. Nathan, *Sybil Exposed*, 98.

66. Schreiber, *Sybil*, 26.

67. Letter to Flora Rheta Schreiber, Flora Rheta Schreiber papers (1916–1988), Lloyd Sealy Library, John Jay College of Criminal Justice, box 12, folder 303, August 2, 1974.

68. Letter to Flora Rheta Schreiber, Flora Rheta Schreiber papers (1916–1988), Lloyd Sealy Library, John Jay College of Criminal Justice, box 12, folder 301, December 12, 1973.

69. Nathan, *Sybil Exposed*, 179.

70. Mike Warnke, with Dave Balsiger and Les Jones, *The Satan Seller* (Plainfield, NJ: Logos International, 1972).

71. Schreiber, *Sybil*, 203.

72. Ibid., 209.

73. Michelle Smith and Lawrence Pazder, *Michelle Remembers* (New York: Congdon & Lattes, 1980), 3.

74. Ibid., 4.

75. Ibid., 3.

76. Ibid., xvii.

77. Ibid., 7.

78. Ibid., 5.

79. Ibid., 10.

80. Ibid., 17.

81. Ibid., 100.

82. Ibid., 118.

83. Ibid., 237.

84. Ibid., 239.

85. *Cardinal S.M.S.* (Saint Margaret's School Yearbook), 1955–1956, 18 (photocopy in author's possession).

86. Larry Kahaner, *Cults That Kill: Probing the Underworld of Occult Crime* (New York: Warner Books, 1988), 200.

87. Kristin McMurran, "A Canadian Woman's Bizarre Childhood Memories of Satan Shock Shrinks and Priests," *People*, September 1, 1980.

88. Shirley Ann Mason therapy diary, Flora Rheta Schreiber papers (1916–1988), Lloyd Sealy Library, John Jay College of Criminal Justice, box 37, folder 1085, May 2, 1958.

89. Damian Inwood, "Author Doesn't Look the Part of a Re-born Child of Satan," *Vancouver Sun*, July or August 1981 [photocopy in author's possession].

CHAPTER 2

1. "#16—McMartin Preschool 1-24-84," VHS tape in the possession of Danny Davis.

2. Kevin Cody, "Virginia McMartin," *Easy Reader*, January 25, 1990, 4.

3. "Benjamin Shula [pseud.]—Mother's Testimony at Grand Jury," vol. 4, 554, March 19, 1984.

4. Kevin Cody, "Virginia McMartin," 4.

5. Mary A. Fischer, "McMartin: A Case of Dominoes?" *Los Angeles Magazine*, October 1989, 126–135, www.byliner.com/read /mary-fischer/a-case-of-dominoes.

6. Debbie Nathan and Michael R. Snedeker, *Satan's Silence: Ritual Abuse and the Making of a Modern American Witch Hunt* (New York: Basic Books, 1995), 71.

7. Jane Hoag, "Supplemental Report re: Victim: Matthew Johnson [pseud.]," 1.

8. Manhattan Beach Police Department, Letter to Parents of Former and Current McMartin Preschool Children, September 8, 1983, available

online at http://law2.umkc.edu/faculty/projects/ftrials/mcmartin/letter
toparents.html.

9. Bob Zink, "Memorandum," review of the deposition of Ruth Owen,
October 5, 1987, 3.

10. Gloria Barton (mother of Sara Barton), diary, 3.

11. Ibid., 2.

12. Ross E. Cheit, *The Witch-Hunt Narrative: Politics, Psychology,
and the Sexual Abuse of Children* (New York: Oxford University Press,
2014), 28.

13. Police report, Manhattan Beach Police Department, 83-04932,
September 16, 1983, 3–4.

14. Nathan and Snedeker, *Satan's Silence*, 74.

15. "McMartin Chronology," *Easy Reader*, January 25, 1990, 12.

16. David, Shaw, "Reporter's Early Exclusives Triggered a Media
Frenzy," *Los Angeles Times*, January 20, 1990, www.latimes.com/food/la
-900120mcmartin_lat-story.html#page=2.

17. "Reporter's Daily Transcript, Monday, August 8, 1988, Volume 265.
The People of the State of California, Plaintiff, vs. Raymond Buckey and
Peggy McMartin Buckey, Defendants," 37, 481.

18. Ibid., 37, 492.

19. Nathan and Snedeker, *Satan's Silence*, 76.

20. Kee MacFarlane and Jill Waterman, *Sexual Abuse of Young Children:
Evaluation and Treatment* (New York: Guilford Press, 1986), xiv.

21. Ibid., 72–74.

22. "Reporter's Daily Transcript, Tuesday, August 9, 1988, Volume
266. The People of the State of California, Plaintiff, vs. Raymond Buckey
and Peggy McMartin Buckey, Defendants," 37, 694.

23. Cheit, *Witch-Hunt Narrative*, 40.

24. "Reporter's Daily Transcript, Tuesday, August 9, 1988, Volume
266. The People of the State of California, Plaintiff, vs. Raymond Buckey
and Peggy McMartin Buckey, Defendants," 37, 694.

25. Manhattan Beach Police Department, Supplemental Report, Jane
Hoag, re. Victim: Matthew Johnson [pseud.], dr. no. 83-04288.

26. Ibid., 4.

27. Ibid., 4.

28. CII interview with Ella Baldwin (pseud.), 1 November 1983, transcript, interviewer Kee MacFarlane, 1.

29. Ibid., 33.

30. Ibid., 37.

31. Ibid., 47.

32. Ibid., 53–54.

33. Ibid., 57.

34. Ibid., 62.

35. Ibid., 71.

36. CII interview with Otis Lawton (pseud.), November 1983, transcript, interviewer Kee McFarlane, 71.

37. Cheit, *Witch-Hunt Narrative*, 45.

38. CII interview with Mark Janes (pseud.), November 30, 1983, transcript, interviewer Kee McFarlane, 9–11.

39. Jane Hoag, Supplemental Report, Jane Hoag, re. Victim: Matthew Johnson (pseud.), November 30, 1983.

40. CII interview with Jenny Brown (pseud.), December 7, 1983, transcript, interviewer KeeMacFarlane, 58.

41. CII interview with Jeremy Morse (pseud.), December 9, 1983, transcript, interviewer Kee McFarlane, 16.

42. Ibid., 22.

43. Ibid., 26.

44. Ibid., 53.

45. Cheit, *Witch-Hunt Narrative*, 50–51.

46. Ibid., 47.

47. Roland Summit and JoAnn Kryso, "Sexual Abuse of Children: A Clinical Spectrum," *American Journal of Orthopsychiatry* 48, no. 2 (April 1978): 237.

48. Ibid., 239.

49. Ibid., 243.

50. Mary Springer, "Most Incest Cases Are Not Reported; Area Has Its Share," *Torrance Daily Breeze*, July 5, 1977, A1.

51. Roland Summit and JoAnn Kryso, "Sexual Abuse of Children: A Clinical Spectrum," 237–251.

52. Roland Summit, "The Child Sexual Abuse Accommodation Syndrome," *Child Abuse and Neglect* 7 (1983): 177–193.

53. CII Interview with Keith Doherty (pseud.), transcript, January 24, 1984, 13–14.

54. Ibid., 17–18.

55. Ibid., 21–22.

56. Ibid., 28.

57. Ibid., 35.

58. Ibid., 37.

59. Ibid., 65.

60. Ibid., 68.

61. Cheit, *The Witch-Hunt Narrative*, 51.

62. *Eyewitness News*, KABC-TV Los Angeles, CA, February 2, 1984.

63. Ibid.

64. Bruce Woodling and Peter D. Kossoris, "Sexual Misuse, Rape, Molestation and Incest," *Pediatric Clinics of North America* 28, no. 2 (1981): 481–499.

65. Wilmes R. G. Teixeira, "Hymenal Colposcopic Examination in Sexual Offenses," *American Journal of Forensic Medicine and Pathology* 2, no. 3 (September 1981): 209–215.

66. Kevin Cody, "McMartin Kids' Doctor Says Physical Abuse a Certainty," *Easy Reader,* January 14, 1988, 20.

67. "In Wake of Sexual Abuse: Unraveling a Nightmare," *American Medical News*, March 22, 1985, 1.

68. Nathan and Snedeker, *Satan's Silence*, 101.

69. Astrid Heger, director, *Response: Child Sexual Abuse—A Medical View*, film (Los Angeles: United Way, 1985).

70. Nathan and Snedeker, *Satan's Silence*, 83.

71. Kevin Cody, "Defense Attacks Abuse Findings by Child Doctor," *Easy Reader*, February 4, 1988, 19.

72. Nathan and Snedeker, *Satan's Silence*, 84–85.

73. *Eyewitness News*, KABC-TV Los Angeles, CA. Videotape "#1—Satz 1 & 2," in possession of Danny Davis.

74. Danny Davis, interview with author, September 19, 2012.

75. Sue Avery, "Spreading Worry: Hotline Kept Busy with Child Abuse Calls—'Public Awareness' on Rise, Says Director," *Los Angeles Times*, April 8, 1984.

76. Lois Timnick, "Abuse in the Nursery School—A License Is No Safety Guarantee," *Los Angeles Times*, April 2, 1984.

77. Lois Timnick, "Safety at Child-Care Centers: Whose Job Is It? Parents Ask," *Los Angeles Times*, June 18, 1984.

78. George Wiley, "The Dilemma of Day Care," *Easy Reader*, September 27, 1984, 18.

CHAPTER 3

1. Patrick Boulay, "Five Arrested as Part of Countywide Child Sex Abuse Ring Investigation," *Jordan Independent*, May 30, 1984, 2.

2. E. R. Shipp, "Minnesota Townspeople Jolted by Sex Scandal with Children," *New York Times*, September 6, 1984, www.nytimes.com/1984/09/06/us/minnesota-townspeople-jolted-by-sex-scandal-with-children.html.

3. Mary Schroeder, "What Should Families Do About Sexual Abusers?" *Jordan Independent*, October 20, 1983, 4.

4. Edward Humes, *Mean Justice: A Town's Terror, a Prosecutor's Power, a Betrayal of Innocence* (New York: Simon & Schuster, 1999), 61.

5. Don Hardy Jr. and Dana Nachman, directors, *Witch Hunt*, film (KTF Films, 2008).

6. Eric Black, "Zeal Sets Up Morris for Criticism and Praise," *Minneapolis Star and Tribune*, October 19, 1984, 16A.

7. Ibid., 1A.

8. *People v. Tony Galindo Perez*, Opinion of the California Court of Appeal, Fifth Appellate District, no. 4381, May 18, 1981.

9. Ibid.

10. *Brown v. Board of Education*, 347 U.S. 483 (1954); *Gideon v. Wainwright*, 372 U.S. 335 (1963); *Reynolds v. Sims*, 377 U.S. 533 (1964); *Miranda v. Arizona*, 384 U.S. 436 (1966).

11. Jonathan Simon, *Governing Through Crime: How the War on Crime Transformed American Democracy and Created a Culture of Fear* (New York: Oxford University Press, 2007), Kindle Edition, location 742.

12. Humes, *Mean Justice*, 65.

13. Ibid., 64.

14. Ross E. Cheit, *The Witch-Hunt Narrative: Politics, Psychology, and the Sexual Abuse of Children* (New York: Oxford University Press, 2014), 119.

15. *In Re Scott and Brenda Kniffen on Habeas Corpus*, Kern County (Calif.) Superior Court, Appeal No. 5 Crim. F004423, October 28, 1993, 13–15.

16. Ibid., 17–19.

17. Debbie Nathan and Michael R. Snedeker, *Satan's Silence: Ritual Abuse and the Making of a Modern Witch Hunt* (New York: Basic Books, 1995), 61.

18. Hardy and Nachman, *Witch Hunt*.

19. Michael Trihey, "Parents Found Guilty of Molestation 289 Times," *Bakersfield Californian*, May 17, 1984, A1.

20. Gary A. Gilbreath, "Letters: Cites Tragic Results in Molester Trial," *Bakersfield Californian*, June 22, 1984, B10.

21. Humes, *Mean Justice*, 362.

22. Paul McEnroe and David Peterson, "Jordan," *Minneapolis Star and Tribune*, October 21, 1984, 23A.

23. Bruce Rubenstein, "'I'm Not the Only One Who's Guilty' Claims Rud in Interview," *Jordan Independent*, August 22, 1984, 14.

24. McEnroe and Peterson, "Jordan," 17A.

25. Ibid.

26. Ibid.

27. Tom Dubbe, *Nightmares and Secrets: The Real Story of the 1984 Child Sexual Abuse Scandal in Jordan, Minnesota* (Shakopee, MN: Memorial Press, 2005), 56.

28. "SMK Interview," September 26, 1983, transcript, 2.

29. "Supplementary Report, Complainant Detective David N. Einertson, Suspect James John Rud," received by attorney's office on November 22, 1983.

30. Arrest Report, Marlene Germundson, DOB 9-8-56, received by attorney's office on November 14, 1983.

31. "KAL Interview," October 20, 1983, transcript, 2.

32. "JMO Interview," October 3, 1983, transcript, 3–4.

33. Paul McEnroe, "Abuse Cases Darken Jordan's Bright Side," *Minneapolis Star and Tribune*, November 18, 1983, 10A.

34. Paul McEnroe, "Sex-Abuse Charges Against Rud Total 108," *Minneapolis Star and Tribune*, November 19, 1983, 7A.

35. Jim Parsons, "Caution Becomes the Rule in Jordan," *Minneapolis Star and Tribune*, November 20, 1983.

36. "Computer Will Document Abuse Investigation Data," *Jordan Independent*, December 15, 1983, 7.

37. Gail Andersen, "Abuse of Children Not More Prevalent in Jordan," *Jordan Independent*, November 24, 1983.

38. Schroeder, "What Should Families Do About Sexual Abusers?" 4.

39. Patrick Boulay, "Shakopee Man Latest Sex Ring Suspect; 8 Now Arrested," *Jordan Independent*, November 24, 1983, 1.

40. Schroeder, "What Should Families Do About Sexual Abusers?" 4.

41. "Out of the Mouths of Babes," with Trish Wood, *Notes from the 5th Estate*, broadcast date January 5, 1993, transcript.

42. Susan Phipps-Yonas, interview with author, May 23, 2013.

43. "Out of the Mouths of Babes," *Notes from the 5th Estate*.

44. "Law Clerks Hired for Rud Case, Foster Parents Needed," *Shakopee Valley News*, February 8, 1984, 1.

45. Nathan and Snedeker, *Satan's Silence*, 94.

46. Hardy and Nachman, *Witch Hunt*.

47. Steve E. Swenson, "Rate of Arrest for Molesting Double in Kern," *Bakersfield Californian*, October 23, 1983, A1.

48. Hardy and Nachman, *Witch Hunt*.

49. Ibid.

50. "Report on the Kern County Child Abuse Investigation," Office of the Attorney General, Division of Law Enforcement—Bureau of Investigation, September 1986, 18–19.

51. Hardy and Nachman, *Witch Hunt*.

52. Humes, *Mean Justice*, 217.

53. Robert D. Hicks, *In Pursuit of Satan* (Buffalo, NY: Prometheus Books, 1991), 263.

54. Humes, *Mean Justice*, 221.

55. Steve E. Swenson, "Officers Certain Child Pornography Is Made in Kern," *Bakersfield Californian*, January 28, 1985, A4.

56. Interview Report, Case No. 85-0181-01A, State of California, Department of Justice, Bureau of Investigation, May 7, 1986, 9.

57. Humes, *Mean Justice*, 222.

58. Nathan and Snedeker, *Satan's Silence*, 99.

59. "Report on the Kern County Child Abuse Investigation," vii.

60. Humes, *Mean Justice*, 222.

61. Hardy and Nachman, *Witch Hunt*.

62. "Report on the Kern County Child Abuse Investigation," viii.

63. Ibid., viii.

64. Humes, *Mean Justice*, 224.

65. Ibid., 226.

66. Dennis J. McGrath, "Jordan Child Abuser Turns State Witness," *Minneapolis Star and Tribune*, August 16, 1984, 1A.

67. "James Rud, Voluntary Statement," August 14, 1984, 1–2.

68. Ibid., 3.

69. Ibid., 5.

70. Ibid., 7.

71. "James Rud, Voluntary Statement, Tape #3," August 15, 1984, 7.

72. Ibid., 19.

73. Josephine Marcotty, "Rud Fails to Identify Child-Abuse Suspect," *Minneapolis Star and Tribune*, August 28, 1984, 1B.

74. Mike Kaszuba, "James Rud Sex-Abuse Testimony Thrown Out," *Minneapolis Star and Tribune*, September 5, 1984, 1A.

75. "State of Minnesota, Commission Established by Executive Order No. 85-10 Concerning Kathleen Morris, Scott County Attorney, Report to Governor Rudy Perpich," 36.

76. Josephine Marcotty, "Both Bentzes Deny Abusing Children," *Minneapolis Star and Tribune*, September 14, 1984, 2A.

77. Bruce Rubinstein, "Sex Abuse Case Analysis: Was Bentz Trial a Witch-Hunt?" *Jordan Independent*, September 26, 1984, 2A.

78. Josephine Marcotty, "Tearful Girl, 12, Confronts Attorney Who Challenges Sex-Abuse Testimony," *Minneapolis Star and Tribune*, September 1, 1984, 1A.

79. Dan Oberdorfer and Josephine Marcotty, "Bentzes Acquitted in Abuse Case," *Minneapolis Star and Tribune*, September 20, 1984, 1A.

80. Kathleen Morris, "Text of Kathleen Morris' Statement," *Minneapolis Star and Tribune*, October 16, 1984, 15A.

81. "State of Minnesota, Commission Established by Executive Order No. 85-10 Concerning Kathleen Morris, Scott County Attorney, Report to Governor Rudy Perpich," 11.

82. Pat Doyle and Paul McEnroe, "Transcripts Allege Child-Porn Ring," *Minneapolis Star and Tribune*, October 18, 1984, 7A.

83. Pat Doyle, "Girl Told Officers of Porno Films, Being Forced to Eat Pets," *Minneapolis Star and Tribune*, October 19, 1984, 1A.

84. Joe Rigert and Kevin Diaz, "BCA to Investigate Reports of Slayings," *Minneapolis Star and Tribune*, October 18, 1984, 1A–9A.

85. Dan Oberdorfer and Joe Rigert, "Morris Withdraws from Cases," *Minneapolis Star and Tribune*, October 19, 1984, 14A.

86. Paul McEnroe, Dan Oberdorfer, and Cheryl Johnson, "Sources Suggest Link to Stories of Child Slayings," *Minneapolis Star and Tribune*, October 16, 1984, 15A.

87. "County Estimates Cost of Sex Abuse Ring Expenditures at $251,266.87," *Jordan Independent*, August 22, 1984, 3.

88. "Out of the Mouths of Babes," *Notes from the 5th Estate*.

89. Britt Robson, "The Scars of Scott County," *Minneapolis St. Paul Magazine*, March 1991, 127.

90. Joe Rigert and Paul McEnroe, "Boys' Admission of Lies Halted Probe of Child Slayings," *Minneapolis Star and Tribune*, November 20, 1984, 6A.

91. Paul McEnroe and David Peterson, "Jordan," *Minneapolis Star and Tribune*, October 21, 1984, 20A.

CHAPTER 4

1. Lois Timnick, "A Town That No Longer Trusts Itself," *Los Angeles Times*, July 29, 1984, B1.

2. "Supplemental Report—02513, Nov. 19 1984," Los Angeles County Sheriff's Department.

3. George Wiley, "McMartin Parents Take Matters, Shovels in Own Hands, Search Lot," *Easy Reader*, March 21, 1985, 3.

4. Investigator's Report, March 28, 1985, Manhattan Beach Police Department.

5. Kevin Cody, "McMartin Children Turn to Press, Defendants Turn to Supervisors," *Easy Reader*, November 14, 1985, 5.

6. John A. Jackson, "McMartin Parent Arrested in Futile Evidence Search," *Easy Reader*, May 9, 1985, 4.

7. John A. Jackson, "McMartin Watch," *Easy Reader*, November 15, 1984, 11.

8. Joan Villa Cziment, "A Community Agonizes over Action in Child Molestation," *Los Angeles Times*, July 22, 1984, SB1.

9. George Wiley, "The Dilemma of Day Care," *Easy Reader*, September 27, 1984, 17.

10. James Quinn, "A Mother's Child-Abuse War," *Los Angeles Times*, July 1, 1984, V1.

11. John A. Jackson, "McMartin Watch," *Easy Reader*, November 15, 1984.

12. John A. Jackson, "McMartin Watch," *Easy Reader*, August 30, 1984, 5.

13. Gary K. Morley and Bruce R. Stevens, "Report on Interview with Brett Wiesberg," Federal Bureau of Investigation, conducted June 21, 1984, 2.

14. Michael A. Randolph, "Report on Interview with Malcolm Robert Lawton [pseud.] and Gloria Sue Lawton [pseud.]," Federal Bureau of Investigation, conducted July 5, 1984, 1.

15. Ibid., 4.

16. "Report on Interview with Judy Johnson," Federal Bureau of Investigation, conducted June 26, 1984.

17. Carl Ingram, "Senate Oks Court Use of TV in Child Sex-Abuse Cases," *Los Angeles Times*, February 5, 1985, SD3.

18. Carl Ingram and Jerry Gillam, "Senate Oks Tough Child Abuse Bill," *Los Angeles Times*, June 15, 1984, A18.

19. Paul Feldman, "Sex Abuse Trials: Glare on Children," *Los Angeles Times*, December 16, 1984, D1.

20. Kevin Cody, interview with author, October 3, 2012.

21. "Child Sexual Abuse Victims in the Courts," US Senate Subcommittee on Juvenile Justice, Committee on the Judiciary, Washington, DC, May 22, 1984, 83.

22. Paul Feldman, "Sex Abuse Trials: Glare on Children," D8.

23. Danny Davis, interview with author, September 19, 2012.

24. Ibid.

25. Ibid.

26. John A. Jackson, "McMartin Watch," *Easy Reader*, September 27, 1984, 8.

27. Paul Eberle and Shirley Eberle, *The Abuse of Innocence: The McMartin Preschool Trial* (Buffalo, NY: Prometheus Books, 1993).

28. John A. Jackson, "McMartin Watch," *Easy Reader*, November 29, 1984, 1, italics in original.

29. John A. Jackson, "McMartin Watch," September 27, 1984, 8.

30. Marilyn Croffi, "Syndicate Jackson!" *Easy Reader*, October 11, 1984, 2.

31. "Testimony of Kee MacFarlane," Child Abuse and Daycare, Joint Hearing Before the Subcommittee on Oversight of the Committee on Children, Youth and Families, US House of Representatives, September 17, 1984, 42.

32. Ibid., 43.

33. Ibid., 44.

34. Nadine Brozan, "Witness Says She Fears 'Child Predator' Network," *New York Times*, September 18, 1984, www.nytimes.com /1984/09/18/us/witness-says-she-fears-child-predator-network.html.

35. "Testimony of Kee MacFarlane," 46.

36. Ibid., 45.

37. Ibid., 46.

38. Peter W. Kunhardt and Kenneth Wooden, producers, "Why the Silence?" *20/20*, ABC, January 3, 1985.

39. Morgan Gendel, "KABC Plans to Preempt '20/20' Show," *Los Angeles Times*, December 24, 1984, D1.

40. John A. Jackson, "McMartin Watch," *Easy Reader*, November 29, 1984, 44.

41. "McMartin Chronology," *Easy Reader*, January 25, 1990, 13.

42. Carol McGraw, "10-Year-Old's Credibility Tested by Allegations," *Los Angeles Times*, April 26, 1985, C2.

43. Carol McGraw, "Macabre Cemetery Rites Told by McMartin Witness," *Los Angeles Times*, April 25, 1985, C6.

44. McGraw, "10-Year-Old's Credibility Tested by Allegations," C1.

45. John A. Jackson, "McMartin Watch," *Easy Reader*, April 4, 1985, 4.

46. John A. Jackson, "McMartin Watch," *Easy Reader*, April 11, 1985, 5.

47. John A. Jackson, "McMartin Watch," *Easy Reader*, September 19, 1985, 15.

48. John A. Jackson, "McMartin Watch," *Easy Reader*, May 9, 1985, 9.

49. John A. Jackson, "McMartin Watch," *Easy Reader*, November 7, 1985, 1.

50. Mary A. Fischer, "McMartin: A Case of Dominoes?" *Los Angeles Magazine*, October 1989, www.byliner.com/read/mary-fischer/a-case-of-dominoes.

51. Kevin Cody, "The McMartin Tapes," *Easy Reader*, November 13, 1986, 1.

52. Ibid., 14.

53. Ibid., 17.

54. Ibid., 18.

55. Kevin Cody, "The McMartin Tapes—Part II," *Easy Reader*, November 20, 1986, 17.

56. Cody, "The McMartin Tapes."

57. Cody, "The McMartin Tapes—Part II."

58. Ibid., 20.

59. Ibid., 18.

60. Kevin, Cody, "The McMartin Tapes—Part III," *Easy Reader*, November 27, 1986, 21.

61. Ibid., 23.

62. Ibid., 21.

63. Ibid., 13.

64. Ibid., 23.

65. Kevin Cody, "Truth About McMartin Witness' Role May Have Been Lost with Her Death," *Easy Reader*, December 25, 1986, 3.

CHAPTER 5

1. Berta Rodriguez, "Sex-Abuse Retrial to Start Monday," *El Paso Times*, March 8, 1987, 1B.

2. Katha Pollitt, "Justice for Bernard Baran," *The Nation*, February 21, 2000, www.thenation.com/article/justice-bernard-baran#.

3. Peter Carlson, "Divided by Multiple Charges of Child Abuse, a Minnesota Town Seethes with Anger," *People*, October 22, 1984, www.people.com/people/archive/article/0,,20088952,00.html; Nadine Brozan, "Witness Says She Fears 'Child Predator' Network," *New York Times*, September 18, 1984, www.nytimes.com/1984/09/18/us/witness-says-she-fears-child-predator-network.html.; Claudia Wallis, "The Child-Care Dilemma," *Time*, June 22, 1987, 54–59.

4. Kenneth Lanning, interview with author, February 4, 2013.

5. Kenneth Lanning, interview with author, February 25, 2013.

6. Ibid.

7. "List of Participants," *Day Care Center and Satanic Cult Sexual Exploitation of Children 2/18–21/85*, packet, copy in author's possession.

8. "Handout: Search Warrants Probable Cause Example," Inspector Seth Goldstein, District Attorney's Ofc., 70 W. Hedding, West Wing, San Jose, CA 95110, copy in author's possession.

9. Sandi Gallant, "Questionnaire," 1985, copy in author's possession.

10. Glenn E. Stevens, "Memorandum—Day Care Center and Satanic Cult/Sexual Exploitation of Children Seminar, February 18–21, 1985," 8.

11. Ibid., 4–5.

12. Kenneth V. Lanning, "The 'Witch Hunt,' the 'Backlash,' and Professionalism," in *The APSAC Advisor* 9, no. 4 (Winter 1996), www.nationalcac.org/professionals/images/stories/handouts2009/lanning,%20ken%20-%20witch%20hunt%20hand%2010.pdf.

13. David Healy, *The Creation of Psychopharmacology* (Cambridge, MA: Harvard University Press, 2002), 317.

14. Janice Haaken, *Pillar of Salt: Gender, Memory, and the Perils of Looking Back* (New Brunswick, NJ: Rutgers University Press, 1993), 77.

15. Joan Acocella, *Creating Hysteria: Women and Multiple Personality Disorder* (San Francisco: Jossey-Bass, 1999), 112.

16. Debbie Nathan, *Sybil Exposed* (New York: Free Press, 2011), 212.

17. Richard P. Kluft and Catherine G. Fine, eds., *Clinical Perspectives on Multiple Personality Disorder* (Washington, DC: American Psychiatric Press, 1993).

18. *Diagnostic and Statistical Manual of Mental Disorders*, 3rd ed. (Washington, DC: American Psychiatric Association, 1980), 257.

19. Ibid., 257.

20. Ibid., 258.

21. E. L. Bliss, "Multiple Personalities: A Report of 14 Cases with Implications for Schizophrenia and Hysteria," *Archives of General Psychiatry*, 37 (1980): 1388–1397.

22. Ian Hacking, *Re-Writing the Soul: Multiple Personality and the Sciences of Memory* (Princeton, NJ: Princeton University Press, 1995), 39–40.

23. Jeffrey Masson, *The Assault on Truth: Freud's Suppression of the Seduction Theory* (New York: Farrar, Straus and Giroux, 1984).

24. Carol Tavris, "The 100-Year Cover Up: How Freud Betrayed Women," *Ms.*, March 1984.

25. Allen Esterson, "Jeffrey Masson and Freud's Seduction Theory: A New Fable Based on Old Myths," *History of the Human Sciences* 11, no. 1 (1998): 1–21, www.esterson.org/Masson_and_Freuds_seduction_theory.htm.

26. Josef Breuer and Sigmund Freud, *Studies on Hysteria*, trans. James Strachey (New York: Basic Books, 2000), 280.

27. Ibid., 299.

28. Sigmund Freud, "Further Notes on the Neuro-Psychoses of Defense," in *Standard Edition of the Complete Psychological Works of Sigmund Freud*, vol. 3 (London: Vintage, 1962), 172–177.

29. Sigmund Freud, "The Aetiology of Hysteria," in *Standard Edition of the Complete Psychological Works of Sigmund Freud*, vol. 3 (London: Vintage, 1962), 204.

30. Hacking, *Re-Writing the Soul*, 83–84.

31. Nathan, *Sybil Exposed*, 216.

32. *Tyson v. Tyson*, 727 P.2d 226 (Washington, 1986).

33. *Diagnostic and Statistical Manual of Mental Disorders*, 3rd ed. revised (Washington, DC: American Psychiatric Association, 1987).

34. Ibid., 269.

35. Ibid., 271.

36. Betty Friedan, *The Feminine Mystique* (New York: W. W. Norton & Company, 1963), 1963.

37. Hacking, *Re-Writing the Soul*, 70.

38. Mike Warnke, with Dave Balsiger and Les Jones, *The Satan Seller* (Plainfield, NJ: Logos International, 1972).

39. Jon Trott and Mike Hertenstein, "Selling Satan: The Tragic History of Mike Warnke," *Cornerstone* 98 (1992), http://web.archive.org/web /20110629063019/http://www.cornerstonemag.com/features/iss098 /sellingsatan.htm.

40. Michael Winerip, "Revisiting the 'Crack Babies' Epidemic That Was Not," *New York Times*, May 20, 2013, www.nytimes.com/2013/05 /20/booming/revisiting-the-crack-babies-epidemic-that-was-not.html.

41. Carolyn Bronstein, *Battling Pornography: The American Feminist Anti-Pornography Movement, 1976–1986* (Cambridge: Cambridge University Press, 2011), 320–321.

42. Catharine MacKinnon and Andrea Dworkin, eds., *In Harm's Way: The Pornography Civil Rights Hearings* (Cambridge, MA: Harvard University Press, 1998), 40.

43. Ibid., 177.

44. Ibid., 338.

45. *The Report of the Commission on Obscenity and Pornography* (New York: Bantam Books, 1970), 32, 29.

46. *Final Report of the Attorney General's Commission on Pornography* (Nashville, TN: Rutledge Hill Press, 1986), li.

47. Ibid., 540–546.

48. Andrea Dworkin Audiotape collection, 1975–1999; New York (New York), Commission on Pornography testimony, January 22, 1986, T-323, tape 19, Schlesinger Library, Radcliffe Institute, Harvard University, Cambridge, MA.

49. Ibid.

50. MacKinnon and Dworkin, *In Harm's Way*, 384.

51. *Final Report of the Attorney General's Commission on Pornography*, 134.

52. Ibid., 199–220.

53. Ibid., 214.

54. Ibid., 215.

55. Ibid., 77.

56. E. N. Padilla, "An Agrarian Reform Sugar Community in Puerto Rico," PhD dissertation, Columbia University, 1951. Ethnographers and other observers have observed similar practices in Thailand, Cambodia, and among lower-class communities in mid-twentieth-century Japan.

57. Interview with Jason Cramer (pseud.), August 28, 1984, interviewers Laurie and Joseph Braga, transcribed by Laurie Alvarado on September 17, 1994, 14.

58. Ibid., 8.

59. W. L. Whittington et al., "Incorrect Identification of *Neisseria gonorrhoeae* from Infants and Children," *Pediatric Infectious Disease Journal* 7, no. 1 (1988): 3–10.

60. Sarah Alexander and Catherine Ison, "Evaluation of Commercial Kits for the Identification of *Neisseria gonorrhoeae*," *Journal of Medical Microbiology* 54, no. 9 (September 2005): 827–831.

61. M. J. Robinson and T. R. Oberhofer, "Identification of Pathogenic Neisseria Species with the RapID NH System," *Journal of Clinical Microbiology* 17, no. 3 (March 1983): 400–404.

62. Debbie Nathan and Michael R. Snedeker, *Satan's Silence: Ritual Abuse and the Making of a Modern American Witch Hunt* (New York: Basic Books, 1995), 194–195.

63. Jan Hollingsworth, *Unspeakable Acts* (New York and Chicago: Congdon and Weed, 1986), 434.

64. Ibid., 369.

65. Nathan and Snedeker, *Satan's Silence*, 171.

66. Interview with Ileana Flores, "Did Daddy Do It?" *Frontline*, January 2001, transcript at www.pbs.org/wgbh/pages/frontline/shows/fuster /interviews/ileana.html.

67. Debbie Nathan, "Revisiting Country Walk," *Institute for Psychological Therapies Journal* 5 (1993), www.ipt-forensics.com/journal/volume5 /j5_1_1.htm.

68. Ibid.; *The State of Florida vs. Ileana Fuster*, Case No. 84-19728B, transcript, November 26, 1985, 60.

69. *The State of Florida vs. Ileana Fuster*, 61–62.

70. Interview with Ileana Flores, *Frontline*.

71. Ileana Flores, Deposition, Taken by Arthur Cohen, 1994, www.pbs .org/wgbh/pages/frontline/shows/fuster/frank/94recant.html.

72. Nathan, "Revisiting Country Walk."

73. Ileana Flores, Deposition, September 1985, www.pbs.org/wgbh/pages /frontline/shows/fuster/frank/85depo.html.

CHAPTER 6

1. Kevin Cody, "Prosecutor Admits Negligence, Buckey Seeks Release," *Easy Reader*, December 18, 1986, 4.

2. Ibid.

3. Lois Timnick, "Former McMartin Case Prosecutor Tells Court of Withholding Facts," *Los Angeles Times*, January 21, 1987, OC 7. (Glenn Stevens was never charged.)

4. Lowell Bergman, producer, "The McMartin Preschool," *60 Minutes*, CBS, November 2, 1986.

5. Ibid.

6. Kevin Cody, "Buckey's Lawyer Wants Trial Out of Los Angeles," *Easy Reader*, February 5, 1987, 3, 15.

7. Kevin Cody, "Double Blow Hits Preschool Parents," *Easy Reader*, February 5, 1987, 3, 23.

8. *Eyewitness News*, KABC-TV Los Angeles, CA, March 28, 1985.

9. Danny Davis, interview with author, September 19, 2012.

10. Kevin Cody, "A Rat in the Hall of Justice," *Easy Reader*, March 19, 1987, 22.

11. Ibid., 23.

12. Jan Hollingsworth, *Unspeakable Acts* (New York and Chicago: Congdon and Weed, 1986).

13. Kevin Cody, "Public's Denial of Child Sex Abuse Examined at Meeting," *Easy Reader*, May 7, 1987, 3, 12–13, 15.

14. *The People of the State of California vs. Raymond Buckey and Peggy McMartin Buckey*, daily transcript, vol. 99, July 13, 1987, 14970.

15. Ibid., vol. 100, 15004.

16. Ibid., 15006.

17. Ibid., 15008–15009.

18. Ibid., 15012–15013.

19. Kevin Cody, "The Alleys of Justice," *Easy Reader*, August 20, 1987, 1.

20. *The People of the State of California vs. Raymond Buckey and Peggy McMartin Buckey*, daily transcript, vol. 109, August 3, 1987, 16344.

21. Ibid., 16350–16351.

22. Ibid., 16369.

23. Paul Eberle and Shirley Eberle, *The Abuse of Innocence: The McMartin Preschool Trial* (Buffalo, NY: Prometheus Books, 1993), 159.

24. Ibid., 48.

25. Ibid., 159.

26. *The People of the State of California vs. Raymond Buckey and Peggy McMartin Buckey*, daily transcript, vol. 110, August 4, 1987, 16525.

27. Eberle and Eberle, *Abuse of Innocence*, 68.

28. Gary Scharrer, "New Trial Possible for Dove," *El Paso Times*, November 14, 1986, 4B.

29. Berta Rodriguez, "Group Helps Parents Cope with Alleged Molestations," *El Paso Times*, November 3, 1985, 1A.

30. Pat Graves, "Dove Gets 20 Years," *El Paso Times*, March 21, 1987, 2B.

31. Debbie Nathan, "The Making of a Modern Witch Trial," *Village Voice*, September 19, 1987, reprinted in Debbie Nathan, *Women and Other Aliens: Essays from the U.S.-Mexico Border* (El Paso, TX: Cinco Puntos Press, 1991).

32. Gary Scharrer, "Social Worker in Molestation Trial Defends Method of Interviewing Boy," *El Paso Times*, March 7, 1986, 1B.

33. Pat Graves, "Social Worker Is Challenged at Abuse Trial," *El Paso Times*, March 17, 1987, 1A.

34. Ibid.

35. Nathan, "The Making of a Modern Witch Trial," 141.

36. Gary Scharrer, "Tearful Testimony: Ex-YMCA Teacher Tells About Typical School Day," *El Paso Times*, March 25, 1986, 2A.

37. Gary Scharrer, "'The Verdict Speaks the Truth': Parents Say They're Satisfied," *El Paso Times*, March 28, 1986, 2A.

38. Nathan, "The Making of a Modern Witch Trial," 142.

39. Ibid.

40. Gary Scharrer, "Deliberations to Resume in Sex Abuse Trial," *El Paso Times*, March 27, 1986, 8A.

41. Debbie Nathan, "Sex, the Devil, and Daycare," *Village Voice*, September 19, 1987, reprinted in Debbie Nathan, *Women and Other Aliens: Essays from the U.S.-Mexico Border* (El Paso, TX: Cinco Puntos Press, 1991).

42. Ibid., 118.

43. Ibid., 119.

44. Gary Scharrer, "New Trial Possible for Dove," *El Paso Times*, November 14, 1986, 4B.

45. VOCAL, "Statement Given to Press," October 20, 1984, 1.

46. Paul Eberle and Shirley Eberle, *The Politics of Child Abuse* (Secaucus, NJ: Lyle Stuart, 1986), 87–88.

47. Ibid., 102.

48. Mary Pride, *The Child Abuse Industry: Outrageous Facts About Child Abuse & Everyday Rebellions Against a System That Threatens Every North American Family* (Westchester, IL: Crossway Books, 1986), vii.

49. Ibid., 31.

50. Brett Drake et al., "Racial Bias in Child Protection? A Comparison of Competing Explanations Using National Data," *Pediatrics* 127, no. 3 (March 1, 2011): 471–478.

51. Pride, *The Child Abuse Industry*, 143.

52. Ibid., 35.

53. Ibid., 115.

54. Debbie Nathan, "Victimizer or Victim: Was Kelly Michaels Unjustly Convicted?" *Village Voice*, August 2, 1988, 33.

55. Jack Jones, "McMartin Trial Witness Held," *Los Angeles Times*, October 10, 1987, A4.

56. *The People of the State of California vs. Raymond Buckey and Peggy McMartin Buckey*, daily transcript, vol. 137, October 9, 1987, 20145.

57. Ibid., 20343–20345.

58. Kevin Cody, "Jurors Not Happy to Hear Trial Going on for a Year," *Easy Reader*, August 11, 1988, 5.

59. Kevin Cody, "Virginia McMartin Takes the Stand," *Easy Reader*, September 10, 1987, 3.

60. Bob Williams, "For Others, Time Eases the Memories," *Los Angeles Times*, July 17, 1988, F1.

61. Bob Williams, "Picking Up the Pieces: A Freed Ex-McMartin Pre-School Teacher Still Haunted by Her Family's Shattered Life," *Los Angeles Times*, July 17, 1988, F1.

62. Kevin Cody, "The 'Mini-Trial' of Peggy Ann Buckey," *Easy Reader*, January 5, 1989, 12.

63. "Peggy Ann Buckey to Resume Teaching," *Los Angeles Times*, February 16, 1989, A4.

64. Kevin Cody, "Peggy Ann Buckey Climbs Back," *Los Angeles Times*, January 5, 1989, 25.

65. Bob Williams, "McMartin Fallout Eases; Preschools Again at Capacity," *Los Angeles Times*, May 1, 1988, R4.

66. James Rainey, "Molestations of 2 More Day-Care Infants Alleged," *Los Angeles Times*, December 2, 1988, SB8.

67. Williams, "McMartin Fallout Eases."

68. Bob Williams, "McMartin Case Cast Wide, Dark Shadow: Charges, Suspicion Resulted in 7 Area Preschools Closing," *Los Angeles Times*, May 1, 1988, R7.

69. Williams, "McMartin Fallout Eases."

70. Nielson Himmel, "Buckey Freed on $1.5-Million Bail After 5 Years in Jail," *Los Angeles Times*, February 16, 1989, 3.

CHAPTER 7

1. *Geraldo—Devil Worship: Exposing Satan's Underground*, NBC, Paramount television broadcast, October 22, 1988.

2. Ibid.

3. Ibid.

4. Ibid.

5. *Geraldo Rivera—McMartin Special*, NBC, Paramount television broadcast, January 29, 1990.

6. Ibid.

7. The culmination of this work is Stephen J. Ceci and Maggie Bruck, *Jeopardy in the Courtroom: A Scientific Analysis of Children's Testimony* (Washington, DC: American Psychological Association, 1999).

8. Ellen Willis, *No More Nice Girls: Countercultural Essays* (Hanover, NH: Wesleyan, 1992), 219.

9. Robert O. Self, *All in the Family: The Realignment of American Democracy Since the 1960s* (New York: Hill and Wang, 2012), 328.

10. Arnold Friedman, "My Story," in *Conviction Integrity Review: People v. Jesse Friedman*, June 2013, Appendix, 538–552, www.nassaucounty ny.gov/agencies/DA/NewsReleases/2013/062413friedman.html.

11. Andrew Jarecki, director, *Capturing the Friedmans*, HBO Video, 2004.

12. Search Warrant Inventory, Inspector J. McDermott, November 3, 1987, 1.

13. "Victim Questionnaire," in *Conviction Integrity Review: People v. Jesse Friedman*, June 2013, Appendix, 287.

14. Jarecki, *Capturing the Friedmans*.

15. Debbie Nathan, "Complex Persecution," *Village Voice*, May 20, 2003, www.villagevoice.com/2003-05-20/news/complex-persecution/full.

16. Jarecki, *Capturing the Friedmans*.

17. Ibid.

18. *Conviction Integrity Review: People v. Jesse Friedman*, June 2013, 18.

19. Friedman, "My Story," 539.

20. Nathan, "Complex Persecution."

21. David Friedman, Western Union Mailgram to Arnold Friedman, April 5, 1988, in *Conviction Integrity Review: People v. Jesse Friedman*, June 2013, Appendix, 433.

22. *Friedman v. Rehal*, 618 F.3d 142 (2nd Cir. 2010), 149.

23. Jarecki, *Capturing the Friedmans*.

24. *Geraldo—Busting the Kiddy Porn Underground*, NBC, Paramount television broadcast, February 23, 1989.

25. Jarecki, *Capturing the Friedmans.*

26. Garnett D. Horner, "Interview with Richard M. Nixon," *Washington Star-News*, November 9, 1972, 1.

27. Lawrence Wright, *Remembering Satan* (New York: Alfred A. Knopf, 1994), 12–13.

28. Ibid., 16.

29. Ibid., 17.

30. Ibid., 99.

31. Ethan Watters, "The Devil in Mr. Ingram," *Mother Jones* 16, no. 4, 30–68.

32. Wright, *Remembering Satan*, 196.

33. Bob Passantino, Gretchen Passantino, and Jon Trott, "Satan's Sideshow: The True Lauren Stratford Story," *Cornerstone* 18, iss. 90 (1990): 23–28, www.answers.org/satan/stratford.html.

34. Lauren Stratford, *Satan's Underground: The Extraordinary Story of One Woman's Escape*, foreword by Johanna Michaelsen (Gretna, LA: Pelican Publishing, 1991), 21.

35. Ibid., 89.

36. Wright, *Remembering Satan*, 26.

37. Ibid., 36.

38. Ibid., 6–7.

39. Debbie Nathan and Michael R. Snedeker, *Satan's Silence: Ritual Abuse and the Making of a Modern American Witch Hunt* (New York: Basic Books, 1995), 169.

40. Paul Ingram, e-mail to author, May 21, 2014.

41. Richard Ofshe, *Making Monsters: False Memories, Psychotherapy, and Sexual Hysteria* (New York: Charles Scribner's, 1994), 167.

42. Wright, *Remembering Satan*, 96.

43. Ofshe, *Making Monsters*, 168.

44. Ibid., 170.

45. Wright, *Remembering Satan*, 196.

46. Ofshe, *Making Monsters*, 169.

47. Richard Ofshe, "Synanon: The People Business," in *The New Religious Consciousness*, eds. Charles Y. Glock and Robert N. Bellah (Berkeley: University of California Press, 1976); Richard Ofshe, "The Social Development of the Synanon Cult: The Managerial Strategy of

Organizational Transformation," *Sociological Analysis* 41, no. 2 (1980): 109–127.

48. Richard Ofshe, with Margaret Singer, "Attacks on Peripheral versus Central Elements of Self and the Impact of Thought Reforming Techniques: Review and Theoretical Analysis," *Cultic Studies Journal* 3, no. 1 (1986), reprinted in *Tort and Religion* (Chicago: American Bar Association, 1989).

49. Wright, *Remembering Satan*, 137.

50. Ibid., 144–146.

51. Justice R. Peterson, *State of Washington v. Paul R. Ingram*. Report of Proceedings, No. 88-1-752. Superior Ct. St of Washington for Co. of Thurston, 1990, 900–918; Karen A. Olio and William F. Cornell, "The Facade of Scientific Documentation: A Case Study of Richard Ofshe's Analysis of the Paul Ingram Case," *Psychology, Public Policy, and Law* 4, no. 4 (1998): 1182–1197.

52. Wright, *Remembering Satan*, 193.

53. Ibid., 194.

54. Paul Ingram, e-mail to author, May 21, 2014.

55. Nik Nerburn, director, *Paul: The Secret Story of Olympia's Satanic Sheriff*, http://vimeo.com/57770807.

56. Ibid.

57. Paul Ingram, e-mail to author, May 26, 2014.

CHAPTER 8

1. "#40—Jury View 4-17-89," VHS, private collection of Danny Davis.

2. Kevin Cody, "Jury Visits McMartin for First Time," *Easy Reader*, April 20, 1989, 5.

3. Lois Timnick, "McMartin Pre-School of Past Returns for Jurors," *Los Angeles Times*, April 20, 1989, A1.

4. Paul Eberle and Shirley Eberle, *The Abuse of Innocence: The McMartin Preschool Trial* (Buffalo, NY: Prometheus Books, 1993), 266.

5. "Buckey Tells of Abuse as a Child," *Los Angeles Times*, May 31, 1989, OC2.

6. Lois Timnick, "Minister Testifies in McMartin Trial," *Los Angeles Times*, June 2, 1989, A2.

7. Memorandum, "Life Magazine Interview of Peggy McMartin Buckey," from Bill Stoops to Dean Gits, March 21, 1988, 12.

8. Peggy McMartin Buckey, "Memo Pad," photocopy in author's possession.

9. Max Toth and Greg Nielson, *Pyramid Power* (New York: Warner Destiny, 1976), 165.

10. *The People of the State of California vs. Raymond Buckey and Peggy McMartin Buckey*, daily transcript, vol. 403, August 2, 1989, 55202–55204.

11. Ibid., vol. 405, August 4, 1989, 55481.

12. Ibid., vol. 403, August 2, 1989, 55204.

13. Ibid., vol. 404, August 3, 1989, 55337–55338.

14. Ibid., vol. 405, August 4, 1989, 55486.

15. Kevin Cody, "Ray Buckey's Secret Love Life Is a Secret No Longer," *Easy Reader*, August 24, 1989, 8.

16. Kevin Cody, "Raymond Buckey: A Life in Limbo," *Easy Reader*, October 5, 1989, 21.

17. Eberle and Eberle, *Abuse of Innocence*, 313.

18. Interview with Kelly Michaels, conducted by Jonas Rappaport, August 8, 1986, video recording, electronic file in author's possession.

19. Ross Cheit, *The Witch-Hunt Narrative: Politics, Psychology, and the Sexual Abuse of Children* (New York: Oxford University Press, 2014), 239.

20. Lynne A. Daley, "Baran Receives Life Term; Parole Possible in 15 Years," *Berkshire Eagle*, February 1, 1985.

21. Kevin Cody, "MMrtn15 catch 1 4licnse platgam inPound courtrm," *Easy Reader*, January 12, 1989, 9.

22. "McMartin Judge Says Case 'Has Poisoned Everyone,'" *Los Angeles Times*, October 14, 1988, C8.

23. Eberle and Eberle, *Abuse of Innocence*, 314.

24. "McMartin Case Near Mistrial as 5th Juror Leaves," *Los Angeles Times*, July 25, 1989, OC, A8.

25. Eberle and Eberle, *Abuse of Innocence*, 291.

26. Ibid., 294.

27. John McCann, "Anatomical Standardization of Normal Prepubertal Children," presentation at Health Science Response to Child Maltreatment Conference, Center for Child Protection, Children's Hospital and Health Center, San Diego, CA, January 21–24, 1988, audiocassette.

28. John McCann et al., "Perianal Findings in Prepubertal Children Selected for Nonabuse: A Descriptive Study," *Child Abuse and Neglect* 13, no. 2 (1989): 179–193.

29. John McCann et al., "Genital Findings in Prepubertal Girls Selected for Non-Abuse: A Descriptive Study," *Pediatrics* 86, no. 3 (September 1, 1990): 428–439.

30. Nancy Kellogg and the Committee on Child Abuse and Neglect, "The Evaluation of Sexual Abuse in Children," *Pediatrics* 116, no. 2 (August 1, 2005): 506–512.

31. Eberle and Eberle, *Abuse of Innocence*, 319.

32. Ibid., 326.

33. Kevin Cody, "In Buckey's Defense," *Easy Reader*, October 26, 1989, 6.

34. Kevin Cody, "Defending the Children," *Easy Reader*, November 2, 1989, 13.

35. Ibid., 16.

36. McMartin Buckey, "Memo Pad."

37. Kevin Cody, "The Courtroom Verdict," *Easy Reader*, January 25, 1990, 2.

38. Lois Timnick, "Not Guilty: Both Buckeys Cleared in Historic McMartin Case," *Los Angeles Times*, January 18, 1990, P1.

39. David Shaw, "Where Was Skepticism in Media?" *Los Angeles Times*, January 19, 1990, A20.

40. David Shaw, "Times McMartin Coverage Was Biased, Critics Charge," *Los Angeles Times*, January 22, 1990, A1.

41. David Freed, "Cost of Case Is Measured in Reputations and Emotions," *Los Angeles Times*, January 19, 1990, A18.

42. "Jurors Say Prosecution Never Demonstrated Buckey Responsibility," *Los Angeles Times*, January 18, 1990, P1.

43. Lowell Bergman, producer, "The McMartin Pre-School Update," *60 Minutes*, CBS, February 4, 1990.

44. Kevin Cody, "Parents Petition to Protest McMartin Verdicts," *Easy Reader*, February 1, 1990, 4.

45. Alexandra Gross, "Ricky Lynn Pitts," *National Registry of Exonerations*, University of Michigan Law School, www.law.umich.edu/special/exoneration/Pages/casedetail.aspx?caseid=3540.

46. James Rainey, "McMartin Jurors Feel Ire of Public over Their Verdicts," *Los Angeles Times*, January 20, 1990, A32.

47. Lois Timnick and Carol McGraw, "Initial Hysteria Provoked Positive Changes in Day Care," *Los Angeles Times*, January 19, 1990, A18.

48. *Larry King Live*, CNN, February 5, 1990, videotape "#31—L. King 2-5-90," in possession of Danny Davis.

49. Lois Timnick, "McMartin Parents Dig Up School in Last-Ditch Search," *Los Angeles Times*, April 28, 1990, B3.

50. Steven R. Churm, "Parents Dig Persistently for Evidence," *Los Angeles Times*, June 5, 1990, B1.

51. "McMartin Preschool Whistleblower Jackie McGauley Exposes Ted Gunderson and Accomplices," *Barbara Hartwell vs. CIA*, March 25, 2010, http://barbarahartwellvscia.blogspot.com/2010/03/mcmartin -preschool-whistleblower-jackie.html.

52. E. Gary Stickel, "Archaeological Investigations of the McMartin Preschool Site, Manhattan Beach, California," The McMartin Tunnel Project, 1993, 104.

53. Ibid., 16.

54. W. Joseph Wyatt, "What Was Under the McMartin Preschool? A Review and Behavioral Analysis of the 'Tunnels' Find," *Behavior and Social Issues* 12 (2002): 29–39.

55. Roland Summit, "The Dark Tunnels of McMartin," *Journal of Psychohistory* 21, no. 4 (1994): 397–416.

56. Lois Timnick, "Child Takes the Stand in Buckey Trial," *Los Angeles Times*, May 10, 1990, B1.

57. Lois Timnick, "McMartin a Talkative Witness for Grandson," *Los Angeles Times*, June 6, 1990, B3.

58. Carol McGraw, "In the End, Jury Gave in to Confusion," *Los Angeles Times*, July 28, 1990, 1.

59. Lois Timnick, "Charges Against Buckey Dismissed," *Los Angeles Times*, August 2, 1990, B1.

CHAPTER 9

1. Ellen Bass and Louise Thornton, eds., *I Never Told Anyone: Writings by Women Survivors of Child Sexual Abuse* (New York: Harper & Row, 1983).

2. Ellen Bass and Laura Davis, *The Courage to Heal: A Guide for Women Survivors of Child Sexual Abuse* (New York: Harper & Row, 1988).

3. Ibid., 22.

4. Ibid., 21.

5. Ibid., 22.

6. Ibid., 113.

7. Ibid., 72.

8. Ibid., 65.

9. Ibid.

10. Ibid., 66.

11. Ibid., 80.

12. Ibid.

13. Ibid., 86.

14. Sigmund Freud, "The Aetiology of Hysteria," in *Standard Edition of the Complete Psychological Works of Sigmund Freud*, vol. 3 (London: Vintage, 1962), 204.

15. Bass and Davis, *Courage to Heal*, 88.

16. Ibid., 347, 345–346.

17. Ibid., 347.

18. Moritz Benedikt, "Beobachtung über Hysterie," in *Zeitschrift für practische Heilkunde* (1864).

19. Franz Anton Mesmer, *Mémoire sur la découverte du magnetism animal* (Paris: Didot, 1779).

20. Henri F. Ellenberger, *The Discovery of the Unconscious: The History and Evolution of Dynamic Psychiatry* (New York: Basic Books, 1970), 13.

21. Ibid., 382.

22. Jean-Martin Charcot, *Iconographie photographique de la Salpêtrière* (Jean-Martin Charcot, 1878).

23. Elaine Showalter, *Hystories: Hysterical Epidemics and Modern Media* (New York: Columbia University Press, 1998), 34.

24. Sigmund Freud, *Standard Edition of the Complete Psychological Works of Sigmund Freud*, vol. 3 (London: Vintage, 1962), 9.

25. Paul Bernard, *Des Attentats à la pudeur sur les petites filles*, Laboratoire de Médecine Légale de Lyon (Paris: Octave Doin, 1886).

26. Paul Brouardel, *Les Attentats aux moeurs* (Paris: J. B. Ballière, 1909).

27. Colin A. Ross, *Multiple Personality Disorder: Diagnosis, Clinical Features, and Treatment* (New York: John Wiley & Sons, 1989), 55, 72.

28. Daniel Goleman, "New Focus on Multiple Personality," *New York Times*, May 21, 1985, www.nytimes.com/1985/05/21/science/new-focus -on-multiple-personality.html?pagewanted=1.

29. Debbie Nathan, "Cry Incest: Victims of Childhood Sexual Abuse," *Playboy* 39, no. 10, October 1992, 84.

30. Ross, *Multiple Personality Disorder*, 217.

31. Onno van der Hart and Barbara Friedman, "A Reader's Guide to Pierre Janet on Dissociation: A Neglected Intellectual Heritage," *Dissociation* 2 (1989): 3–16.

32. Bessel van der Kolk and William Kadish, "Amnesia, Dissociation, and the Return of the Repressed," in Bessel van der Kolk,

Psychological Trauma (Washington, DC: American Psychiatric Press, 1987), 173–190.

33. Daniel Brown, Alan W. Scheflin, and D. Corydon Hammond, *Memory, Trauma Treatment, and the Law* (New York: Norton, 1998).

34. Sigmund Freud, "Repression," in *Standard Edition of the Complete Psychological Works of Sigmund Freud*, vol. 14 (London: Vintage, 1962), 146–158; Josef Breuer and Sigmund Freud, *Studies on Hysteria*, trans. James Strachey (New York: Basic Books, 2000), 116 (emphasis in the original).

35. M. J. Eacott and R. A. Crawley, "The Offset of Childhood Amnesia: Memory for Events That Occurred Before Age 3," *Journal of Experimental Psychology: General* 127 (1998): 22–33.

36. Elizabeth Loftus and Terrence Burns, "Mental Shock Can Produce Retrograde Amnesia," *Memory and Cognition* 10 (1982): 318–323.

37. John Yuille and Judith Cutshall, "A Case Study of Eyewitness Memory of a Crime," *Journal of Applied Psychology* 71 (1986): 291–301.

38. Judith Herman, *Father-Daughter Incest* (Cambridge, MA: Harvard University Press, 1981).

39. Lenore Terr, "What Happens to Early Memories of Trauma? A Study of Twenty Children Under Age Five at the Time of Documented Traumatic Events," *Journal of the American Academy of Child and Adolescent Psychiatry* 27 (1988): 96–104.

40. John Briere and Jon Conte, "Self-Reported Amnesia for Abuse in Adults Molested as Children," *Journal of Traumatic Stress* 6 (1993): 21–31.

41. Richard McNally, *Remembering Trauma* (Cambridge, MA: Belknap Press of Harvard University Press, 2003), 197.

42. Elizabeth Loftus, Sarah Polonsky, and Mindy Fullilove, "Memories of Childhood Sexual Abuse: Remembering and Repressing," *Psychology of Women Quarterly* 18 (1994): 67–84.

43. Daniel Brown, Alan Scheflin, and Charles Whitfield, "Recovered Memories: The Current Weight of the Evidence in Science and in the Courts," *Journal of Psychiatry and Law* 27 (1998): 5–156.

44. Charles Wilkinson, "Aftermath of a Disaster: The Collapse of the Hyatt Regency Hotel Skywalks," *American Journal of Psychiatry* 140 (1983): 1134–1139.

45. Brown, Scheflin, and Hammond, *Memory, Trauma, Treatment, and the Law*, 156.

46. Stephen Dollinger, "Lightning-Strike Disaster Among Children," *British Journal of Medical Psychology* 58 (1985): 375–383.

47. Ross, *Multiple Personality Disorder*, 252.

48. Ibid., 233.

49. Ibid., 269.

50. Ibid., 275.

51. Ibid., 276.

52. Walter C. Young et al., "Patients Reporting Ritual Abuse in Childhood: A Clinical Syndrome, Report of Thirty-Seven Cases," *Child Abuse and Neglect* 15 (1991): 181–189; Walter C. Young, Letter, *Child Abuse and Neglect* 15 (1991): 611–613.

53. Debbie Nathan, *Sybil Exposed* (New York: Free Press, 2011), 225.

54. Nathan, "Cry Incest."

55. Susan Faludi, *Backlash: The Undeclared War Against American Women* (New York: Doubleday, 1991), 338–339.

56. Elizabeth Loftus and Katherine Ketcham, *The Myth of Repressed Memory: False Memories and Allegations of Sexual Abuse* (New York: St. Martin's Griffin, 1996), 152.

57. Colin A. Ross, *The Osiris Complex: Case-Studies in Multiple Personality Disorder* (Toronto, Canada: University of Toronto Press, 1994), 165.

58. Ibid., 166.

59. Ibid., 169.

60. Ibid., 175.

61. Ellen Willis, "Coda," in *The Essential Ellen Willis*, ed. Nona Willis Aronowitz (Minneapolis: University of Minnesota Press, 2014), 488–489.

62. Gloria Steinem, *Revolution from Within: A Book of Self-Esteem* (Boston: Little, Brown, and Company, 1992), 78.

63. Elizabeth S. Rose, "Surviving the Unbelievable: A First-Person Account of Cult Ritual Abuse," *Ms.*, January/February 1993, 41.

64. Ibid., 43.

65. Letters, *Ms. Magazine*, May/June 1993, 7.

66. Anita Lipton, "Recovered Memories in the Courts," in *Recovered Memories of Child Sexual Abuse: Psychological, Social, and Legal Perspectives on a Contemporary Mental Health Controversy*, ed. Sheila Taub (Springfield, IL: Charles C. Thomas, 1999), 165–210.

67. Brown, Scheflin, and Hammond, *Memory, Trauma Treatment, and the Law*, 398, 538.

68. Ross E. Cheit, *The Witch-Hunt Narrative: Politics, Psychology, and the Sexual Abuse of Children* (New York: Oxford University Press, 2014), 390.

69. Joan Acocella, *Creating Hysteria: Women and Multiple Personality Disorder* (San Francisco, CA: Jossey-Bass, 1999), 15.

CHAPTER 10

1. Kenneth V. Lanning, "Investigator's Guide to Allegations of 'Ritual' Child Abuse," Behavioral Science Unit, National Center for the Analysis of Violent Crime, Federal Bureau of Investigation, FBI Academy, Quantico, Virginia, 1992.

2. Mary A. Fischer, "McMartin: A Case of Dominoes?" *Los Angeles Magazine*, October 1989, www.byliner.com/read/mary-fischer/a-case -of-dominoes.

3. Paul Eberle and Shirley Eberle, *The Abuse of Innocence: The McMartin Preschool Trial* (Buffalo, NY: Prometheus Books, 1993), 362.

4. "Kelly Michaels: The End of Innocence," *48 Hours*, CBS, May 5, 1993.

5. Dorothy Rabinowitz, "A Darkness in Massachusetts—II," *Wall Street Journal*, March 14, 1995, http://online.wsj.com/news/articles /SB122635339100615063.

6. *Commonwealth vs. Violet Amirault / Commonwealth vs. Gerald Amirault*, 424 Mass 618, Middlesex County, October 9, 1996–March 24, 1997, http://masscases.com/cases/sjc/424/424mass618.html.

7. Dorothy Rabinowitz, "From the Mouths of Babes to a Jail Cell: Child Abuse and the Abuse of Justice—A Case Study," *Harper's*, May 1990, 54.

8. B. A. Robinson, "Geraldo Rivera: Satanic Ritual Abuse and Recovered Memories," *ReligiousTolerance.org*, November 7, 2007, www .religioustolerance.org/geraldo.htm.

9. Gilbert Cates, director, *Do You Know the Muffin Man?*, produced by Daniel Freudenberger, Avnet/Kerner Company Productions, 1989.

10. Mick Jackson, director, *Indictment*, HBO, February 21, 2012.

11. Mike Barber and Andrew Schneider, "Detective a Man Who Charmed, Harmed," *Seattle Post-Intelligencer*, February 23, 1998, 10.

12. Charges against Glassen were eventually dropped.

13. Kathryn Lyon, *Witch Hunt: A True Story of Social Hysteria and Abused Justice* (New York: Avon Books, 1998), xl.

14. Peter Bull, producer, "When Children Accuse: Who to Believe?" *Turning Point*, ABC News, November 14, 1996.

15. Don Hardy Jr. and Dana Nachman, directors, *Witch Hunt,* film (KTF Films, 2008).

16. Dorothy Rabinowitz, "Martha Coakley's Convictions," *Wall Street Journal,* January 14, 2010, http://online.wsj.com/news/articles/SB100014 24052748704281204575003341640657862.

17. Radley Balko, "Kern County's Monstrous D.A.," *Reason.com,* December 21, 2009, http://reason.com/archives/2009/12/21/kern-countys -monstrous-da.

18. Peter J. Boyer, "Children of Waco," *New Yorker,* May 15, 1995, 42.

19. Richard Beck, "The Friedmans," *n+1,* iss. 18, Winter 2013.

20. Jordan Smith, "Believing the Children," *Austin Chronicle,* March 27, 2009, www.austinchronicle.com/news/2009-03-27/believing-the -children.

21. Chuck Lindell, "Fran Keller to Be Freed in Satanic Abuse Case," *Austin American-Statesman,* November 26, 2013, www.statesman.com /news/news/local/fran-keller-to-be-freed-in-satanic-abuse-case/nb5S2.

22. Stephen J. Ceci and Maggie Bruck, *Jeopardy in the Courtroom: A Scientific Analysis of Children's Testimony* (Washington, DC: American Psychological Association, 1999), 108.

23. Ibid., 90.

24. Elizabeth Loftus and Katherine Ketcham, *The Myth of Repressed Memory: False Memories and Allegations of Sexual Abuse* (New York: St. Martin's Press, 1994).

25. Elizabeth Loftus and Jacqueline Pickrell, "The Formation of False Memories," *Psychiatric Annals* 25 (1994): 720–725.

26. Retro Report, producer, "McMartin Preschool: Anatomy of a Panic," *New York Times,* March 9, 2014, www.nytimes.com/video/us /100000002755079/mcmartin-preschool-anatomy-of-a-panic.html.

27. Ross Cheit, *The Witch-Hunt Narrative: Politics, Psychology, and the Sexual Abuse of Children* (New York: Oxford University Press, 2014), 14.

28. Ibid., 14, 195.

29. Ibid., 285.

30. Ibid., 328.

31. W. L. Whittington et al., "Incorrect Identification of *Neisseria gonorrhoeae* from Infants and Children," *Pediatric Infectious Disease Journal* 7, no. 1 (1988): 3–10.

32. Sarah Alexander and Catherine Ison, "Evaluation of Commercial Kits for the Identification of *Neisseria gonorrhoeae,*" *Journal of Medical Microbiology* 54, no. 9 (September 2005): 827–831.

33. "Gonorrhea Laboratory Information Characteristics of *N. gonorrhoeae* and Related Species of Human Origin," Centers for Disease Control and Prevention, December 10, 2013, www.cdc.gov/std /gonorrhea/lab/ngon.htm.

34. Cheit, *The Witch Hunt Narrative*, 145.

35. Ibid., 89.

36. Ibid., 360.

37. Kyle Zirpolo, as told to Debbie Nathan. "I'm Sorry," *Los Angeles Times*, October 30, 2005, http://articles.latimes.com/2005/oct/30 /magazine/tm-mcmartin44.

38. Jennifer (pseud.), interview with author, April 17, 2014. All subsequent quotations are also from this interview.

39. Kenneth Pope, "Recovered Memory or Just a Giant Con Trick?" *New Zealand Herald*, September 9, 1998, A13.

40. Diana E. H. Russell, "The Great Incest War: Moving Beyond Polarization," 1999, www.dianarussell.com/the_great_incest_war.html.

41. Emily Bazelon, "Abuse Cases, and a Legacy of Skepticism—'The Witch-Hunt Narrative': Are We Dismissing Real Victims?" *New York Times*, June 9, 2014, www.nytimes.com/2014/06/10/science/the-witch -hunt-narrative-are-we-dismissing-real-victims.html.

42. Eliana Gil and Toni Cavanagh Johnson, *Sexualized Children: Assessment and Treatment of Sexualized Children and Children Who Molest* (Rockville, MD: Launch Press, 1993), xiii.

43. David Finkelhor, Richard Ormrod, and Mark Chaffin, "Juveniles Who Commit Sex Offenses Against Minors," *Juvenile Justice Bulletin*, US Department of Justice, Office of Justice Programs. December 2009, www.ncjrs.gov/pdffiles1/ojjdp/227763.pdf.

44. Emily DePrang, "Life on the List," *Texas Observer*, May 31, 2012, www.texasobserver.org/life-on-the-list.

45. Bruce Rind, Philip Tromovitch, and Robert Bauserman, "A Meta-Analytic Examination of Assumed Properties of Child Sexual Abuse Using College Samples," *Psychological Bulletin* 124, no. 1 (1998): 22–53.

46. Ibid., 36.

47. Ibid., 46.

48. Ibid., 47.

49. Scott O. Lilienfeld, "When Worlds Collide: Social Science, Politics, and the Rind et al. (1998) Child Sexual Abuse Meta-Analysis," *American Psychologist* 57, no. 3 (March 2002): 178.

50. Bruce Rind, Philip Tromovitch, and Robert Bauserman, "Condemnation of a Scientific Article: A Chronology and Refutation of the Attacks and a Discussion of Threats to the Integrity of Science," *Sexuality and Culture* 4 (2000): 14.

51. Laura Schlessinger, "Analysis of Pedophilia Junk Science at Its Worst," in *The Dr. Laura Program* (radio broadcast), March 15, 2000, Sherman Oaks, CA: Premiere Radio Networks; Simon A. Cole, "Unpopular Psychology," *Lingua Franca*, no. 10, February 2000, 12.

52. Carol Tavris, "The Uproar over Sexual Abuse Research and Its Findings," *Society* 37, no. 4 (2000): 15–17.

53. R. McCarty, "A Brief Comment by APA Executive Director for Science," *Psychological Science Agenda* 12, no. 6 (1999): 3.

54. Judith Levine, *Harmful to Minors: The Perils of Protecting Children from Sex* (Minneapolis: University of Minnesota Press, 2002), 3.

55. Ibid., 128.

56. Ibid., 89.

57. Deborah Roffman, "Harmful to Minors (book review)," *Psychology Today*, August 1, 2002, www.psychologytoday.com/articles/200208/harmful-minors-book-review.

58. Robert Stacy McCain, "Promoting Pedophilia: Attempts to Legitimize Adult-Child Sex on Rise," *Washington Times*, April 19, 2002, A2.

59. "Statement by Robert Knight," Concerned Women for America, April 25, 2002, press conference, www.cwfa.org/statement-by-robert-knight.

60. Soraya Nadia McDonald, "Shanesha Taylor, Arrested for Leaving Children in Car During Job Interview, Speaks," *Washington Post*, June 23, 2014, www.washingtonpost.com/news/morning-mix/wp/2014/06/23/shanesha-taylor-arrested-for-leaving-children-in-car-during-job-interview-speaks.

61. Deon Guillory, "North Augusta Mother Charged With Unlawful Conduct Towards a Child," *News Channel 6 WJBF.com*, July 1, 2014 (updated 12 August 2014), www.wjbf.com/story/25915218/north-augusta-mother-charged-with-unlawful-conduct-towards-a-child.

62. CNN Wire Service, "'Didn't Think I Was Doing Anything Wrong': Mom Arrested for Allowing 7-Year-Old Son to Go to Park Alone," *Fox6Now.com*, July 29, 2014, http://fox6now.com/2014/07/29/mother-arrested-after-allowing-7-year-old-son-to-go-to-park-alone.

63. Emily Ekins, "UPDATED/Poll: 68 Percent of Americans Don't Think 9-Year-Olds Should Play at the Park Unsupervised," *Reason-Rupe*

Poll, August 19, 2014, http://reason.com/poll/2014/08/19/august -2014-reason-rupe-national-survey.

64. "The Decline of Marriage and Rise of New Families," Pew Research Center, November 18, 2010, www.pewsocialtrends.org/files/2010/11/pew -social-trends-2010-families.pdf.

65. Ellen Willis, "Marriage on the Rocks," in *No More Nice Girls: Countercultural Essays* (Hanover, NH: Wesleyan, 1992), 68.

66. Sigmund Freud, *Five Lectures on Psychoanalysis* (New York: Norton, 1961), 22.

INDEX

as medical problem, 4, 6, 11, 22, 124
See also child sexual abuse; ritual
abuse
*Child Abuse Industry, The: Outrageous
Facts About Child Abuse &
Everyday Rebellions Against a
System That Threatens Every
North American Family* (Pride),
162
Child Abuse Prevention and
Treatment Act (1974), 9, 11, 238
childhood amnesia, 225–226, 227
childhood sexuality, 257, 259
Child Pornography and Sex Rings
(Burgess), 119
Child Protection Act (1984), xv
Children's Institute International (CII),
38, 40–41, 48, 49, 54, 56, 58, 59,
96, 103, 127, 154, 165, 171, 204,
206, 243, 249, 251
billing California for interviews and
medical examinations, 60
number of children interviewed, 93
(*see also* interviews with children:
number of)
Children's Path Preschool, 63
children unsupervised, 263–264
child sexual abuse, 136, 238
and antifeminism, 264
children as sexual predators,
256–257
as doubling every year, 103
as epidemic, xii–xiii, 7
and family members/close friends,
76, 96, 159, 209, 219, 223, 232, 233
and fundamentalism, 184
games as cover for, 36–37 (*see also*
naked games)
genitalia of victims, 202
ignoring, xvi, 17, 127
meaning of terms "child" and
"abuse," 258
and mental illness, 124
and parental negligence, 95–96
physical/medical evidence of abuse,
xv, xix, xxii, 37, 57–60, 72, 83,

94–95, 97, 110, 111, 123, 141,
150, 154, 155, 202–203, 204, 248
searches concerning, 153–154
Seduction Theory concerning, 15,
16
sex offender status, xxii, xxiii–xiv
skepticism concerning, 152–153,
154 (*see also* McMartin
Preschool: doubts about guilt
concerning)
statute of limitations concerning,
232
stigma associated with, xvi–xvii
as not traumatic, 227–228
as underreported, 52
See also child abuse; interviews with
children; ritual abuse
"Child Sexual Abuse Accommodation
Syndrome, The" (CSAAS)
(Summit), 50–53, 145, 157
Christianity/Christians, xxiv, 23,
27, 122, 181, 184. *See also*
evangelicals
Chrysalis journal, 15
Church of Living Water, 186, 189
CII. *See* Children's Institute
International
Cincinnati, 5
Cioffi, John, 95, 96
civil lawsuits, 97, 209, 233, 237, 242,
243, 254, 262
civil rights, 133, 162, 242
Clinton, Bill, 247
Coakley, Martha, 246
Cody, Kevin, 150–151, 152, 163
Coleman, Lee, 162
colposcopes, 58, 59, 123, 155
Comprehensive Child Development
Act, 8
Comprehensive Textbook of Psychiatry,
124
computers, 76, 173, 174, 175, 180
Concerned Women for America, 262
confessions, 29, 83, 86, 105, 144, 145,
151, 163, 188, 189, 190, 191, 192
false confessions, 190, 191

Rivera, Geraldo, 169–171, 179, 186,
    210, 244
Roberts, Charlie, 158
Roll, Colonel James, 104
Ross, Colin, 223, 224, 229–230, 235
Rubin, Lael, 62, 99, 109, 110–111, 112,
    113, 122, 139, 149, 151, 153, 163,
    165, 199, 204, 205, 249
    withholding information from
    defense attorneys, 147–148
Ruby, Michael, 63
Rud, James, 73, 74–75, 76, 83–87, 89,
    90, 251
Rush, Florence, 7, 15, 125, 133
Russell, Diana, 256

Sachs, Roberta, 231
sadomasochism, 237
St. Cross Episcopal Church (Hermosa
    Beach), 63, 106, 109, 150, 213
Salem, Massachusetts, xx–xxi
    and witch trials, xx–xxi
Sally Jessy Raphael (television show),
    192
Salmon, Matt, 259
Salpêtrière hospital in Paris, 221
Satanic Bible, The (LaVey), 23
satanism, xiv, xvi, xx, 23, 24, 25–26, 29,
    80–82, 105–106, 108, 122, 130,
    149, 150, 154, 169–171, 184–185,
    187, 189, 191, 210, 220, 224, 230,
    231, 236, 256
    See also ritual abuse
Satan Seller, The (Warnke), 23, 130
Satan's Silence: Ritual Abuse and the
    Making of a Modern American
    Witch Hunt (Nathan and
    Snedeker), ix
Satan's Underground (Stratford),
    184–185
Saturday Evening Post, 5, 6
Satz, Wayne, 56–57, 61, 150, 166,
    205–206
scapegoating, 100, 117, 149, 160
Schlessinger, Dr. Laura, 259
Schreiber, Flora Rheta, 17, 19, 21–22

science, 261–262
    scientific advances, 248, 249
Scottsdale, Arizona, 263
Sealander, Judith, 6
search warrants, 61, 63, 91, 112, 120
secrecy, 44–46, 51, 53, 54, 62
Secret Trauma, The (Russell), 256
Senate Judiciary Committee, xii, xiii
Senate Subcommittee on Children and
    Youth, 9–11
Sewall, Samuel, xxi
sex education, 261, 263
sex offenders, 247. See also pedophilia;
    rape
sex rings, 72, 73–77, 78, 80, 81, 82–83,
    87, 88, 245, 251, 267
    cost of sex ring investigations, 90
"Sexual Abuse of Children, The: A
    Feminist Point of View" (Rush),
    125
Sexual Assaults on Young Girls
    (Bernard), 222
sexual harassment, 131
Sexualized Children: Assessment and
    Treatment of Sexualized Children
    and Children Who Molest
    (Johnson), 256–257
sexual politics, 162
sexual revolution, xxiv, 7, 14, 138,
    265
Shaw, David, 205–206
Silence of the Lambs (Starling), 118
Silverman, F. N., 3
single parents, 172, 260, 263, 265
Sixth Amendment, 98, 99
60 Minutes news program, 148–149,
    156, 209
SLAM. See Stronger Legislation
    Against Molesters
Smith, Michelle, 24, 105, 223
Snedeker, Michael, ix, 58, 79
social panic, 99–100, 149, 215
social/political change, 117, 181, 233,
    234, 268
social workers, xi, xv, xix, xx, 7, 10, 49,
    70, 78, 80, 91, 119, 124, 126, 157

CREDIT: Josephine Livingstone.

RICHARD BECK is an
associate editor at *n+1*. He
lives in New York.